Crossing Cultures

D0086087

What is culture?
Why does it matter?
And how do we teach across cultures?

As a result of increasing organizational interculturalism, the challenge of communicating across cultures is one that teachers face on a daily basis. But how do we help ourselves when preparing for intercultural challenges? And what are the best methods of acquiring the skills required to be effective international managers?

Crossing Cultures offers teachers and trainers a unique set of proven methods for developing the skills required by both students and practitioners when striving to be effective members and managers in cross-cultural situations. Comprehensively structured to provide a framework for teaching, every chapter features its own teaching module embedded in robust discussion of its theoretical source, as well as a working definition and specific directions for practice. The "master teachers" who offer these modules highlight the potential difficulties, typical dialogues, and the variations required for different audiences, while approaching the fundamentals of culture from diverse disciplines, including anthropology, sociology, management, psychology, and strategy.

First and foremost a book for teachers, *Crossing Cultures* is also a book for their students, bringing together the best authors in the field to illustrate what understanding and action is required to successfully cross cultures.

Nakiye Avdan Boyacigiller is Dean of the Graduate School of Management at Sabanci University, Istanbul, Turkey. She has 17 years experience of teaching at San José State University, USA.

Richard Alan Goodman was Professor of Technology and Strategy at The Anderson School, UCLA, USA. He also chaired an affinity group of 54 faculty from 33 universities on cultural issues.

Margaret E. Phillips is Associate Professor of International Business at the Graziadio School of Pepperdine University. She is a teacher, a scholar, and a consultant in international management.

Crossing Cultures

Insights from Master Teachers

**Edited by Nakiye Avdan Boyacigiller,
Richard Alan Goodman, and
Margaret E. Phillips**

With a foreword by Jone L. Pearce

Routledge
Taylor & Francis Group

NEW YORK AND LONDON

The work in this book is derived and expanded from a Workshop on Teaching Crossing Cultures held at the University of California at Los Angeles (UCLA). This work has been financially supported by the United States Department of Education through their funding of the UCLA Center for International Business Education and Research (CIBER) under the direction of José de la Torre. The UCLA CIBER program has in turn funded the CIBER Cross Cultural Colleagium (C4), a decade-old affinity group of 54 faculty at 33 universities.

First published 2003
Simultaneously published in the UK, USA and Canada
by Routledge
29 West 35th Street, New York, NY 10001
and by Routledge
11 New Fetter Lane, London EC4P 4EE

Routledge is an imprint of the Taylor & Francis Group

© 2003 Nakiye Avdan Boyacigiller, Richard Alan Goodman, and Margaret E. Phillips selection and editorial matter; individual chapters, the contributors

Typeset in Baskerville by Wearset Ltd,
Boldon, Tyne and Wear, UK
Printed and bound in Great Britain by The Cromwell Press,
Trowbridge, Wiltshire

All rights reserved. No part of this book may be reprinted or reproduced or utilized in any form or by any electronic, mechanical, or other means, now known or hereafter invented, including photocopying and recording, or in any information storage or retrieval system, without permission in writing from the publishers.

Library of Congress Cataloging in Publication Data
A catalog record of this book has been requested

British Library Cataloguing in Publication Data
A catalogue record for this book is available from the British Library

ISBN 0-415-30818-6 (hbk)
ISBN 0-415-30819-4 (pbk)

CWIL

GN
345.65
.C76
2003

Dedication

It is with great sadness, but also with sincere gratitude, that we dedicate this book to our late co-author, Dick Goodman. Dick was our teacher and advisor, but he felt more comfortable in the role of colleague, collaborator, and friend. He taught us much about organizations, culture, research, and teaching ... but most importantly, about the joy of learning together.

We thank you Dick, for your humor and human-ness, and for your tolerance and inclusiveness of people and ideas – we will never forget you, or your many lessons.

Contents

List of contributors   xv
Foreword by Jone L. Pearce   xvii
Acknowledgments   xix

PART I
Not the beginning   1

1   Culture, passion, and play   3
    RICHARD A. GOODMAN, MARGARET E. PHILLIPS, AND
    NAKIYE AVDAN BOYACIGILLER

PART II
Framing the culture concept: What is culture?/
How can we characterize it?   11

2   Are we the same or are we different? A social-
    psychological perspective of culture   13
    SHARON G. GOTO AND DARIUS K.-S. CHAN

Instructor level: novice to extremely experienced
Audience: all ages and levels of sophistication
Objectives: to quickly demonstrate the existence of cultural
    differences and the diversity of cultural identity, and to
    provide a platform for deepening the students'
    sophistication
Process: experiment and discussion

3   **What is culture and why does it matter? Current
    conceptualizations of culture from anthropology**   20
    MARY YOKO BRANNEN

    Instructor level: intermediate to extremely experienced
    Audience: advanced undergraduates, graduates, and
        advanced professionals
    Objectives: to define culture and acculturation and explore
        their impact on organizational life
    Process: lecture/reflection

4   **One's many cultures: a multiple cultures perspective**   38
    SONJA A. SACKMANN AND MARGARET E. PHILLIPS

    Instructor level: intermediate to extremely experienced
    Audience: advanced undergraduates, graduates, and
        advanced professionals
    Objectives: to explore the notion of individuals simultaneously
        being members of more than one cultural group, and to
        consider the multiple cultures within organizations
    Process: exercise and reflective discussion

5   **Learning about our and others' selves: multiple identities
    and their sources**   49
    BERNARDO M. FERDMAN

    Instructor level: novice to extremely experienced
    Audience: all ages and levels of sophistication
    Objectives: to learn about one's own and others' multiple
        cultural identities and to build skills for discerning them
    Process: exercise and reflection

**PART III
Culture scanning and sense-making: how do we
"learn" and characterize culture?**   63

6   **Context–culture interaction: teaching thick descriptions
    of culture**   65
    JILL KLEINBERG

    Instructor level: intermediate to extremely experienced
    Audience: all ages and levels of sophistication

Objectives: to learn to see patterns that are culturally, not
  personally nor psychologically, based
Process: field work

7   **Cultural scanning: an integrated cultural frameworks
    approach**   76
    MARGARET E. PHILLIPS AND NAKIYE A. BOYACIGILLER

Instructor level: intermediate to extremely experienced
Audience: all ages and intermediate to advanced levels of
  sophistication
Objectives: to sharpen the understanding of cultural
  assumptions by providing a pragmatic integrated
  framework for debriefing simulations, field experiences
  or other cross-cultural exposures
Process: framework applied to simulations/field experience

8   **Teaching cultural sense-making**   89
    ALLAN BIRD AND JOYCE S. OSLAND

Instructor level: intermediate to extremely experienced
Audience: all ages and levels of sophistication
Objectives: to move students from simple labeling to deeper
  interpretive capabilities recognizing the dynamic and
  paradoxical nature of culture
Process: learning-stage-based, multiple methods

9   **Examining culture change through *Fiddler on the Roof***   101
    JENNIFER RONEY

Instructor level: novice to extremely experienced
Audience: all ages and levels of sophistication
Objectives: to learn about the dynamics of culture change
  derived from external pressures
Process: film-based experiential exercise

PART IV
The experience of crossing cultures 109

10 Using the hero's journey: a framework for making sense of
the transformational expatriate experience 111
JOYCE S. OSLAND

Instructor level: novice to extremely experienced
Audience: all ages and levels of sophistication
Objectives: to learn the basic structure of preparation for,
exploration of, and return from a new culture
Process: classroom exercise

11 Apples and Oranges: an experiential exercise in crossing
cultures 128
STEPHEN R. JENNER

Instructor level: novice to extremely experienced
Audience: all ages and levels of sophistication
Objectives: to simulate an experience of crossing culture
Process: experiential exercise

12 Building transpatriate skills: the *Star Trek* case 135
GERARD L. ROSSY AND MARGARET E. PHILLIPS

Instructor level: intermediate to extremely experienced
Audience: all ages and intermediate to highly sophisticated
learners
Objectives: to develop and assess personal skills needed for
crossing culture and develop organizational competencies
to support expatriate assignment
Process: video case

13 Cultural transitions: a biopsychosocial model for cultural
adaptation 145
SUSAN FUKUSHIMA AND SUI WA TANG

Instructor level: novice to extremely experienced
Audience: all ages and levels of sophistication
Objectives: to learn the causes and costs of the stress involved
in crossing cultures
Process: assigned reading and lecture

PART V
Going deeper: developing a global mindset   **155**

14   **Turning frogs into interculturalists: a student-centered developmental approach to teaching intercultural competence**   157
JANET M. BENNETT

Instructor level: intermediate to extremely experienced and instructor teams
Audience: all ages and levels of sophistication
Objectives: to help students progress through various stages toward developing sophisticated intercultural competence
Process: assessment and exercises for different stages

15   **Shaping the global mindset: designing educational experiences for effective global thinking and action**   171
MARTHA L. MAZNEVSKI AND HENRY W. LANE

Instructor level: novice to extremely experienced
Audience: all ages and levels of sophistication
Objectives: to learn to recognize underlying connections (universals and differentiators) between and among cultures using a developmental process that relies on increasing self-awareness on the part of the learner
Process: assortment of exercises and techniques

16   **Limitations of the culture perspective in teaching international management: the case of transition economies**   185
TATIANA KOSTOVA

Instructor level: intermediate to extremely experienced
Audience: all ages and intermediate to high levels of sophistication
Objectives: to learn that institutional analysis is a necessary supplement to cultural analysis for more complete international understanding
Process: short cases and lecture

17 Reflective silence: developing the capacity for meaningful
    global leadership   201
    NANCY J. ADLER

    Instructor level: novice to extremely experienced
    Audience: all ages and levels of sophistication
    Objectives: to learn the value of reflective silence and the
         process of reflection
    Process: in-class exercises

PART VI
The cultural context of work: collaborative
relationships today   219

18 Building multicultural teams: learning to manage the
    challenges of homogeneity and heterogeneity   221
    CRISTINA B. GIBSON

    Instructor level: novice to extremely experienced
    Audience: all ages and levels of sophistication
    Objectives: to learn and experience the impact of
         homogeneous and heterogeneous teams
    Process: team projects

19 Teaching culture "on the fly" and "learning in working"
    with global teams   235
    JULIA C. GLUESING

    Instructor level: advanced to extremely experienced
    Audience: working professionals and geographically dispersed
    Objectives: to use moments of intercultural tension to pause
         and diagnose cross-cultural issues to promote team
         development
    Process: interventions with "in-situ" teams

20 Teaching mindful intercultural conflict management   253
    STELLA TING-TOOMEY

    Instructor level: intermediate to extremely experienced
    Audience: all ages and levels of sophistication
    Objectives: to develop conflict resolution skills in cross-cultural
         settings
    Process: experiential exercise

21 **Effective cross-cultural leadership: tips and techniques for
    developing capacity**   269
    MEENA SURIE WILSON

    Instructor: intermediate to extremely experienced
    Audience: all ages and levels of sophistication
    Objectives: to learn and apply frameworks that develop cross-
        cultural adaptability
    Process: exercises, dialogue, and reflection

PART VII
**The cultural context of work: impacts on functional
performance**   281

22 **Global ethics**   283
    HEIDI VERNON

    Instructor level: intermediate to extremely experienced
    Audience: all ages and levels of sophistication
    Objectives: to learn that ethics differ by culture and to
        understand the ethics of self and others
    Process: caselets

23 **Negotiating culture**   293
    ROBERT S. SPICH

    Instructor level: advanced to extremely experienced
    Audience: all ages and levels of sophistication
    Objectives: to learn about the negotiating process when
        multiple cultures are represented
    Process: simulation

24 **Conceptualizing and designing a course in international
    human resource management**   300
    COLETTE A. FRAYNE

    Instructor level: advanced and experienced
    Audience: advanced undergraduates and above, professionals
    Objectives: to present propositions on how to handle the
        cultural question in a multicultural complex business
        negotiations course
    Process: course design for mixed didactic/experiential
        learning

25 Incorporating culture in joint-venture and alliance instruction: the Alliance Culture Exercise 310

J. MICHAEL GERINGER AND COLETTE A. FRAYNE

Instructor level: intermediate to extremely experienced
Audience: advanced undergraduates, graduate students, and
  working professionals
Objectives: to learn to use an outcomes framework to assess
  cultural evolutionary possibilities within a joint venture or
  alliance
Process: framework and exercise

26 Teaching culture in the capstone strategy course 319

ALLAN BIRD

Instructor level: intermediate to extremely experienced
Audience: advanced undergraduates, graduate students, and
  working professionals
Objectives: to learn to interweave cultural issues within a
  complex integrative capstone to improve decision making
  and implementation capabilities
Process: course design and case method

PART VIII
Not the end 327

27 As we go forward 329

RICHARD A. GOODMAN, MARGARET E. PHILLIPS AND
NAKIYE AVDAN BOYACIGILLER

Contributors

Nancy J. Adler Faculty of Management, McGill University, Montreal, Quebec, Canada

Janet M. Bennett Intercultural Communications Institute, Portland, OR, USA

Allan Bird College of Business Administration, University of Missouri–St. Louis, St. Louis, MO, USA

Nakiye Avdan Boyacigiller College of Business, San José State University, San José, CA, USA and Graduate School of Management, Sabanci University, Istanbul, Turkey

Mary Yoko Brannen Department of Organization and Management, College of Business, San José State University, San José, CA, USA

Darius K.-S. Chan Psychology Department, Chinese University of Hong Kong, Shatin, Hong Kong SAR, China

Bernardo M. Ferdman California School of Organizational Studies, Alliant International University, San Diego, CA, USA

Colette A. Frayne The Albers School of Business and Economics, Seattle University, Seattle, WA, USA

Susan Fukushima The Anderson School at UCLA, University of California–Los Angeles, Los Angeles, CA, USA

J. Michael Geringer Orfalea College of Business, California Polytechnic University–San Luis Obispo, San Luis Obispo, CA, USA

Cristina Gibson Center for Effective Organizations, University of Southern California, Los Angeles, CA, USA

Julia C. Gluesing Cultural Connections, Inc., Troy, MI, USA

Richard A. Goodman The Anderson School at UCLA, University of California–Los Angeles, Los Angeles, CA, USA

Sharon G. Goto Department of Psychology, Pomona College, Claremont, CA, USA

Stephen Jenner School of Business, California State University, Dominguez Hills, Carson, CA, USA

Jill Kleinberg The School of Business, University of Kansas, Lawrence, KN, USA

Tatiana Kostova International Business Department, Moore School of Business, University of South Carolina, Columbia, SC, USA

Henry W. Lane College of Business Administration, Northeastern University, Boston, MA, USA

Martha L. Maznevski IMD, Lausanne, Switzerland

Joyce S. Osland Department of Organization and Management, College of Business, San José State University, San José, CA, USA

Margaret E. Phillips The George L. Graziado School of Business and Management, Pepperdine University, Malibu, CA, USA

Jennifer Roney Pacific University, Forest Grove, OR, USA

Gerard L. Rossy Department of Management, College of Business and Economics, California State University–Northridge, Northridge, CA, USA

Sonja A. Sackmann Department of Economics, Management and Organization Sciences, Universität der Bundeswehr, Munich, Germany

Robert Spich The Anderson School at ACLA, University of California–Los Angeles, Los Angeles, CA, USA

Sui Wa Tang Department of Psychiatry, University of Hong Kong, Hong Kong SAR, China

Stella Ting-Toomey Department of Speech Communication, California State University at Fullerton, Fullerton, CA, USA

Heidi Vernon College of Business Administration, Northeastern University, Boston, MA, USA

Meena Surie Wilson Center for Creative Leadership, Greensboro, NC, USA

Foreword

Jone L. Pearce

We always have loved travelers' tales. There is something about the ways foreigners are different from us while also being recognizably like us that beguiles. Yet, as we have learned, such tales tell us much more about the teller than the exotic others. This makes it difficult for teachers of international management. Students arrive expecting delightful tales of foreigners. They might expect to just get by in accounting or statistics courses, but they do expect to be entertained in an international management class. How to do so without perpetuating a superficial exoticism? This book adopts a philosophy, backed up with useful tools, that enables teachers to do just that. *Crossing Cultures* takes on the ambitious task of helping us convey understanding without complacency, and knowledge without arrogance. This book moves us closer to these goals in a way that is insightful, stimulating, and really, very useful.

This work is a twenty-first century tale. It assumes that we all are now cosmopolitans, or as they tell it, carry multicultural imprints. That is, today we have not only the culture we were born into, but also many familiar foreign ones, learned as we live among neighbors from different backgrounds and absorb different cultures from a globalized mass media and literature. Our classrooms now hold students who have had lessons in multicultural tolerance since elementary school (and many who have not). We have students who have lived and worked in other cultures for decades, while others have received all of their cultural imprints solely from the tales of others, not all of them with lessons of tolerance. How to help such diverse cosmopolitans to look deeper and see more? Can we keep them engaged and motivated by the tale, without mesmerizing and pacifying?

Nakiye Boyacigiller, Dick Goodman, and Maggi Phillips have developed a genuinely innovative way to help us all approach this task; it is an approach that puts reflection and reformulation at the forefront. First, they offer the why, not just the how. Accomplished teachers of anthropology, learning, conflict management, ethics, negotiation, human resources management, and alliance formation have been gathered here and asked to share their best course sessions addressing crossing cultures. By bringing together such diverse specialists, there is more genuine intellectual insight here than I have found in most scholarly books on culture. As they say, they "engage complexity with dialogue," and the inclusion of so many different approaches to culture gives us the tools to get the conversation going, in our own minds as much as in the classroom.

Yet what is genuinely exciting is the way the material is presented. Each master teacher provides (1) the intellectual background for the subject matter covered in the session, (2) a description of the how-to for the classroom exercise, and (3) common dilemmas the instructor sometimes has with the session. Thus, each chapter, on its own, is extremely useful. In each, we can see the intellectual underpinnings and, depending on the group, can choose to teach them; we can evaluate exercise outcomes, as well as find help in addressing dysfunctional responses.

Further, this book is ambitious while remaining refreshingly modest. Boyacigiller, Goodman, and Phillips describe how they have tried to grapple with the complexity of teaching culture to avoid false epiphanies, an arrogance that is closed to learning, and how not to overplay that seductive "culture card." They recognize that the topic is one of immense intellectual complexity, but that students come to a class on culture expecting exotic tales, and maybe some fun. They give us tools, clearly labeled for easy access, and then let us decide how we will use them. This respect for the book's readers, as much as the combination of intellectual heft and practical tools, is what leads me to call this a twenty-first century work. It is innovative, engaging and useful, and I hope it will serve as a model.

March 17, 2003
Irvine, California

Acknowledgments

In early 1991, José de la Torre, the founding director of the UCLA Center for International Business Education and Research (CIBER), invited a small group of colleagues to lunch, where he encouraged us to form a culture-focused effort in support of the CIBER mission. Embracing this mission of bringing together disciplines from across university campuses to support education in international business, the CIBER Cross Cultural Colleagium (C4) was born. Several years later, our C4 "godfather" offered us additional CIBER support to convene an international seminar to further our work on teaching culture. From this C4 activity, this book has arisen. We owe an enormous debt to José's insight, stimulation, encouragement, and passion, and his steadfast belief in our endeavors, and we wholeheartedly thank him.

Residing under the UCLA CIBER umbrella has provided C4 with wonderful protection from direct exposure to the harsher elements of fundraising and competition for support. But our experience has actually been more akin to being under a double-layered Chinese parasol – the second, upper layer of which is the United States Department of Education. The CIBER program, designed by the DOE in a wonderfully creative fashion, has flourished across the country, including at UCLA, nourished and tended by DOE Program Manager Susanna Easton. Recognizing early the uniqueness of the C4 project at UCLA, Susanna has been a particularly strong supporter and forceful contributor to the evolution of our group. Over-arching the UCLA CIBER, Susanna and the DOE have continually provided intellectual support and, of course, financial resources earmarked for C4. Like a lovely double-layered parasol, these have protected C4 while allowing us to move about in fresh air and light so our ideas might grow and flourish. We are grateful beneficiaries of the Department of Education CIBER program and of Susanna Easton's confidence and support. We thank them sincerely.

For more than a decade, C4 has met three times a year for extensive discussions of a wide range of issues cultural. The "floating" membership of C4 includes 54 colleagues at 33 universities. The C4 community has been incredibly stimulating to our work on culture – both research and teaching – and to that of most of the contributors to this book. We are extremely grateful to be part of this community of culture scholars, and we thank all our C4 colleagues for their active participation in and loyalty to this group. Special thanks go to C4 members Allan Bird, Colette Frayne, and Mike Geringer, for hosting our teaching mini-conference at Cal Poly San Luis Obispo, the prototype for the international seminar that fostered this book.

Our other professional communities have been supportive as well. The genesis for this book began in teaching workshops at the annual and international meetings of the Western Academy of Management and at the Academy of International Business. We thank these organizations and colleagues from around the world who expressed interest in our ideas, showed strong support for a broader discussion of teaching culture, and encouraged us to collect and contribute our accumulated knowledge in a more tangible form.

We obviously owe our thanks to all the contributors to our book. They have been patient and responsive, their contributions have been thoughtful and carefully developed, and their insights have been stimulating and impressive. As we have worked to help them shape these modules, we have felt continually excited by their ideas and inspired by their passion for their work.

We are extraordinarily grateful to Lynn Mayeda. She not only warmly embraced the forty pages of instructions from the publishers, but also provided the support we needed to go from authors' manuscripts to the submitted publisher's document. This is, in itself, a job requiring not only conscientious attention to detail but smart management of the flow of documents and editorial corrections. Lynn, we thank you – you are a true heroine.

Without the support of these special people and the many unnamed associates of us all, this volume would not have been possible. However, it is our students who were and are the motivation for this book, so it is them we must thank most profusely. The positive feedback we get from them inspires us all to be better teachers and lifelong learners.

Part I

Not the beginning

Chapter 1

Culture, passion, and play

*Richard A. Goodman, Margaret E. Phillips, and
Nakiye Avdan Boyacigiller*

Introduction

This book is "not the beginning," but only a consolidating pause in our
individual journeys toward understanding and teaching about cultural
crossings. It is driven by our intellectual curiosity, our academic interests
and the accident of our birthright. As a Turkish–American in California,
Paris, and Istanbul, a New Yorker in the U.S. Midwest, or a Jamaican–
Californian – we naturally grew into this field from our personal experiences and challenges. Muslim, Jew, Christian – our own cross-cultural lives
focused our attention and shaped our interests. Later as industrial relations specialist, strategist, organization theorist – we contextualized our
disciplines within our own multicultural worlds.

In our professional lives of research, teaching, and consulting, we engaged
with issues cultural and issues international, embedded in issues organizational. We found ourselves at the nexus of several disciplines – borrow-
ing a concept here and a concept there – adapting those we found to the
pragmatic realities of organizational life. We soon discovered that the way
forward was to "virtually" assemble a cohort of differently trained or differently experienced colleagues with whom to share our evolving "knowledge
of the ineffable" (culture) and our evolving struggle with how to create
effective learning experiences – learning for ourselves, for our students,
and for people living and working in organizations.

We expect many of you came to the teaching of crossing cultures in
much the same way. Some of you may be novices, recently requested to
"internationalize" your courses; some may have expanded their human
relations training responsibilities to include preparation of executives for
expatriate assignment; some may have extensive personal international
experience, be trilingual, carry multiple passports, and have academic
appointments and teaching responsibilities at universities in several countries. Whatever your range or scope of experience and exposure, we know
you, like us, have noticed that the world has become more intercultural

and interdisciplinary and recognize that it will continue to be so as we move forward in the twenty-first century. We know you, like us, find a range of challenging cross-cultural work and life situations now form the background of many organizational activities. And we appreciate that, every day, like us, you are confronted with these challenges, yet lack easily available, substantive approaches to meet them.

We bring to you this book of insights – philosophical, theoretical, applied, and very practical – to meet these challenges, to allow expanded exposure to ideas, concepts, and processes developed by experienced teachers and scholars of cross-cultural and international organization and management, and to increase opportunities for collegial interaction and engagement. Our goal is to help us all, as teachers and learners, make a major leap forward in our understandings of issues cultural and in our ability to help our students learn and develop the requisite skills to be effective members in and managers of twenty-first-century organizations.

Origins of this book

The voices you hear in *Crossing Cultures: Insights from Master Teachers* are those of our network of colleagues who are members or affiliates of the UCLA Center for International Business Education and Research (CIBER) Cross Cultural Colleagium (C4). This affinity group of 54 scholars from 33 universities comes from a wide variety of backgrounds and approaches the fundamental issues of culture from a variety of disciplines (such as anthropology, sociology, international business, management, psychology, strategy, theatre, and psychiatry, to name but a few.) For over a decade, concepts and methods, data and experience, working and teaching about issues cultural have been a substantive basis for intellectual "play" among this set of colleagues. We have been privileged to be founding members, contributors, and colleagues to this eclectic set of scholars for whom culture is not only a focus for work, but also a passion. That passion extends not only to the exploration but also to the teaching of culture concepts and the development of skills for successful culture crossings. Since the inception of C4, we have worked and played with notions and processes for developing skills and capabilities within our students. Finally, we felt it was time to bring together the best in teaching materials from our best teachers. We did so, first in workshop and now in text.

We convened a three-day seminar involving 50 master teachers from across North America and overseas. Here we discussed our approaches to teaching about cultural crossings, as well as our dilemmas. We did this in full plenary for all three days. No one wanted to leave the room – except to eat. (We are passionate about eating as well!) The intensity and passion of the sessions surprised all observers, though not the participants. We, after all, were having the time of our lives. This is exactly why we became academics – to think, to feel, to share, to help, to support, and to have fun!

We came together with the goal of *promoting conscious competence* among teachers in this field. Within our workshop, we focused on exploring and elaborating our philosophies, sharing methods and teaching tools, building and enriching each of our approaches and techniques. The level of passion at the meeting arose because these "master teachers" had much to teach and much *to learn* from one another. *Crossing Cultures: Insights from Master Teachers* is the result.

Key tenets of this book

This book is not only a direct derivative of our teaching workshop, it is also a representation of the unique character and collegial style of C4. We have endeavored in our instructions to our colleagues and in our own editing to reflect the key tenets of C4 – tenets that we have grown to view as fundamental to our understandings of the nature of culture in organizations and to productive processes for its exploration. We believe:

1   The focal concept of "culture in organization" should be the idea of *working together*. Thus, our objectives are to increase cross-cultural skills for successful working relationships within organizations.
2   A second central tenet we hold is the understanding that, unlike the anthropological roots of the organizational culture metaphor, organizations are not isolated self-contained communities that carry a single, monolithic culture. Nor, like the traditional focus of the international management field, are organization members assumed to carry and employ only their national cultural mindset. Rather, each member of the organization is assumed to carry multiple cultural imprints and schemas, all of which are available to them as they engage in their work. These include cultures that are, for example, geographically based (e.g., national, regional), societal subgroups (e.g., ethnic, sex, religion), cross-organizational (e.g., industry, profession, discipline), organizational, and sub-organizational (e.g., functional, hierarchical, project-based). Thus, individuals in the organization live with and within *multiple cultures.*
3   A core element of working together in multiple cultural settings is the need to learn about the cultures that compose the organization. Thus, a third tenet (and, of course, one of the main reasons for this book) is the *need for learning cultures*. This need goes well beyond learning the codified artifacts available in descriptions of one culture or another. Rather, it is about learning the cultures that exist within the organizational setting, and recognizing that such cultures are in constant flux as organizational membership changes over time. Learning

about a gestalt is an ongoing exploration and requires frequent reflection and reformulation of one's understandings.

4   An unresolved question, but a central tenet, is the question of cultural salience. We all recognize that we shift our behavior from one situation to another based upon our "choice" of which cultural schema should dominate – an unconscious, but highly developed competence. *Oscillating salience* depicts our understanding of individual behavior in organizations. This is the existential truth. The current question, then, is, "What triggers the operative salience within a given situation?"

5   The foregoing explanations lead directly to the fifth tenet. Working together, learning culture, living with multiple cultures of oscillating salience requires the willingness to *engage complexity.* This is, perhaps, a meta-tenet.

6   *Dialogue* is our sixth tenet. To study culture, it is important to engage in dialogue across disciplines, across institutions, and across roles. C. West Churchman tells a wonderful parable about the blind men and the elephant. We are all familiar with the basic tale, but Churchman brings a very different perspective to the parable. He points out the arrogance of the storyteller. The parable only makes sense to the teller and the listener because the storyteller appears to know the "truth." We treasure the value of dialogue with others in a co-equal flow of information, perspective, and insight, because such dialogue helps us better understand the "thing" we have labeled an elephant. We study and work with "informants" who help us see the shape of this elephant more clearly. But we recognize that culture is an ephemeral "elephant" and that our informants are ever crafting and individually interpreting through their own socially constructed realities. Thus, we have come to recognize the vain and futile stance of the storyteller.

   Dialogue also refers to a "process." The process of learning and discovery through dialogue is central for both novice and initiated, especially in the cross-cultural field. Dialogue is important at both the personal and intellectual ends of the spectrum. We characterize dialogue as sharing, caring, and listening with respect. It requires change from a mode of academic confrontation to a learning orientation. Professionals and novices can learn from each other; executives and academics can learn from each other; students and teachers can learn from each other. Confrontation, in the form of respectful yet passionate interaction, can yield to stimulation and from there to insight and enlightenment.

7   *Grappling with dilemmas* is an inherent characteristic of teaching in this area. How can we teach learning culture in a fast yet deep and meaningful fashion? How do we create learning environments that

recognize the inherent complexity of culture yet allow for some parsimony to our session designs? How do we minimize the ugly risk of stereotyping? How do we give our students the sense of power to say "I'm confident that I know enough to go to Germany and negotiate" while not being arrogant enough to believe that they "truly" do know enough and, thus, will remain open to new learning? Can one focus on the complexities of culture with a fairly young homogeneous student population? How do we limit "false epiphany" where you find something that looks sophisticated and comprehensive and you use it, and then it freezes your inclination and ability to learn? How do we ensure that our students not "overplay the culture card" and recognize the important institutional factors that also may be at play? It is requisite that we continue to surface dilemmas in both concept and process to allow dialogue and, hopefully, new insight to develop around them.

8   All the above tenets speak to a primary outcome of culture and also the main feature of C4 – a sense of *community*. Fundamentally, C4 is a group of colleagues who periodically engage together in intensive and extensive conversation and exploration. A sense of fellowship, fun, and intellectual play characterizes these relationships. These exchanges are supplemented by many additional and ongoing connections that infuse our other professional activities, our travels, and our personal interactions. Scholarship, collegiality, and friendship are the source, glue, and outcomes of the C4 community. We hope that readers of this book will extend the nature, reach, and scope of our virtual community!

9   *Passion* permeates our work and is reflected directly in the nature and intensity of our interactions. This seems to emanate from the personal connections to the topic of culture in the life situation or experience of each C4 member. Additionally, the experience of presenting to an audience of diverse and articulate professionals who learn from helping and constructively challenging the presenter is quite exciting and exhilarating, as is the experience of being an active participant in that exchange. This passion that strengthens the relationships between C4 members and solidifies our commitment to the group is that which we hope you the reader bring and/or develop in the process of engaging with ideas within this book.

"Master teachers"/master learners

When soliciting contributions for the book we looked for people who shared many of the values above, had reputations as strong teachers and take a rigorous approach to their teaching, and who dealt with subject matter that we felt needed to be a part of the book. The core group of master teachers are members of C4 and affiliates who participated in our workshop, colleagues and friends who share common values around the importance of scholarship and community. We expanded our set of contributors a bit beyond that scope, seeking in particular to extend our international and interdisciplinary reach.[1]

We should note that despite the somewhat immodest title of "master teachers," each and every one of the authors is a "master learner" as well. Master teachers most often have a thirst for lifelong learning. As one of our colleagues notes, even high-performance athletes need coaches. People want to have new things to try in class without having to construct them for themselves all the time. So we offer this "cookbook," but please note: it is not just a bunch of new recipes, but a sourcebook like *James Beard's Theory and Practice of Good Cooking*[2] that offers the "why" rather than just the "how." It is to this end that we asked the authors to surface, in their modules, the underlying principles and philosophical orientations in their learning and to grapple with the dilemmas they face in their teaching.

Structure of the teaching modules

This book provides a framework to address different issues regarding cultural interactions: conceptual definitions; learning and characterizing cultures; experiencing cultural crossings; the development of a broader global mindset; intercultural collaboration; and, cultural impacts on functional performance in organizations. For each issue, our "master teachers" were asked to provide a teaching module representing their best teaching idea and embedded in a robust discussion detailing:

- the philosophical or theoretical source of the idea or exercise;
- how it reflects their working definition of culture;
- how they use the module (including, as appropriate, specific directions for instructors and students); and,
- variations for different audiences (i.e., undergraduates or executives, in classroom or *in situ*) and typical student dialogues or responses.

Authors were also asked to highlight the typical difficulties they encounter when using the module and how they adjust to these difficulties when they arise. An annotated table of contents provides further guidance as to instructor level, audience, objectives, and process for each module.

Our charge to our readers

We hope that you will approach this book with the mental model of inquisitiveness and experimentation. Many of us have been grappling with issues around how to best teach cross-cultural management for years. Whether you are an expert organization behavior or management instructor but a novice to international management, or you are a veteran trainer of expatriates for overseas assignments, we expect you too have been grappling with some of these very issues. We hope that, by deeply engaging with the material, you will begin to think about the various issues raised in the modules and how you would deal with them with your own students and in your own learning. We trust you will be provoked to experiment with what is here and share it with others in your own intellectual community. We also invite you to share your new learning with specific authors and with all who have contributed to this book, toward the end of expanding our community of colleagues and our understanding of the complexities of crossing cultures.

Notes

1 While we believe we have involved a stellar set of authors, we recognize the need for more geographic and disciplinary diversity among authors and colleagues as we address these topics.
2 Beard, J. (1977) *James Beard's Theory and Practice of Good Cooking*, New York: Alfred A. Knopf.

Part II

Framing the culture concept

What is culture?/How can we characterize it?

A fundamental principle of this book is to permit "definitional robustness" to inform our collective appreciation. Each author was requested to identify their own definition of culture as part of the module they were writing about. True to this principle we have created as the first part a series of teaching modules that come from different perspectives and that engage in the adaptation of their perspectives to teaching about culture and culture's impact within organizations and between organizations.

Goto and Chan bring to bear a social-psychological perspective that bridges between the individual and the cluster of individuals. By starting with individually generated data they easily show a class where the clusters of shared values exist. This is a powerful and easily presented technique that supports the idea that "there is a difference" at the values level and is a powerful starting point for the exploration of these differences.

We have asked Mary Yoko Brannen to explicate how she as a trained social anthropologist selects from, adapts, and transitions the basic issues of her field into a most valuable lesson at the organizational level. Thus, she challenges the static and monocultural assertions of many and argues for dynamic and multicultural assumptions as more relevant to organizational life.

Sackmann and Phillips offer a "multiple cultures" view of organizational life, a developing perspective in the field of international cross-cultural management. They provide a practical process for discussion of this perspective, one that has been used successfully both with students at various academic levels and with practitioners. Here, the focus is on heightening the learners' awareness of the multiple cultures carried both by individuals and by organizations and deepening their understanding of the impact of these multiple cultures within work settings.

Ferdman, whose point of view is social-psychological, provides us with a "personalized" class exercise that brings the idea of one's multicultural identity directly to each student. Whereas the case above allowed the student to intellectualize multicultural identity, this module helps each of us to personalize the issue through creating guided pictures of ourselves. Through recognizing group-level and individual differences in ourselves and others, Ferdman helps us understand the sources of the inherent diversity in us all.

Chapter 2

Are we the same or are we different?

A social-psychological perspective of culture

Sharon G. Goto and Darius K.-S. Chan

Introduction

This chapter introduces a teaching tool that illustrates "culture" through the eyes of social psychologists. In doing so, we will first define culture, then use the Twenty Statements Test (TST) to illustrate the theoretical and methodological intricacies of this conceptualization. The TST has long been useful in research; but we believe that the TST is a promising instrument for teaching as well, particularly given this individually based perspective on culture.

Background

What is culture? There is a tendency to base culture on national and racial or ethnic boundaries. However, this approach tends to artificially homogenize a population's diversity. For example, both authors are Asian. Yet, one is a fourth generation Japanese–American, the other is Hong Kong Chinese. Using race to place the two authors within the same category would be simplistic, neglecting differences in ethnicity and acculturation experiences. Furthermore, if we are looking for similarities or differences across cultures, knowing that the co-authors are Asian does not provide information or understanding beyond the category. That is, categories are not informative in and of themselves. For these reasons, many social psychologists have defined culture in the terms of subjective culture (Triandis 1972).

The "subjective culture" framework views individuals as the primary building blocks upon which cultural groups are based. Every individual brings to the table a series of past experiences. These past experiences are based on socialization and knowledge of what is reinforced by important others like co-workers, peers, social groups, and family members. Often, these past experiences, either explicit or tacit, influence the positions a person may take. When commonalities along these lines exist in an aggregate of people, we identify it as culture. That is, culture exists at the intersections of people's experiences and expectations. Organizational culture, for example, is built on the foundations of individuals interacting within an organizational setting. Subjective culture then defines a culture as those sharing common attitudes, values, and norms for behavior. Given this definition, the co-authors might share a similar culture, not based on phenotype, but rather on shared attitudes. Why attitudes, values, and norms? These constructs are *constructs of choice* for social psychologists. Beyond mere categories, knowing and understanding the attitudes held by a group of people or the pressure an individual faces from co-workers can help clarify why decisions are made and practices are enacted.

Geert Hofstede's (1980) work with IBM employees provides a very familiar usage of culture as subjective culture. Hofstede found four dimensions that were useful as boundaries of subjective culture: power distance, uncertainty avoidance, masculinity/femininity, and individualism/collectivism. This last dimension has generated much interesting cross-cultural and cultural research. Collectivism, which is related to an interdependent construal of the self is generally seen as subjective culture where interrelationships with others and groups are valued over that of independence. In contrast, individualism, which is related to an independent construal of the self, values independence and separation from others over connectedness (Markus and Kitayama 1991). Nations that exemplify collectivist characteristics are Spain and Korea. The United States and Australia typify individualistic cultures.

A commonly used measure of collectivism is the Twenty Statements Test (TST) (Ip and Bond 1995; Triandis, McCusker and Hui 1990; Rhee, *et al.* 1995). This requires answering the question, "Who am I?" twenty times. The responses to the statements, "I am...," are then coded as being either "independent" (i.e., individualistic) or "group" (i.e., interdependent or collectivist).

The TST can be used effectively to initiate discussions and further understanding about culture. We have used this tool in undergraduate classrooms, in cultural trainings for community-based organizations, and in business settings. Since the TST is open-ended and easily influenced by discussion, we suggest it be used to illustrate cultural differences and capture an audience's attention. To this end, first administer the TST either as shown in the handout in Appendix 2.1 or ask the class or audience to respond to the statement, "I am" in the margins of their notebook.

Upon completion, train the audience to code their own responses by explaining the "group" versus "individual" distinctions as described below. For each response, provide a code of "I" which represents individual responses or "G" which represents group responses. Group responses denote *common fate* between similar respondents. For example, if a policy were put in place to affect education, all "students" would be affected.

Examples of group responses are "daughter," "student," "female," and "Japanese." In contrast, individual responses do not connote interdependence, but are attributes of that person. For example, "I am funny" or "I am hungry" are to be coded as individual responses. Interesting discussion may ensue regarding how to code an allocentric response such as "I am family-oriented." I recommend including this in the "G" category, due to connotations of common fate. An alternative is to omit similar responses from further analysis since it does not fall cleanly into either category. Finally, they are to calculate the percentage of their responses that are "G." This is their personal score of collectivism.

The instructor can then begin talking about "what is culture?" and specifically how culture might be understood to affect and be represented in individuals and in groups, as aggregates of individual people. This may be followed by discussions about cross-national differences in collectivism, cultural diversity, cross-cultural methodology, or dynamic aspects of culture.

Discussion of TST for the instructor

As a teaching tool, the TST carries many benefits. First, it is participative, easy to administer to large groups, and requires very little preparation. Although a copy of a handout is provided, students can use the margins of their notebooks, and they can code their responses immediately.

Beyond being user-friendly, the TST can illustrate bold differences in national boundaries. In our experience, U.S. samples generally respond with about 20 percent "group" self-descriptions (sometimes the mode is 0 percent), whereas in China a 60 percent "group" response is not uncommon, particularly among older populations. A show of hands easily indicates the modal percentage of "group" responses in the classroom. North American students are often surprised to hear the high percentages of other countries. (Note: depending on the intent of the instructor other groupings for analysis can be used, such as gender, organization, education, or regional identity.)

The TST can also illustrate the diversity of culture within a given group. For example, although the mode of group statements is around 20 percent, within a classroom we have found the percentage of group statements to range from 0 to 80 percent. Oftentimes, Asian-American students respond strongly toward collectivism, much like students in China (Trafimow, Triandis and Goto 1991; Rhee, *et al.* 1995). Furthermore, some European-American students are much more collectivist than the Asian-American students!

The range of responses is also informative. For example, if the range is narrow (e.g., all respondents fall in the 20–30 percent group), then the construct of collectivism can be thought to be strongly proscribed by the culture. A wider range might indicate the influence of several factors like the particular family or workgroup dynamics operating within the larger culture.

The TST can illustrate the dynamic nature of culture, thereby avoiding the tendency to think of culture as static. Studies have suggested that although an individual may be primarily individualistic or primarily collectivist, they are not purely so (Trafimow, Triandis and Goto 1991). Furthermore, this may be situationally driven (Hong, *et al.* 2000). That is, an individual might have a "bin" of many different self-descriptions that are primarily collectivist. Yet, this individual also has some individualistic self-descriptions in their repertoire that may be elicited by environmental cues. Therefore, at times this individualist can act collectivistically. This notion can be illustrated by "priming" the participants or class. First, ask them to spend a few minutes thinking about things that make them similar to others. You may even ask them to jot ideas down. This focuses their attention on collectivism. If you then ask them to do the TST, the percentage of group responses should be higher than if they were not primed. This also works if you prime for individualism (ask them to think about things that make them different from others).

The TST is also useful in discussions of cultural methodology. First, the TST has been shown to have construct validity. Recall the definition of subjective culture as shared attitudes, values, and norms. An onion skin metaphor illustrates their theoretical interrelations – at the innermost layer, most central to the individual are notions of the self, the next layer is values, followed by attitudes, and behavioral norms. These theoretically linked facets of subjective culture have been empirically supported through Chan's (1994) COLINDEX. In this study, the proportions of group descriptions as elicited by the TST were positively correlated with collectivist values [i.e., determined using Schwartz's (1992) values (e.g., harmony)] and traditional measures of collectivist attitudes (Triandis, *et al.* 1986), and negatively correlated to individualistic values (e.g., hedonism) and individualistic attitudes. Therefore, the TST is a simple, open-ended and codable task that lacks demand characteristics, and maintains construct validity.

Interestingly, it can easily be used in other languages. Because the TST relies on open-ended, projective techniques, only the initial statement ("I am") needs translation. The respondent can fill in the blank in their native tongue and then either the respondent or a second person fluent in that language can code the data. If the TST is used comparatively (e.g., employees in the U.S. versus Singapore), the TST remains relatively easy to administer as only the percentages of "individual" versus "group" responses are needed. Only if the content of the responses were deemed essential for a given purpose would back-translation become necessary. In this case, there may be challenges to the "meaning" of what represents an individual versus group-oriented response. That is, perhaps responding, "I am a student" connotes group membership in one culture, but is a very individually based endeavor in another culture. Respondents within a given culture should negotiate the appropriateness of meanings. This exercise in meaning can be incorporated as a class exercise on conceptual equivalence.

Furthermore, there may be limitations of language itself. Asking "I am" in Cantonese almost forces the respondent to answer with a noun if the respondent is to be grammatically correct (D. K.-S. Chan, personal communication, April 2001). A noun is more likely to be coded as a group response. More importantly, the TST can be used to illustrate the dangerous nature of imposed etics (i.e., presumed universals from one culture that are imposed onto others). In many East Asian and collectivist cultures, the notion of "the self" as context-free, invariant, and non-relational is artificial. Asking the seemingly neutral question, as "I am..." may impose an individualistic framework on a collectivist individual, forcing the void of context (Fiske, *et al.* 1998). Perhaps "We are..." might be more appropriate. Perhaps allowing for a context "if _____, then I am _____" would be more appropriate.

Finally, the TST and subjective cultures are useful as a theoretical tool for understanding current and introducing future orientations of culture. For example, what happens when cultures clash? Should we expect cultural conflicts in negotiations between individuals from a collectivist culture and individuals from individualistic cultures? In the U.S., increasing cultural diversity has been a source of conflict (and reward). Can we understand the intricacies of a diversifying workforce by understanding how collectivists operate or fail to operate effectively in an individualist culture? What will cultural diversity look like in a collectivist culture? Just as the TST and collectivism are useful for understanding current issues of culture, they are also useful as a concrete tool for imagining and understanding future situations.

Collectivism represents a single aspect of culture. As shown, the TST can be easily and effectively adopted to introduce elementary notions of culture. However, to avoid the risk of stereotyping, perhaps the best use is as a building block in a series of conversations about culture. Used in conjunction with other cultural dimensions and teaching tools, the TST will enable an increasingly sophisticated understanding of the rich and varied textures of culture.

Appendix 2.1 Handout for the Twenty Statements Test

Please answer the following questions by completing the sentence, "I am…" twenty times. Please work quickly, and proceed from one response to the other with ease. If you "get stuck" do not force your responses.

1 I am _____
2 I am _____
3 I am _____
4 I am _____
5 I am _____
6 I am _____
7 I am _____
8 I am _____
9 I am _____
10 I am _____
11 I am _____
12 I am _____
13 I am _____
14 I am _____
15 I am _____
16 I am _____
17 I am _____
18 I am _____
19 I am _____
20 I am _____

Source: Adapted from Triandis, McCusker and Hui 1990.

Further reading

Hong, Y.-Y., Morris, M. W., Chiu, C. Y. and Benet-Martinez, V. (2000) "Multicultural minds: a dynamic constructivist approach to culture and cognition," *American Psychologist*, 55 (7): 709–20.

Markus, H. R. and Kitayama, S. (1991) "Culture and the self: implications for cognition, emotion, and motivation," *Psychological Review*, 98 (2): 224–53.

Trafimow, D., Triandis, H. C. and Goto, S. G. (1991) "Some tests of the distinction between the private self and the collective self," *Journal of Personality and Social Psychology*, 60: 649–55.

References

Chan, D. K.-S. (1994) "COLINDEX: a refinement of three collectivism measures," in S. C. Choi, Ç. Kagitçibasi, U. Kim, H. C. Triandis and G. Yoon (eds), *Individualism and Collectivism: Theory, Method, and Applications*, Thousand Oaks, CA: Sage.

Fiske, A. P., Kitayama, S., Markus, H. R. and Nisbett, R. E. (1998) "The cultural matrix of social psychology," in D. T. Gilbert, A. P. Fiske and G. Lindzey (eds), *Handbook of Social Psychology*, 4th edn, Hillsdale, NJ: Lawrence Erlbaum.

Hofstede, G. H. (1980) *Culture's Consequences: International Differences in Work-related Values*, Beverly Hills, CA: Sage.

Hong, Y.-Y., Morris, M. W., Chiu, C. Y. and Benet-Martinez, V. (2000) "Multicultural minds: a dynamic constructivist approach to culture and cognition," *American Psychologist*, 55 (7): 709–20.

Ip, G. W. M. and Bond, M. H. (1995) "Culture, values and the spontaneous self-concept," *Asian Journal of Psychology*, 1: 29–35.

Markus, H. R. and Kitayama, S. (1991) "Culture and the self: implications for cognition, emotion, and motivation," *Psychological Review*, 98 (2): 224–53.

Rhee, E., Uleman, J. S., Lee, H. K. and Roman, R. J. (1995) "Spontaneous self-descriptions and ethnic identities in individualistic and collectivistic cultures," *Journal of Personality and Social Psychology*, 69: 142–52.

Schwartz, S. H. (1992) "Universals in the content and structure of values: theoretical advances and empirical tests in 20 countries," in M. P. Zanna (ed.), *Advances in Experimental Social Psychology*, San Diego, CA: Academic Press, pp. 1–65.

Trafimow, D., Triandis, H. C. and Goto, S. G. (1991) "Some tests of the distinction between the private self and the collective self," *Journal of Personality and Social Psychology*, 60: 649–55.

Triandis, H. C. (1972) *The Analysis of Subjective Culture*, New York: Wiley.

Triandis, H. C., Bontempo, R., Betancourt H., Bond, M., Leung, K., Brenex, A., Georgas, J., Hui, C. H., Marin, G., Setiadi, B., Singha, J. B. P., Verma, J., Spangenberg, J., Touzard, H. and de Montmollin, G. (1986) "The measurement of etic aspects of individualism and collectivism across-cultures," *Australian Journal of Psychology*, 38: 257–67.

Triandis, H. C., McCusker, C. and Hui, C. H. (1990) "Multimethod probes of individualism and collectivism," *Journal of Personality and Social Psychology*, 59 (5): 1006–20.

Chapter 3

What is culture and why does it matter?

Current conceptualizations of culture from anthropology

Mary Yoko Brannen

Introduction

The objective of this chapter is to provide a theoretical and practical orientation to teaching about culture in today's complex cultural organizations. The study of organizations as cultural phenomena derives from a long tradition in the social sciences. In sociology, Durkheim (1933), Harris (1979), and Weber (1947) provided important analyses of the relationship between culture and industrialization. In anthropology, researchers in a specialization called "urban anthropology" focus on organizational sites. Many studies are comparative, in which national systems of work organization and philosophy are contrasted (for example, Dore 1973; Nakane 1967; Ong 1987; and Sahlins 1985). In addition, within the last few decades there has been a return to sites that are decidedly urban and multicultural (for example, Appadurai 1998; Douglas and Wildavsky 1982; Harris 1979; Lamphere 1987; and Willis 1977). The more recent research is changing the way culture is seen in anthropology by breaking down the boundaries between ourselves and our cultural "others." Culture is being viewed as permeable with ample variation within as well as between cultures.

In organizational studies, there has been a keen interest in studying the organizational phenomena of culture since the late 1970s. Notable works in organization studies include Frost *et al.* (1985), Hatch (1993), Jelinek, Smircich and Hirsch (1983), Kunda (1991), Martin (1992), Schein (1985), Smircich (1983), and Van Maanen (1975, 1976, 1982, 1988), as well as the more practitioner-oriented work on corporate culture such as Deal and Kennedy (1982), Ott (1989), and Peters and Waterman (1982). In addition, Japanese-owned U.S. companies, prevalent in the late 1980s, added to the complexity of studying organizations as cultural phenomena as they represented "bicultural" work organizations – neither necessarily "Japanese" nor "American." Indeed, such bicultural organizations were the precursors of today's complex cultural "global" organizations made up of multiple cultures linked together by mission rather than history, location or time. This is the advent of the metanational organization (Doz, Santos and Williamson 2001), characterized by virtual teams, global development teams, and organizational knowledge transfer across space and time in which the boundaries between previously discrete units, such as nations, cultures, and organizations, have become obscured (Lyotard 1984).

In order to make sense, be prepared for, and function relatively smoothly within the relatively new organizational dynamics that take place in such complex cultural settings, it is useful to approach the topic with the tools that fit extant culture theory. However, teaching tools that emphasize cultural dynamics are scarce. Much of the organizational culture literature has treated U.S. organizations as predominantly monocultural entities – assuming a culturally homogeneous workforce. Some of the literature has pointed to the existence of subcultures in organizations (Whyte 1948 and Turner 1972 laid down the theory; Smircich 1983, Gregory 1983, Martin and Siehl 1983, Van Maanen and Barley 1984 are some often-cited examples of case studies of the phenomenon). Yet, even these studies operate under the assumption that there is one dominant organizational culture that circumscribes all other "mini-cultures."

Much of the practitioner-oriented literature on corporate culture views culture as something that must be transmitted to newcomers to the organization to ensure their success. This view of culture does not allow for the case in which the newcomers to the organization are the ones in power, such as in the case of foreign mergers and acquisitions of U.S. concerns. Since top management (or the people in power) in the U.S. have historically been white middle-to-upper-class males, research in organizational culture has reflected this condition by treating the dominant culture as uniform and generalizable. Although business organizations in the United States have always been culturally diverse, the examination of such diversity has been overlooked, perhaps a consequence of an ideological faith in acculturation of "others" to the "standard" of white males.

Similarly, the tendency to generalize to the monolithic whole exists in the field of cross-cultural (or comparative) management where the word "culture" is more often than not used synonymously with "nation," and national cultural traits are treated as systematically predictable behavioral patterns (Child 1981). While this extensive literature provides a substantial amount of descriptive material on understanding how people of different national cultures behave in organizations, and even helps to predict the types of conflict that are likely to arise from cross-national organizational encounters, these studies generally ignore the fact that work organizations produce their own cultures.

The cross-cultural management literature that looks at the interaction of two national cultures in one organizational setting quickly falls back into what the anthropologist Eric Wolf (1982: 34), calls a "two billiard ball" understanding of culture. Both national cultures are treated as monolithic entities that either collide with each other, leading to unsuccessful ventures, or miss grazing each other, remaining intact in their original cultural forms (Brannen 1998). As Shaw (1990) has pointed out, there is a need for a dynamic model for understanding the interaction between foreign managers and host-country employees. Although quite a while ago Nancy Adler (1986) suggested a "synergistic model" as a new theoretical approach to researching cross-cultural organizational interactions, very little empirical work has been done to formalize such a model.

To summarize, there are four general theoretical limitations of the current management literature to understanding the cultural dynamics of today's complex cultural organization:

1   our present understanding of culture is parochial;
2   culture (organizational or national) is assumed to be consistent in thought and behavioral manifestations across a specified cultural grouping of individuals;
3   there is limited understanding of the interface between national culture and organizational culture; and,
4   cultures are seen as static, not allowing for the reinterpretation of the original cultural contract.

Recent theoretical developments in anthropology with regard to understanding and researching culture provide certain solutions to these limitations in the management literature on culture.

Theoretical contributions from recent anthropological theory

Two general trends, arising from what some anthropologists have called a "crisis in anthropology" (Fox 1991; Marcus and Fisher 1986), promise valuable contributions to culture theory in organization studies and provide a more robust theoretical framework for making sense of the cultural dynamics in today's complex cultural organizations. One trend, centering on ethnographic methodology, takes up the central issue of ethnographic authority and how studies about culture should be represented (e.g., Clifford 1988; Clifford and Marcus 1986; Said 1978). The other trend centers on theory and represents a new tradition referred to as "political economy" that revitalizes the hitherto under-emphasized or altogether ignored cultural components of history and politics (e.g., Ong 1987; Roseberry 1989; Sahlins 1985; Wolf 1982). Both of these trends push the field toward an understanding of cultural phenomena as dynamic, interconnected, mutable, and multi-layered. The traditional static definition of culture as "a system of shared meanings enacted by a particular group of people" (Schein 1985), then, needs updating.

A current definition of culture from anthropology that reflects these new trends is offered by Aihwa Ong (1987):

> "Culture" is taken as historically situated and emergent, shifting and incomplete meanings and practices generated in webs of agency and power. Cultural change is not understood as unfolding according to some predetermined logic (of development, modernization, or capitalism) but as the disrupted, contradictory, and differential outcomes, which involve changes in identity, relations of struggle and dependence, including the experience of reality in situations wherein groups and classes struggle to produce and interpret culture within the industrializing milieu.
>
> (Ong 1987: 2–3)

Though Ong is writing about large-scale social systems, her approach to defining culture and cultural change appropriately explicates these constructs for current complex organizational cultural settings and provides a useful base for developing teaching materials to overcome the limitations of previous representations of culture for understanding organizational behavior in international contexts.

Teaching aids to explicate the culture concept in today's complex cultural organizations

The following is a sample narrative for teaching about culture in today's complex cultural organizations. Each point serves to address and provide a counterbalance to one or more of the four limitations of current culture theory discussed above:

I   Cultural parochialism – Cultural interconnectedness
II   Cultural homogeneity – Cultural complexity and embeddedness
III Culture as monolithic – Variance within culture
IV   Culture as static – Culture as dynamic.

The key limitation and the counterbalanced view listed above are referred to by Roman numeral in the narrative discussion below.

1 Breaking down the notion of the "world as global village" – toward the notion of a cultural interconnectedness (1) and dynamics (IV)

Introduction

The world as "global village" is an expression used so often that the phrase itself has become a cliché. As such, most of us take for granted much of the outcome of globalization. We navigate our lives daily through a panoply of cross-cultural choices, such as which nation's food to eat, what foreign film to watch, or what country's fashions to wear. Most of us even quite comfortably intermix foreign words in our daily vocabulary, like when we say something analogous to "it's a Zen sort of thing," or "he's a real macho kind of guy."

For this exercise I use an up-to-date visual example of cultural homogenization such as a picture of McDonald's in Russia or Starbuck's in Tiananmen Square. I have also successfully used a cartoon from *The New Yorker* magazine that shows an older couple at a travel agent's office with posters of downtown São Paulo, Tokyo, and Paris each city depicted as mirror images of the others. The accompanying narrative I use for this is the following.

Narrative

Here, a couple, perhaps planning their second honeymoon, is at a travel agency. If they were to choose where to go by the posters above the travel agent's desk they might as well flip a coin – São Paulo, Tokyo, Paris all look the same!

Discuss the notion of globalization

There are many topics that can be brought up in this discussion. These include the benefits and costs of globalization, issues of efficiency, issues of cultural hegemony, and of the global integration versus local respon- siveness continuum (Prahalad and Doz 1987). Most important here is to develop an understanding that cultures are active not passive recipients of firms' offerings. As such, firms' offerings are often "recontextualized" (that is, given new meaning) as they are received and integrated into new cultural environments (Brannen 2003).

Here I go on to talk more deeply about homogenized cultural artifacts uncovering the significant differences that underlie them. One of my favorite examples to use is that of vending machines in various countries. Vending machines themselves are homogenized industrial artifacts that look and function the same in different cultural venues. In fact they are traveler-friendly because one does not need to speak the local language to choose and execute a purchase. However, the contents of vending machines vary widely across cultures. For example, in Japan one can purchase beer, sake, whiskey, hot hamburgers, underwear, and other convenient items not found in vending machines in the United States. This difference can serve as a way to get at the cultural misperceptions – a good question to ask the class is, "What would you presume about the Japanese culture based on the items one can purchase in vending machines there?" Students often say that there must be a lot of juvenile alcoholics in Japan or that Japanese must not care about under-age drinking, or that the punishment for under-age substance abuse must be incredibly severe to offset abuse, etc. This discussion then can bring up how our perceptions of other cultures are biased by our own cultural assumptions. This in turn can lead into a discussion of analyzing other cultures by going deeper than the artifacts themselves to uncover the values and assumptions underlying them. For example, the Japanese value convenience and space-saving solutions. They do not have ample food storage in their homes, therefore being able to go down to a vending machine to get sake or beer when a guest comes over is a useful solution. In addition, Japan is a shame-oriented society like many collectivist cultures and therefore social pressure alone is a strong deterrent for abusing alcohol consumption by means of under-age use of vending machines.

2 Building up an understanding of cultural differences that matter – toward the notion of cultural complexity (II) and embeddedness (III)

Introduction

But, one important locale where global navigation happens less smoothly is the transnational firm. In this setting, the culture, or the taken-for-granted rules and scripts that govern how people interact, is not so clear. And, as firms around the globe continue to internationalize, it is in this setting that more and more of us are likely to experience the more poignant effects of the "global village."

Narrative

In order to demonstrate the effects of culture on organizational behavior, let's have a pop quiz, at it were. Please get out a blank piece of paper. I will put on the screen a series of open-ended sentences. As I do so, please finish the sentences with the first thoughts that come to mind.

I then present the following:

- When I'm angry I . . .
- If I don't agree with an idea I . . .
- When someone in my team has done a good job I . . .
- If someone hasn't been pulling his/her load I . . .
- A meeting is to . . .

Discussion

There are several ways to present this. One way is to go through each open-ended question and have the students respond to each in a succinct fashion. Then uncover the culturally general responses supplied. In the example of Table 3.1, Japanese cultural responses are supplied.

Alternatively, the instructor can substitute other cultural responses as indicated by the specific teaching context. Compare and contrast the answers the students come up with and the Japanese (or whatever culture used) general cultural responses. The responses can be uncovered all at once or one response at a time. Either way, the discussion should get at the core national cultural values and assumptions that underscore differences between cultures (the U.S. and Japan for example) that determine our behaviors surrounding the managerial situations outlined in the "pop quiz." This provides an understanding of the embeddedness of culture at the national or organizational, and individual levels. The level of the individual is made patent by the variance in individual responses within the same cultural framework – for example the difference between two American students' responses. When such within-culture differences occur, the instructor can have the students reflect on the various cultural influences they personally have that make up their individual cultures of origin.

Typically in a U.S. teaching setting, the majority of the students will have responses that are quite opposite those of a typical Japanese. The typical U.S. responses are as in Table 3.2.

A useful means of debriefing this exercise is to tie in the responses to core national cultural values. This can be done in a variety of ways. One

Table 3.1 Japanese cultural responses

When I'm angry I . . .	grin and bear it
If I don't agree with an idea I . . .	say that it's interesting and I'll think about it
When someone in my team has done a good job I . . .	reward the group
If someone hasn't been pulling his/her load I . . .	leave it up to group pressure
A meeting is to . . .	formalize a decision

Table 3.2 U.S. cultural responses

When I'm angry I...	show it
If I don't agree with an idea I...	say so
When someone in my team has done a good job I...	reward the individual
If someone hasn't been pulling his/her load I...	sanction the individual
A meeting is to...	make a decision

way is to ask the students what core values their responses underlie. Another way is to use one of the cultural frameworks for analyzing cultural differences, such as Hofstede's four dimensions as outlined in *Culture's Consequences* (1980) or Kluckhohn and Strodtbeck's core cultural orientations as outlined in *Variations in Value Orientations* (1961). If there is a lot of variance in the responses of the class, one can use this disparity to analyze differences between cultures as represented by the class composition, as well as emphasize difference within cultures.

3 Understanding cultural embeddedness (II) or peeling off the layers of the onion

Introduction

Here, I provide the traditional definition of organizational culture from Schein (1985) as a "straw man," as it were, to then add to this simple definition of culture the various complexities that cultural embeddedness contributes to the construct.

> What is culture?
> Culture is the pattern of shared values, expectations, and behaviors developed and learned by a group of people interacting over time.

Aihwa Ong's definition (presented in the "Theoretical contributions" section of this chapter above) might be provided at the end of the series as an updated definition.

I generally use the pop quiz above as an illustration of how the different focal points of culture affect organizational behavior. Each of the answers provided to the open-ended questions is a cultural artifact or organizational behavior.

Using Figure 3.1, I first discuss how there are different focal points of culture – national, organizational and individual, in particular, and many others can be added, such as occupational, industrial, sub-cultural groupings.

Culture at three levels

Along with Figure 3.1, I present the following:

- National culture
    - Hofstede's dimensions of "national" culture
        - Power distance, Uncertainty avoidance, Individualism–Collectivism, Masculinity–Femininity
    - Sub-national cultures
- Organizational culture
    - The culture of Matsushita and Sony versus "Japanese" culture
- Individual culture
    - Function of different affiliations, extent of socialization, learned through experience . . . stereotypes

I then show how Schein's three-level model of culture (presented below) can be used both as a diagnostic tool to uncover the basic cultural assump-

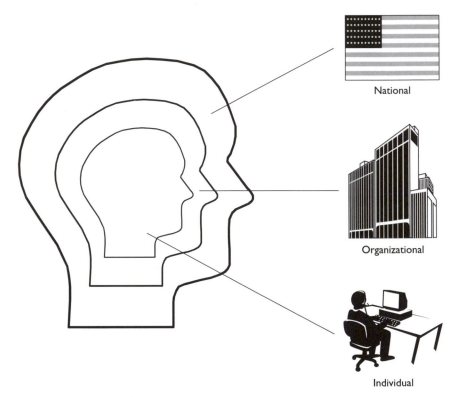

Figure 3.1 Cultural levels.

tions of an organization, and as a comparative tool to heighten our understanding of organizational cultural differences that matter when managing across cultures.

Understanding culture

- Artifacts
  On the surface, that can be "sensed" easily
- Values
  That can be inferred or articulated
- Assumptions
  Hidden – about man and the environment, about human nature, human roles and relationships, reality, time, risk-taking,...

This is also very helpful for discussing underlying core cultural assumptions that inform organizational behavior and helps students understand the basis of their individual responses to the pop quiz above.

Discussion

The ensuing discussion should lead to the uncovering of the basic values and core assumptions upon which behaviors are predicated. For example, using the first sentence in the quiz above, "When I'm angry I...." – Japanese generally "grin and bear it." This is a behavior that belies a cultural value that outward displays of emotion are bad. This value in turn belies a basic core assumption that conflict should be avoided. One can analyze in this way each one of the quiz statements and endings provided both in the Japanese general response and in the student's own response.

4 Discovering cultural dynamics (IV) and understanding variance within culture (II)

Introduction

Here the aim is to break down the notion of monolithic cultural attributes that are static over time and build up the understanding that the way we view another culture is both (1) integrally tied to our own cultural assumptions, and (2) since culture is a group-level phenomenon, it is enacted by individuals who represent varied degrees of connection with the general cultural attributes. This also serves as a way to discuss some of the weaknesses of cultural stereotyping.

Perception

First, I provide a second definition of culture as a HELP system (Gluesing 1995). I find this definition useful in underscoring the role of perception in cultural reasoning. I present this definition as follows:

> Culture as learned HELP
> **H** – habits: determine the unconscious shared behaviors of people in a cultural group;
> **E** – expectations: represent the tacit shared understandings;
> **L** – language: both verbal and nonverbal;
> **P** – perception: governs how we understand both ourselves and others.

Second, I emphasize the effect of our cultural perspective on perception with the following statement:

> Perception
> The cultural perspective that people bring with them to an interaction affects not only their own behaviors but also their perceptions of the behaviors of others.

Third, I give the following example of perceptual relativity. Table 3.3 lists two distinct cultural groups' (cultures A and B) descriptions of a third cultural group – Americans. These descriptions were collected from three Procter & Gamble work teams after two years of working together. Each team (cultural group) was asked to list the key cultural attributes of the other two groups. Culture A is Brazilian. Culture B is English. I generally ask the class to guess the identities of national cultural groups A and B.

Table 3.3 How others see Americans

Group A	Group B
reserved	friendly/outgoing
rushed/time-conscious	relaxed/easygoing
realistic/hard-headed	optimistic
team worker	independent
quality-conscious	output-oriented
unemotional	emotional
serious/businesslike	fun-loving/joking
self-controlled	self-indulgent

Table 3.4 Billiard balls

	U.S.	Japan	Germany
Hierarchy	Rank	Age	Expertise
Time	Short-term	Long-term	Long-term
Decision-making	Top-down	Consensus	"Consens und Orden"
Problem-solving	Objective	Subjective	Objective
Risk-taking	High	Low	Low

The billiard ball model

I use the metaphor of cultural billiard balls to discuss the use-value and shortcomings of generalized descriptions of national cultures (cultural stereotypes). I use Table 3.4 to show a comparison of the general organizational cultural responses of Japanese, Americans, and Germans at a particular German–Japanese joint venture in Cologne, Germany (Brannen and Salk 2000). Any aggregate cultural comparison will do for this exercise. The general goal is to discuss the use-value of cultural stereotyping. When we know nothing of the other culture, stereotypical information is useful because it gives us a point of departure in making sense of the other. The information can tell us where our cultural responses might either "collide," leading to unsuccessful interactions, or "roll parallel" with one another, exposing areas of cooperation. However, generalized cultural information does not tell us how individuals within cultures will respond to certain situations or what type of organizational culture might emerge in joint ventures, mergers, or acquisitions between companies representing distinct national cultural groups.

Variations within cultures

Individuals exhibit a range of personal fit with their national cultures of origin, reflecting their ongoing particular cultural histories in various contexts and subgroup combinations (Brannen 1998). Therefore, individuals exhibit national cultural attributes ranging from those that might be considered "marginal" within a given national culture to those that would be considered "hyper-normal" or embodying mainstream national cultural attributes to a very strong degree (Table 3.5). In other words, individuals navigate and situate themselves in organizational settings by taking hyper-normal, normal, or marginal-normal stances in terms of a

Table 3.5 Cultural zones

"Hyper-normal"	Outliers within the culture holding more extreme beliefs (HN)
"Cultural norm(al)"	The dominant attitude set (CN)
"Marginally normal"	Outliers not so committed to "normal" beliefs (MN)

given cultural dimension (Figure 3.2). For these reasons, aggregate cultural descriptions may not be representative of organizational cultures nor of the cultures of origin of the individuals who make up the organization. Thus, a given national or organizational culture will always be an imperfect mirror reflection of the other.

Discussion

Here, I reiterate the advantages and limitations of the aggregate model of culture (billiard-ball model). Issues of perception or frame of reference and variations within cultures are two of the more significant caveats. An effective and helpful wrap-up of this section is to discuss ways in which one can become more aware of our perceptual blinders. There are several exercises that help facilitate a fruitful discussion, including the Johari Window exercise and the Cultural Shield exercise. The former is well outlined in Schneider and Barsoux's textbook *Managing Across Cultures* (2000). The exercise has the student list the key attributes of his or her cultural make-up and then ask a person from a different culture to describe the student's culture as well. The student then compares and contrasts how he/she sees it versus how another sees it. The latter exercise is performed as follows. Draw a shield on one side of a piece of paper and divide it into six areas. In each area write a question that gets at a person's perception of themselves. These questions should help the student get at his/her core cultural assumptions (e.g., "The one best thing someone can say about me is..." or "The most important thing in the world to me is..." or "What is the one thing money cannot buy?"). After filling out his/her shield, ask the student to develop a list of his/her own core cultural assumptions that underlie the answers of his/her "cultural shield." The shield is a metaphor for the armor we use to protect ourselves from the challenges of everyday life encounters.

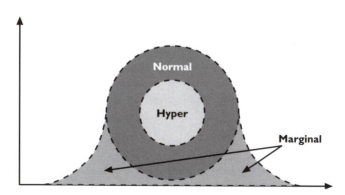

Figure 3.2 Person-fit with cultural norm.

5 A new model of negotiated culture (I and IV)

Introduction

When members from two distinct national or organizational cultures come together a "negotiated culture" emerges. The negotiated culture that emerges will not be a blend or hybrid culture. It will obviously be related to the cultures of origin represented, but it will not reflect one or the other culture in its entirety.

Given cultures A and B, the negotiated cultural outcome will be neither A nor B nor A + B, but some other outcome more like a mutation containing parts of both parents as well as some aspects of its own idiosyncratic making.

Negotiated culture

Culture in global ventures is negotiated over time between members having differing cultural orientations regarding work.

> THUS, given cultures A and B,
> $A \& B \neq A, B, \text{ or } A + B$
> BUT,
> an adaptation of both A and B

An organization that is the result of an international merger or acquisition (e.g., an international joint venture) is a contested terrain where groups of individuals compete to assert their norms and practices. What determines the kind of organizational culture that will result in such instances? There are many sources of power and influence that contribute to the evolution of the organizational culture.

Table 3.6 Sources of power and influence

Field power External environment	Arena power Internal environment

• Cultural
• Historical
• Political
• Legal
• Economic
• Institutional
	• Venture structure
	  – Subsidiary, international joint venture, etc.
	• Organizational structure
	  – Formal
	  – Informal
	    • In-group cultural ties
	    • Home-office ties
	• Interpersonal
	  – Centrality, criticality, expertise
	  – Language

These can be broken down into external and internal influences. External environmental influences such as national culture and the political, legal, historical, and institutional factors, I call "field power," and they are generally considered "given" of a firm's operating condition. Internal organizational influences such as venture structure, organizational structure and interpersonal sources of influences, I call "arena power." Firms have more control over the conditions within the micro-arena of the organization itself than over those in the field or external environment. Those aspects in the external environment of the organization are more stable and are generally non-negotiable. Managers have more influence over aspects of organization internal to the arena of the firm.

Cultural hybrids

Many individuals in today's complex cultural organization are what we call "cultural hybrids" (Gluesing 1995). These individuals have learned at least two cultural "HELP" systems. As such, these individuals provide valuable resources in negotiating merged organizational cultures as cultural brokers (see Figure 3.3).

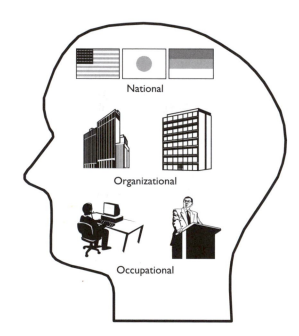

- People experienced in moving from one cultural frame of reference to another

- Learned another HELP system

- Acquired bridging skills

National

Organizational

Occupational

Figure 3.3 Cultural hybrid.

Theoretical and practical wrap-up and discussion

People turn to cross-cultural studies to help them navigate across cultural borders. Cross-cultural studies proliferate in all the social sciences. These studies generally share the assumption that, despite globalization of the world economy, differences in thinking and social action exist between people of different nations and that such differences matter, especially when it comes to executing transnational projects. Whether the transnational activity involves crossing borders to negotiate favorable trade policies, insure just usages of foreign aid, successfully manage overseas operations, effectively transfer technology, or provide cross-cultural guidance to expatriate individuals and families, people need cultural knowledge. With cultural knowledge, they can understand or predict, as the case may be, the consequences of the cross-cultural interactions.

Current views on culture from anthropology show us a way of breaking away from the tendency to mythologize and stereotype other cultures by understanding the complexities of the culture concept including our interconnectedness, cultural embeddedness and the dynamics by which culture evolves in today's complex cultural organizations. By providing a model for seeking knowledge of other cultures that is self-reflexive, anthropologists offer organizational scholars ways to break down traditional parochial, monolithic and static conceptualizations of culture.

These current conceptualizations on culture from anthropology notwithstanding, teaching the culture concept in such a way that students understand cultural complexity, dynamics, embeddedness, and so on is not problem-free. Out of the many challenges I have faced in attempting to do so, perhaps the most difficult are making the students conscious of stereotyping and of using the word "culture" as a cognate to mean national culture. The exercises provided here on the role of perception, cultural relativity, and embeddedness are ones that have proven successful in getting my students to move beyond the tendency to over-generalize culture, toward an understanding of their own role in perceiving, enacting and negotiating culture.

References

Adler, N. J. (1986) "Cross-cultural research: the ostrich and the trend," *The Academy of Management Review*, 8: 226–32.

Appadurai, A. (1998) *Modernity at Large: Cultural Dimensions of Globalization*, Minneapolis: University of Minnesota Press.

Brannen, M. Y. (1998) "Negotiated culture in binational contexts: a model of culture change," *Anthropology of Work Review*, 2, Winter/Spring, XVIII: 6–18.

Brannen, M. Y. (2003) "When Mickey loses face: recontextualization, semantic fit and the semiotics of foreignness," working paper, San José State University.

Brannen, M. Y. and Salk, J. E. (2000) "Partnering across borders: negotiating organizational culture in a German–Japanese joint-venture," *Human Relations*, 53 (4): 451–87.

Child, J. (1981) "Culture, contingency and capitalism in the cross-national study of organizations," in L. L. Cummings and B. M. Staw (eds), *Research in Organizational Behavior*, 3, Greenwich, CT: JAI Press, pp. 303–56.

Clifford, J. (1988) *The Predicament of Culture: Twentieth-Century Ethnography, Literature, and Art*, Cambridge, MA: Harvard University Press.

Clifford, J. and Marcus, G. (eds) (1986) *Writing Culture*, Berkeley: University of California Press.

Deal, T. E. and Kennedy, A. A. (1982) *Corporate Cultures*, Reading, MA: Addison-Wesley.

Dore, R. (1973) *British Factory, Japanese Factory*, London: Allen and Unwin.

Douglas, M. and Wildavsky, A. (1982) *Risk and Culture*, Berkeley: University of California Press.

Doz, Y., Santos, J. and Williamson, P. (2001) *From Global to Metanational: How Companies Win in the Knowledge Economy*, Cambridge, MA: Harvard University Press.

Durkheim, E. (1933) *The Division of Labor in Society*, New York: Free Press.

Fox, R. G. (1991) *Recapturing Anthropology: Working in the Present*, Santa Fe: School of American Research Press.

Frost, P. J., Moore, L., Louis, M. R., Lundberg, C. and Martin, J. (eds) (1985) *Organizational Culture*, Beverly Hills, CA: Sage.

Gluesing, J. (1995) "Fragile alliances – negotiating global teaming in a turbulent environment," doctoral dissertation, Wayne State University, electronic version, Digital Dissertations UMI Proquest.

Gregory, K. (1983) "Native-view paradigms: multiple cultures and culture conflicts in organizations," *Administrative Science Quarterly*, 28: 359–76.

Harris, M. L. (1979) *Cultural Materialism*, New York: Random House.

Hatch, M. J. (1993) "The dynamics of organizational culture," *Academy of Management Review*, 18 (4): 657–93.

Hofstede, G. (1980) *Culture's Consequences, International Differences in Work-related Values*, Beverly Hills, CA: Sage.

Jelinek, M., Smircich, L. and Hirsch, P. (eds) (1983) "Organizational culture," *Administrative Science Quarterly*, 28: 3.

Kluckhohn, F. R. and Strodtbeck, F. L. (1961) *Variations in Value Orientations*, Evanston, IL: Row, Peterson.

Kunda, G. (1991) *Engineering Culture: Control and Commitment in a High-Tech Corporation*, Philadelphia, PA: Temple University Press.

Lamphere, L. (1987) *From Working Daughters to Working Mothers*, Ithaca, NY: Cornell University Press.

Lyotard, J. F. (1984) *The Postmodern Condition: A Report on Knowledge*, Minneapolis: University of Minnesota Press.

Marcus, G. and Fisher, M. (1986) *Anthropology as Cultural Critique: An Experimental Moment in the Human Sciences*, Chicago: University of Chicago Press.

Martin, J. (1992) *Cultures In Organizations: Three Perspectives*, New York: Oxford University Press.

Martin, J. and Siehl, C. (1983) "Organizational culture and sub-culture: an uneasy symbiosis," *Organizational Dynamics*, 12: 52–64.

Nakane, C. (1967) *Kinship and Economic Organization in Rural Japan*, New York: Athlone Press.

Ong, A. (1987) *Spirits of Resistance and Capitalist Discipline: Factory Women in Malaysia*, Albany: State University of New York Press.

Ott, S. J. (1989) *The Organizational Perspective*, Homewood, IL: The Dorsey Press.

Peters, T. J. and Waterman, R. H. (1982) *In Search of Excellence*, New York: Harper and Row.

Prahalad, C. K. and Doz, Y. (1987) *The Multinational Mission*, Cambridge, MA: Harvard University Press.

Roseberry, W. (1989) *Anthropologies and Histories*, New Brunswick, NJ: Rutgers University Press.

Sahlins, M. (1985) *Islands in History*, Chicago: University of Chicago Press.

Said, E. W. (1978) *Orientalism*, New York: Pantheon Books.

Schein, E. (1985) *Organizational Culture and Leadership*, San Francisco: Jossey-Bass.

Schneider, S. and Barsoux, J. F. (2000) *Managing across Cultures*, San Francisco: Jossey-Bass.

Shaw, J. B. (1990) "A cognitive categorization model for the study of intercultural management," *Academy of Management Review*, 15 (4): 626–45.

Smircich, L. (1983) "Concepts of culture and organizational analysis," *Administrative Science Quarterly*, 28: 339–58.

Turner, B. (1972) *Exploring the Industrial Subculture*, New York: Herder and Herder.

Van Maanen, J. (1975) "Police socialization," *Administrative Science Quarterly*, 20: 207–28.

Van Maanen, J. (1976) "Breaking in: socialization to work," in R. Dubin (ed.), *Handbook of Work, Organization, and Society*, Chicago: Rand McNally, pp. 67–130.

Van Maanen, J. (1982) "Fieldwork on the beat," in J. Van Maanen, J. Dabbs and R. Faulkner (eds), *Varieties of Qualitative Research*, Beverly Hills, CA: Sage, pp. 103–51.

Van Maanen, J. (1988) *Tales of the Field: On Writing Ethnography*, Chicago: University of Chicago Press.

Van Maanen, J. and Barley, S. R. (1984) "Occupational communities: culture and control in organizations," in B. M. Staw and L. L. Cummings (eds), *Research in Organizational Behavior*, 6. Greenwich: JAI Press.

Weber, M. (1947) *Wirtschaft und Gesellschaft*, 3rd edn, Tübingen: J. C. B. Mohr.

Whyte, W. F. (1948) *Human Relations in the Restaurant Business*, New York: McGraw-Hill.

Willis, P. (1977) *Learning to Labor*, New York: Columbia University Press.

Wolf, E. (1982) *Europe and the People without History*, Berkeley: University of California.

Chapter 4

One's many cultures
A multiple cultures perspective

Sonja A. Sackmann and Margaret E. Phillips

Introduction

The objective of this teaching module is to provide students with a comprehensive framework of the concept of culture as applied to organizations. The framework includes the various levels of culture that may be carried by an individual and that may, therefore, impact life in organizations. Thus, it provides a basis for understanding the complex and dynamic interplay of cultural issues at the organizational and suborganizational levels and for choosing the most appropriate actions in a given setting.

Audience

Depending on the depth and selection of readings, the module can be taught to undergraduate and graduate students, students at the doctoral level, as well as practitioners and executives. The module works well as an introductory session to culture, cultural issues, and cultural dynamics.

Philosophical foundations and conceptual frame

Culture as a concept was originally developed in the field of anthropology. In the first phase of its application to organizational settings, culture was predominantly considered a property of a nation (e.g., Nath 1986; Roberts and Boyacigiller 1984). In the 1960s and 1970s, and even more so in the 1980s, culture was also applied to an organization, that is, an organization was considered to have one culture (e.g., Deal and Kennedy 1982; Peters and Waterman 1982). Since that time, the concept of culture applied to organizations has been further differentiated, and insights gained from studies in disciplines such as sociology have been integrated as well. Study of distinct organizational subcultures has a long tradition in sociology, with special attention being given to professions and occupations (e.g., Van Maanen 1979; Van Maanen and Barley 1984; Trice and

Beyer 1993). While these studies have focused on pre-selected groups, research that has allowed cultural boundaries to surface has shown that subcultures in organizational settings may emerge within a variety of boundaries, such as tenure and hierarchy (Martin, Sitking and Boehm 1985), functional identity (Sackmann 1991), ethnicity (Gregory 1983), gender (Blackhurst 1986; Eberle 1997), role (Rusted 1986), plant site (Bushe 1988), work group (Kleinberg 1994) and "countermovement" (Dent 1986). In addition, industry (Grinyer and Spender 1979; Phillips 1994; Laurila 1997), geographical region (Weiss and Delbecq 1987), and economic region (Hickson 1993), as well as ideologies (Aktouf 1988; Westwood and Kirkbride 1989), may influence culture at the organizational level. Based on these studies and their insights, a more differentiated view of the concept of culture applied to organizational settings emerged: the "multiple cultures perspective" (Boyacigiller *et al.* 1996, 2003). From this perspective, culture in organizational settings is considered a complex, dynamic phenomenon whose carriers may be members of several subcultures (Boyacigiller *et al.* 1996, 2003; Sackmann 1991, 1997; Sackmann and Phillips 1992).

Conception of culture

This "multiple cultures" perspective is based on the following definition of culture:

> The core of culture is composed of explicit and tacit assumptions or understandings commonly held by a group of people; a particular configuration of assumptions/understandings is distinctive to the group; these assumptions/understandings serve as guides to acceptable and unacceptable perceptions, thoughts, feelings and behaviors; they are learned and passed on to new members of the group through social interaction; culture is dynamic – it changes over time.
>
> (Boyacigiller *et al.* 2003)

The multiple cultures perspective is based on the premise that culture is a collective socially constructed phenomenon that is created and negotiated by its members. Its core is composed of cognitive elements such as basic beliefs, assumptions, or cultural knowledge that guide the group members' thinking, feeling and actions. Artifacts such as physical manifestations, verbal and nonverbal behaviors, and symbolic events are at a more visible level of culture and are part of the cultural network. In addition, the multiple cultures perspective implies that a shared cultural mindset may emerge or exist whenever a set of basic assumptions or beliefs is held in common by a group of people. As such, individuals are most likely carriers of multiple cultures, since they belong to various cultural groupings at any given moment in time. We have argued that, depending on the issue at hand, a different cultural identity may become salient (Boyacigiller *et al.* 1996, 2003).

Preparation and materials

The participants are assigned two readings in advance:

- Sackmann and Phillips (2002), an academic overview of the perspective;
- Goodman, Phillips, and Sackmann (1999), a practical application of the perspective to a multinational project team.

For doctoral students, we replace Sackmann and Phillips (2002) with Boycigiller *et al.* (2003), to allow an overview of the major streams of international cross-cultural management research: cross-national comparison; intercultural interaction; and, the multiple cultures perspective. For this group, we also assign Sackmann (1997), a collection of research studies detailing the multiple cultures salient in organizational settings.

The following materials are desirable to run the module:

- flipchart paper;
- markers (one for each participant);
- masking tape;
- walls on which flipchart papers can be attached.

Description of the teaching module and teaching process

1   We give a short introduction to the module (refer to *Philosophical foundations and conceptual frame* section above), and present our objective as follows. Provide participants with a framework of culture in organizational settings:

- a map for "reading" and understanding cultural issues in organizations;
- implications for effective management of cultural issues in organizations;
- indications for more effective self-management.

2   Then we ask the participants (students/practitioners/executives) to introduce themselves by each naming three key cultural mindsets they carry, including the specific setting in which each of the three mindsets is important and why they are important in that particular setting. This may be done either verbally or on a flipchart paper with the

name of the person on the top and the three key mindsets given underneath. Generally, we prefer the written version since this allows us to return to it and elaborate later.

3   We initiate a discussion about the Goodman, Phillips and Sackmann (1999) article and have participants identify the various cultural mindsets involved in the project team, including any they might recognize that are not noted in the article. During the discussion, we list the mentioned identities on a board or flipchart paper, and we make sure that each participant has an understanding of those different identities.

4   Once these cultural identities are sufficiently noted, we ask participants for their understanding of culture. We list the central elements of their descriptions visibly on a flipchart paper or board. Then we give a definition of culture (see *Conception of culture* above), highlighting the key elements in the following manner:

Culture:

- explicit and tacit *assumptions*;
- shared by a *group* of people;
- *distinctive* to the group;
- *guide* acceptable and unacceptable *perceptions, thoughts, feelings, behaviors*;
- *learned* by all members and *passed on* to new members in *dynamic* social *interaction*.

We explain the critical elements italicized and their implications in an organizational setting. Reference to the project team in the Goodman *et al.* article, as well as the descriptions of culture provided by the participants, works well.

5   We then explain the multiple cultures perspective using Figure 4.1, *The Cultural Context of an Organization*. In this introduction, we remind the participants of the various levels of culture that may impact organizations and we highlight the following key points, asking the participants for examples, giving our own examples, and referring to the relevant literature at each level of analysis:

- Culture exists at several levels, even if we may not be aware of them at the moment (e.g., we may ask participants to complete the following sentence: "Culture at the organizational level is influenced by *(level)* therefore *(potential effect)*").
- The key issue is the question of the salient cultural identity of the members of the organization, and individual cultural identity may be issue-specific.
- Do not decide too quickly that the national or organizational level is the salient culture when confronted with a certain issue or

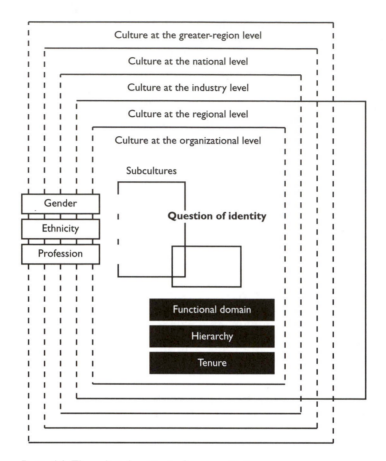

Figure 4.1 The cultural context of an organization.

problem. Probe the issue and explore whether other levels of culture may be involved. People tend to identify, even blame, the most visible (and verbally or label-wise the socially most acceptable) level of culture, when in fact other levels may be the real cause of the problem.

- In conducting research, it is important to make a conscious choice which level to focus on and to be aware of potential influences from other levels.
- When evaluating research results, it is important to ask the levels questions: could the results also be influenced by another cultural level (e.g., nation, organization, industry, profession)?

The last two points are particularly important in discussions with doctoral students, but also have relevance for students and practitioners.

Using Table 4.1, we discuss the underlying premises of this perspective as presented in Sackmann and Phillips (2002), including the impetus for the perspective, the key research questions it addresses, the underlying assumptions, and the frameworks and methods it employs.

Depending on the nature of the participants, the discussion of these underlying premises may be more academic and research-oriented or more applied. With a more academically interested audience (e.g., doctoral students), we compare the premises of the other two research perspectives in international cross-cultural management: cross-national comparison and intercultural interaction (Boyacigiller *et al.* 1996, 2003), see Table 4.2.

During these discussions, it is important to give examples that relate to participants' current work or life situation and to mention implications of each of the premises discussed. For student participants, these implications are, again, more academic and research-oriented; for practitioners and executives these implications need to address real work–life issues.

6   We then ask participants to go back to their initial introduction and elaborate on the three key cultural mindsets they had mentioned in their introduction (participants may change the mindsets that they mentioned initially). We ask them to describe the specific context in which they come to bear, how and why they acquired them, when they become most important, and why. If they changed one or several of the mindsets they mentioned initially, we want them to explain why they did so and why the new culture is more important. To guide the discussion, we ask each participant to draw a representation of him-herself on flipchart paper and place each of their cultural mindsets in

Table 4.1 Premises of the multiple cultures perspective

Impetus	• globalization • workforce diversity
Research questions	Many cultures are present within organizations: • which become *salient*? • when/why/how does this occur?
Assumptions	• organizations = multiplicity of cultures • an individual holds membership in many cultures • salience of any culture is empirical question
Frameworks	• *a priori* • empirically derived • emergent
Methods	• hybrid, multiple methods • seek "insider's view"

Table 4.2 Premises of the research perspectives in international cross-cultural management

Premise	Research perspective		
	Cross-national comparison	Intercultural interaction	Multiple cultures
Impetus	• U.S. economic dominance • expanding global markets	• changing balance of global economic power • foreign direct investment • attention to employee differences	• globalization • workforce diversity
Research questions	How do managerial attitudes and behaviors differ across nations?	When members of two national cultures interact, what is the nature of the new organizational culture that evolves or emerges?	Many cultures are present within organizations: • which become *salient*? • when/why/how does this occur?
Assumptions	• nation-state = culture • cultural identity is given, single, permanent • significant differences are culturally-based	• culture = group-level phenomenon • national culture and organization context important • cultural groups evolve or emerge	• organizations = multiplicity of cultures • an individual holds membership in many cultures • salience of any culture is an empirical question
Frameworks	universal categories of culture	process models	• *a priori* • empirically derived • emergent

Methods	• natural science model – positivist, empirical
	• large-scale, multi-variate analysis
	• culture = independent variable = nation state
		• inductive methods
		  – ethnography
		  – participant observation
		• qualitative data analysis
			• hybrid, multiple methods
			• seek "insider's view"

Source: Adapted from Boyacigiller *et al.* (1996, 2003).

a bubble around the drawing, including the specifications mentioned above.

7   In another round of discussion, we ask participants to focus on potential conflicts that may arise from the various mindsets. For example,

conflicts may arise from a "fit problem" (a key mindset becomes salient in a socially inappropriate situation, e.g., a mother of a sick child who, due to a last-minute child-care crisis, has to take the child along to a crucial work-group meeting) or a "crowding problem" (conflicting cultural mindsets both become salient in a particular setting, e.g., desiring to be a good citizen of your department and a strong contributor to a cross-functional project team but project team goals conflict with intra-departmental interests).

Depending on the group of participants, this discussion about conflicting mindsets may lead to a small-group task focused on a particular conflicting mindset-salience issue, with the assignment to develop potential solutions for handling the issue. These are then presented to the entire group.

8   We then focus on implications of the multiple cultures perspective. We explore two aspects with the participant:

a   implications of membership in an organization with multiple cultures, and
b   implications of managing people with multiple cultural identities.

With doctoral students, we address a third aspect:

c   implications of the multiple cultures perspective for organizational research.

To drive these discussions, we use the following questions:

1   With regard to cultural salience, many cultures are present within organizations and are carried by individuals simultaneously:

   •   Which become salient?
   •   When do they become salient?
   •   How do they become salient?
   •   Does task/problem/question influence salience?
   •   What causes salience to vary?

2   How might we deal with multiple cultures simultaneously?
3   How should we deal with multiple cultural identities?
4   How can we deal with complex cultural reality?
5   Does this help us to understand organizational life better?

9   In a last step, we ask participants to chart for themselves the critical insights they gained from the session and the implications for:

a   their "mindset-wellbeing"
     Here, participants usually identify insights relevant to both their work life and their personal and family life.
b   their organization's effectiveness

Here, participants might identify mindsets impeding an intended change process.

In addition, we ask participants to identify up to three actions they feel may change or improve a current situation. Here, personal change toward dealing more effectively with their multiple identities is often proposed, as well as organizationally oriented change.

Potential follow-up assignment

Have participants write up their own case using one critical task or project in their work organization and identifying the various cultural mindsets they and others carry that influence the work.

Dilemmas

We continue to grapple with certain issues as we work with the ideas presented in this module. Conceptually, critical empirical and theoretical questions remain (e.g., the cultural salience questions raised for discussion above, the links between the multiple cultures perspective and role theory). Practically, in the presentation of this module the following dilemmas arise:

- Participants (like many researchers in the field of international cross-cultural management) still tend to employ ubiquitous cross-cultural research results embedded in the cross-national comparison perspective to cite the fundamental importance of national culture.
- We need to be continually aware of personal biases and avoid overusing certain examples (e.g., being women/mothers/professionals). Here we suggest keeping notes on other types of examples or problems proven to be potent generators of discussion.
- Some participants may have a strong need for homogenization, feel uncomfortable with such a postmodern, loosely coupled patchwork of partial identities, and, therefore, resist further exploration. We struggle to help these participants accept ambiguity (a key skill for success in crossing cultures) versus immediately applying mechanisms of cognitive dissonance reduction.
- Discussion may trigger deep-rooted problems or intra-personal conflicts in participants who may then need help afterwards to sort out their personal situation. Here, again, we find ourselves reliant on good facilitation skills and cross-cultural sensitivity and sensibility.

References

Aktouf, O. (1988) "Corporate culture, the Catholic ethic, and the spirit of capitalism," paper presented at The Proceedings of the Standing Conference on Organizational Symbolism, Istanbul.

Blackhurst, M. (1986) "The role of culture in affirmative action strategy," paper presented at the International Conference on Organizational Symbolism and Corporate Culture, Montreal.

Boyacigiller, N. A., Kleinberg, M. J., Phillips, M. E. and Sackmann, S. A. (1996) "Conceptualizing culture," in B. J. Punnett and O. Shenkar (eds), *Handbook for International Management Research*, New York: Blackwell, pp. 157–208.

Boyacigiller, N. A., Kleinberg, M. J., Phillips, M. E. and Sackmann, S. A. (2003) "Conceptualizing culture: elucidating the streams of research in international cross-cultural management," in B. J. Punnett and O. Shenkar (eds), *Handbook for International Management Research*, 2nd edn, Ann Arbor: University of Michigan Press.

Bushe, G. R. (1988) "Cultural contradictions of statistical process control in American manufacturing organizations," *Journal of Management*, 14 (1): 19–31.

Deal, T. E. and Kennedy, A. A. (1982) *Corporate Cultures*, Reading, MA: Addison-Wesley.

Dent, J. F. (1986) "A case study of emergence of a new organizational reality," paper presented at the International Conference on Organizational Symbolism and Corporate Culture, Montreal.

Eberle, T. S. (1997) "Cultural contrasts in a democratic nonprofit organization: the case of a Swiss reading society," in S. A. Sackmann (ed.), *Cultural Complexity in Organizations: Inherent Contrasts and Contradictions*, Thousand Oaks, CA: Sage, pp. 133–59.

Goodman, R. A., Phillips, M. E. and Sackmann, S. A. (1999) "The complex culture of international project teams," in R. A. Goodman (ed.), *Modern Organizations and Emerging Conundrums: Exploring the Post Industrial Sub-culture of the Third Millennium*, San Francisco: New Lexington Press, pp. 23–33.

Gregory, K. (1983) "Native-view paradigms: multiple cultures and culture conflicts in organizations," *Administrative Science Quarterly*, 28: 359–76.

Grinyer P. H. and Spender, J. C. (1979) "Recipes, crises, and adaptation in mature businesses," *International Studies of Management and Organization*, 9 (3): 113–33.

Hickson, D. J. (ed.) (1993) *Management in Western Europe*, Berlin: Walter de Gruyter.

Kleinberg, J. (1994) " 'The crazy group': emergent culture in a Japanese–American binational work group," in S. Beechler and A. Bird (eds), *Research in International Business and International Relations*, Greenwich, CT: JAI Press (special issue on Japanese management), vol. 6: 1–45.

Laurila, J. (1997) "Discontinuous technological change as a trigger for temporary reconciliation of managerial subcultures: a case study of a Finnish paper industry company," in S. A. Sackmann (ed.), *Cultural Complexity in Organizations: Inherent Contrasts and Contradictions*, Thousand Oaks, CA: Sage, pp. 252–72.

Martin, J., Sitking, S. B. and Boehm, M. (1985) "Founders and the elusiveness of a cultural legacy," in P. J. Frost, L. F. Moore, M. R. Louis, C. C. Lundberg and J. Martin (eds), *Organizational Culture*, Beverly Hills, CA: Sage, pp. 99–124.

Nath, R. (1986) "The role of culture in cross-cultural and organizational research," in R. N. Farmer (ed.), *Advances in International Comparative Management*, Greenwich, CT: JAI Press, vol. 2: 249–67.

Peters, T. J. and Waterman, R. J., Jr. (1982) *In Search of Excellence: Lessons from America's Best-run Companies*, New York: Harper and Row.

Phillips, M. E. (1994) "Industry mindsets: exploring the cultures of two macro-organizational settings," *Organization Science*, 5 (3), August: 384–402.

Roberts, K. H. and Boyacigiller, N. A. (1984) "Cross-national organizational research: the grasp of the blind men," in B. M. Staw and L. L. Cummings (eds), *Research in Organizational Behavior*, Greenwich, CT: JAI Press, vol. 6: 423–75.

Rusted, B. (1986) "Corporate entertainment as social action: the case of a service organization," paper presented at the International Conference on Organizational Symbolism and Corporate Culture, Montreal.

Sackmann, S. A. (1991) *Cultural Knowledge in Organizations: Exploring the Collective Mind*, Newbury Park, CA: Sage.

Sackmann, S. A. (ed.) (1997) *Cultural Complexity in Organizations: Inherent Contrasts and Contradictions*, Thousand Oaks, CA: Sage.

Sackmann, S. A. and Phillips, M. E. (1992) "Mapping the cultural terrain in organizational settings: current boundaries and future directions for empirical research," CIBER working paper #92–05, Los Angeles: Center for International Business, Anderson Graduate School of Management, University of California, Los Angeles.

Sackmann, S. A. and Phillips, M. E. (2002) "The multiple cultures perspective: an alternate paradigm for international cross-cultural management research," paper presented at and published in the Proceedings of the Western Academy of Management International Conference, July.

Trice, H. M. and Beyer, J. M. (1993) *The Cultures of Work Organizations*, Englewood Cliffs, NJ: Prentice-Hall.

Van Maanen, J. (1979) "The fact of fiction in organizational ethnography," *Administrative Science Quarterly*, 24, 539–50.

Van Maanen, J. and Barley, S. (1984) "Occupational communities: culture and control in organizations," in B. M. Staw and L. L. Cummings (eds), *Research in Organizational Behavior*, Greenwich, CT: JAI Press, vol. 6: 287–365.

Weiss, J. and Delbecq, A. (1987) "High-technology cultures and management: Silicon Valley and Route 128," *Group and Organization Studies*, 12 (1), March: 39–54.

Westwood, R. I. and Kirkbride, P. S. (1989) "Jonathan Livingston Seagull is alive and well and living in Hong Kong: cultural disjuncture in the symbolization of corporate leadership," paper presented at the International Conference on Organizational Symbolism and Corporate Culture, Fontainebleau, France.

Chapter 5

Learning about our and others' selves

Multiple identities and their sources

Bernardo M. Ferdman

Introduction

This chapter describes a three-hour workshop in which participants explore the multiple sources of their identity and those of their class-mates, focusing in particular on the social categories, group memberships, and other affiliations that together both make them unique and connect them to other people. The workshop includes two related but separate components, "Sources of our identity," and "Learning about others." Although the workshop was designed for and is described in the context of a semester-long course, *Cultural Diversity in the Workplace*, it can be adapted for many other uses.

The first part of the chapter describes the workshop objectives, and includes directions for the teacher, instructions for students, a list of the reading assignments, and examples of key handouts. The second part of the chapter reflects on the exercise and contextualizes it in relation to the key issues and concepts employed, particularly with regard to the view of culture and cultural identity that it seeks to transmit to students. Finally, the third part of the chapter briefly considers some challenges and dilem-mas involved in using this activity in the classroom.

Part One: Workshop objectives, directions, and materials

Overview and objectives

The workshop is titled *Sources of Our Identity: Exploring Our and Others' Selves*. It is usually the third session of a 15-week course, Cultural Diversity in the Workplace, required of all doctoral and master's students in the San Diego programs of Alliant International University's California School of Organizational Studies (usually in the first or second year). My orienta-tion to the course is that it is important for all students to find something of interest in it, and that they should learn much about diversity and inclusion not just from the content of the course, but also from how I run it.

The goal is for students to learn, in a personal way, how individuals (including themselves) typically derive much of their identity from group memberships and, at the same time, how there is a great deal of diversity within such identity groups. The focus of the workshop, as I present it to students, is: building skills for inquiring about our differences, both of ourselves and of others.

This is a relevant excerpt from the course description and learning goals included in the syllabus:

> This course focuses on the complex dynamics of ethnic, racial, gender, and other diversity in organizations as seen from the vantage points of social science and organizational studies. We will adopt multiple levels of analysis to critically explore the current state of theory, research and application regarding the role and treatment of differences and the creation of inclusion in the workplace ... A guiding assumption and focus for the course is that awareness, understanding, and skills regarding cultural diversity are cornerstones of effective and ethical professional practice in organizational psychology and related fields ... Learning in the course is geared both to the personal and to the professional – as we consider the nature and implications of cultural diversity, the way these are intertwined and inseparable comes to the fore.

The course syllabus includes the reading assignment and questions to think about for the workshop session (see Appendix 5.1).

Workshop design and directions

The workshop includes two major portions: (1) *Sources of our identity* (about one hour), and (2) *Learning about others* (about two hours). Table 5.1 presents an outline of the design and its components. In the first part, I make a brief presentation (and if possible, ask the teaching assistant to provide an illustration), then ask the students to draw a picture of their own sources of identity, share these with one other classmate, and then engage in a large group discussion. In the second part, after a short introduction, students interview each other following strict time guidelines, meet in their small project groups to process what happened, and take part in a large group discussion.

Table 5.1 Workshop design and time needed

Workshop: Exploring our and others' selves	Time needed (total: $2\frac{1}{2}$ hrs. to $3\frac{1}{2}$ hours)
Overview of session design and objectives	5 minutes
Sources of our identity	Total: 55 to 80 minutes
Brief input (including example)	15 to 30 minutes
Draw a picture of you	15 minutes
Share in pairs	10 to 15 minutes
Large group discussion	15 to 20 minutes
Learning about others	Total: 100 to 130 minutes
Set-up	15 to 25 minutes
Interviews	40 minutes
Small groups	25 minutes
Journal	5 to 10 minutes
Large group discussion	15 to 30 minutes

Sources of our identity

The components of *Sources of our identity*, the workshop's first major portion, are described next.

BRIEF PRESENTATION/LECTURETTE

This lecturette provides an introduction to the different types of group-ings among people and addresses the various dimensions of identity, including both personal or individual aspects and social identities, with the primary focus on the latter. (See Figure 5.1 for the visual.) I give a brief explanation for each dimension, usually with a personal illustration of how that has made a difference for me personally. I also hand out a summary of Loden and Rosener's (1991) notion of primary and secondary dimensions of diversity. The goal is to have students see that, although we are each at once similar to everyone else (we are all human) and like no one else (we are all unique), a key focus in learning about diversity is our similarity to and connection with groups of people. This makes us both similar to and different from others.

I point out that part of what makes us unique is the specific configura-tion of identities that each of us has and their impact on each other (Ferdman 1995). Thus, being a man is a somewhat different experience for me than for a man in a different cohort or who grew up elsewhere, or who is gay, or who has no children. At the same time, I share some con-nections with those other men that people who are not men do not, and other people view and treat us as men. I also make additional points about the varying degrees of awareness that we may have of our various sources of identity, the ways in which particular identities are more or less salient

Sources of Our Identity

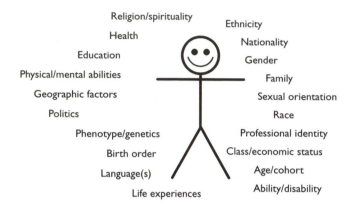

Figure 5.1 Sources of our identity.

Source: Adapted from The Kaleel Jamison Consulting Group, Inc.

in different contexts, and the changes in both our awareness and the salience over our lifespan, especially as one identity interacts with another (for example, becoming a parent changed the experience of being Jewish, being a professor, and being a consultant for me). Finally, the teaching assistant briefly presents an illustration of his/her own configuration of identities, using a poster or easel pad similar to Figure 5.1, but replacing the category names with his or her own identities. (I do this myself if the teaching assistant is not available.) This is important, because it both begins to sensitize students to the multiplicity and complexity of identity and it primes them to listen to the detailed stories of others.

DRAW YOUR OWN PICTURE

I now ask students to draw their own picture (using Figure 5.2), and to begin to answer these questions:

1   Which identities are you most/least aware of?
2   Which identities are others most/least aware of?
3   Which identities are you most/least comfortable with?

(These questions can vary depending in part on the nuances I would like to bring out and the time available.)

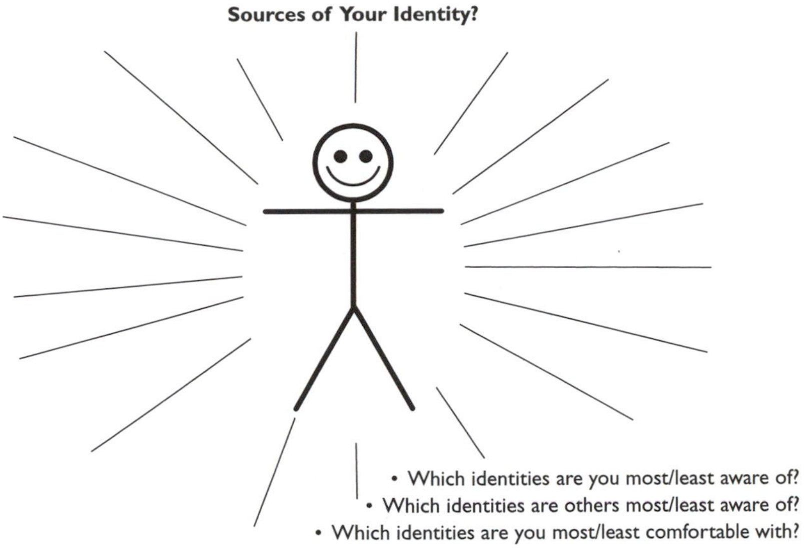

Sources of Your Identity?

- Which identities are you most/least aware of?
- Which identities are others most/least aware of?
- Which identities are you most/least comfortable with?

Figure 5.2 Sources of your identity.

Source: Adapted from The Kaleel Jamison Consulting Group, Inc.

SHARE IN PAIRS

I then ask students to each find a partner who is not in their fieldwork group and who preferably appears to be very different from them (in whatever way they choose to define this), and to share their pictures in those pairs (sharing whatever they feel comfortable revealing and keeping private whatever they are not comfortable revealing).

LARGE GROUP DISCUSSION

This is designed to bring out key insights about identities, their configuration, how they become obscured or highlighted in different contexts or at different times, and other similar issues. (As a substitute when time is short, or additionally so as to hear everyone's voice right away, I sometimes first ask for one insight from each person, going around the room: What is one insight you've had today about identity in the context of diversity? This is also useful if the workshop has to be stopped here and continued at a subsequent class session.)

Learning about others

The following sections describe the major components of the second part of the workshop, *Learning about others*.

SET-UP (INTRODUCTION)

In this introduction, I once again explain the purpose and the overall design. Students are told that they will be working in their fieldwork project teams (formed the previous week), and that they will have the opportunity to interview one of their fellow group members as well as to be interviewed and to observe one or more interviews. I go on to lead a brief discussion (or simply give a lecturette, depending on time) about inquiry and interviews. Topics covered include setting up the interview, confidentiality, body language, empathy, comfort level, timing, types of questions, checking assumptions, tone, and the importance of sharing of oneself. The goal here is for students to begin to think about the many components involved in interviewing others, including the human relationship aspects. They will get to know their fellow team members as individuals and in the context of a task that is quite relevant to what they will have to do for their project.

I conclude the introduction/set-up by letting students know that their task in conducting an interview will be as follows (presented on an easel pad):

> To learn about significant experiences and milestones in the interviewee's journey to becoming who she/he is today. [One can also add, focusing in particular on her or his experiences of privilege, or, focusing in particular on his/her cultural identity.]

After presenting this on an easel pad (or on an overhead), I give students about 5 to 10 minutes to develop, individually, a strategy and a list of questions for an 8-minute interview that will accomplish the interview task.

INTERVIEWS

In this part the students actually conduct the interviews. In my experience this portion of the session works best when it is very strictly timed. Students will always want more time, but this is not necessary to get the benefit of the activity. First, students are asked to meet in their fieldwork groups, and then each group is asked to select a Person A, B, C, etc. At this point, the role assignments for each time period are distributed, as shown in Table 5.2. Each time period (using strict timing) consists of an 8-minute interview and one or two minutes for making individual notes regarding observations,

Table 5.2 Role assignments for interviews

For groups of four: Time period	Person A	Person B	Person C	Person D
1	Interviewee	Interviewer	Observer	Observer
2	Observer	Observer	Interviewee	Interviewer
3	Observer	Interviewee	Interviewer	Observer
4	Interviewer	Observer	Observer	Interviewee

For groups of three: Time period	Person A	Person B	Person C
1	Interviewee	Interviewer	Observer
2	Interviewer	Observer	Interviewee
3	Observer	Interviewee	Interviewer
4	Talk about process of interviewing, insights for group project		

feelings, and thoughts (to be ready for processing in the small group discussion later). Then, groups are given about 45 seconds to one minute to get ready to switch roles, before getting a signal to begin the next round. (If necessary, the interviews can be as short as six minutes.) Usually, I call out a warning one minute before the interview period is up.

SMALL GROUPS

After all the interview rounds are completed, students continue to meet in their groups, but now talk about their experience. The assignment, posted on an easel pad, is as follows:

Discuss in group:

- What was it like being interviewed?
- What was it like being an interviewer?
- What could you see as an observer?
- What led to more genuine dialogue/sharing?

To share with large group later: Learning about effective interviewing.

JOURNAL

At the conclusion of the small group discussion, students are given five minutes to journal (i.e., note for their own use) their answers to the following questions (posted on an easel pad):

- What would you like to work on to develop/enhance your interviewing skills?

- What are your initial thoughts about how you will do this?
- Into what aspects of yourself would you like to delve more deeply?

LARGE GROUP DISCUSSION

Finally, the workshop concludes with a large group discussion reflecting on the complete experience. This conversation typically brings out important insights about, e.g., timing, empathy, assumptions. Depending on time, I might kick off the discussion by asking students to brainstorm regarding key insights they had about interviewing and learning about others, and listing these on the board. During this discussion, students often realize that some questions "work" better than others. They typically mention how amazed they were to learn so many new things about people that they have been around for some time. Finally, conversation often hinges around how challenging it can be to go beyond their own assumptions as to what particular labels, experiences, and the like mean, and to elicit the interviewee to provide his/her own meanings and interpretations. For example, they often describe their reluctance in the interviewee role to open up if they were not asked the "right" questions, in the "right" way.

At the end of the discussion, I typically hand out resource packets that include the following:

- Interview protocols used in my research (for individual and group interviews).
- Sample interview questions for (a) "non-dominant-culture employees," (b) "dominant-culture employees," (c) leaders and policy-makers (from Gardenswartz and Rowe 1994).
- Five ways to ask questions (from Gardenswartz and Rowe 1994).
- Additional examples of interview questions, surveys, etc.
- Additional articles about interviewing and formulations of questions.

Part Two: Reflections and theoretical notes

This seemingly simple and straightforward activity is actually quite multi-layered. Among other themes, it addresses the multiplicity and complexity of identity and its many sources, the diversity and uniqueness of experience even within the same identity groups, the role of the individual in constructing and interpreting cultural identity, and the key role of dialogue in the process of knowing about our own self-identities and those of others. As a way to learn about culture and cultural identity, it challenges unitary approaches to those constructs that do not recognize the wide variety that exists within any one group, while at the same time requiring participants to confront the reality of group-based differences.

Most importantly, it asks every student to be a participant in and contributor to diversity. At the end of the workshop, most students realize that every individual is internally diverse and adds to the diversity of the group as a whole.

The issue of multiplicity and complexity is quite critical to address in any treatment of cultural diversity. Traditional and certainly colloquial approaches to diversity often revert to over-simplified categorization systems that obscure more than they reveal. While certainly there is some social meaning to the broad racial categories that have been in use in the United States, for students to truly learn about cultural diversity, they must go beyond such classification systems to learn how these and other categories actually apply to the experiences of individuals. Increasingly, these categories are less and less meaningful (Ferdman 2001) and are being replaced with a greater number of labels that are self-assigned by people. Not only do people prefer to name their own categories, but also individuals belong to many categories at once. By seeing these juxtaposed in relation to themselves and others, this notion becomes more grounded in reality for participants.

Another idea that underlies the activity is that membership in the same identity group can be experienced in a variety of ways (even by the same individual over time and across settings). In this activity, participants both construct themselves alone (in the first part) and construct themselves in direct interaction with another (as they are interviewed in the second part). This allows them to experience both the possibilities and the limitations to self-definition. They learn how they simultaneously must be and need not be bounded by shared categories. Two Latinos in the class, three women, or five 20-year-olds will find that they are similar in some ways, and very different in other ways. In the conversations in which they share their pictures identifying sources of identity, participants often discover similarities with those who on the surface seemed very different, and also discover great differences with those who appeared on the basis of initial assumptions to be very similar. Related to this is the issue of how one group membership interacts with another (Ferdman 1999; Ferdman and Gallegos 2001). For example, being a woman will be experienced differently by a 55-year-old African-American heterosexual grandmother than by a 22-year-old White single lesbian.

The third issue, regarding individuals' roles in constructing themselves, is based in large part on my previous work (Ferdman 1990, 1995, 2000; Ferdman and Horenczyk 2000) in which I have written extensively about the concept of cultural identity, which I see, at the individual level, as the reflection of culture as it is constructed by each of us. Specifically, cultural identity for me is one's individual image of the behaviors, beliefs, values, and norms – in short, the cultural features – that are thought to characterize one's group(s), together with one's feelings about those features and one's understanding of how they are (or are not) reflected in oneself (Ferdman 1990). Essentially, this is a psychological account of how individuals personalize their group that reflects the realities of multicultural societies in that it does not assume within-group homogeneity. As such, it can enhance our understanding of cultural transitions, such as those that go along with immigration (Ferdman and Horenczyk 2000). According to this view, culture is not static or fixed, but rather is continuously transformed. As we come into contact with each other – both within and between groups – we constantly change culture and its elements. As Nagel points out:

> Culture is not a shopping cart that comes to us already loaded with a set of historical, cultural goods. Rather we construct culture by picking and choosing items from the shelves of the past and the present ... In other words, cultures change: They are borrowed, blended, rediscovered, and reinterpreted.
>
> (Nagel 1994: 162)

According to Nagel, ethnic cultures (as well as ethnic boundaries and identities) are negotiated, defined, and produced through social interaction inside and outside ethnic communities. I would suggest that this is the case for most, if not all, social identities.

These last points also speak to the role of dialogue (e.g., Isaacs 1999) in both the construction and the learning process. It is difficult, I believe, for us to know ourselves, without engaging in conversation and without reflecting on our interactions with others. The process of identifying key aspects of the self, then talking about them with each other, requires participants to become conscious of the degree to which this may be true for them. Moreover, it requires students to go beyond facile generalizations about groups, and engage with those who are present in the room with them. They must engage with each other; and for this engagement to be productive, it must be culturally aware and sensitive, and it must be dynamic and interactive. Scripts, or general rules for interaction, simply will not suffice.

Ultimately, the collective construction that I hope results for the class is recognition that diversity is truly about every individual. Participants must deal with the tension that exists in accepting the reality of both group-level differences and individual differences – neither is sufficient alone when trying to understand diversity.

Part Three: Challenges and dilemmas

There are a number of challenges and dilemmas that arise in using this activity. I discuss three of these here.

The first challenge is the constant pressure of time. Students are often frustrated that they do not have more time to generate aspects of their own identity, to talk about these with classmates, or to interview each other. I also grapple with this, because there is certainly a benefit to the specific learning that they do about each other. Ultimately, the challenge is to allow for this while also both drawing out the conceptual learning and facilitating the generation of student insights into the implications for themselves and others. For this to happen, enough time must be given to processing the content.

A second challenge has to do with the need that some participants will have to transcend group memberships, and the resulting debates that can ensue when other students seek to disabuse them of the idea that group memberships are irrelevant. More generally, the challenge is to support the group in avoiding either/or thinking or becoming polarized around particular positions. The dilemma I often grapple with has to do with the degree to which I am or should be directive or bring out my points explicitly. If I take students through the process and support them in reaching their own insights, the learning can be deeper. Yet, at times, this can also encourage unhealthy debate among participants. Ultimately, I have dealt with this by making sure in the prior session to establish clear ground rules for engagement and safety in the classroom and by presenting material on dialogue (e.g., Isaacs 1999) and on difficult conversations (Patton 1999).

The third challenge arises after the interviewing activity. One key insight students often have as part of the interviewing portion of the experience is that they realize how difficult it is to ask good questions that really bring out the interviewee. They learn that there is much more learning to be done. My way of handling this in part is via the packet of sample questions I offer. My dilemma regards the question of how to get the students to the next level so that they develop their own expertise, rather than just taking the packet I offer and choosing a few questions for their fieldwork. I continue to struggle with and have not quite resolved this dilemma; I partly address it through my comments and suggestions in response to the students' fieldwork plans, which encourages them to adapt the questions to the particular objectives of their project.

Conclusion

Over the years that I have used it, I have found the workshop provides a solid, memorable, and rewarding base for students to begin to learn about some of the complexities of diversity and culture. I hope that it will do the same for those readers who use it.

Appendix 5.1 Reading assignment

Readings
SOURCES OF OUR IDENTITY: EXPLORING OUR AND OTHERS'
DIFFERENCES (INTERVIEWING WORKSHOP)

Taylor Cox, Jr. (1993). Group identities in the self-concept. *Cultural Diversity in Organizations: Theory, Research and Practice* (Chapter 4, pp. 43–63). San Francisco: Berrett-Koehler.

Taylor Cox, Jr. and Ruby L. Beale (1997). *Developing Competency to Manage Diversity: Readings, Cases and Activities* (Chapter 4, pp. 51–77). San Francisco: Berrett-Koehler.

Donald C. Klein (1994). Collective dis-identity. In Elsie Y. Cross, Judith H. Katz, Frederick A. Miller, and Edith W. Seashore (eds), *The Promise of Diversity: Over 40 Voices Discuss Strategies for Eliminating Discrimination in Organizations* (pp. 272–9). Burr Ridge, IL: Irwin.

Bernardo M. Ferdman (1995). Cultural identity and diversity in organizations: bridging the gap between group differences and individual uniqueness. In M. Chemers, S. Oskamp and M. A. Costanzo (eds), *Diversity in Organizations: New Perspectives for a Changing Workplace* (pp. 37–61). Thousand Oaks, CA: Sage.

Andrea Fontana and James H. Frey (1994). Interviewing: the art of science. In N. K. Denzin and Y. S. Lincoln (eds), *Handbook of Qualitative Research* (pp. 361–76). Thousand Oaks, CA: Sage.

Optional:
Elisha Y. Babad, Max Birnbaum and Kenneth D. Benne (1983). *The Social Self: Group Influences on Personal Identity.* Beverly Hills, CA: Sage. [Part I. Initial considerations. (Especially the following sections: "Self-definition and group memberships," "A method of inquiry into the social self," "Skills for self inquiry," and "Exploring life history.")]

Jeanne Marecek, Michelle Fine and Louise Kidder (1997). Working between worlds: qualitative methods and social psychology. *Journal of Social Issues, 53,* 631–44.

Lyn Mikel Brown (1997). Performing femininities: listening to White working-class girls in rural Maine. *Journal of Social Issues, 53,* 703–23.

Suggested questions to think about
Sources of Our Identity: Exploring Our and Others' Differences (Interviewing workshop)

Focus: building skills for inquiring about our differences, both of ourselves and others.
Objectives: a) to learn about processes of inquiry as initial preparation for conducting interviews as part of the fieldwork assignment; b) to delve experientially into the nature and range of the diversity in each of our selves and in our group.

1 Who are you? What makes you who you are?
2 What are some of the social components of your identity? Have these developed/changed over time? How? Why?
3 If someone wanted to find out more about who you are, what types of questions would they have to ask? How would they have to ask them?

References

Ferdman, B. M. (1990) "Literacy and cultural identity," *Harvard Educational Review*, 60: 181–204.

Ferdman, B. M. (1995) "Cultural identity and diversity in organizations: bridging the gap between group differences and individual uniqueness," in M. Chemers, S. Oskamp and M. A. Costanzo (eds), *Diversity in Organizations: New Perspectives for a Changing Workplace*, Thousand Oaks, CA: Sage, pp. 37–61.

Ferdman, B. M. (1999) "The color and culture of gender in organizations: attending to race and ethnicity," in G. N. Powell (ed.), *Handbook of Gender and Work*, Thousand Oaks, CA: Sage, pp. 17–34.

Ferdman, B. M. (2000) " 'Why am I who I am?' Constructing the cultural self in multicultural perspective," *Human Development*, 43: 19–23.

Ferdman, B. M. (2001) "Multiple and complex ethnocultural identities: what are we talking about and why should we care?" in B. M. Ferdman (Chair), *Multiple and Complex Ethnocultural Identities in Plural Societies: Implications for Intergroup Relations*, symposium presented at "International Perspectives on Race, Ethnicity, and Intercultural Relations," second Biennial Conference of the International Academy of Intercultural Relations, Oxford, MS, April.

Ferdman, B. M. and Gallegos, P. I. (2001) "Latinos and racial identity development," in C. L. Wijeyesinghe and B. W. Jackson III (eds), *New Perspectives on Racial Identity Development: A Theoretical and Practical Anthology*, New York: New York University Press, pp. 32–66.

Ferdman, B. M. and Horenczyk, G. (2000) "Cultural identity and immigration: reconstructing the group during cultural transitions," in E. Olshtain and G. Horenczyk (eds), *Language, Identity, and Immigration*, Jerusalem: Hebrew University Magnes Press, pp. 81–100.

Gardenswartz, L. and Rowe, A. (1994) *The Managing Diversity Survival Guide: A Complete Collection of Checklists, Activities, and Tips*, Burr Ridge, IL: Irwin Professional Publishing.

Isaacs, W. N. (1999) *Dialogue and the Art of Thinking Together*, New York: Doubleday.

Loden, M. and Rosener, J. B. (1991) *Workforce America! Managing Employee Diversity as a Vital Resource*, Burr Ridge, IL: Irwin Professional Publishing.

Nagel, J. (1994) "Constructing ethnicity: creating and recreating ethnic identity and culture," *Social Problems*, 41: 152–76.

Patton, B. M. (1999) "Difficult conversations with less anxiety and better results," *Dispute Resolution Magazine*, Summer: 25–9.

Part III

Cultural scanning and sense-making
How do we "learn" and characterize culture?

In the previous section, we focused upon the concept of culture itself and provided perspectives from several disciplinary platforms. These platforms allowed us different windows for analysis and provided different teaching challenges. Here we have selected four modules that take us to the next step – teaching how to "learn culture." Specifically, we look at the fundamental dilemma of how to learn about a tacit issue that is also dynamic, ever changing, and different in different contexts.

The raw material we have is context, symbol, and behavioral trace. The four modules all aim at training the individual to gather and interpret cultural data. Each learner is encouraged to put away natural inclinations and become enmeshed first into descriptive data gathering and then into inferential analysis. Deep appreciation of a culture develops over time. Thus, description and inference are meant to lead to "tentative" cultural hypotheses. The cultural hypothesis set can then be elaborated when the learner next "visits" the same culture.

An anthropological approach to understanding work organizations is presented in Kleinberg's simulated fieldwork immersion. Here the learner is asked to avoid inferences that are at the individual level in favor of inferences that recognize the group's role in the behavior observed. This skill in distinguishing the cultural from the psychological and the social is a first step in the anthropological process.

When the learner can begin to "see" behavioral patterns, the next step in sense-making is to embed this skill into a more systematic appreciation. Phillips and Boyacigiller use simulation and fieldwork to demonstrate the use of an integrated cultural framework for accelerating learners' appreciation of what they observe. In employing frameworks, learners are asked to take the observational data and categorize them based upon an integration of a number of frameworks, while keeping in mind that the frameworks themselves provide only a necessarily rudimentary understanding.

Bird and Osland offer a series of lecture topics, some based upon fieldwork, that aid cultural sense-making through increasingly sophisticated analysis. They drill down from a framework base through stereotyping to the identification of cultural paradoxes. This recognizes and reinforces the issue of context and helps the learner comprehend that people behave differently in different contexts. Thus, context is seen as a required modifier of the inference process.

Roney uses story and film to provide the learner with the further challenge of drawing inferences about cultures that are changing over time. While traditions seem stable, there is constant interaction with external events that drive traditions to change and be modified. Thus, meaning is an ever-evolving concept. Roney uses film to create a shared, albeit distant, experience for the class to focus upon as they consider the stability and dynamics of basic values.

Fundamental to this section is the idea that "real" cultural learning is a long-term project, one that most students and executives cannot achieve in the very short periods of their education or even over a few years of experience in the field on "foreign" assignment. We offer these modules because they are methods for accelerating the learner's evolving appreciation.

Chapter 6

Context–culture interaction
Teaching thick descriptions of culture

Jill Kleinberg

Introduction

This module presents an exercise to help students develop an intuitive understanding of culture as a social construct. Though a critical concept for business students to understand, culture is an elusive concept, difficult for most students to grasp. For this reason, when I began teaching about the implications of culture in business and organizational contexts, I developed this experiential exercise in which the student is asked to surface and describe the culture of a particular organizational setting. It has remained a key tool in several courses I teach at the undergraduate and/or graduate levels. These courses include Organizational Behavior, Comparative and Cross-cultural Management, Cross-cultural Negotiation, and a seminar on Organizational Ethnography.

The exercise is ethnographic in nature and directly draws on the conceptualization of culture presented by anthropologist James P. Spradley in his book *Participant Observation* (1980), a text designed to show the beginning student how to do ethnographic fieldwork. This particular concept of culture came to the attention of organizational researchers in a groundbreaking *Administrative Science Quarterly* special issue on organizational culture (Gregory 1983). Spradley's basic definition of culture is consonant with that definition which has come to be accepted by many organization and management scholars. Our discourse inevitably reflects underlying assumptions about culture as a social construct (Boyacigiller *et al.* 2003; Kleinberg 1998). These assumptions encompass notions of:

1   what culture is,
2   what culture does,
3   how culture comes into being,
4   how culture can be "discovered," and
5   how culture can be conveyed in words (i.e., "represented") so others are able to comprehend its content and significance.

Spradley's book on doing ethnography deals explicitly with each of these challenging issues, and the cultural analysis exercise adapted from his framework gives students the opportunity to work intimately on all of these aspects of a theory of culture.

The concept of culture

Students prepare for the exercise by reading and discussing the first three chapters of Spradley's book, *Participant Observation*, at least two weeks before the written cultural analysis assignment is due.[1] Students, therefore, have ample opportunity to clarify Spradley's concept of culture as well as to ask questions about how to do the assignment.

According to Spradley, ethnographers must be concerned with three fundamental aspects of human experience when they study a culture: cultural knowledge, cultural behavior, and cultural artifacts. Cultural knowledge is the core or essence of culture. It can be conceptualized as a set of dynamic mental constructs or "cognitive sketch maps" (Frake 1977), the components of which are shared by a group of people. This is "the acquired knowledge people use to interpret experience and generate behavior" (Spradley 1980: 6). Cultural knowledge may be explicit or tacit. Figure 6.1 shows Spradley's schematic representation of what cultural

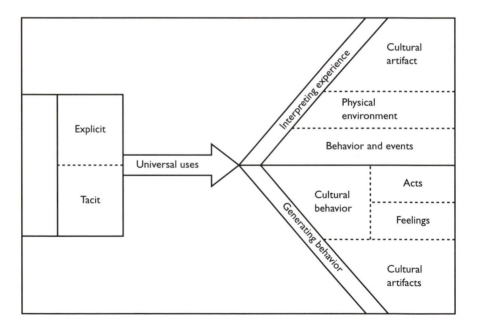

Figure 6.1 The two levels of cultural knowledge.

Source: Adapted from Spradley 1980: 8.

knowledge is and what it does. I refer to "cultural knowledge" inter-changeably with the terms "shared understandings," "shared sense-making," and "shared assumptions." Cultural knowledge is the "insider's" point of view (Spradley 1980: 4).

In class discussion, I frequently use the example of the "typical" college classroom to illustrate the construct of cultural knowledge. At the explicit level of consciousness, people may communicate cultural knowledge with relative ease, as in the meanings attached to the respective social cat-egories of "teacher" and "student," or the meanings attached to cultural artifacts (the things people make and use) like desks, pens, and paper. If an "outsider" were to ask a student to explain appropriate classroom behavior, the student might readily refer to the fact that the social setting has two kinds of participants – a teacher whose role it is to transmit know-ledge and students whose role it is to acquire knowledge. The student might proceed to tell the interlocutor that those in the learner role know that they are expected to enter the classroom, take a seat at a desk, and set out paper and pen so that they can take notes.

Tacit cultural knowledge, however, lies outside our awareness, as in the shared understanding that each student tends to acquire his/her habitual place to sit among the array of desks in the classroom. Even the social cat-egories of teacher and student are comprised of numerous unconscious understandings, such as various shared understandings about how a student should exhibit "respect" for the teacher.

Spradley calls on the theory of symbolic interactionism (Blumer 1969) to explain emergent cultural knowledge, or how culture comes into being. The "meaning" of, or the way people "make sense" of people, places, events and so forth, is an interpretive process that is accomplished through social interaction. "Culture, as a shared system of meanings, is learned, revised, maintained and defined in the context of people inter-acting" (Spradley 1980: 9).

To help illustrate this concept, I have sometimes arranged with a student to come to class early and sit that day in the place normally occu-pied by one of the other students. This leads to lively discussion about how people behaved and felt in response to the violation of tacit cultural know-ledge regarding seating arrangements. Students become aware of the process by which cultural knowledge is reinforced (or changed) through social interaction – in this case, looks of surprise and other body language indicating the sense of awkwardness of the person who finds someone sitting at "his" desk.

Cultural behavior, as shown in Figure 6.1, consists of actions and feel-ings, and the production and use of cultural artifacts as guided by cultural knowledge. Students often have difficulty determining when behavior can be considered "cultural." It helps to think of cultural behavior as "pat-terned" behavior that tends to recur in similar situations. Using once again the classroom example, the common behavior of a student raising his/her hand and being recognized by the instructor before speaking is an illustration of cultural behavior guided by the cultural knowledge that this is the appropriate way to participate in class discussion. The fact that a student might forgo this expected cultural behavior demonstrates an important point that cultural knowledge is not prescriptive – it is, in Frake's words, "a set of principles for map making and navigation" (1977: 6–7, quoted in Spradley 1980: 9), which may or may not be applied, depending on the situation. It is recognized, of course, that there may be social costs for failing to act according to widely shared understandings about appropriate behavior.

Analyzing an organizational scene

In the following paragraphs, I will reproduce (in italics) my one-page assignment description for the Cultural Analysis of an Organizational Scene, interspersing it with pedagogical commentary. Because of the complexity of the culture concept, and because the concept is so critical to the perspective on organization I want to convey to students, my emphasis in this exercise is on learning rather than on rigid performance criteria. I encourage them to have fun with it through their choice of "organizational scene" and through extensive class discussion of the ethnographic experience.

Cultural Analysis of an Organizational Scene (100 points)

Objectives

- *To understand the concept of culture presented by Spradley.*
- *To develop ethnographic observational and analytical skills.*
- *To consider the relevance of the concept of culture and these observational and analytical skills to being an effective member of an organization.*

As preparation for the exercise, I emphasize that I am introducing them to an ethnographic approach commonly associated with the discipline of anthropology but increasingly utilized in both business and organizational research and practice (e.g., Baba 1998). Discussion before and after students have completed the exercise highlights ways that one can develop the ability to be simultaneously participant and observer, a skill which is acquired only through disciplined practice. It highlights as well the process by which one arrives at inferences about the cultural knowledge of a group of people.

It is important to stress that, like any ethnographic enterprise, this exercise asks students only to make inferences about cultural knowledge. The mental constructs, the cognitive sketch maps that comprise culture, cannot be observed directly. They can only be inferred from the cultural behavior and cultural artifacts and from the speech utterances (a kind of cultural behavior) of those who are being observed by the ethnographer.

Assignment

> *Choose a social setting to observe. It can be a setting you are very familiar with or one that is new to you. Examples include such diverse settings as a University of Kansas class, a yoga class, a religious gathering, a football game, an apparel store, a grocery store, a bar, or a family get-together.*

While students initially show trepidation about this assignment, mainly because it requires them to work with unfamiliar concepts and because there is no template for carrying it out, most become enthusiastic when they begin to think about the setting that they will study. Our class discussion revolves around the advantages and disadvantages (also addressed by Spradley) of choosing a setting in which one is a full participant versus a setting where one can be a passive observer. We talk about the pitfalls of choosing a setting about which, whether or not one is a participant, one has prior knowledge – that is, the dilemma of how to keep one's existing cultural knowledge from infusing the ethnographic analysis. Usually I am asked if a scene like a yoga class or a family get-together can be considered "organizational," thus leading to discussion of a broad interpretation of what constitutes an organization. I encourage students to choose a setting that interests them and many opt for one which they anticipate will intrigue fellow class members in later discussion.

> *Conduct participant observation for approximately <u>two hours</u>. (The observations may be at different times. For purposes of this assignment, rely <u>only</u> on what you observe; do not "interview" participants in the setting.) Collect ethnographic data by observing the actors' cultural behavior (including speech messages) and the cultural artifacts that are relevant to the setting. Ask yourself <u>detailed</u> ethnographic questions about what people are doing and what people are using (e.g., are you observing similar behaviors on the part of a number of participants in the scene?). Make a record of your observations. If possible, take notes while you are observing. If this is not possible, make notes of what you have seen and heard immediately after completing the observation. Analyze the observed cultural behavior (i.e., patterned behavior exhibited by a number of participants in the social setting) to make inferences about the cultural knowledge, explicit and tacit, which underlies the observed cultural behavior and cultural artifacts.*

Many students initially wonder how they can learn enough about underlying cultural knowledge after just two hours of observation. They typically approach the exercise with the expectation that their resulting analysis must be "accurate." I assure students that, in this attenuated time-frame, they should strive less for accuracy than for the most plausible inferences about cultural knowledge based on the available data.

Nonetheless, I stress how critical it is to work with good data, as ethnographic analysis is contextually embedded. Good data are minutely detailed and accurate descriptions of what people were observed to do and say and of the physical environment of the setting. For example, in addition to the numerous actions that accomplish a social transaction such as ordering and paying for a drink at a coffee bar, the observer should note facial expressions and other body language as well. Careful observation requires concentration and discipline.

Students often feel overwhelmed by this call for detail. They ask, for example, how it is possible to describe a whole football game in such depth. This leads to a discussion of focus. The most successful analyses tend to be focused comparatively narrowly. I usually do not ask students to attach their field notes to the written ethnographic account, although doing so could enhance their motivation to attend conscientiously to making an ethnographic record. Before they begin the assignment, however, we talk about devising mnemonic systems for helping one remember observations if notes cannot be made immediately.

The most challenging aspect of the exercise is drawing inferences about cultural knowledge. First of all, even after extensive discussion and illustration, the notion of cultural knowledge eludes many students. They resist intangible abstractions of this sort, especially when the abstraction is so amorphous and seemingly arbitrary as cultural knowledge. Going back to the classroom-seating example, a common student response uses reasons or psychological motivations ("we always sit in the same place because it makes us feel more secure") rather than a true inference about cultural knowledge, etc. When I propose, as an inference about cultural knowledge, a statement like "There is a shared understanding that each class member has his/her own place to sit," I observe many incredulous looks. This is too simple. This is too obvious. Is this more than a variant description of observed behavior? Some other shared understandings that typically can be inferred from observed behaviors in my classes include the following:

1   it is not appropriate to sit in someone else's informally designated seat;
2   if someone sits in your seat, it is appropriate for you to choose a different seat for that particular class meeting;
3   appropriate seating choices do not include the first two rows of desks facing the teacher;

4   personal belongings should be distributed on one's desk or on the floor near one's desk; and,

5   it is not appropriate to place personal belongings on another desk in the classroom, even an uninhabited one.

So, in addition to mastering the difficult analytical mechanics of inferring cultural knowledge, students face the problem of "representation" or "writing culture" (Boyacigiller *et al.* 2003; Van Maanen 1988). That is, they must struggle with putting into words statements that reflect the way members of a group make sense of a particular organizational scene.

Identifying cultural knowledge as either explicit or tacit presents another problem. I want students to try to make this distinction. The distinction is important because tacit cultural knowledge is most resistant to change and often reflects our most deeply held convictions. In my own research, managers working in Japanese-owned and -managed subsidiary companies in Southern California expressed the greatest moral indignation when their respective tacit cultural assumptions about work were violated by the cultural other (Kleinberg 1989). The shared assumptions that I have inferred above with regard to classroom seating arrangements in my opinion clearly constitute tacit cultural knowledge.

> *After analyzing the data, write an "ethnography" or cultural analysis of the observed setting. Keep in mind that the written ethnographic account needs to supply enough description of observed behavior to support the inferences that you make about the cultural knowledge that helps guide that behavior. I favor depth of analysis over breadth. Spradley's terminology with regard to the concept of culture offers convenient tools for doing this description and analysis. Utilize these tools in order to strengthen your ethnographic account!*
>
> *Your cultural analysis will be evaluated on four dimensions. These are: (1) demonstrated effort in finding and carefully observing an appropriate social setting; (2) demonstrated understanding of Spradley's concept of culture; (3) demonstrated understanding of the process of making inferences about cultural knowledge; and (4) effective writing, in terms of organization, grammar, punctuation, and spelling.*
>
> *Be prepared to discuss in class your experience of doing ethnography as well as the culture that you discovered in the setting you observed.*

Typically about two-thirds of the draft ethnographic accounts I receive reflect an adequate understanding of the concept of culture and/or how to write a statement that captures the essence of the cultural knowledge that has been inferred through ethnographic analysis. Most of these still leave ample room for improvement. Common problems with regard to the fundamental concept of culture are the tendency to represent culture in terms of reasons or psychological motivations and to confuse cultural knowledge and cultural behavior.

For those students who demonstrate at least a rudimentary grasp of Spradley's conceptual framework, the main problems in their ethnographic accounts center on organization, analytical depth, and representation of culture. In addition, I invariably receive some analyses that are infused with the student's prior cultural knowledge.

One paper that stays in my mind offered a generic cultural analysis of a football game that illuminated the complex rules and extensively utilized the jargon (folk terminology) of the game. My comments, of course, queried what the student actually saw and heard at the specific football game he presumably observed for the assignment. The analysis failed to provide the detailed description of actual observed behaviors.

What stance, then, should a student take along the continuum of possibilities between cultural insider and cultural outsider? If Starbucks is the organizational scene being studied, does the ethnographer-in-training, adopt a tabula rasa strategy, putting aside their insider knowledge about key cultural artifacts, such as coffee, cups, and money? Or, does the ethnographer assume a midway stance as a cultural insider who knows about the paraphernalia surrounding coffee and knows about money, but who has (as much as possible) divested themself of preconceptions concerning the shared assumptions that guide behavior in a coffee bar? Either stance is acceptable. Most organizational scenes studied by students resonate to some extent with the observer's prior experience. The objective of the exercise is to comprehend something previously unknown, to achieve insights that would not have been possible without using an ethnographic lens.

And what does a good cultural analysis look like? There are important choices to make about how to organize the analysis and how to represent the construct of culture. I normally ask students to read certain organizational ethnographic writings in order to help them understand the concept of culture in an organizational context and to show them the form that a cultural analysis might take.[2] One ethnographic account I frequently assign is Van Maanen's analysis of the culture of ride operators at Disneyland (1991). The excerpt below illustrates how Van Maanen constructs his cultural analysis; it concerns shared sense-making with regard to the relative social status of different types of ride operators.

> Uniforms also correspond to a wider status ranking that casts a significant shadow on employees of all types. Male ride operators on the Autopia wear, for example, untailored jumpsuits similar to pit mechanics' and consequently generate about as much respect from peers as the grease-stained outfits worn by pump jockeys generate from real motorists at gas stations.
>
> (Van Maanen 1991: 62)

Van Maanen's analysis evokes the mode of "thick description" practiced by anthropologist Clifford Geertz. Organization scholars interested in culture often quote Geertz's definition of culture, which is wholly compatible with the definition offered earlier in this chapter.

> Believing, with Max Weber, that man is an animal suspended in webs of significance, I take culture to be those webs, and the analysis of it to be therefore not an experimental science in search of law but an interpretive one in search of meaning.
>
> (Geertz 1973: 5)

To Geertz, thick description means the layered unfolding in writing of what people have been observed or been reported to have done; what they have been heard or been reported to have said – in the past as well as in the present. The description is crafted in such a way that the webs of significance that are culture become apparent to the reader subtly as the text unfolds. "Thick" description is necessary because "most of what we need to comprehend a particular event, ritual, custom, idea, or whatever is insinuated as background information before the thing itself is directly examined" (Geertz 1973: 9).

Because they have enjoyed Van Maanen's ethnography of ride operators, some students use it a model for their cultural analysis assignment. I steer most toward a style resembling the "cognitive anthropologists" such as Spradley, however. I believe that this is the simplest, cleanest way for a novice to work through the process of discovering and representing culture. Compared to a Geertzian approach, cognitive anthropologists' reconstructions of shared understandings tend to be articulated more clearly. One of my own ethnographic accounts of emergent cultures in the Japanese–American bi-national work context may be assigned to serve as a model (e.g., Kleinberg 1994a, b).

Making distinct inferences about cultural knowledge is a central concern. I give an illustration from my own research below. One domain of cultural knowledge that I inferred comprises assumptions that flesh out the Japanese expatriate managers' understanding that Americans present a number of specific managerial problems (Kleinberg 1994b).

Americans are a problem

- Inflexibility
- Narrow interpretation of responsibility
- Concern for power and money
- Self-interest above group welfare.

In the article, I explicate the meaning of each of the sub-domains of cultural knowledge through textual thick description, thereby clarifying the logic for making these particular inferences. I do this by relying heavily, but not exclusively, on the words of Japanese managers whom I interviewed or conversed with informally.

It is important to keep in mind, however, that the cultural analysis assignment asks students <u>only to observe</u> an organizational scene. They are instructed not to interview participants in the scene.[3] My reasons for limiting the ethnographic data that students have to work with are the short timeframe of the ethnographic project and the fact that they are not trained to conduct ethnographic interviews. Although students feel that it would be easier if they could ask questions their lack of training would result in the collection of extremely compromised data and drive analyses tending even more toward inferences that emphasize psychological motivation. Focusing just on what they see people do and hear people say actually simplifies the process of making inferences about cultural knowledge. The circumscribed design of the exercise heightens students' awareness that they are trying to uncover a cognitive phenomenon, much of which is underneath the consciousness of the people under observation. I tell the students:

> *Describe what you saw and heard. Milk that description as much as possible for inferences about underlying cultural knowledge. You have a six-page limit and, therefore, you must carefully choose what to include in your description. Do not waste space on a lot of description that will not directly relate to the inferences that you make. Be sure, however, to provide enough description for me to see <u>why</u> you have drawn the inferences about cultural knowledge that you have drawn. Take some risks. You don't have to be right about your inferences. <u>What is important is that you internalize the framework for discovering and representing culture.</u>*

Notes

1 Assigned chapters are: (1) Ethnography and culture; (2) Ethnography for what?; and, (3) The ethnographic research cycle. Students also read Miner's (1956) classic tongue-in-cheek essay on "the Nacierma," where Americans are portrayed as superstitious natives.
2 Other useful examples of writing organizational culture are found in the following publications (this is not an exhaustive list): Frost, *et al.* 1991; Kunda 1992; Sackmann 1991.
3 The method of ethnographic data gathering commonly known as "participant observation" normally includes both observation and interviewing.

References

Baba, M. L. (1998) "Anthropologists in corporate America: 'knowledge management' and ethical angst," *The Chronicle of Higher Education* (8 May): B4–B5.

Blumer, H. (1969) *Symbolic Interactionism*, Englewood Cliffs, NJ: Prentice-Hall.

Boyacigiller, N. A., Kleinberg, M. J., Phillips, M. E. and Sackmann, S. A. (2003) "Conceptualizing culture: elucidating the streams of research in international cross-cultural management," in B. J. Punnett and O. Shenkar (eds), *Handbook of International Management Research*, 2nd edn, Ann Arbor: University of Michigan Press.

Frake, C. O. (1977) "Plying frames can be dangerous: some reflections on methodology in cognitive anthropology," *Quarterly Newsletter of the Institute for Comparative Human Development*, 3: 1–7.

Frost, P. J., Moore, L. F., Louis, M. R., Lundberg, C. C. and Martin, J. (eds) (1991) *Reframing Organizational Culture*, Newbury Park, CA: Sage.

Geertz, C. (1973) *The Interpretation of Cultures*, New York: Basic Books.

Gregory, K. L. (1983) "Native-view paradigms: multiple cultures and culture conflicts in organizations," *Administrative Science Quarterly*, 28: 359–76.

Kleinberg, J. (1989) "Culture clash between managers: America's Japanese firms," *Advances in International Comparative Management*, vol. 4, Greenwich, CT: JAI Press, pp. 221–44.

Kleinberg, J. (1994a) "The crazy group: emergent culture in a Japanese–American binational work group," *Research in International Business and International Relations*, vol. 6, Greenwich, CT: JAI Press, pp. 1–45.

Kleinberg, J. (1994b) "Practical implications of organizational culture where Americans and Japanese work together," *National Association for the Practice of Anthropology Bulletin*, 14: 48–65.

Kleinberg, J. (1998) "An ethnographic perspective on cross-cultural negotiation and cultural production," *Advances in Qualitative Organization Research*, vol. 1, Greenwich, CT: JAI Press, pp. 201–49.

Kunda, G. (1992) *Engineering Culture: Control and Commitment in a High-Tech Corporation*, Philadelphia, PA: Temple University Press.

Miner, H. (1956) "Body ritual among the Nacirema," *American Anthropologist*, 58: 503–7.

Sackmann, S. A. (1991) *Cultural Knowledge in Organizations: Exploring the Collective Mind*, Newbury Park, CA: Sage.

Spradley, J. P. (1980) *Participant Observation*, New York: Holt, Rinehart and Winston.

Van Maanen, J. (1988) *Tales of the Field: On Writing Ethnography*, Chicago: University of Chicago Press.

Van Maanen, J. (1991) "The smile factory: work at Disneyland," in P. J. Frost, L. F. Moore, M. R. Louis and J. Martin (eds), *Reframing Organizational Culture*, Newbury Park, CA: Sage, pp. 58–76.

Chapter 7

Cultural scanning

An integrated cultural frameworks approach

Margaret E. Phillips and Nakiye A. Boyacigiller

Introduction

This teaching module introduces cultural scanning, a tool for learning how to "learn culture." The module focuses on explaining the process of cultural scanning and the content of an "integrated framework for cultural analysis" (IFCA) which we use to discern key dimensions of a focal group's culture. Cultural scanning promotes a proactive approach to cultural learning and systematic, deliberate cultural comparisons.

The lecturette

1 The logic and process of cultural scanning

a Rationale for learning how to "learn culture"

Central to cross-cultural competency is the need to know how to "learn" other cultures. This implies "learning" for the purpose of understanding, interacting, and navigating in cultures different from our own. It is now quite common for

> people of many nationalities ... [to] lead multicultural teams, work on multi-country projects, and travel monthly outside their home countries. In any year, they may work in Paris, Shanghai, Istanbul, Moscow, or Buenos Aires with colleagues from a different set of countries.
> (description of work at Eastman Kodak Company, cited in Delano
> 2000: 77)

While there is a need to acquire sophisticated and in-depth cultural knowledge, today's manager has a more pressing need to acquire these understandings quickly and efficiently. Managers also need to remain in a proactive, learning mode as they encounter and interact with employees, partners, suppliers, and customers in and from new or different cultural contexts. Therefore, to be effective in organizations today, we must "learn how to 'learn culture'" (Teagarden 1994).

b The process of learning culture is "messy"

To learn a culture new to us, our central task is to "decipher the 'content' of the culture" (Schein 1990: 12). But the process of doing so is rather messy. As we prepare for and cross into a foreign culture, we are continuously gathering information about it. As we go about collecting this vast amount of information, it is difficult to know what elements are key to understanding and navigating within that new culture. As human beings, our inclination is to focus on those things most *important* in our own cultures, most *different* from our own cultures, or most *obvious or easily identifiable* in the other culture. This often leads us to a rather superficial and ethnocentric analysis, because some key elements of the foreign culture may not be important to or different from our own, nor may they be obvious to or easily identifiable by someone wearing our personal cultural lenses.

c The "onion" definition of culture

We can employ the following definition of culture:

> "culture" is a set of explicit and tacit assumptions or understandings commonly held by a group of people; a particular configuration of assumptions is distinctive to the group; these assumptions/understandings serve as guides to acceptable and unacceptable perceptions, thoughts, feelings and behaviors; they are learned and passed on to new members of the group through social interaction; they change over time, although the tacit assumptions which are the core of culture are most resistant to change.
>
> (Boyacigiller *et al.* 1996: 172)

We see that culture is like an "onion", with multiple layers that can be peeled away to find the more intangible, abstract, and tacit set of assumptions at the core. The outer, substantially larger layer of the onion is composed of the culture's immediately tangible manifestations, or artifacts. Unlike assumptions, artifacts are not abstract renderings of the culture. Rather, they are physical (e.g., instruments, symbols, logos, dress, office design), behavioral (e.g., rites, rituals), and verbal (e.g., language, stories) representations of elements of the culture. Beneath the external layer of artifacts is the layer of values. These are *preferred* behaviors, objectives, and outcomes – "*ideals*," "what *should* be done." They are fewer and much more abstract than artifacts. While some values can be consciously articulated (e.g., rules and regulations, laws, corporate mission statements), most (e.g., norms) are invisible until they are violated.

d Attributes of a culture scan

To decipher the content of a culture we need a <u>process</u> to guide our attention to certain artifacts and values in the unfamiliar culture that we could use – in as systematic and objective a manner as humanly possible – to infer this new culture's set of assumptions. To this end, we teach the process of <u>Cultural Scanning</u> using the <u>Integrated Framework for Cultural Analysis</u> (IFCA). The IFCA:

- identifies the types of assumptions known to compose the core of a cultural mindset;
- is useful in recording and organizing the vast array of cultural data we collect through observation of and experience within a cultural context;
- helps us to interpret the underlying meaning of these cultural manifestations, revealing the belief system of the cultural group.

Theoretically and practically, use of the IFCA for cultural scanning allows us to understand the key "central tendencies" of the culture and enables us to interact and navigate more successfully within that culture. More importantly, it forces us into a proactive learning mode as we approach and enter cultures foreign to us, because it requires us to constantly refine and modify our interpretation of assumptions as we, through observation and experience, collect new data.

2 The integrated framework for cultural analysis (IFCA)

The IFCA (see Table 7.1) unites into one overarching structure several frameworks for cultural analysis developed by culture researchers from a variety of disciplines, including anthropology (Kluckhohn and Strodtbeck 1961; elaborated in Phillips (1994) and Schein (1990)), communications theory (Hall and Hall 1990), social psychology (Hofstede 1980), and international management (Hofstede and Bond 1988; Trompenaars 1993). These frameworks are composed of "dimensions" (concise sets of issues, e.g., time, relationships, communication, power) that are both common to all human groups and have different meanings or interpretations in different cultures. We have integrated the various frameworks to allow attention to an expanded range of cultural dimensions, as well as to the depth of understanding derived from multiple authors' perspectives on the same dimension. This gives you the ability to construct a more broadly grounded "road map" of a culture, known as a <u>sociotype</u>. Unlike a stereotype, a sociotype is your consciously held, currently as-accurate-as-possible, intentionally modifiable-upon-further-experience description (not evaluation) of the culture you are learning (from Adler 2002: 81).

Table 7.1 Integrated Framework for Cultural Analysis – explanation of dimensions

Free will / Determinism

a relationship with environment (K&S / S / T) dominance / subjugation / harmony (K&S / S)	Feeling of group toward its environment Can control / controlled by / balance or congruence
b uncertainty avoidance (H)	Low–high tendency to avoid uncertainty in organizations

Sources of truth

a origins of truth (S / P)	Where group seeks "right" answers, e.g., scientific test, law, guru, tradition, trial / error
b universalism / particularism (T)	Rules of wide generality vs. an emphasis on context

Nature of time (K&S / S / T)

a past (H&H / K&S / S) / present (K&S / S) / future (H&H / K&S / S) short- / long-term future (H&B)	Time orientation Focus = near-term / far-future; define "short" / "long"
b monochronic / polychronic (H&H)	Does one thing at a time / simultaneous actions
c linear / cyclical (S)	String of activities / repeated set of activities

Nature of human nature (K&S / S) General expectations of people's character / intentions

a good / evil / neutral variable by individual (K&S / S)	Anticipated nature of all or defined sets of people Each individual differs – some good, some bad
b mutability (K&S / S)	Can people change? Who? How?
c "us" / "them" (P / S)	In-group / out-group distinctions

Nature of work relationships (K&S / P / S / T)

a individualistic (H / K&S) / collectivistic (H) / hierarchical (K&S / P / S)	Individually oriented / group-oriented / status-based ranking; lineal
b power distance (H)	Low / high acceptance of power differences
c ascription / achievement (T)	Basis for conferring status: merit / worth determined by who one is / by what one has done
d specific / diffuse (T)	Context of relationship: bounded / spans domains

Purpose of work (K&S / P / S)

a doing / being / becoming (K&S / S)	For extrinsic rewards Acceptance / enjoyment of here and now; fate Personal growth and self-actualization
b masculinity / femininity (H)	Materialistic, aggressive, "doing" Nurturing, concerned about quality of life, "being"

Communication

a high / low context (H&H)	Amount of information implicit in situation of messages
b fast / slow messages (H&H)	Message form: slow = must be deciphered (e.g., book) fast = straightforward (e.g., headline)
c neutral / emotional (T)	Degree to which emotions are visibly expressed

*H&H = dimension contributed by Hall & Hall; H = Hofstede; H&B = Hofstede & Bond; K&S = Kluckhohn & Strodtbeck; P = Phillips; S = Schein; T = Trompenaars.

To introduce students to the work from which the IFCA was derived, we usually assign one of the many chapters on culture available in such texts as Adler (2002), Deresky (2000), or Cullen (2002), or excerpts from the original work of the various authors of the frameworks.

For easier application by students, we have translated the focus of each major dimension into a series of questions that guides the scanning process (see Table 7.2). For an exercise in comparative cultural analysis, students are given a handout listing these questions with space to record their findings regarding relevant artifacts and values and their interpretations of meaning (i.e., assumptions in use) for each cultural group. Table 7.2 gives an example of such an analysis for the Rossy–Phillips *Star Trek* cross-cultural management video case study of Chapter 12 in this volume.

The assignment

We teach cultural scanning to a variety of different groups in a variety of different settings, and we tailor the cultural data-gathering experience to the group. The experience generally involves scanning the cultures of one or two groups, organizations, or organizational units. We find a comparative cultural analysis across two or more cultural groups most effective for highlighting cultural differences to demonstrate the implications for management practice and organization design. For example, Table 7.2 shows that the nature of work relationships is hierarchical in both cultures, but in the Klingon culture this hierarchy is used for control; high power-distance solidifies the formality of relationships, and the captain's position is quasi-autocratic. In contrast, the chain of command in Starfleet culture is used for information; lower power-distance characterizes the less formal relationships in this technocracy, where decisions are made based on expert knowledge. It is this detailed knowledge, not solely the position of the organization on the particular dimension, that provides the substance of the *sociotype* and that conveys the "meanings," straightforward and nuanced, ascribed by the culture.

Below are a few examples of cultural scanning assignments we use for different audiences.

Organization Behavior or International Management course for undergraduate or graduate students (including executive education)

1   Debriefing experiential exercises (e.g., BaFá BaFá – Shirts 1977) or observation assignments (e.g., two schools in the university, two different retail stores, two different units of the students' organization, *Star Trek* video case used in Chapter 12).

Table 7.2 Sample culture scan with guiding questions

	Starfleet culture	Klingon culture

Free will
• Control
  – Can environment be controlled?
  – Is behavior controlled by self, social norms, rules, or by whims of others?
  – Is harmony important?
  – Can circumstances change? How?
• Uncertainty avoidance
  – How much do people strive to limit uncertainty in their lives?
  – How important are rules and procedures?
	Control:
	– technical domination based on standards; state-of-art knowledge
	– in harmony with other "life forms"
	Change:
	– does occur, but can be studied and understood
	– can learn
	Uncertainty recognized:
	– inherent in mission to seek out/explore new life forms
	– rules mitigated by trust, experience
	– thoughtful risk-taking is good
		Control:
		– dominant – must be to reduce risk/threat
		– black/white rules
		Change:
		– individual's honor determined by family honor, tradition, "has worked for thousands of years"
		Uncertainty:
		– reduced/avoided through aggressiveness and confrontation to ensure domination

Sources of truth
• Origins of truth
  – Where do people go for directions/ answers?
  – Who do they go to?
• Universalism
  – What can be questioned and what can't?
  – Are rules situation-specific or generally applied?
  – Is context important when judging right/wrong?
	– experts/experienced
	– learning; cooperative analysis with reporting through chain of command
	– learning orientation promotes questioning
	– rules modifiable if rational reason
		Go to:
		– next level in hierarchy for orders
		– Klingon code of honor for answers
		Who: senior officer or Klingon High Command
		Little or nothing can be questioned;
		– no need: answers are black and white
		– rules are universally applied

Table 7.2 continued

	Starfleet culture	Klingon culture
Time • Is attention paid to – past? present? future? – Which is most important? • Do people do – many things at once? – one thing at a time? • How are priorities set? • What is considered "prompt"?	Present: service to the Federation Longer-term: "seek out new life" More polychronic: perform a variety of activities More linear: past does not necessarily predict future	Present: serving the Pagh; Future: dying an "honorable death" More monochronic than Starfleet (i.e., either "in battle" or "not in battle") Somewhat cyclical: live/fight/die difficult to imagine new or different patterns Priorities: defend Klingons Prompt: upon order of a superior
Human nature • Are others viewed as individuals or as members of a homogeneous group? • What are expectations about other people? – are they positive? Can "good" people change? – are they negative? Can "bad" people change? • How are strangers treated?	Individuals/strangers – all given a chance to show ability Positive – loyalty to the mission of Starfleet – technical competence – learning-oriented	Others/strangers – negative; viewed with suspicion Klingons: neutral/individual – good = dying honorably, strong, loyal, parents died with honor – bad = weak, show feelings, traitor, parents did not die with honor
Work relationships • Do people work individually? in groups? • Does workspace (e.g., location, size, objects) reveal status? • Are most interactions based on – the formal hierarchy? – informal relationships? • How important are family ties as opposed to achievement in determining an individual's status? • Who do people admire/envy/fear?	Individual tasks contribute to team effort – has chain of command but uses hierarchy for information – decisions based on expertise; a technocracy Formal/informal relationships; low power-distance Achievement based on knowledge/expertise confers respect Admire – qualities/character of Picard/Riker	Individual tasks in hierarchical structure – hierarchy used for control Formal relationships Personal position in hierarchy is basis for status; – "a Klingon is his work, not his family" Admire – those who die with honor High power-distance – fear Captain Kargon – captain autocratic, but can be challenged by second in command

Table 7.2 continued

	Starfleet culture	Klingon culture
Purpose of work		
• Do people value	– "becoming"	– "doing" for reward of honorable death; "a Klingon is his work, not his family"
– aggressiveness, competitiveness, and material rewards?	– personal growth desirable	– masculine dominant; women are masculine
– social interaction and attempts to improve quality of work life?	– learning important	– aggressiveness, strength determines position
– learning and growing on the job?	– masculine and feminine behavior	
Communications		
• To what degree is information explicitly stated and details spelled out?	Low context	High context
	– "etiquette" rather than hard-and-fast rules	– many rules unspoken but must be followed
• Are communications	Fast and accurate messages	Fast messages with black/white interpretation
– fast and concisely stated? (e.g., headlines, bullet points, voice mail)	– information file	– little contextual data
– slow? (i.e., requiring interpretation, attentive to relationship building)	Relatively few significant nonverbals	Nonverbals: physical location of speaker; limited range
• What nonverbal behavior (e.g., body language, eye contact, tone of voice)		
– helps you understand what someone tells you?		
– is contrary to information you are being told?		

a   Students work individually or in small groups to identify the assumptions of each cultural group experienced or observed on each dimension and to provide evidence (artifacts and values) to support their claims.

b   Suggested debrief questions for shared experience (e.g., whole class exercise):

- Chart the cultural assumptions of the two groups in an interactive discussion.
- Identify key differences in assumptions you found between the two cultures.
- What does the sociotype derived from the culture scan suggest you do when entering that particular culture?
- What would you have done differently if you had the sociotype information in advance?
- How effective would this sociotype be in guiding your interactions with *one* member of the other culture? (This question helps to illustrate the problem of stereotyping.)
- What behaviors does this suggest might be most productive when entering a culture new to you?

c   For individual assignments, ask students to chart the cultural assumptions and identify key differences, then convey in writing their insights and conclusions from the experience.

2   Developing team reports on a country emphasizing the cultural underpinnings of managerial practices.

Students produce a briefing book for a training program to prepare a home-country manager for an expatriate assignment. The briefing book should focus on management and explain management practices from a comparative/contextual perspective. A key element of the briefing book is the *sociotype* developed from a culture scan of data gathered about the country. For example, students studying Japan may discuss how conflict is dealt with indirectly, often through intermediaries and during after hours socializing, as one might expect in a high-context, diffuse culture.

MBA course in Organization Theory and Design

As a portion of an organizational analysis or design/redesign project, students perform a culture scan on their organization or organizational unit and integrate it with analyses they have performed from other theoretical perspectives. The key question here is: "How does your cultural analysis inform, confirm, and/or expand your findings from your other analyses?"

Pre-departure training for study abroad

Students scan and compare home country culture with target-country culture in advance of departure and upon arrival.

a   Students work with others (e.g., exchange or returning students) from their host country to prepare a cultural scan from data collected prior to their departure, and continually update it following arrival in the host country to help acclimate and reduce the effects of culture shock.

b   For study trips (e.g., to Mexican maquiladoras along the California border) students prepare a comparative scan of their home-country culture (i.e., U.S. business culture) and the culture of the destination country from data collected prior to departure (i.e., Mexican business culture). Then they scan the culture of the destination location (i.e., Tijuana business culture) during the study trip.

Coaching managers in situ

The culture scan has also been successfully used in coaching managers in the analysis of their organization or organizational unit and in the assessment of cultural differences in a merger situation.

In each of the above learning situations, the emphasis is on developing a fairly systematic reading of the culture(s) at hand as the basis of organizational analysis or managerial action. The focus is not on the culture scan itself, rather on the conclusions one can derive from it. For example, in the team's country report, the intent is for students to use the culture scan to make a first best guess as to how managers in the focal country approach decision-making, leadership and motivation, and other aspects of management.[1] In most of the above examples, we use the culture scan in a comparative fashion (country/culture X is more achievement-oriented than country/culture Y) – emphasizing less the specific answer than the learning gained from the comparison. The intent is also to give the students/managers a sense that culture is tractable, learnable, and that the differences/similarities across cultures have important implications for managerial sense-making and action.

Dilemmas

While we find cultural scanning to be a powerful tool for understanding culture, there are several important caveats to using this approach.

With regard to our use of the <u>integrated cultural dimensions</u>, we grapple with several issues of a philosophical and pedagogical nature:

a   *The "integrated" framework:* Our approach to developing the integrated framework was a pragmatic one, motivated by our teaching. The framework does not have an empirical basis. Hence, some of the dimensions are more theoretically robust than others (e.g., individualism/collectivism), and we are concerned whether this is appropriate. We also tend to use some of the dimensions with somewhat of a different connotation than in the original research, driven as we are by pragmatic teaching concerns rather than theoretical purity.[2] Some may find this objectionable and question whether this is really an "integrated" framework.

b   *The balance between complexity and simplicity:*

   • Have we included too many dimensions or too few?
   • Is the current conceptualization too cumbersome?
   • Alternatively, in our search to develop a parsimonious list of cultural dimensions, have we erred on the side of trivialization of culture?

c   *Levels of analysis issue:* From a practical standpoint, should the questions or probes used to scan be different at different levels of analysis?

d   Does the IFCA lead to a focus on *cultures as static and unchanging* rather than as in constant interaction with one another (Brannen and Salk 2000)?

e   What about *cultural paradoxes*? Does the integrated framework underplay the incidence of cultural paradoxes (Osland and Bird 2000)? We think not. Provided that the culture scan is based upon multiple observations of a dimension in different circumstances and, most importantly, that the emphasis is placed on the process, not the answer. Thus, if a student encounters collectivist behavior in a culture where individualism tends to be the dominant assumption, they should try to understand the logic behind this, rather than disparage the new data. In this way, engaging in cultural scanning actually assists the process of identifying and understanding cultural paradoxes.

With regard to the process of <u>cultural scanning</u>, we face the following issues:

f   *Sociotypes vs stereotypes:* We are most troubled by the possibility that we may be encouraging our students' predilection to focus on looking for "the right answer" – with the "answer" becoming more important than the process of learning. This results in a focus on key words (assumptions) as "answers" rather than as shorthand for the underpinning knowledge and the rich sociotype of interwoven meanings. More important, while the culture scan is a tool for sociotyping and a powerful first step in understanding cultures, we worry that it may also facilitate stereotyping. We spend much time in our classes trying to ensure that this does not happen by constantly focusing on the group as the bearer of the culture, not the individual. Nevertheless, it is a risk.

g *Overemphasis on cultural factors:* Despite our protestations not to "overplay the culture card," we find within our largely U.S.-based student groups[3] a predilection to underemphasize institutional factors such as the economic context, political and legal systems, and history.

Conclusion

Notwithstanding our dilemmas with the cultural scanning process, our development and use of the IFCA is driven by our belief that:

> there is no such thing as an established list of those elements of societal cultures that are most related to ways of organizing and managing, a list that ends all discussion and can be learned by heart ... However, there are elements that recur frequently enough to suggest that they are of primary import ... Their manifestations have to be ... managed by everyone, whether or not their job is managerial.
>
> (Hickson and Pugh 1995: 20)

It is toward this vital and practical end that we teach the process of cultural scanning as a tool for learning how to "learn culture."

Notes

1 When performing national cultural scans, only a few countries have ample published work from which to draw conclusions regarding management practices (Thomas, Shenkar and Clarke 1994). Therefore, students find the culture scan process invaluable for developing sociotypes of countries for which data on management practices are scarce.
2 For example, we include space as an artifact of the relationships dimension, rather than as a separate dimension as in the original work by Hall and Hall (1990).
3 While we both are on faculties of universities with international cultural diversity, both universities are located in the U.S., which may account for this.

References

Adler, N. J. (2002) *International Dimensions of Organizational Behavior,* 4th edn, Cincinnati, OH: South-Western College Publishing.

Boyacigiller, N. A., Kleinberg, M. J., Phillips, M. E. and Sackmann, S. A. (1996) "Conceptualizing culture," in B. J. Punnett and O. Shenkar (eds), *Handbook for International Management Research,* Cambridge, MA: Blackwell.

Brannen, M. Y. and Salk, J. E. (2000) "Partnering across borders: negotiating organizational culture in a German–Japanese joint-venture," *Human Relations*, 53 (4): 451–87.

Cullen, J. B. (2002) *Multinational Management: A Strategic Approach*, Cincinnati, OH: South-Western College Publishing.

Delano, J. (2000) "Executive commentary," to J. S. Osland and A. Bird, "Beyond sophisticated stereotyping: cultural sensemaking in context," *Academy of Management Executive*, 14 (1): 77–8.

Deresky, H. (2000) *International Management: Managing across Borders and Cultures*, 3rd edn, Upper Saddle River, NJ: Prentice-Hall.

Hall, E. T. and Hall, M. R. (1990) "Key concepts: underlying structures of culture," *Understanding Cultural Differences: Germans, French and Americans*, Yarmouth, ME: Intercultural Press, pp. 1–31.

Hickson, D. J. and Pugh, D. S. (1995) *Management Worldwide: The Impact of Societal Culture on Organizations around the Globe*, London: Penguin.

Hofstede, G. (1980) "Motivation, leadership, and organization: do American theories apply abroad?" *Organizational Dynamics*, 9 (1): 42–63.

Hofstede, G. and Bond, M. (1988) "The Confucius connection: from cultural roots to economic growth," *Organizational Dynamics*, 16 (4): 4–21.

Kluckhohn, F. R. and Strodtbeck, F. L. (1961) *Variations in Value Orientations*, Evanston, IL: Row, Peterson.

Osland, J. S. and Bird, A. (2000) "Beyond sophisticated stereotyping: cultural sensemaking in context," *Academy of Management Executive*, 14 (1): 77–8.

Phillips, M. E. (1994) "Industry mindsets: exploring the cultures of two macro-organizational settings," *Organization Science*, 5 (3): 384–402, with appendices.

Schein, E. H. (1990) "Organizational culture," *American Psychologist*, February: 109–19.

Shirts, R. G. (1977) *BaFá BaFá: A Cross Culture Simulation*, Del Mar, CA: Simile II (Simulation Training Systems).

Teagarden, M. (1994) Quote from panel discussion at the Fourth Annual Centers for International Business Education and Research (CIBER) Conference on Language for Business and Economics, Los Angeles, CA, February.

Thomas, A. S., Shenkar, O. and Clarke, L. (1994) "The globalization of our mental maps: evaluating the geographic scope of JIBS coverage," *Journal of International Business Studies*, 25 (4): 675–86.

Trompenaars, F. (1993) *Riding the Waves of Culture: Understanding Diversity in Global Business*, Chicago: Irwin.

Chapter 8

Teaching cultural sense-making

Allan Bird and Joyce S. Osland

Introduction

Cultural dimensions (Hall and Hall 1990; Hampden-Turner and Trompenaars 1993; Hofstede 1980; Kluckhohn and Strodtbeck 1961; Parsons and Shils 1951; Ronen and Shenkar 1985; Schwartz 1992; and Triandis 1982) are the foundation of many cross-cultural courses and training programs. Table 8.1 presents 23 dimensions commonly used to compare cultures, which are typically presented in the form of bipolar continua. These etic values provide people with ways of distinguishing between cultures and serve as a basic building block for understanding culture. Teaching people to categorize whole cultures using these dimensions, however, may have the unanticipated consequence of promoting stereotyping, albeit on a more sophisticated level. Long-term sojourners and many cultural scholars find it increasingly difficult to make useful generalizations about other cultures since so many exceptions and qualifications to the stereotypes, both cultural and individual, come to mind. In reality, cultures are both complex and paradoxical. As researchers and professors, we often overlook Kluckhohn and Strodbeck's caveat that cultural behavior is contingent upon the context. The model presented in this chapter provides a process-oriented way for people to understand culture and focus their attention on being more effective in intercultural interactions.

This teaching module has the following objectives:

- Move students beyond sophisticated stereotyping to a more complex understanding of culture.
- Introduce students to the paradoxical nature of culture and the importance of context.
- Equip students with a model to make sense of cultural behavior and paradoxes.
- Teach students to observe and learn behavioral scripts.

Table 8.1 Common cultural dimensions

Subjugation to nature	Harmony	Mastery of nature
Past	Present	Future
Being	Thinking	Doing
Evil human nature	Neutral or mixed	Good
Hierarchical	Collectivistic	Individualistic
Private space	Mixed	Public
Monochronic time		Polychronic time
Low-context language		High-context language
Low uncertainty-avoidance		High uncertainty-avoidance
Low power-distance		High power-distance
Short-term orientation		Long-term orientation
Collectivism		Individualism
Femininity		Masculinity
Universalistic		Particularistic
Neutral		Affective
Diffuse		Specific
Achievement		Ascription
Individualism		Communitarian
Inner-directed		Outer-directed
Long-term		Short-term
Hierarchy		Egalitarianism
Embeddedness		Autonomy
Mastery		Harmony

Sources: Kluckhohn and Strodtbeck (1961); Hall and Hall (1990); Hofstede (1980); Parsons and Shils (1951); Hampden-Turner and Trompenaars (1993); Trompenaars (1994); Schwartz (1992).

In the following sections, we will outline the specific steps we take to present the main concepts in the module.

Decoding culture

To work successfully across cultures, we introduce the necessity of decoding cultural behavior with the aid of the value dimensions included in Table 8.1. Students are expected to learn the various frameworks and be able to recognize them. Since this skill requires practice and learning to look at behavior differently, we test them with weekly quizzes utilizing cross-cultural vignettes, cultural assimilators, and videos until they have mastered the ability to decode cultural behavior. When using the Gannon (2001) text, we provide students with a worksheet containing all the value dimensions so they can determine them for each country described in the book.

Sophisticated stereotypes and helpful stereotypes

Once students are making progress in decoding value dimensions, we explain the concept of sophisticated stereotypes (Bird and Osland 2000). These occur when people try to explain complex cultures with the short-hand of etic frameworks. For example, when we teach students and managers how to perceive the Israelis using Hofstede's (1980) dimensions, they may come to think of Israelis only in terms of small power-distance, strong uncertainty-avoidance, moderate femininity, and moderate individualism. In this manner, we reduce a complex culture to a sophisticated stereotype people may be tempted to apply to all Israelis in all contexts.

We ask, "How is using a sophisticated stereotype like Hofstede's description of a country's culture any better than the negative stereotypes we often hear about other cultures (dirty, lazy, dishonest, etc.)?" and "Are stereotypes ever helpful?" We conclude that the value dimensions that lead to sophisticated stereotypes are a necessary but insufficient tool to understand culture. Culture is too paradoxical and complex for etic frameworks alone.

Cultural stereotypes can be helpful – *provided* we acknowledge their limitations. They are more beneficial in making comparisons between cultures than in understanding the wide variations of behavior within a single culture. Adler (2001: 81) encourages the use of "helpful stereotypes," which have the following limitations. They are:

1   consciously held;
2   descriptive rather than evaluative;
3   accurate in their description of a behavioral norm;
4   the first "best guess" about a group prior to having direct information about the specific people involved;
5   modified based on further observations and experience.

We draw attention to Ratiu's (1983) comparison of "the most internationally effective" and "least internationally effective" MBA students at INSEAD. He found that the former group changed their stereotypes of other nationalities as a result of interacting with them while the latter group did not. We then note that the limitations of sophisticated stereotypes become most evident when we confront cultural paradoxes. This is the moment we realize our understanding is incomplete, misleading, and potentially dangerous.

Cultural paradoxes

Cultural paradoxes are defined as situations that exhibit an apparently contradictory nature based on the expectations we have for cultural behavior (Bird and Osland 2000). We often introduce this concept with a cultural assimilator about bar behavior in Japan (Brislin and Cushner 1996). It illustrates that the Japanese act in a highly formal (uncertainty-avoiding) way when dealing with others in a business setting. But in the context of after-hours drinking with friends, they are often much more informal and direct. We provide other examples of cultural paradoxes to make the point that we can find instances of both ends of any bipolar value within the same culture, depending on the context. For example, U.S. culture with its historical value of equality is a low-power-distance culture, but many U.S. CEOs are autocratic, something that is perceived as acceptable in that role and context.

Next, we ask students to come up with their own examples of cultural paradoxes, which we put on the board. With graduate classes or very curious undergraduates, we lead a discussion, asking "What would explain these paradoxes?" Role differences, unresolved cultural issues, individual rather than group behavior, real versus espoused values, Western insistence on framing culture as bipolar, and value trumping are usually responsible (Bird and Osland 2000).

Value trumping

Value trumping is the recognition that in specific contexts certain sets of values take precedence over others. Bird and Osland (2000) promote a holistic, contextual view of culture in which values coexist as a constellation, but their salience differs depending on the situation. Using the gestalt concept of figure-ground, at times a particular value becomes dominant (figure), while in other circumstances this same value recedes into the background (ground) (Tripathi 1988). In India, for example, collectivism is figural when individuals are expected to make sacrifices for their families or the larger society – for example, Hindu sons who postpone marriage until their sisters marry or daughters who stay single to care for their parents. In this case, collectivism trumps individualism. In other circumstances, however, collectivism fades into the background and individualism comes to the fore and is figural when Indians focus more on self-realization and spirituality – for example, elderly men who detach themselves from their family to seek salvation (Tripathi 1988). Individualism trumps collectivism at this point in their lives. Foreigners who do not understand enough about the cultural context to interpret why or when one value takes precedence over another perceive such behavior as paradoxical. Within one's own culture, learning such nuances occurs more or less automatically, and we do not expect consistency.

A true understanding of the logic of another culture includes comprehending the interrelationships among values in a given context. The challenge is in how to teach a perspective that will encourage people to look for these interrelationships and provide a mechanism for identifying them.

Metaphors in teaching culture

At this point, we introduce two analogies that guide our approach to teaching culture. One is the ideal of *culture learning as putting together a jigsaw puzzle*. Though one may have the picture on the puzzle box as a guide, making sense of each individual piece and understanding where and how it fits is exceedingly difficult. As more pieces are put into place, however, it is easier to see the bigger picture and understand how individual pieces mesh. Similarly, as one acquires more and varied experiences in the new culture, one can develop an appreciation for how certain attitudes and behaviors fit the "puzzle" and create an internal logic of the new culture.

We point out that the danger with sophisticated stereotyping is that it may lead individuals to think that the number of shapes that pieces may take is limited and that pieces fit together rather easily. As Barnlund notes, "Rarely do the descriptions of a political structure or religious faith explain precisely when and why certain topics are avoided or why specific gestures carry such radically different meanings according to the context in which they appear" (Barnlund 1975: 6).

One of the best descriptions of "the peeling away of layers" that characterizes deeper cultural understanding is found in a fictionalized account of expatriate life written by an expatriate manager, Robert Collins (1987). He outlines ascending levels on a Westerner's perception scale of Japanese culture that alternate, in daisy-petal-plucking fashion, between seeing the Japanese as significantly different or not really that different at all. Collins's description reflects the spiraling way people learn a different culture, our second metaphor for teaching culture.

If we accept that cultures are paradoxical, then it follows that learning another culture often occurs in a *dialectical fashion – thesis, antithesis, and synthesis*. This is the second metaphor we use. Thesis entails a hypothesis involving a sophisticated stereotype. Antithesis is the identification of an apparently oppositional cultural paradox. Synthesis involves making sense of contradictory behavior – understanding why certain values are more important in certain contexts. Behavior appears less paradoxical once the foreigner learns to frame situations and match them with the appropriate schemas in the same way that members of the host culture do. Collins's (1987) description of the Westerner's perception scale in comprehending Japanese culture illustrates one form of dialectical culture learning, an upwardly spiraling cycle of cultural comprehension.

The cultural sense-making model

We begin with an example of a cultural paradox. For example, in the past, Costa Rican customers preferred ATMs over human tellers because "at least the machines are programmed to say 'good morning' and 'thank you.'" We ask the class for their hypotheses about this question: "Why is it that so many Latin American cultures are noted for warm interpersonal relationships and a cultural script of *simpatía* (positive social behavior) while simultaneously exhibiting seeming indifference as service workers at times in both the private and public sectors?" Then we introduce the cultural sense-making model as a way to answer this question, and we challenge students to see whether the paradoxes they observed and listed can also be explained by this model.

The cultural sense-making model, shown in Figure 8.1, conveys a holistic understanding of culture and explains how culture is embedded in context. Context is also embedded in culture, so one could argue that the entire model is situated within the broader culture. For simplicity's sake, however, we choose to focus only on the sense-making that occurs in deciphering cultural paradoxes. Cultural sense-making is an ongoing process involving an iterative cycle of sequential events: framing the situation, making attributions, and selecting a script; all under-girded by constellations of cultural values and cultural history.

Framing the situation

The process begins when an individual identifies a context and then engages in indexing behavior, which involves noticing or attending to stimuli that provide cues about the situation. In determining what to attend to and what to ignore, an individual "frames the situation." For example, to index the context of a meeting with a Finnish colleague, one might consider characteristics such as prior events (his recent visit to campus during which he became acquainted with my family and participated in family outings); the nature of the collegial relationships in academic settings in Finland (relationships often appear informal and easy-going, but still maintain a level of reserve and austerity not common to U.S. academic settings); the specific topic under discussion (problems with setting up interviews at Finnish companies); and, the location of the interaction (my office).

Making attributions

The next step is attribution, a process in which contextual cues are analyzed in order to match the context with an appropriate schema. The matching process is moderated or influenced by one's social identity

Expectations:

What type of situation am I entering?

- An initial meeting
- A conference call
- An informal conversation
- Reporting on tasks completed

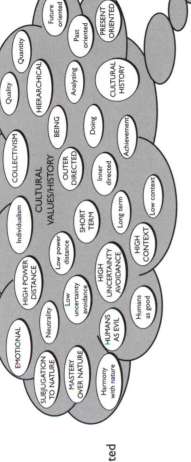

Framing the Situation

- We develop expectations about a situation before entering it. These expectations are based on past experiences and on what we think we know about the situation.
- Upon first coming into the situation, we take in the scene, scanning for relevant cues that confirm our expectations are correct.
- Based on that initial scan, we quickly establish a frame for the situation.

Making Attributions

- We make attributions about the situation and about the "other" based on the frame we build and the cues we perceive.
- Our attributions are influenced by our self-identity: our ethnicity, religion, social class, past experiences, etc.
- Attributions about the "other" are influenced by our attitudes and beliefs about their identity: their ethnicity, religion, social class, etc.

Selecting a Script

- Based on the frame and attributions we have made, we select a script to guide us through the situation.
- The script we select is chosen from a repertoire developed through past experiences.
- The selection of a script is influenced by our ability to draw similarities between this situation and past experiences.

Figure 8.1 The cultural sense-making process.

(e.g., ethnic or religious background, gender, social class, organizational affiliation) and one's history (e.g., experiences and chronology). One considers the question, "Who is this person and how does he or she view the situation?" A senior Chinese manager who fought against the Japanese in World War II will make different attributions about context and employ a different schema when he meets with a Japanese manager than will a South Korean manager of his generation, or a junior Malaysian manager whose personal experience of Japan is limited to automobiles, electronics, and sushi.

Selecting a script

Schemas are cultural scripts, "a pattern of social interaction that is characteristic of a particular cultural group" (Triandis *et al.* 1984). They are accepted and appropriate ways of behaving, specifying certain patterns of interaction. From personal or vicarious experience, we learn how to select a schema. By watching and working with bosses, for example, we develop scripts for how to act when we take on that role ourselves. We learn appropriate vocabulary and gestures, which then elicit a fairly predictable response from others.

The influence of cultural values

Schemas reflect an underlying hierarchy of cultural values. For example, Russian subordinates working for U.S. managers who have a relaxed and casual style and who openly share information and provide opportunities to make independent decisions, will learn specific scripts for managing in this fashion. The configuration of values embedded in this management style consists of informality, honesty, equality and individualism – values that are at variance with aspects of Russian values. At some point, however, these same U.S. managers may withhold information about a sensitive personnel situation because privacy, fairness and legal concerns would trump honesty and equality in this context. This trumping action explains why the constellation of values related to a specific schema is hierarchical. It also helps us understand why cultural decoding by the Russian subordinates may be so difficult.

The influence of cultural history

When decoding schemas, we may also find vestiges of cultural history and tradition. Mindsets inherited from previous generations explain how history is remembered (Fisher 1997). For example, perceptions about Indonesia's colonial era may still have an impact upon schemas, particularly those involving interactions with Westerners, even though that country gained its independence generations ago.

We explain the Costa Rican example in this manner. When bank tellers interact with clients (indexing context) many of them (e.g., members of various in-groups, civil servants making attributions) do not greet customers and make eye contact, but concentrate solely on their paperwork (selecting schema). The values that underlie this schema are in-group/out-group behavior and power (cultural values). In collectivist cultures such as Costa Rica, members identify strongly with their in-group and treat members with warmth and cooperation. In stark contrast, out-group members are often treated with hostility, distrust, and a lack of cooperation. Customers are considered as strangers and out-group members who do not warrant the special treatment given to in-group members (family and friends). One of the few exceptions to simpatía and personal dignity in Costa Rica, and Latin America generally, is the rudeness sometimes expressed by people in positions of power. In this context, the cultural values of high power-distance trumps simpatía. Unlike many other contexts in Costa Rica, bank tellering does not elicit a cultural script of simpatía, and state-owned banks do not have a history of training employees in friendly customer service (cultural history) at this time.

Using the cultural sense-making model

We use videos and cases that show problematic cross-cultural interactions. Student groups take the perspective of different actors and graph their behavior using the model. Then they explain how the characters should have framed the situation, what attributions they should have made, and what script would be most effective. They present these two analyses to the class.

To further highlight the role of the sense-making model in taking students beyond sophisticated stereotypes, we use language that focuses on forming and testing hypotheses about contextual behavior: What are your hypotheses for why Spanish workers take long siestas in the afternoon and work later in the evening? How can you find out if your hypotheses are correct?

Teaching behavioral scripts

Once students have mastered the steps associated with cultural sense-making, we change the emphasis to learning schemas for specific contexts. We introduce a variety of activities to sharpen their skills in cultural observation and behavioral flexibility. Prior to sending them out to observe a different culture, we teach students to observe and decode more like anthropologists. We do not expect them to obtain an in-depth understanding of another culture in a short period, but we hope to hone their observation skills and increase their cultural curiosity. We want them to notice different scripts and start making linkages between values and behavior.

In "wrong way/right way" exercises, student teams are instructed to deliberately demonstrate incorrect behavior in a particular cultural context; they ask others to point out the mistakes and then replay the scene using correct behaviors. To model the crucial behavior of asking for help in understanding cultural vagaries, students use cultural mentors to explain situations they choose to learn about. For instance, how do effective managers in Mexico encourage workers to perform at a high level? Why does that work for them? Variations in the mentors' answers and the qualifications attached to answers lead students to more complex understanding of the other culture.

Audience focus

We adapt the order of the topics and the emphasis we give to them based on the amount of exposure the audience has had to other cultures and their motivation for understanding cultural behavior.

For an audience with limited cross-cultural experience, we ask them to observe a local culture (e.g., a Vietnamese student attended all the public St. Patrick's Day celebrations in her town and then wrote a paper on what she had learned about Irish culture). We give more attention to stereotypes and identifying cultural paradoxes within their own culture, and progress to examples we provide from other cultures. With a provincial audience, we sometimes begin this module with student stereotypes about different cultures. We follow the example of a Latin American history professor who passes out clay in the first class and asks students to create something that captures the essence of another culture. He asks the students from the U.S. to form something that represents Mexico and has the international students make an object that represents the United States. Students explain their creations and then discuss whether their work portrays a stereotype or reality. This leads into a discussion of stereotypes, their roots, their presence in the workplace, and their implications for cross-cultural interactions. Students have an opportunity to see how people from other cultures perceive their own culture and to hear how the use of stereotypes affects them.

With a more culturally experienced audience, we begin with cultural value differences and then ask them to generate their own paradoxes. We spend more time on the theory with graduate students. With executives, however, we begin with experienced cultural difficulties and devote more time to practical applications.

Impact on our teaching

One dilemma is that some students have great difficulty analysing and decoding cultural incidents. We suggest they read cultural assimilators Brislin and Cushner (1996) and Storti's books on *Cross-cultural Dialogues* (1994) and *Figuring Foreigners Out* (1999). Occasionally, we have to remember that not all students are as fascinated with culture as we are and keep the focus on the practical utility for them. As a result of using the model, however, we spend less time talking or lecturing to students and more time trying to develop situations and activities in which students can apply what they are learning. Our teaching has taken on a more practical application orientation. The sense-making model takes abstract, sometimes vague, notions of culture and cultural dimensions and gives students a way to focus on the not-so-vague and less-abstract beliefs and behaviors of individual actors in specific situations. Using the cultural sense-making model has led us, paradoxically, to encourage students to give less weight to cultural explanations when seeking to understand the behavior of people from cultures other than their own. Because it focuses on the perceptions, attributions and behaviors of specific individuals in specific situations, the model requires students to consider others as individuals. Students learn to look at people in a situation and not see *Germans*, but *a German* acting in *a particular situation*. Students find the *process* of making sense of other cultures as fascinating as we do.

References

Adler, N. (2001) *International Dimensions of Organizational Behavior*, Boston: Kent.

Barnlund, D. (1975) *Public and Private Self in Japan and the United States*, Yarmouth, ME: Intercultural Press.

Bird, A. and Osland, J. S. (2000) "Beyond sophisticated stereotyping: Cultural sensemaking in context," *Academy of Management Executive*, 14 (1): 65–87.

Brislin, R. and Cushner, K. (1996) *Intercultural Interactions: A Practical Guide*, 2nd edn, Thousand Oaks, CA: Sage.

Collins, R. J. (1987) *Max Danger: The Adventures of an Expat in Tokyo*, Rutland, VT: Charles E. Tuttle.

Fisher, G. (1997) *Mindsets: The Role of Culture and Perception in International Relations*, Yarmouth, ME: Intercultural Press.

Gannon, M. and Associates (2001) *Understanding Global Cultures: Metaphorical Journeys through 17 Countries*, Thousand Oaks, CA: Sage.

Hall, E. T. and Hall, M. R. (1990) *Understanding Cultural Differences*, Yarmouth, ME: Intercultural Press.

Hampden-Turner, C. and Trompenaars, A. (1993) *The Seven Cultures of Capitalism*, London: Currency/Double Day.

Hofstede, G. (1980) *Culture's Consequences: International Differences in Work-related Values*, Beverly Hills: Sage.

Kluckhohn, F. and Strodtbeck, F. L. (1961) *Variations in Value Orientations*, Evanston, IL: Row, Peterson.

Parsons, T. and Shils, E. (1951) *Toward a General Theory of Action*, Cambridge, MA: Harvard University Press.

Ratiu, I. (1983) "Thinking internationally: a comparison of how international students learn," *International Studies of Management and Organization*, 13: 139–50.

Ronen, S. and Shenkar, O. (1985) "Clustering countries on attitudinal dimensions: a review and synthesis," *Academy of Management Review*, 10: 435–54.

Schwartz, S. H. (1992) "Universals in the content and structure of values: theoretical advances and empirical tests in 20 countries," in M. Zanna (ed.), *Advances in Experimental Social Psychology*, 25, 1–66, New York: Academic Press.

Storti, C. (1994) *Cross-Cultural Dialogues: 74 Brief Encounters with Cultural Difference*, Yarmouth, ME: Intercultural Press.

Storti, C. (1999) *Figuring Foreigners Out: A Practical Guide*, Yarmouth, ME: Intercultural Press.

Triandis, H. C. (1982) "Dimensions of cultural variations as parameters of organizational theories," *International Studies of Management and Organization*, 12 (4): 139–69.

Triandis, H. C., Betancourt, H., Lisansky, J. and Marin, G. (1984) "Simpatía as a cultural script of Hispanics," *Journal of Personality and Social Psychology*, 47 (6), 1363–75.

Tripathi, R. C. (1988) "Aligning development to values in India," in D. Sinha and H. S. R. Kao (eds), *Social Values and Development: Asian Perspectives*, New Delhi: Sage, pp. 315–33.

Trompenaars, F. (1994) *Riding the Waves of Culture*, Burr Ridge, IL: Irwin.

Chapter 9

Examining culture change through *Fiddler on the Roof*

Jennifer Roney

Introduction

The circumstances of culture change are complex and varied and they present a major challenge for multinational firms. This teaching module introduces one approach to teaching about culture change. By exploring the classic film *Fiddler on the Roof* (Jewison 1971) the module specifically addresses two major forces that affect cultural change: external pressures and intergenerational conflict. From the module, students learn key concepts for identifying the factors of change and managing them effectively.

Film, in general, serves to powerfully connect students to the film's context, making the material more relevant to the video-age student body (Summerfield 1993). The film *Fiddler on the Roof* presents a rich portrayal of culture change in a tight traditional Jewish community (Anatevka). The stability of this community stands in stark contrast with the rapidly changing environment surrounding it.

Fiddler on the Roof takes place in the countryside outside of the city of Kiev just prior to the communist revolution of the early 1900s. Concurrently, each of the three daughters of a dairy farmer named Tevye engage in a romance that tests traditional community values. Tevye must decide how to respond to the external changes, as well as to three different challenges from his daughters. The film ends traditionally when the entire community is forced to leave their homes behind as part of an effort to displace Jews from the region.

The film demonstrates changes of individual beliefs about what is right and wrong, change in traditions prompted by the diffusion of new ideas and opportunities (accepted most easily by the younger generation), change of roles and relationships, and major, disruptive societal change. The challenges and varied perceptions and level of integration shown in this film are analogous to important issues, such as old-economy firms and values in the new economy, and the dramatic changes facing individuals and firms in countries undergoing massive transformations (e.g., China, or the Eastern European countries).

Presentation of the film

This lesson occurs in the middle of a cross-cultural or international management course. Prior to this class, students have learned what culture is and the levels at which it is manifest. (Early in the term, I sometimes use the introductory song "Traditions" to discuss what culture is.) In addition, students have learned what it is like to experience culture differences (culture shock).

As specific preparation, I ask students to watch *Fiddler on the Roof* in their own time and suggest video stores and the campus multi-media center as sources for copies. Seeing the entire film is critical to providing the context from which the students can understand the various issues that influence change. After they have seen the entire film, I can use short clips to remind them of particular incidents and their context.

In the beginning of the session, a brief history of the events of the period is presented and a general discussion is held. To set a strong foundation for discussion I ask them to identify roles that are critical to the underpinning of this culture, and how these roles reinforce and perpetuate the cultural values. These questions are quite helpful:

- What roles seem to be important to the people in Anatevka? Why?
- How are these roles important to survival of this society?
- How do these roles support the religious beliefs shared by the members of this society?

Critical roles include:

- the rabbi as the interpreter of the society's core values;
- Tevye as the opinion leader and mediator with the outside environment;
- the matchmaker as the force that perpetuates the critical marriage rituals.

I like to focus on the role of women and the beliefs that center on the desirability of education for women and marrying outside their own faith. A discussion of these issues leads nicely into the discussion of change, particularly because it provides a micro-level analysis and a good comparison of the three daughters. Perchik's words, "Girls should learn too. Girls are people," and the religious townsman's reply "How radical!" is a good place to begin a discussion of these issues. This discussion easily evolves into issues of change and the factors that affect change in the society.

Culture change

The terms below serve as the foundation for the full culture change discussion. They are drawn from the cultural anthropology literature of Barrett (1991) and Bee (1974).

- Diffusion – the spread of cultural traits or artifacts from one society to another.
- Cultural crystallization – the crystallizing of cultural patterns (first-mover advantage).
- Intracultural variation – the diversity of behavior, beliefs and attitudes within particular societies.
- Integration – when various elements of a society "fit together"; often has a restraining influence on social change.
- Cultural inertia – cultural patterns tend to endure because they serve certain groups.

Diffusion

This film provides a good opportunity to identify diffusion of new ideas and technologies as an impetus for change.

I start with ideas introduced by Perchik, the student visiting from Kiev. He brings a new way of looking at many of the traditions of Anatevka including courtship rituals (particularly arranged marriages), Sabbath rituals, wedding rituals (including dowry), appropriate behaviors between men and women, dress, dance, and celebration rituals. His ideas are resisted by many but are cautiously considered by the well-respected and more forward-thinking dairy farmer, Tevye. Tevye's curiosity and willingness to welcome Perchik into his home provides the opportunity for diffusion of Perchik's ideas to Tevye's daughters and wife, and other villagers. Either the clip where Perchik first enters the community or where he is dancing with Hodel, is good for reminding the class about how Perchik's ideas were introduced. My discussion focus is on what factors supported diffusion of these ideas (e.g., Perchik's passion, Tevye's curiosity, a changing external environment?) and what might have prevented their diffusion (e.g., the rabbi banning information from the outside or outsiders, Perchik not being Jewish or not having something to offer Tevye, like the lessons for his daughters?).

This film also provides a good example of the diffusion of new technology, in this case the sewing machine. The sewing machine can increase the economic potential of Motel the tailor. This then provides a basis for his break with tradition by asking for the hand in marriage of Tevye's eldest daughter, Tzeitel. Tevye faces a dilemma whether to stand fast or to allow his daughter's wishes to dominate. All the while, he recognizes the risk to her financial future should this new technology not provide the supposed benefits. After discussing the decision by Tevye, I ask the students:

- How did the villagers react to the new sewing machine when it arrived?
- How do you think they will respond to other new technologies should they become aware of them?
- What factors make this technology acceptable, where others might not be?

The film clip showing the sewing machine's arrival encourages the students to consider the greater implications of a shift in economic status. What does this do to the traditions in the society? This gives the students an opportunity to see the connections between change and the traditions, and to appreciate how those connections reinforce the societal purposes of the traditions. We also explore other technologies and the factors that would affect their acceptance to give students an opportunity to hypothesize where the limits might be and at what point a society will resist change. This is discussed in greater detail later in the session.

Cultural crystallization

The crystallization process occurs after there is general acceptance of the change. Earlier changes tend to show first-mover advantage, and then act as a resistance to other changes. Here is a good opportunity to generalize by using the students' personal experiences. I ask them to identify changes that were introduced and accepted into their home organizations and then reflect how these changes acted to either resist or impede other changes.

Intracultural variation

We discuss the various reactions to Tevye's decision to reject the butcher and accept Motel as Tzeitel's husband. I ask the students to hypothesize why Tevye's wife, the butcher, his daughters, and others each responded differently to this change. This leads to a discussion of vested interests and varying levels of comfort with ambiguity and change. These differences, "intracultural variation," explain in part why ideas are not diffused uniformly throughout the community. Though people share cultural values, the way they interpret those values and the degree to which they act on them differ. In addition, the roles individuals play influence the way they interpret the introduction of new ideas and technologies.

Integration and resistance to change

Understanding resistance to change is critical to understanding cultural change in societies and organizations. Resisting change and "strangers'" ways has been important to the survival of the Jewish culture throughout history and this is reinforced through the rituals presented in the film. Highlighting this point is Tevye's ironic comment, "Our forefathers have been forced out of many, many places at a moment's notice. Maybe that is why we always wear our hats."

Changes that occur in society, particularly changes to basic traditions and beliefs, are believed by community members to present a threat to the society and its survival. The Jewish culture and specifically the culture of Anatevka has strong cultural integration. The integration of daily practices, relationships, social roles and religious beliefs holds the society together and creates significant resistance to change. The introduction of new ideas oftentimes does not apparently "fit" with existing behaviors, beliefs and values. Here Tevye's response to the different value challenges that each of the three daughters presents (with their choice of husbands) becomes the focus of discussion. The discussion questions posed to small student groups are: compare and contrast the three nontraditional marriages, then identify which cultural values were challenged by each. These are usually quite lively discussions.

Following these small group discussions, I ask the full assembly of students:

- What emboldened the daughters to challenge tradition?
- On what bases do these marriages challenge the society of Anatevka?
- What do they threaten within the society?
- Why doesn't Tevye accept the marriage of his daughter Chava to the non-Jew?
- How is this different from the other daughters?

This discussion evolves from the recognition of the power of diffusion of new ideas in the community to more focused issues. Tzeitel's choice of Motel challenged the tradition of arranged marriages and perhaps Tevye's reputation. (Tevye does not view this as a threat to the fabric of the Anatevka society and his main concern is the reaction of his wife.) The marriage of the second daughter, Hodel, to Perchik, presents a greater threat to tradition since Perchik did not ask for Tevye's permission but only his blessing. (Once again, Tevye sees this as a threat to his own authority but not to the basis of their society. He is concerned about his daughter's safety and security but is willing to accept the risk to give her a choice.) It is only the marriage of his third daughter, Chava, which truly challenges community values – those forbidding inter-faith marriages as a fundamental threat by potentially dissolving the community. (The external political changes occurring during this period emphasize this point and highlight the "us" versus "them" belief.) This challenge is too great for Tevye to accept and thus he rejects not only the marriage but his daughter as well. Chava's choice of a husband is actually better as far as providing for her financial needs than that of her sisters, and this contrast highlights what is important to Tevye and the values of the community. I like to play the clip where Tevye says, "A bird may love a fish, but where would they build a home together?"

Cultural inertia

I also introduce another factor that serves to resist change: cultural inertia. I ask:

- Who has the greatest stake in maintaining the status quo in this society?

The answers to this question can be the religious leaders including the rabbi, the men, the older members, the wealthiest in the society, or even the Russians. I ask students to think about who has the most to lose in their own organizations or the organizations they have read about. Why do these individuals resist change? To deepen the discussion I ask:

- What do they have to lose?
- What could happen if things change?
- Why would they resist change even if it may be the best thing for the society or organization?
- What are the potential implications of cultural inertia?
- How did cultural inertia affect the people of Anatevka?

Cultural inertia is a very powerful force against change because those in power, who have the greatest capacity to initiate and support change, are the least likely to want to risk the implications of change and thus will resist it. Ultimately, the cultural leaders of Anatevka were slow to see the change in the external environment and thus were unprepared for the implications. I then ask the students:

- To what extent should a society seek to adapt to changes in the external environment?

Concluding the class

To conclude my class module on cultural change I broaden the discussion to tie the concepts discussed using *Fiddler on the Roof* to a more contemporary topic of cultural change and resistance to change. I ask questions like the following:

- How does the information age, including the diffusion of the Internet, affect the rate and degree of change in cultures? Give evidence of where you see people getting more alike.
- Where in society today do you see people resisting the forces that draw them together?
- What do societies do to resist outside influences? Why do they do this?

These questions produce a very rich discussion about what the forces of change are, how they are being diffused, and who has the most to lose and gain from this change. I like to supplement this discussion with an article called "Jihad vs. McWorld" (Barber 1992). It highlights the forces for globalism and localism and identifies the simultaneous nature of these forces. This article is given at the end of the culture change class to allow students to uncover the issues for themselves during the class discussion, without influencing the process. The article, however, provides some very good examples of both global and local forces and the growing tension between them. It also offers evidence for powers that tend to resist change on a grander scale, which provides an effective way to conclude the culture change module.

Reflections and dilemmas

Culture change is a topic of great importance to organizations that must learn to change quickly to respond to a rapidly changing external environment. It is important to give students basic tools with which to explore the changes they must manage. The concepts introduced in this module were chosen to provide some basic terms and empirically based theory to shape the understanding of cultural change. *Fiddler on the Roof* is a rich cultural experience to watch and it comes to life for students as they discuss the changes while using the change concepts introduced in class.

However, making a musical about a Jewish village in Czarist Russia relevant to twenty-first-century managers is the key dilemma for teaching culture change in this way. Are the types of changes and responses to change representative in this film? Students are challenged to make connections to contemporary situations throughout, whether the connections are with situations in their own companies or in the business news. My students, graduate and undergraduate, full-time and fully employed, generally have very little difficulty finding the relevance of *Fiddler on the Roof* to present contemporary organizational change. Film is a powerful medium, and this one is particularly effective in providing a rich shared context from which to explore a range of cultural issues, especially cultural change.

This film highlights a small village of oppressed Jews in Europe in the early twentieth century. Given the conflicts in the Middle East in the early twenty-first century some concern may arise from emotions regarding more current events. To avoid this, I make clear to my students that this is a case study and like any case study is simply a model for us to apply the concepts which we are learning. Second, I find that the era which this film portrays is removed enough from the present to distance the issues (despite the fact that the historical context has influenced the present situation). Finally, I encourage students to share their personal reflections as they apply themselves to the material we are learning and discourage emotional responses. This model fits well into the basic framework that defines my entire course, so students are prepared by the time they see this film to focus on analysis before judgment and to allow situations to generate questions for further exploration.

References

Barber, B. R. (1992) "Jihad vs. McWorld," *The Atlantic Monthly*, March.

Barrett, R. A. (1991) *Culture and Conduct: An Excursion in Anthropology*, Belmont, CA: Wadsworth.

Bee, R. L. (1974) *Patterns and Processes: An Introduction to Anthropological Strategies for the Study of Sociocultural Change*, New York: The Free Press.

Jewison, N. (1971) *Fiddler on the Roof*, Hollywood, CA: Metro-Goldwyn-Mayer Studios Inc. Video: ASIN 6304151306.

Summerfield, E. (1993) *Crossing Cultures through Film*, Yarmouth, ME: Intercultural Press.

Part IV

The experience of crossing cultures

In Parts II and III, we explored the characterization of culture and provided training modules for making sense of a situation through a cultural lens. This part provides training modules focused upon the actual experience of crossing into a new culture for an extended period of time.

In the first module, Osland offers a process to appreciate the heroic nature of crossing cultures and returning. Through this experience, she provides a "journey" focus that explicates a number of stages in the process and reflects upon the stress and transformational possibilities of an expatriate experience.

Rossy and Phillips provide a quite effective media-based module that reinforces the cultural lens and framework as well as providing insight into the difficulties caused by unfamiliarity. Their use of two "intergalactic" cultures gives the learner a robust experience to analyze while allowing the instructor to avoid the presumed familiarity students often bring to cultural subject matter.

Jenner then offers a simulation experience that allows learners to test themselves in attempting to decipher a unique and different culture. In this, as with the two previous modules, the realities of the journey are conveyed and deepened, and the "stress" factors are identified.

Fukushima and Tang bring a robust psychoanalytic perspective to Part IV in a model of the basic nature of the stressors in cross-cultural endeavors. As they integrate two frameworks for describing psychological and physiological responses to crossing cultures, they reveal the significant risks and costs attendant to the poorly prepared, casually selected, unsupported expatriate. Toward moderating these consequences, they offer training and coping strategies at each step of their model.

Chapter 10

Using the hero's journey

A framework for making sense of the transformational expatriate experience

Joyce S. Osland

Introduction

As organizations become more international, the expatriate experience is shaping the lives and careers of an increasing number of people. Yet the sojourn literature seldom describes the subjective nature of the experience, the journey inward. The purposes of this teaching module are to:

- provide a better understanding of the complex, transformational nature of the expatriate experience;
- help prospective expatriates obtain more realistic ideas of what to expect and benefit from the experience of those who have gone before them;
- furnish current and returned expatriates with a framework for making sense of their experience.

The framework – the myth of the hero's journey

The metaphor that helps many expatriates make sense of their experience is the myth of the hero's journey (Campbell 1968). Joseph Campbell, renowned expert on mythology, studied myths from all over the world and identified their common plots and stages. All hero's adventure myths – one of the most common mythical themes – have the same basic plot: *separation* from the world, *initiation*, which involves penetration to some source of power, and a life-enhancing *return*. For example, "Jason sailed through the Clashing Rocks into a sea of marvels, circumvented the dragon that guarded the Golden Fleece, and returned with the fleece and the power to wrest his rightful throne from a usurper" (Campbell 1968: 30). Mythical heroes either seek to find their destiny outside their known world or inadvertently stumble into another world. In either case, there is an "awakening of the self," as mystics have termed it (Underhill 1911).

Heroes are helped by magical friends who guide them past the dangerous guardians of a different world. Next, they undergo a series of trials that ends with a decisive victory and brings them to the realization of a higher consciousness or a power hidden within them. After this transformation, heroes return home from their journey with the power to share with their compatriots the boons (benefits or blessings) they acquired on their adventure, such as the gift of fire or spiritual illumination.

Though it may seem an unlikely comparison at first glance, expatriate business people have much in common with mythical heroes, and their experience overseas has much in common with the stages of the hero's adventure myth. Expatriates consider and eventually accept the request to go abroad (The Call to Adventure), leaving behind the domestic office of the organization and the social support of an established life. They embark on the fascinating, adventurous but initially lonely overseas assignment (Crossing the First Threshold). The location is often shrouded in the ambiguity of unknown languages and customs (The Belly of the Whale). The expatriates' tasks are challenging, often well beyond what they would have been asked to accomplish in their own country in terms of autonomy and in the degree and breadth of responsibility. If they are fortunate, cultural mentors help them understand the other culture and provide the reassurance that they will succeed at their challenges (The Magical Friend). Unfamiliar obstacles of all stripes and colors confront expatriates (The Road of Trials). These obstacles force them to question their own identity, their values, and their assumptions about numerous aspects of everyday life previously taken for granted. Some of these obstacles appear in the form of paradoxes the expatriates must learn to resolve, such as how much of their identity they must give up to be accepted by the other culture. When they perform their tasks successfully and learn to adapt to another culture, expatriates experience a solid sense of satisfaction, mastery, and self-efficacy. Among other changes, they return with greater understanding of foreign lands, increased self-confidence and interpersonal skills, and tolerance for differences in people (The Ultimate Boon). Their return home is often marked by a sense of loss at leaving behind the magical charm and fulfillment of the sojourn (The Return). Some companies treat them as heroes and make use of the skills they developed or honed abroad; others do not (Osland 1995a, b).

Although expatriates never refer to themselves as heroes, their stories contain numerous examples of "hero talk," such as their pride in succeeding at difficult work assignments, "making it on their own," feeling "special," and taking pride in their ability to acculturate and adapt to change. The myth of the hero's journey does not describe the experience of all expatriates – some go abroad for reasons that have nothing to do with the quest for adventure or personal growth. The metaphor does, however, provide a greater understanding of the experience of numerous expatriates who are enacting heroism – for those who perceive an overseas assignment as a call to adventure and an opportunity to experience something that is not available in their own culture.

Audience focus

This framework has been used with various audiences – in speeches to people with an interest in overseas work, class sessions for international management courses at both graduate and undergraduate levels, workshops for school counselors, international students, MBA students, and U.S. students preparing to study abroad. The session design varies in terms of the particular emphases made in the introduction and the overarching questions that guide the session. These changes reflect the interests relevant to different groups. For example, with MBA students I emphasize the literature on expatriates and the particular "hole" this research was designed to fill. I also ask them to write down the answers to two questions as we go through each stage of the framework:

1   If this is the experience that many expatriates will face, what criteria should we use to select prospective expatriates?
2   How should human resources departments handle expatriates?

I generally ask for their answers at the end of the session and emphasize the lessons for companies (Osland 1995a, b; Mendenhall and Oddou 1991; Black *et al.* 1999; and Harvey 1999).

My focus with people who have either been abroad or are going abroad is more personal. For the former group, does the framework seem valid to them? Did they pass through these stages and, if so, what was it like? What were the most important lessons they learned abroad? For those who are considering going overseas or training to be sent abroad, the focus is on whether or not this sounds like the type of experience they can manage. How would they expect to respond? How might this relate to similar challenges they have successfully handled in the past? What can they do to minimize the negative effects of the cycle and maximize the positive? I ask people going abroad to write down the action steps they plan to take overseas.

Audience preparation and reading

Another audience difference relates to whether or not they have read anything about the framework before the session. If they have read nothing, I include expatriate quotations in my lecture so it comes alive for them. If they have read the book or an article, I simply present a quotation from Campbell for each stage and its implications for expatriates.

Ideally, the participants would have read something about the framework ahead of time, but this is not necessary. Professors can choose the level of reading they wish to assign along this continuum from no reading at all, to Table 10.1 (described next), to the *Training and Development* article (Osland 1995b), the *Human Resource Management* article (Osland 2000) or *The Adventure of Working Abroad* book (Osland 1995a). If they wish to tie in the expatriate experience with global leadership, they can use the book chapter, "The quest for transformation: the process of global leadership development" (Osland 2001). That chapter focuses primarily on the transformation process that occurs in the initiation phase of the journey.

Lecture material

Table 10.1, entitled "The myth of the hero's adventure and the expatriate experience," is the basis for my lecture portion of a session. I use different categories depending on the audience and the available time. The table presents the pertinent stages of the hero's journey myth, an example of that stage from the movie *Star Wars*, an expatriate example that describes what they go through in each stage, and the significance of each stage for expatriates.

Star Wars is a good example of a hero's journey plot, probably because Joseph Campbell was a good friend of George Lucas and advised him on the film. Other movies with a hero's journey plot are *Dancing with Wolves* and *Braveheart*. I have found that U.S. audiences are most familiar with *Star Wars*, and it seems to work well with other audiences.

How the framework fits into the expatriate literature

To see how this framework fits with the rest of the expatriate literature, please see the literature review written by Mendenhall *et al.* (2002). Although some hybrid models exist, most expatriate adjustment theories can be classified in four categories:

1   learning models;
2   stress-coping models;
3   personality-based models;
4   developmental models.

The learning-based models imply that the key to adjustment is for expatriates to learn the ways of the new culture to which they are assigned. Oberg's (1960) culture shock model is quite well known and views adjustment as an illness. In contrast, more recent research has focused on adjustment as a normal stress reaction to uncertainty, information overload, and loss of control. Personality-based models focus on identifying expatriate competencies and looking at relationships with the Big Five personality dimensions[1] (Ones and Viswesvaran 1997). Some of the development models assume that contact with another culture causes

Table 10.1 The myth of the hero's adventure and the expatriate experience

Stages in the myth	Star Wars example	Expatriate example	Significance for expatriates
I. DEPARTURE *The Call to Adventure* The hero either decides to pursue a quest because something is lacking or stumbles into an adventure	Luke hears the call: "Help me Obi-Wan Kenobi. You are my only hope"	Potential expatriates are asked to move to their assignments overseas: some accept the call while others refuse the opportunity	– Importance of a visceral response to the call – One must be ready for the adventure – Strong desire to go as a selection criterion for expatriate and family
Or			
Refusal of the Call The hero turns down the call due to self-interest	C-3PO refuses: "No more adventures"		
The Magical Friend In mythology supernatural figures explain how to get beyond difficult obstacles or provide assurance that the hero will not be harmed	Ben Kenobi: "I have something for you" [a Jedi sword] "Let the Force guide you"	This type of assistance is found in local cultural mentors, experienced resident expatriates, social nodes (international schools, churches, clubs) and career mentors at HQ; they provide protection, help, and encouragement	– Lack of knowledge about the other culture and the stress of initial adjustment feels like a forced return to childhood and dependency – Cultural mentors interpret the local culture and provide advice Benefits of having a cultural mentor: expatriates were 1 more fluent; 2 perceived themselves as better adapted to work and general living conditions; 3 more aware of expatriate paradoxes; 4 more highly rated on performance evaluations by superiors and selves

Table 10.1 continued

Stages in the myth	Star Wars example	Expatriate example	Significance for expatriates
Crossing the First Threshold This stage begins when mythical heroes step outside their normal world and enter the unknown	Ben Kenobi gets the spaceship past the town guards using the Force	Expatriates leave behind the known for the unknown and cross both physical and cultural boundaries	– Period of uncertainty, stress, and difficulty as they figure out how to set up their lives and get things done at work – Period of unexpected surprises and failed expectations – Period of novelty, strangeness, exhilaration and accelerated learning *Threshold Guardians:* 1 Lack of language ability 2 Cultural impermeability 3 Headquarters constraints 4 Expatriate community
Belly of the Whale (sub-stage) In this stage, heroes are swallowed alive, falling into an abyss of some sort over which they have no control. Later on they are resurrected	Bar scene: Han Solo's spaceship is sucked into the enemy space station	Expatriates decide how deeply to immerse themselves into the other culture and open themselves up to its influence	This stage represents the psychological leave-taking of their own culture – Period of learning about one's culture and self – Expatriates discover their own system of rationality and cultural patterns are not universally appropriate – Easily identified acculturation strategies – Pecking order – "ideal" expatriate is bicultural and well acculturated

Table 10.1 continued

Stages in the myth	Star Wars example	Expatriate example	Significance for expatriates
II. INITIATION *The Road of Trials* Mythical heroes are confronted with numerous obstacles and tests	Cellblock scene including a fight with storm-troopers, octopus, and garbage compacter	The obstacles encountered in their daily lives as well as the paradoxes inherent in the expatriate experience	– Expatriates can relate a litany of trials relating to logistical, acculturation, and language difficulties – Some expatriates complain bitterly about "hardships" and return home – Successful expatriates use patience, positive attitude, and humor to deal with trials – Expatriates experience paradoxes that are only problematic until they learn to determine which side is more effective in a given situation

The Ultimate Boon
In myth, the hero's consciousness is transformed by trials or illuminating revelations, penetrating to a source of power, a higher consciousness. It is a process of death and rebirth, and includes these aspects:
1 The need for sacrifice
2 The move from dependence to independence
3 Discovery of a universal power within
	Luke risks his life to rescue Princess Leia and uses the Force to blow up the space station. In the process he is transformed from a boy into a Jedi Knight	Expatriates are transformed by their experience (which partly explains why it is difficult to return home). The higher consciousness for them is a bicultural perspective and the knowledge they possessed the inner resources to rise to this challenge	– Expatriates can quickly report how they changed abroad:
			  positive changes in self
			  changed attitudes
			  improved work skills
			  increased knowledge
			  closer family relationships
			– They also make sacrifices, move from dependence to independence, and find inner resources they were not aware they had
			– Their transformation process is described as "letting go" and "taking on"

Table 10.1 continued

Stages in the myth	Star Wars example	Expatriate example	Significance for expatriates
III. THE RETURN *Crossing the Return Threshold* There are three sub-stages: 1 The hero's refusal to return (the reluctance some heroes feel to leave the mystic realm and return to their former life) 2 The crossing of the return threshold (the difficulty in sharing the illumination they have gained with people back home who have not undergone the same life-changing experience) 3 Master of two worlds (the higher consciousness and ability to function in both known and formerly unknown worlds)	Luke escapes to the rebel base Luke can fly using either high-tech instruments or the Force	This represents the repatriation and readjustment stage for expatriates. Some expatriates are called home before their tour of duty expired or before their work was accomplished	Coming home was difficult for these reasons: "You can't go home again" "Little fish in a big pond" Readjustment to decreased autonomy Uncertainty about the job or move Lack of interest in their experiences Idealization and false expectations The testing period Missing life abroad – Repatriation is a problem of differentiation and integration. A bicultural perspective means looking at the world with a different lens and a broader perspective

Note
This material is taken from Osland (1995a).

individuals to psychologically disintegrate, regroup, and then attain a higher level of development and maturation. This is reminiscent of Lewin's (1947) unfreezing, moving, and refreezing process of change. The hero's journey framework is a developmental model involving grounded theory and qualitative research. This metaphor makes no pretense of assigning time markers to each stage, because personal transformation is an unpredictable and nonlinear process (Mendenhall 1999). The hero's journey model goes beyond adjustment, a more frequent focus in expatriate research, to underscore the importance of the broader concept of personal transformation.

Conception of culture

Crossing cultural boundaries occurs not only when we traverse national borders but also when we move to a region with a different subculture, when we work with a different ethnic group in our own country, when we are exposed to new organizational or occupational cultures, or when we leave home to go to college. While the journey may be most dramatic when we cross national borders, the stages in the hero's journey also pertain to these other examples of crossing cultures. Therefore, all participants can think of a personal example when they crossed some kind of cultural boundary and embarked on a hero's journey.

Alternative teaching designs

Introduction

While the introduction varies slightly for different audiences, I generally mention that I studied this theme because most of the expatriate literature failed to reflect the essence of what many people consider to be the most significant experience of their lives. This research tried to capture the oral tradition of expatriates and their subjective experience so others would know what to expect and could avoid common mistakes.

I tell students that expatriates often sit around and swap stories about what happened to them and other expatriates, which leads to the Favorite Expatriate Story exercise.

Our favorite expatriate story

Tell your own favorite story and ask participants to listen carefully for underlying themes. Try to use a story that has many of the stages of the hero's journey in it. Then ask, "What can we learn from a story like this? What themes did you hear in this story?" and write their answers to each question on the board.

Then ask the participants to tell their favorite expatriate stories. Ask to hear interesting stories and have the participants identify common themes. This process models how my research on expatriates was done.

The themes I heard again and again from expatriates when I lived overseas were:

- mastery that results from successfully grappling with a foreign language, cracking the code of another culture, and learning to be effective at work;
- the heroic flavor of their tales about rising to difficult occasions and accomplishing what had previously seemed impossible;
- the paradoxes they pondered;
- their personal transformation as a result of opening themselves up to another culture.

This led me to test whether the hero's journey myth was a useful framework for understanding the expatriate experience. I did this by listening to the stories of returned expatriates and doing content analysis on their stories. Next, I briefly explain the stages in the hero's journey, using a graphic that portrays all the stages.

Shared example

Either ask students/participants to watch the first *Star Wars* film (or some other movie with a hero's journey plot) prior to the session or show specific clips from this video during the session.

Shared experience

Ask the group who has lived or worked overseas and where this occurred. Then ask the participants who have not lived overseas to form a pair with someone who has.

In-depth presentation of the framework

For each stage, provide:

1 Campbell's description;
2 ask what that stage would be in the *Star Wars* film;
3 explain the stage's significance for expatriates according to the research (Osland 1995a, b);
4 explain its relationship to expatriate issues in general.

Table 10.1 provides the necessary information for this presentation.

Personal hero's journey story

Ask participants to think about an expatriate experience or, if they have not lived overseas, a "domestic" hero's journey to which they can apply the framework. At the end of each stage description, allow them time to write about that stage of their own experience using the prompt questions in Appendix 10.1: Questions for Audience.

Swapping stories

At the end of the description of each stage in the framework, have the pairs (experienced and inexperienced) tell each other about the stages in their personal hero's journeys. Allow about ten minutes for these discussions. Ask for a few of them to be shared with the whole group when their paired discussion ends ("Who just heard an interesting story about a magical friend?"). This gives you a chance to tie their story to the model in a different way or to add more information about expatriates. Make sure you give equal value to expatriate and domestic stories so those students without international experience do not feel ignored.

Completing the expatriate paradox instrument

Participants fill out the Awareness of Paradox Instrument (Appendix 10.2) and discuss their answers in small groups or simply report which ones they have answered to the entire group. "Raise your hand if you answered yes to the first paradox." Count the hands and fill in an overhead showing the paradoxes and what percentage of the class experienced them.

Application to international students

If you have international students in the classroom and want to better integrate them, ask the local students what it was like when they studied overseas (if they did). How did they feel as an international student? What was the hardest thing they faced? What made their experience positive? Then ask the international students in your classroom about their experience in your country and on your campus (without putting them on the spot). Either lead a discussion or break the class into small groups to discuss these questions, "What could we do to make international students feel more welcome?" "How could we facilitate their hero's journey?"

Time and design

Time is the determining factor in choosing among the design alternatives offered in the above section. An all-day design allows you to use video clips, swap audience stories for each stage, and report on interview findings.

Paper assignment

Participants write a paper on their personal hero's journey, describing each stage and how (if) it applied to their experience. In the conclusion they explain whether or not using the framework has helped them make sense of their experience in a different way.

Expatriate interview assignment

Using some of the same questions from the original research on this framework (see the appendix of *The Adventure of Working Abroad*, Osland 1995a, b), students interview expatriates to see first-hand whether the hero's adventure framework fits their experiences. The questions used most commonly by students are shown in Appendix 10.3: Student Interview Questions. They type up each question followed by the response; at the end of the assignment, they explain why the framework does or does not fit the data they gathered from their expatriate. Students read *The Adventure of Working Abroad* (Osland 1995a, b) before they do their interviews. They bring the interviews to class, and we go over the stages in class and discuss what they learned about each stage. Students seem to enjoy sharing their data, and this makes the expatriate experience more tangible for those who have no international experience or who have never worked abroad. This provides students with a better idea about whether they should accept an overseas position.

Self-assessment assignment

Students make a survey form from the selection criteria on pages 202–3 of *The Adventure of Working Abroad* (Osland 1995a) and evaluate themselves on each item, using a 1–5 Likert scale. They write in depth about their strong and weak points as a candidate, develop an action plan for self-improvement, and conclude by determining whether they would be a good candidate for an overseas assignment.

Teaching dilemma/questions

The only dilemma I have ever experienced with this module occurred when a participant said, "I travel all over the world for my job and I don't see any differences. Why are you making such a big deal about being an expatriate?" There is a difference between traveling to a country and actually living and working there, but this may be an example of a person in the denial-of-differences stage of Bennett's model of intercultural sensitivity (Chapter 14). Rather than defend my view on this, I asked other students to respond to this comment.

Students often ask, "What about third-country nationals who never go home but simply transfer to other countries?" Does the framework fit them too? Obviously, they do not go through the return stage; they simply begin the cycle again when they transfer to a new country.

Since the hero's journey is not an apt metaphor for all expatriates, students sometimes ask about other metaphors to describe different types of expatriates. I have not done any research on this question but would recommend it as an area for future research.

Appendix 10.1 Questions for audience

Sit next to someone who has lived or worked overseas. Share your stages with your partner.

CALL TO ADVENTURE Call to Learning. Think of a time when you:

- embarked upon a lengthy adventure, or
- lived in a different culture, overseas or within the boundary of your own country

Identify your own Hero's or Heroine's Adventure and relate it to the presentation

CROSSING THE THRESHOLD
What was crossing the threshold like for you?
Were there any threshold guardians?

THE BELLY OF THE WHALE
Based upon your own experiences or from watching other expatriates, can you categorize them based upon their immersion in another culture? How would you characterize your own acculturation strategy? Why did you choose or fall into that strategy?

MAGICAL FRIEND
How many of you had a cultural mentor?
Who was that person and how did they help you?

THE ROAD OF TRIALS
Please fill out The Awareness of Paradox Instrument and share your answers with your group. Total your answers and write them on the Group Report, which I'll collect as you discuss these questions:
Which paradoxes have you experienced (either overseas or at home)?
Are there others that do not appear on this list?
What are similar paradoxes that you face in your own profession? (optional question depending on audience)
What lessons can you draw from thinking about these paradoxes?

ULTIMATE BOON
Did you change as a result of your hero's adventure? If so, how?

THE RETURN
What was your own return like?
Does the concept of differentiation and integration apply to your experience?
What facilitated/hindered your return?

SUMMARY QUESTIONS
Does the framework of the hero's adventure myth fit/resonate with your own experience? If so, are there any benefits to using this framework?

Appendix 10.2 The awareness-of-paradox instrument

Check the paradoxes you have experienced.

1   Possessing a great deal of power as a result of your role but down-playing it in order to gain necessary input and cooperation.
2   Generally thinking well of the local culture while at the same time being very savvy about being taken advantage of by them.
3   Feeling caught between the contradictory demands of the headquarters on the one hand and the demands of the local culture and the local situation on the other.
4   Seeing the general stereotype about the local culture as valid but also realizing that many individuals do not fit that stereotype.
5   Giving up some of your own cultural ideas and behaviors in order to be accepted or successful in the other culture while at the same time finding some of your core ethnic values becoming even stronger as a result of exposure to another culture.
6   Feeling at ease anywhere but belonging nowhere.
7   Becoming more and more "world-minded" as a result of exposure to different values and conflicting loyalties, but becoming more idiosyncratic as to how you put together your own value system and views on life.
8   Trying to represent your organization as best you can in order to succeed but also realizing that the "ideal" values you act out may not exist back at Headquarters/the administrative office.
9   Being freed from many of your own cultural rules and even from some of the local culture's norms but not being free at all from certain local culture customs which you must observe in order to be effective.

Appendix 10.3 Student interview questions

Tell me about your (last) overseas assignment, from the time when you first learned about the possibility of going to _____? (Let them talk until they run dry.)

1. What did you think when you first heard you were going to __?
2. What were the first few days like?
3. Were there things that surprised you about the way people thought or worked?
4. What was your first big "aha!" about the culture?
5. How would you sum up your first six months?
6. Whom did you know at this point?
7. Did you have someone who could explain the local culture to you and that you could confide in?
8. How did people see you?
9. Can you describe your relationship with your co-workers?
10. What did you think about your job?
11. Can you describe your relationship with your home organization?
12. What was the most important thing you learned in those first six months?
13. What did your family/wife/husband think about living in _____?
14. Do you think other Americans/_____ you saw abroad encountered or experienced difficulties of living and working in another culture that were:
    _____ Very similar to yours
    _____ Similar
    _____ Not similar
    _____ Very different
    Why?
15. Was it easy for you to be accepted by the local people? Why?
16. Do you correspond with anyone from _____? If so, whom?
    _____ Other people of my nationality
    _____ Host-country nationals
    _____ Third-country nationals
17. How would you describe your living situation?
    _____ Lived in a compound of expatriates
    _____ Lived in a neighborhood composed primarily of expatriates
    _____ Lived in a neighborhood composed primarily of host-country nationals
18. What type of non-work activities did you participate in? With whom did you do them?
19. How many co-workers (above, beside or below you in the hierarchy) did you have to deal with on an average day in order to accomplish your work objectives? What nationality were they?
20. Did you feel you changed as a result of working abroad? If so, how?
21. What was it like to come home?
22. Do you feel you get to use the skills you acquired abroad in your current job?
23. Would you go abroad again? Why?
24. If you had to select people to work abroad, what characteristics would you look for?
25. What advice would you give to a friend who was on his or her way to a foreign assignment?
26. What advice would you give to a person ending a foreign assignment about returning home?
27. What advice would you have for HR departments about handling expatriates?

Note

1 "The Big Five personality dimensions" refers to those traits thought to be universal: (1) emotional stability; (2) extraversion; (3) openness to experiences; (4) agreeableness; (5) conscientiousness (Costa and McCrae 1992).

Further reading

Black, J. S., Mendenhall, M. and Oddou, G. (1991) "Toward a comprehensive model of international adjustment: an integration of multiple theoretical perspectives," *Academy of Management Review*, 16: 291–317.
Black, J. S., Gregersen, H., Mendenhall, M. and Stroh, L. (1999) *Globalizing People through International Assignments*, Reading, MA: Addison-Wesley.
Marx, E. (2001) *Breaking through Culture Shock: What You Need to Succeed in International Business*, Yarmouth, ME: Intercultural Press.
Oberg, K. (1960) "Cultural shock: adjustment to new cultural environments," *Practical Anthropology*, 7: 177–82.
Parker, B. and McEvoy, G. (1993) "Initial examination of a model of intercultural adjustment," *International Journal of Intercultural Relations*, 17: 355–79.
Storti, C. (2001) *The Art of Crossing Cultures*, Yarmouth, ME: Intercultural Press.
Tung, R. (1998) "American expatriates abroad: from neophytes to cosmopolitans," *Journal of World Business*, 33 (2): 125–44.

References

Black, J. S., Gregersen, H., Mendenhall, M. and Stroh, L. (1999) *Globalizing People through International Assignments*, Reading, MA: Addison-Wesley.
Campbell, J. (1949) *Hero with a Thousand Faces*, Princeton, NJ: Princeton University Press.
Costa, P. T. and McCrae, R. R. (1992) *Revised NEO-Personality Inventory (NEO-PI-R) and NEO Five Factor Inventory (NEO-FFI) Professional Manual*, Odessa, FL: Psychological Assessment Resources, Inc.
Harvey, M. (1999) "Repatriation of corporate executives," *Journal of International Business Studies*, 20 (1): 131–44.
Lewin, K. (1947) "Frontiers in group dynamics," *Human Relations*, 1: 5–41.
Mendenhall, M. (1999) "On the need for paradigmatic integration in international human resource management," *Management International Review*, 39 (3): 65–88.
Mendenhall, M. and Oddou, G. (1991) "Managing your expatriates: what the successful firms do," *The Human Resource Planning Journal*, 14: 301–8.
Mendenhall, M., Kuhlmann, T., Stahl, G. and Osland, J. (2002) "A review of the expatriate adjustment theory literature: implications for future research and practice," in M. Gannon and K. Newman (eds), *Handbook of Cross-cultural Managem_t*, Oxford: Blackwell, pp. 155–83.
Oberg, K. (1960) "Cultural shock: adjustment to new cultural environments," *Practical Anthropology*, 7: 177–82.
Ones, D. S. and Viswesvaran, C. (1997) "Personality determinants in the prediction of aspects of expatriate job success," *New Approaches to Employee Management*, 4: 63–92.

Osland, J. (1995a) *The Adventure of Working Abroad – Hero Tales from the Global Frontier*, San Francisco: Jossey-Bass.

Osland, J. (1995b) "The adventure of working abroad," *Training and Development*, November: 47–51.

Osland, J. (2000) "The journey inward: expatriate hero tales and paradoxes," *Human Resource Management*, Summer–Fall, 39, 2–3: 227–38.

Osland. J. (2001) "The quest for transformation: the process of global leadership development," in M. Mendenhall, T. Kuhlmann and G. Stahl (eds), *Developing Global Business Leaders: Policies, Processes and Innovations*, Quorum Books, pp. 137–56.

Underhill, E. (1911) *Mysticism: A Study in the Nature and Development of Man's Spiritual Consciousness*, New York: Dutton.

Chapter 11

Apples and Oranges
An experiential exercise in crossing cultures[1]

Stephen R. Jenner

Introduction

Apples and Oranges is a synthesis and redesign of two experiential exercises, BaFá BaFá (Shirts 1994) and Barnga (Thiagarajan 1990), that seeks to accomplish many of the same objectives in a much shorter time period (a 40–75-minute class session) and uses readily available materials. As in BaFá BaFá, participants are divided into two "cultures" with different sets of rules, one emphasizing being part of a close, affectionate family, the other stressing competition for wealth. As in Barnga, playing cards are used to play a game, but the rules are different for the two groups.

The purposes of the Apples and Oranges exercise are to simulate characteristics of cross-cultural experiences (e.g., foreign-language barriers) and to induce responses usually generated or provoked by that experience (e.g., culture shock). The exercise provides a group of participants with a common culture-crossing experience to discuss and analyze as participants reflect on their own responses and behavior. The debriefing almost invariably reveals negative stereotyping of cultural differences.

The exercise is intended for an undergraduate course in organizational behavior or comparative management, but can be used with other participants. The instructions are very simple and easy to learn, and they can be varied depending on the audience and the imagination of the facilitator.

Advance preparation

Although no advance preparation of participants is required, the facilitator can assign readings and discuss the leading theories of culture, cross-cultural communication, and how to "scan" or learn another culture. Alternatively, the facilitator can introduce the conceptual framework for the exercise summarized below.

The conceptual framework

Given the growing cultural diversity of the workforce, there has been great interest in issues related to cross-cultural communication (Bell 1988; Coombs and Sarason 1998; Cox 1991; Hames 1998; Johnston and Packer 1987). The concept of culture used in the definition of cultural diversity can encompass the "primary dimensions" of gender, age, race, sexual orientation, ethnicity, and physical ability, as well as the "secondary dimensions" of educational background, geographic location, income, marital status, military experience, parental status, religious beliefs, and work experience (Gardenswartz and Rowe 1994). Others use the concept of "multiple cultures" to describe many of the same categories, as well as national, industrial, organizational, and family "cultures" (Boyacigiller *et al.* 1996; Phillips 1994). The author of BaFá BaFá also refers to "different corporations, departments or cultures" (Shirts 1994).

People have differing expectations, values, attitudes, and fundamental assumptions about the world. We are embedded in organizations, which have institutional memories. Individual biographies and the organizational "war stories" of decisive moments are critically important in understanding an actor's assumptive universe. Actors are cultural products, and their repertoires of behaviors and understandings vary. Culture is also constantly changing outside the organization so that it is not necessarily "shared." Rather than assuming that collectivities are made up of people with common experience and a shared internalized experience, we need to understand the assumptive universe of individuals and their particular "cultural agreement" with their organization.

The goal is to explain individual and organizational behavior, specifically employee selection, socialization, status, "good performance," control mechanisms, decision-making procedures, purpose of meetings, negotiating behavior, and approaches to functions such as marketing, production, and operations management. Rather than approaching culture theoretically (Archer 1996), we should pragmatically and empirically develop an approach that "works" to explain behavior. The Apple and Oranges exercise is one step toward that end.

Setting and materials required

These are:

- two physically separate spaces (e.g., inside/outside classroom);
- one whiteboard, chalkboard, or flipchart in the debriefing space;
- ordinary playing cards (poker or bridge) – ten cards per player (Note: Jokers are saved for the Apple Culture);
- some unit of "coin," such as plastic poker chips (any color);

- for each participant, one copy of the Values and Norms of Apple and of Orange Cultures (see Appendices 11.1 and 11.2);
- name tags, if the participants are not familiar with one another;
- group size: 10–50 participants;
- time required: 40–75 minutes.

Procedure

1   Very briefly introduce the exercise and divide into two cultures – Apples and Oranges (5 minutes). The following is one possible introductory statement:

> This experiential exercise is a lot of fun and yet you will learn a very serious lesson about crossing cultures. It is very important that you follow the Values and Norms of your culture carefully and stay in your role at all times.

2   In order to mix groups, have participants count off alternately as Apples and Oranges. Distribute name tags if necessary.

3   Separate the groups into the two physically discrete spaces. Distribute ten playing cards, ten chips (leave extras on a table in case more are needed), and the appropriate group Values and Norms handout (Appendices 11.1 and 11.2), and quickly review the appropriate handout with each group. Have participants learn and practice the Values and Norms of their new culture. After the group practice session, collect the Values and Norms handouts. Remind the participants not to show or discuss their Values and Norms with visitors, and that sitting down or playing familiar card games is against the Values and Norms of both cultures (10 minutes).

4   Select visiting teams of 4–5 people maximum (this can be left to the group).

5   Begin enacting the cultures.

6   Exchange visiting teams for 3 minutes at a time. For example, if there were a total of 30 participants divided into two teams of 15, then they would exchange "tourists" 5 at a time for three repetitions. Although they may observe and interact, they may not ask directly about the Values and Norms of the other culture.

7   Upon return, visitors should report on what they observed and what they think the behavior may mean – "Why did they behave that way?" (Two minutes for each visiting team.) Continue to send teams and have visitors report until everyone has visited the other culture (10–25 minutes).

Discussion, debrief, analysis

This takes 20–35 minutes, depending on group size.

1 Sitting in two groups in the same room, members of Apple Culture describe Orange Culture using adjectives as the facilitator writes them on the board. (Option: each person writes an adjective on a card and the facilitator writes them on the board.)
2 Members of the Orange Culture describe the Apple Culture using adjectives as the facilitator writes them on the board.
3 Members of Apple Culture describe their feelings about Orange Culture, and the facilitator writes them on the board.
4 Members of the Orange Culture describe their feelings about Apple Culture, and the facilitator writes them on the board.
5 Members of Apple Culture attempt to describe Values and Norms of the Orange Culture – the rules of the trading game. The descriptions are likely to be negative judgments that characterize interactions with members of the other culture as irrational and unpleasant.
6 Members of Orange Culture attempt to describe Values and Norms of Apple Culture. This group will tend to respond competitively by making their own negative judgments.
7 Members of Apple Culture explain their own Values and Norms to members of Orange Culture, and vice versa. As each group concludes, distribute copies of their Values and Norms handout to the other group. (Option: to speed the process, just distribute the other culture's Values and Norms handout to each group, allow clarifying questions, and move on to step 8.)
8 The facilitator points out the tendency to use one's own values to describe and interpret another culture. It should be emphasized that another culture may be different but is not necessarily worse.

    The following questions also may be discussed:

- What did you think was going on?
  Discuss internal as well as external attribution and the need to ask about both.
- What caused the weird situation?
  Discuss how it is common to think: Did I read the rules wrong? Was I not paying attention? Were they cheating?
- What did you feel?
  Discuss tolerance for ambiguity and the fact that all humans respond emotionally to ambiguity.
- What did you do about it?
  Discuss options, such as appreciative inquiry. Ideally, tourists could develop strategies and tactics for crossing cultures and use the short debriefing sessions before successive visits to guide the

next group of tourists. A systematic inquiry of the other group's values and norms as well as their language would reveal patterns of behavior.

9 Conclude the exercise with some summary comments and/or a quote such as, "Cross-cultural managers should not be like travelers – collectors of the exotic or shocking – but rather seekers of understanding." (Adapted from Storti (1990), *The Art of Crossing Cultures*, p. 30.)

10 As follow-up, participants could be given assignments using foreign-language television, radio, newspapers, film, literature, as well as face-to-face interviews, to learn more about other cultures.

Continuing dilemmas

Though the time, materials, and ease-of-use issues of complex simulations like BaFá BaFá and Barnga are resolved by this exercise, a few challenges still remain:

- What are the boundaries of the concept of "culture"?
- Is "culture" everything?
- What is not "culture"?
- How can people so quickly learn to disrespect others, even their friends, when the others come from another "culture"?

Despite these dilemmas, the emotional and intellectual experience of crossing cultures remains strong for the participant.

Appendix 11.1 Handout: Values and Norms of the Apple Culture

1	Members of the Apple Culture always greet one another with a gentle hug and ask about each other's families as they move around the room.
2	Apple people always stand close to each other in small clusters and they touch shoulders frequently.
3	Members who are older have higher status and they should always be respected and allowed to take the lead in conversation.
4	Apple people really enjoy playing a game with the cards in which both players show one of their cards. If the suits match, the person who started the game pays a chip to the other, if they don't match the other person pays a chip. No matter who wins, both players are always smiling and laughing. Sometimes players give chips and cards spontaneously to their playing partners.
5	Socialize after playing.
6	The Joker is only used to punish another person who violates the Values and Norms of your culture. For example, if another player gets too serious about winning the game, you should hold up the Joker and then guide him or her gently by the arm out of the room without further interaction.

Appendix 11.2 Handout: Values and Norms of the Orange Culture

1	Your culture values winning – gaining the most chips is the purpose of interacting with other people. You NEVER show your hand of cards to anyone, and you always remain serious and focused on winning as often as possible.
2	Members of the Orange Culture have an unusual language. To initiate the card game, hop in front of another person; then raise your arms alternating left and right while repeating the word "orange" to indicate the number of the card they would like to complete their hand of cards. The person responding taps his or her nose to indicate willingness to trade, or shrugs to indicate unwillingness to trade. Point to the sky to ask for a repeat of the offer.
3	By trading cards, try to get the four odd-numbered cards, 3, 5, 7, 9 with one from each suit. When you complete the series, collect five chips from your opponent and exchange your cards for four more from your opponent.
4	Keep playing and try to win as many times as possible.

Note

1 Preparation of this module was supported in part by resources from the Dean of the School of Business at California State University, Dominguez Hills. The author also acknowledges the helpful suggestions of Maggi Phillips, Sara Jenner, Mark Mallinger, Nancy Adler, Richard Boyd and Joanne Preston.

References

Archer, M. S. (1996) *Culture and Agency: The Place of Culture in Social Theory* (revised edn), Cambridge: Cambridge University Press.

Bell, E. L. (1988) "Racial and ethnic diversity: the void in organizational behavior courses," *Organizational Behavior Teaching Review*, 13 (4): 56–67.

Boyacigiller, N. A., Kleinberg, M. J., Phillips, M. E. and Sackmann, S. A. (1996) "Conceptualizing culture," in B. J. Punnett and O. Shenkar (eds), *Handbook for International Management Research*, Cambridge, MA: Blackwell, pp. 157–208.

Coombs, G. and Sarason, Y. (1998) "Culture circles: a cultural self-awareness exercise," *Journal of Management Education*, 22 (2): 218–26.

Cox, T. (1991) "The multicultural organization," *The Executive*, 5 (2): 34–47.

Gardenswartz, L. and Rowe, A. (1994) *The Managing Diversity Survival Guide*, Burr Ridge, IL: Irwin.

Hames, D. S. (1998) "Training in the land of Doone: an exercise in understanding cultural differences," *Journal of Management Education*, 22 (3): 430–6.

Johnston, W. B. and Packer, A. E. (1987) *Workforce 2000: Work and Workers for the Twenty-First Century*, Indianapolis, IN: Hudson Institute.

Phillips, M. (1994) "Industry mindsets: exploring the cultures of two macro-organizational settings," *Organization Science*, 5 (3): 384–402.

Shirts, R. G. (1994) *BaFá BaFá: A Cross-Cultural Simulation*, San Diego, CA: Simulation Training Systems.

Storti, C. (1990) *The Art of Crossing Cultures*, Yarmouth, ME: Intercultural Press.

Thiagarajan, S. (1990) *Barnga: A Simulation Game on Cultural Clashes*, Yarmouth, ME: Intercultural Press.

Chapter 12

Building transpatriate skills

The *Star Trek* case

Gerard L. Rossy and Margaret E. Phillips

Introduction

Skills such as intercultural awareness, sensitivity, resilience, flexibility and openness are becoming necessary core competencies for individuals actively participating in either the global marketplace or the increasingly multicultural domestic workplace. Employees (and students) need to develop an expanded set of personal competencies to build and sustain effective relationships with their workplace colleagues. These skills are of particular urgency and importance to key managerial and technical staff on *transpatriate* assignments and to facilitate *inpatriate* inclusion.[1] Individuals must prepare themselves and learn to prepare others to operate successfully in these ever more complex cross-cultural settings. This case study from the popular *Star Trek: The New Generation* television series is designed to address these issues and to accomplish the following general objectives:

*   increase awareness of and sensitivity to the pervasive, yet largely unconscious, influence of culture on individual and group perception, thought, feeling, and behavior;
*   recognize the effect of personally held cultural assumptions on communication with persons whose thoughts, perceptions, and actions are guided by a different set of assumptions;
*   identify the specific skills needed to communicate and accomplish goals in a cross-cultural context; and,
*   develop the process skills needed for selecting, mentoring and training others to operate effectively in cross-cultural settings.

Audience preparation and framework for analysis

We begin by providing participants with a common definition of culture. In providing a framework for this exercise we employ the following definition:

> Culture is defined as a distinctive set of explicit and tacit assumptions commonly held by a group of people. These assumptions/understandings serve as guides to acceptable and unacceptable perceptions, thoughts, feelings and behaviors. They are learned and passed on to new members of the group through social interaction and can change over time.
>
> (Boyacigiller *et al.* 1996: 172)

We also provide participants with one or more conceptual frameworks for analyzing culture. Frameworks for cultural analysis come from anthropology (Kluckhohn and Strodtbeck, as elaborated in Phillips 1994 and Schein 1990), communications theory (Hall and Hall 1990), and social psychology (Hofstede 1980). Each of these frameworks focuses on dimensions that reveal part of a culture's core set of assumptions. Specifically, Hall and Hall's (1990) framework focuses on context, message speed, space, and time. Schein's (1990) and Phillips's (1994) frameworks include time and space dimensions. Hofstede's (1980) framework identifies four dimensions: individualism/collectivism; masculinity/femininity; power distance; and, uncertainty avoidance. Although any of these will provide a useful structure for analysis, we prefer to use Phillips and Boyacigiller's "integrated framework for cultural analysis," introduced in Chapter 7 of this book.

Any of these frameworks can be used with this case study to perform a culture scan. The purpose of conducting such a scan is to uncover the values and artifacts that locate a specific culture along each salient dimension. From such scans we can infer the basic assumptions of a culture that define its norms of behavior. An example of the application of one of these frameworks for conducting a culture scan and constructing a broadly grounded map of the culture, called a "sociotype," is found in the Phillips and Boyacigiller chapter.

Session design and issues

We have successfully used this case study with international managers in our consulting activities and with multinational classes of graduate business students. In all cases, the majority of participants were familiar with the *Star Trek* television series. Because of this familiarity there is generally broad acceptance of and enthusiasm for this case.

The 47-minute video case is analyzed in four sections, each focusing on a different facet of a cross-cultural assignment:

1   selection and preparation for an expatriate assignment;
2   scanning a culture to develop a sociotype and an understanding of its underlying assumptions;

3   identifying and overcoming barriers to working in another culture;
4   developing organization and individual strategies for adapting to
     other cultures.

With graduate students we have conducted the analysis within a three-hour class session; with executives we have used an all-day design. Both designs work well.

The three-hour design focuses on learning the concept of culture, developing sociotypes, and identifying the impact of culture on behavior. It is essentially aimed at giving students experience in applying concepts. This also provides the group with a "common experience" to discuss and analyze in depth. The fact that it is a truly alien experience avoids the dilemma resulting from individual biases that come from personal familiarity with a culture – none of the participants is likely to have served in *Starfleet*!

The one-day design permits the additional inclusion of specific (to the organization or to individuals) multicultural issues, the formulation of management strategies for developing or enhancing cross-cultural skills within the organization, and the redesign of organization processes (e.g., recruitment/selection/placement, training and development, measurement and evaluation, reward systems, formal reporting structures and informal networks) to facilitate transpatriate assignment. The all-day design also allows for the use of a greater variety of supporting materials and activities such as additional video clips and exercises.

In advance of the exercise, we usually assign students readings such as:

• Goodman, Phillips, and Sackmann (1999) "The complex culture of international project teams";
• Portions of Hall and Hall (1990) *Understanding Cultural Differences: Germans, French and Americans*;
• Adler and Bartholomew (1992) "Managing globally competent people";
• Hofstede (1980) "Motivation, leadership, and organization: do American theories apply abroad?" or a textbook introduction to the work of Hofstede (e.g., Adler 2002).

We also have found the Cross-Cultural Adaptability Inventory (Kelley and Meyers 1992) to be a very useful supplementary tool. It provides the participants with a practical framework and vocabulary for discussing cross-cultural skills and it helps them relate these concepts directly to their own personality traits and behavior. This significantly increases individual interest and motivation, and it helps further reify these abstract concepts. As advance preparation, we instruct each participant to do the following:

- Complete the Cross-Cultural Adaptability Inventory (CCAI) by circling your personal responses to each item on the scoring sheet, totaling each column on the second page of the scoring sheet, and graphing your inventory results on the circular "Profile" graph. Compare your skill development on the four dimensions (emotional resilience, flexibility/openness, perceptual acuity, and personal autonomy).
- Read the CCAI Action Planning Guide for self-development suggestions along each dimension.
- Choose, then perform one action step for each CCAI dimension. For any dimension, you may design your own action step, rather than choosing one suggested in the Guide. (CCAI Action Planning Guide suggests, for example, developing emotional resilience by keeping a journal of positive statements of yourself, flexibility/openness by practicing doing things at a slower than usual pace, perceptual acuity by paying attention to others' body language, and personal autonomy by creating a rank-ordered list of your personal values.)
- Write one paragraph for each dimension describing:
    - the action step you took, and what you learned from the experience;
    - what you need to do to further develop yourself along this dimension prior to accepting an overseas assignment.

At the start of the class session, students can submit anonymously their scores on each dimension, from which class averages can be calculated. During the class session, their individual CCAI profiles and the group composite profile can then be compared with the perceived profiles of the characters in the case. In this way participants can tie theoretical concepts and case learning points to their own profiles of their cross-cultural skills. The completion of the CCAI is not mandatory but it will add a personal dimension that will enhance the learning experience and help individuals more easily relate the material to their own experience.

We have found few dilemmas in using this video case, regardless of audience. Occasionally, there is an individual who does not like science fiction. However, we ask them to "play along" for the sake of the exercise and the other participants. Generally, these individuals become engaged once the exercise is under way.

Timing is the primary dilemma we face in presenting this video case. Often the students become intensely engaged in certain parts of the discussion, limiting our movement through the range of topics we had planned to discuss. To resolve this issue, we generally have identified in advance those debrief questions which are critical for that particular group to address and those that are secondary, to be addressed only if time permits.

The video case

Star Trek: The Next Generation, Episode 34, "A Matter of Honor," screenplay by Burton Armus, directed by Rob Bowman.
Story synopsis is available from *The Star Trek Episode Guide Hypercard Stacks* (Landis 1991–4).

First part of the video

Instructions prior to starting the video

Explain that this *Star Trek* episode involves a situation where one of the officers of the Starship *Enterprise* takes a temporary assignment as an exchange officer on an alien (Klingon) ship. Ask the participants (students) to observe the process through which he is selected and how he prepares for the assignment. Tell students to look for specific comments and behaviors that reveal cultural assumptions and norms. Encourage them to watch the film carefully rather than try to take detailed notes – each of the four segments of the video is short enough to allow good recall within the group.

Start the videotape at the beginning of episode 34. (We find that it is worth the extra time to show the opening credits as the music and visuals help set the mood.)

First Stop – just before Commander Riker is transported to the Klingon Warbird *Pagh* and after Chief O'Brien says: "You're not afraid are you? . . . I would be."

Discussion questions (and suggested answers)

1   *What are the purposes and potential advantages of the Starfleet Command Officer Exchange Program?* To gain more in-depth understanding of the Klingon culture and to develop officers that can work effectively with their Klingon counterparts. To build bridges between the Federation and the Klingon Empire.

2   *Is Commander Riker an appropriate candidate for the Starfleet Officer Exchange Program? Why?* Probe to have students identify Riker's attitudes and beliefs, his personal attributes, and his previous relevant experience and training. (For example, Riker enjoys personal challenges and opportunities to do what no one else has done before. He believes that he can be a more effective Starfleet Officer and can benefit the *Enterprise* by learning more about the Klingons. He sees the exchange program as a learning opportunity and his curiosity and interest help compensate for

normal feelings of anxiety in encountering new situations.) This may also be an appropriate place to discuss their preliminary assessment of how Riker might score on the CCAI dimensions. Keep a record of this information on the board or on a flipchart for later referral.

3   *Clearly Riker is curious and enthusiastic. Are curiosity and enthusiasm sufficient for success in such a program?* Enthusiasm and motivation are important but not sufficient. Success also requires having the requisite knowledge and skills. Enthusiasm should be tempered with knowledge, skills, preparation, and an understanding of the potential problems and pitfalls involved in cross-cultural assignments.

4   *Who chooses Riker for the program and what might be the underlying reason for choosing him?* It appears that Captain Picard may have had Commander Riker in mind when he invited him to the Phaser Range. Picard does not ask Riker directly but rather probes his interest in the assignment indirectly by asking him whom he would assign. In doing so he allows Riker to "volunteer" and he gains some insight into Riker's understanding of the challenges he will face before making a commitment.

5   *How does Commander Riker prepare for his assignment? Provide specific examples and explain.* He inquires about the beliefs and customs of the other culture. He practices culturally appropriate behaviors (Klingon meal). He studies the norms and practices of the role he is about to play. And he uses Lt. Worf (a Klingon native) as a "cultural guide."

The second part of the video

Instructions prior to starting the second part

Tell the group that during this next part Commander Riker will be interacting with several members of the Klingon Warbird, *Pagh*. Ask them to observe how he behaves with each and assess the degree to which they think his actions are effective.

Second Stop – after Commander Riker's first meal aboard the Klingon Warbird *Pagh*.

Discussion questions (and suggested answers)

1   *Riker has now had the opportunity to interact with several members of the crew of the* Pagh. *What is Riker doing well to cross into the Klingon culture?* He asks general questions; actively observes and participates; tries out new behaviors; listens to feedback from his hosts; relates and compares his experiences to his own culture; he expresses those things that are

surprising and do not fit his expectations, and he asks questions about them. He uses a shared emotion, humor, to help build his relationships with the Klingons. And he begins to use Lt. Klag as a local "cultural guide" to help him better understand his new environment.

2   *What could Riker have done differently in his interactions with Lt. Klag?* He could have recognized Klag's sensitivity about his father's loss of honor sooner and stopped probing the issue. He progressed from understanding to trying to change a value that is deeply ingrained in the Klingon culture.

3   *Are there any other things Riker could or should do to enhance his effectiveness in dealing with the Klingons?* Within the constraints of the Klingon hierarchy, he should try to build a relationship with as many officers as possible. He also might consider wearing a Klingon uniform so as to fit in better with his peers.

4   *With this additional information (from the second part of the video), has your initial assessment of Riker's capabilities for this assignment changed? If so, how?* Link this discussion back to earlier discussion of Riker's personal attributes, as were listed on the board. Would anyone change their assessment of his strengths and weaknesses?

5   *Another way of thinking about someone's potential in cross-cultural situations is to look at his or her profile on the CCAI. Based on your initial impressions of Riker, how do you think he would rate on each CCAI category. Emotional resilience?* High, because he appears to have confidence in himself and his ability to navigate in a new culture. *Flexibility and openness?* High, because he volunteers for the assignments, suggesting a willingness to experience and learn from new situations. He has shown ability to quickly assimilate new information and adjust his behavior accordingly. *Perceptual acuity?* He seems particularly sensitive to nonverbals (dinner scene) and he is ambidextrous (uses both hemispheres of the brain; in the opening scene he fires his phaser with both his right and left hands). *Personal autonomy?* He is willing to stand up to and confront both Captain Kargan and Lt. Klag. Also when Chief O'Brien asks him if he is afraid, he says no and seems surprised that someone would think he should be.

[Here you can also compare the class average on each dimension with their perceived profiles of the characters. Individuals can compare their own CCAI profiles with these.]

Third part of the video

Begin the third part of the video, asking the group to continue their observations of Riker and the Klingon officers with whom he interacts.

Third Stop – before the *Pagh* goes into battle with the *Enterprise* (immediately after Captain Kargan says: "Arm all weapons. Prepare to attack.")

Discussion questions (and suggested answers)

1   *What were the barriers faced by Commander Riker in carrying out his role as Executive Officer of the* Pagh? Kargan doubts his loyalty and his intentions. Therefore he doesn't accept Riker's explanation that the *Enterprise* has come to help.
2   *What are the underlying causes of these barriers?* Lack of trust because they haven't had enough time or experience with one another to build that trust. Both Kargan and Riker are seeing the situation from their own cultural perspective and using their own cultural beliefs to interpret the events. Also Kargan using his beliefs to impute the intentions of both Riker and the *Enterprise.*
3   *Which of these barriers does he (try to) overcome and how?* He tries to overcome Kargan's lack of trust in him by offering to act as a Klingon officer, i.e., to serve, and, if necessary, to die with the crew of the *Pagh.*
4   *Which Klingon officer is most difficult for Riker to work with? Why? How does Riker deal with him?* Captain Kargan, because he most strongly holds the traditional values of the Klingon Empire. By reflecting in his own behavior those values that Kargan most respects, i.e., standing up for your beliefs and being willing to die honorably with "your" crew. He deals with him by accommodating, not assimilating (he doesn't "go native").

Fourth Stop – end of film.

After the video

Discussion questions (and suggested answers)

1   *What are the key similarities and differences between Starfleet culture and Klingon culture?* Instructor should have students apply cultural framework they have learned (e.g., Hofstede (1980), Trompenaars (1993), Schein (1990)), or use Phillips and Boyacigiller's "integrated framework for cultural analysis."
2   *Do the similarities help and/or hinder Riker's transition? How?* Because they both operate in hierarchies, Riker had an easier time understanding his role and being accepted in that role. On the other hand, the different way the levels in the Klingon hierarchy relate to one another (i.e., power distance) made complete integration more difficult for Riker. Riker is willing to make mistakes, but mistakes are

not permissible in the Klingon culture. Starfleet seeks harmony and relationships based on trust. The Klingons need to be dominant and therefore tend to distrust other cultures.

3   *How do Riker's experiences aboard the* Pagh *change his attitude toward the Klingons?* In spite of his difficult experience, Riker gains greater understanding and develops new respect and admiration for the Klingons. (Emphasize the value and long-term benefit of struggling through adaptation in another culture – "Learned when *not* to duck.")

4   *The most interesting relationship displayed is that between Riker and Lt. Klag. Are either of them "typical officers" within their own organizations? Why, or why not?* These two officers, who made a personal intercultural connection, could be characterized as "outliers" within their respective cultures. To a great extent this facilitated their relationship and helped them to build a common bond.

5   *Would you (participant or student) volunteer for the Starfleet Officer Exchange Program? Do you believe Captain Picard would select you? What would you need to do to enhance your chances of being selected?*

6   *Based on Riker's experience, what should Starfleet do to better prepare officers for future exchange assignments?*

Use the discussion of Questions 5 and 6 to complete debriefing of the case and to relate it back to real-world applications.

Note

1   "Transpatriate assignments" are successive international postings. "Inpatriates" are host-country and third-country national managers transferred into the home-country offices of a multinational corporation (Harvey and Buckley 1997).

Further reading

Adler, N. J. and Ghadar, F. (1990) "Strategic human resource management: a global perspective," in R. Pieper (ed.), *Human Resource Management in International Comparison*, Berlin/New York: de Gruyter, pp. 235–60.

Black, J. S., Gregersen, H. B. and Mendenhall, M. E. (1992) *Global Assignments: Successfully Expatriating and Repatriating International Managers*, San Francisco: Jossey-Bass.

De La Torre, J. (1994) "Multinational companies will need trans-national managers," *Los Angeles Times*, 24 July: D2.

Hamel, G. and Prahalad, C. (1990) "The core competence of the corporation," *Harvard Business Review*, 68 (2): 79–91.

Sackmann, S. A. (ed.) (1997) *Cultural Complexity in Organizations: Contrasts and Contradictions*, Thousand Oaks, CA: Sage.

References

Adler, N. J. (2002) *International Dimensions of Organizational Behavior*, 4th edn, Boston: Kent.

Adler, N. J. and Bartholomew, S. (1992) "Managing globally competent people," *Academy of Management Executive*, 6 (3): 52–65.

Boyacigiller, N. A., Kleinberg, M. J., Phillips, M. E. and Sackmann, S. A. (1996) "Conceptualizing culture," Chapter 7 in B. J. Punnett and O. Shenkar (eds), *Handbook for International Management Research*, Cambridge, MA: Blackwell.

Goodman, R. A., Phillips, M. E. and Sackmann, S. A. (1999) "The complex culture of international project teams," in R. A. Goodman (ed.), *Modern Organizations and Emerging Conundrums: Exploring the Post Industrial Sub-culture of the Third Millennium*, San Francisco: Lexington Books, pp. 23–33.

Hall, E. T. and Hall, M. R. (1990) "Key concepts: underlying structures of culture," part 1 in *Understanding Cultural Differences: Germans, French and Americans*, Yarmouth, ME: Intercultural Press, pp. 1–31.

Harvey, M. G. and Buckley, M. R. (1997) "Managing inpatriates: building a global core competency," *Journal of World Business*, 32 (1): 35–52.

Hofstede, G. (1980) "Motivation, leadership, and organization: do American theories apply abroad?" *Organizational Dynamics*, 9 (1): 42–63.

Kelley, C. and Meyers, J. (1992) *CCAI: Cross-Cultural Adaptability Inventory*, Minneapolis, MN: National Computer Systems Inc.

Landis, D. R. (1991–4) *The Star Trek Episode Guide Hypercard Stacks*, version 2.1, Oak Mountain Software, http://members.aol.com/oakmtsw/index.html.

Phillips, M. E. (1994) "Industry mindsets: exploring the cultures of two macro-organizational settings," *Organization Science*, 5 (3): 384–402, with Appendices.

Schein, E. H. (1990) "Organizational culture," *American Psychologist*, February: 109–19.

Tromenaars, F. (1993) *Riding the Waves of Culture: Understanding Diversity in Global Business*, Chicago: Irwin.

Chapter 13

Cultural transitions

A biopsychosocial model for cultural adaptation

Susan Fukushima and Sui Wa Tang

Introduction

With the increasing globalization of business, crossing cultures is becoming more commonplace. Functioning effectively in a different culture is both complex and challenging. During the transition period of adapting to a new culture, the vast majority of people will experience mild emotional reactions and stress-related physiological symptoms. These reactions are so ubiquitous that Kalvero Oldenberg introduced the term "culture shock" in 1960 to describe them (Marx 1999: 5).

The type and intensity of the symptoms of "culture shock" will depend on the psychological make-up and experiences of the individual, the amount of difference between the new culture and the culture of origin, as well as the duration and purpose of the assignment. Most people will successfully overcome "culture shock," and many may be psychologically enriched as a result of their intercultural experiences. However, about 10 percent of the population will develop significant difficulties, including psychosis, alcoholism, substance abuse, or depression (Kealey 1996). This may reflect the interaction of a prior predisposition to the development of these disorders with the stresses of intercultural adaptation.

Rosalie Tung (1998), in her work with expatriates, has reported that the median length of time required for adjustment to a new culture is 6–12 months. About 5 percent of overseas employees will never adjust to the new culture, and 6–8 percent will return early from an overseas assignment. In general, senior management will take the longest period of time to adjust, since jobs at this level require more extensive contacts with people in the host country and the duration of the assignment is typically longer.

For American businesses, the failure of key personnel to adjust to a new culture has important ramifications.

- The cost of such failed international assignments is three to five times the employees' annual salary, costing anywhere from $200,000 to $1.2 million (Solomon 1994).

- While the rate of early returnees has dropped over the past decade, the indirect costs of employees who are underperforming can include mismanagement of customer relationships, disrupted relations with overseas nationals, damage to the company's image, and a negative impact on successors (Solomon 1994).
- Repatriation turnover is high. Black, Gregersen, and Mendenhall (1992) found that 74 percent of American repatriates expected to leave employers within a year of repatriation and 26 percent were actively seeking employment. This high turnover robs companies of the experience employees acquire while on an overseas assignment, particularly if international career assignments are being used for overall career development purposes.
- From the standpoint of the employee, the cost of a failed assignment might include a damaged career path and the disruption of family relationships. The failure of spouse and children to adapt to the new culture is often cited as a main reason for early return (Kealey 1996).

Given the extent of the problem, this module will describe how people react to change in terms of stress and the stress-response. It will discuss and synthesize two theoretical models taken from the psychological literature that may be useful in dealing with recruitment, training, and ongoing support of overseas business personnel that will help to minimize the effects of culture shock.

The stress-response

In preparing personnel who are going overseas, understanding how humans react to change is important. Any change, whether positive or negative, introduces the concept of stress. Hans Selye first popularized the term "stress" in the 1950s. He defined stress as "the nonspecific response of the organism to any pressure or demand" (Kabat-Zinn 1990: 236). In order to meet these demands or pressures, the organism will undergo a generalized physiological response, which Selye called the General Adaptation Syndrome or the Stress-Response. Selye felt that stress was a natural part of life and could not be avoided.

Although the word "stress" is now used frequently, it is often used to refer to both an event and the consequences of that event. For clarity, we refer to stressful events as "stressors" and the resulting stress as the "stress-response."

The stress-response evolved as the body's way of dealing with short-term physical emergencies. Walking across the savannah, a human confronted by a lion would mobilize his or her energies to fight or flee. Described initially as a "fight or flight" response, the stress-response enables energy from storage sites to be rapidly mobilized to provide the muscles and brain with energy. When a person encounters something stressful, the cerebral cortex sends messages to another part of the brain, the hypothalamus, which stimulates the sympathetic nervous system. The adrenal glands are also stimulated and secrete corticoids. As a consequence, a cascade of neurochemical and hormonal reactions occurs which increases heart rate, blood pressure, muscle tension and breathing. Blood is shunted away from the digestive system and extremities. The net effect is to increase the transport of nutrients and oxygen to the muscles and brain. The pupils dilate and hearing is more acute. Long-term processes such as growth, reproduction, and immunity are inhibited. When the emergency is past, the stress-response is turned off and the body returns to equilibrium. This is called the relaxation response.

As long as the organism perceives a threat, the body remains aroused. If the stress-response is not turned off at the end of a stressful event, it can become damaging. A chronic stressor (e.g., a chronic life-threatening illness in oneself or another significant person, a messy divorce, or a major reorganization or downsizing at work) causes an ongoing stress-response, which can increase the risk of disease or increase the effects of a disease.

Almost any system in the body can be damaged by a chronic stress-response. An overly active cardiovascular system contributes to hypertension and heart disease. Changes in the lungs may increase the symptoms of asthma or bronchitis. The loss of insulin may be a factor in the onset of adult diabetes. Stress can cause decalcification of the bones, osteoporosis, and increase the susceptibility to fractures. Inhibition of the immune and inflammatory systems can increase the individual's susceptibility to colds and exacerbate cancer and AIDS. Suppression of the reproductive system can cause a loss of libido, cessation of menstruation, a failure to ovulate in women, and impotency in men. A prolonged stress-response can worsen conditions such as arthritis, chronic pain, and diabetes.

Besides physical emergencies, psychological and social stressors can set off the stress-response in humans (Sapolsky 1998). Deadlines, financial worries, overwork, and anxieties about relationships are only a few of the stressors that can evoke the stress-response. The stress-response is precipitated not only by the problems themselves but also by the expectation of these problems. Richard Lazarus defined this class of stressors as "a particular relationship between the person and the environment that is appraised by the person as taxing or exceeding his or her resources and endangering his or her well-being" (Kabat-Zinn, 1990: 239). The individual evaluates a situation and determines how difficult it is. If he or she feels lacking in the resources to cope with it, the situation becomes stressful.

One of the key psychological factors identified as triggering a stress-response is the loss of control and unpredictability (Sapolsky 1998). Because it is the way the event is perceived that is important, it may not be the actual control, but the belief that the individual has no control that triggers the stress-response. What loss of control and unpredictability have in common is that they expose the organism to novelty. Novelty causes arousal and vigilance as the individual searches for new rules of control and prediction. Novelty makes it difficult to predict the usual cause and effect results of behavior.

The situation is even more complex in that psychological factors are not only stressors, but can modulate the stress-response. Not everyone sees the same event in the same way, and two identical stressors can seem more or less stressful if they are perceived differently by different individuals. The same event can be more stressful to a person who has fewer resources for dealing with it than another person who has greater coping resources.

Social factors can also modulate the response to stress. Outlets for expression such as hobbies, athletics, and aesthetic or spiritual activities can reduce the stress-response. The amount of social support can be significant in the amount of stress a person experiences.

When crossing cultures, people are thrown into a situation which is novel: the rules and roles of the culture are ambiguous, the ability to communicate and predict the consequences of one's actions no longer follow. This lack of predictability and loss of control is a psychological stressor that predisposes to a stress-response. Further, there can be changes in social support and outlets for dealing with the stress of the change so that normal coping mechanisms are no longer as useful or adequate. The stress-response is mobilized and we have "culture shock."

The Rahe model

Richard Rahe proposed the model in Figure 13.1 in 1974 (Rahe 1995). It incorporates the salient points of the stress as previously described. This model describes the importance of the interpretation of experience and how this gives rise to different levels of adaptation and stress/disease. It conceptualizes the impact of an event as being filtered through a series of lenses (steps). Much like a polarizing filter that can reduce or augment selected light rays, at each step, the lens diffracts the impact of part of the stressor. If enough of the stressor is diffracted, adaptation results. If it is insufficient, the person is prone to develop illness or mental distress.

In Step One of the model, the perceived significance of the life-event can alter the magnitude of the stressor. Such alterations depend on prior experience with the event, on current social supports, biographical assets, and constitutional factors. Whether an individual explains things by assigning causality to external factors or feels that an event is under his or her control (attributional style) may also play a role (Seligman 1990).

When people feel threatened, they will react by mobilizing psychological defenses (Step Two). These defenses are unconscious patterns of

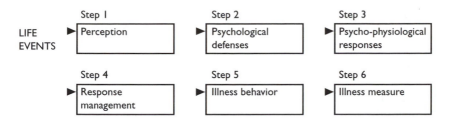

Figure 13.1 The Rahe model.

Source: Adapted from Rahe 1995.

behavior. If adaptive, these defenses can diffract away signals resulting from perceived recent life-events that typically stimulate a variety of psycho-physiological responses (Step Three). This is where the stress-response outlined earlier enters into the picture.

If these psycho-physiological symptoms are interpreted as potentially dangerous to the person's health, they are called symptoms. Step Four in the model is analogous to a color filter that absorbs light rays of certain frequencies – that is, certain response-reduction (coping) techniques can absorb selected symptoms.

A positive lens in Step Five indicates a focusing on persistent symptoms, which are then identified as disease.

Most persons successfully manage Steps One, Two, and Four in making transitions and do not develop an illness. However, when psychological defenses (Step Two) are ineffective and attempts at coping (Step Four) are unsuccessful, a person is at high risk for near-future illness (Steps Five and Six).

The Rahe model is presented as being a sequential process, although adaptation is probably iterative rather than sequential. Despite this limitation, the Rahe model allows the process of adaptation to be broken down into discrete steps. It suggests that the number of stressors we are exposed to, our physiological make-up, and psychological filters through which we see the world (i.e., our coping skills) will make us differentially vulnerable to stress. Thus, the greater the perceived stressor, the more rigid the defense employed to deal with the stressor, and the more maladaptive the coping behavior, the more dysfunctional the resultant response will be.

The other limitation of the Rahe model is that it is presented as a medical model. Culture shock is not a disease *per se*. However, the use of this model is helpful in understanding the adaptation of overseas workers. The identification of maladaptive coping behaviors and the development of physical or mental symptoms would be a signal for some kind of intervention.

The cognitive behavioral model

The Rahe model can be expanded with the cognitive behavior model (Figure 13.2). Developed by Beck (1995), the model hypothesizes that people's emotions and behaviors are influenced by their perceptions of events. Thus, it is not the situation, but the way in which a situation is interpreted, that determines how people feel.

In Beck's formulation, core beliefs are the fundamental and deep understanding that people develop about themselves, other people, and the world. They come into being as people try to make sense of their environment and organize their experience in a coherent way. These beliefs vary in their accuracy and functionality.

The core beliefs influence the development of an intermediate class of beliefs that have to do with rules, attitudes, and assumptions. These beliefs influence perceptions of a situation, and in turn, how we think, feel, and behave.

Automatic beliefs are the most superficial level of cognition. They are the actual words or images that go through a person's mind that are situation-specific. These automatic thoughts generate emotional responses, influence behavior, and lead to physiological responses.

How does this translate into a cultural context? The stress of changing cultures often leads to the emergence of dysfunctional cognitive schemas (cognitive distortions) that then affect thoughts, behavior, and psychophysiological responses. These can lead to depression, anxiety, physical illness, and substance abuse.

For example (adapted from Beck 1995), when an individual is exposed to a new culture, his or her usual mode of behaving may not always be effective. Under these conditions, there are a variety of reactions that a person may have. Person A may feel a sense of excitement and challenge. Person B might use denial to avoid the sense of differences and feel, "There's no problem ... we're all human." Person C might feel demoralized by their inability to deal with the new culture and become anxious with the unconscious core belief of "I'm incompetent." Thus, the initial perception of people will vary and lead to different core beliefs, some of which may be dysfunctional. Figure 13.3 shows such an example of a dysfunctional belief.

Core belief ▶ Intermediate beliefs ▶ Automatic thoughts ▶ Reaction:

SITUATION/STRESS

Emotional
Behavioral
Physiological

Figure 13.2 The Beck cognitive behavior model.

EXPOSURE TO A NEW CULTURE

▼

Core belief: I'm incompetent

▼

Intermediate belief: If I don't understand something perfectly, then I'm dumb

▼

Automatic thought: This is too hard. I'll never understand this.

▼

Reactions

Emotional ▶ Anger, sadness

Behavioral ▶ Alcohol abuse

Physiological ▶ Heaviness in abdomen

Figure 13.3 Illustration of effects of dysfunctional belief using the cognitive behavior model.

Cognitive behavioral theory assumes that the dysfunctional core beliefs can be unlearned and new beliefs, more reality-based and functional, can be learned. The cognitive behavioral model starts with the automatic thoughts that are closest to awareness. Once these are identified, the goal is to correct faulty or illogical thinking by repeated confrontation of the dysfunctional cognitive schemas with discrepant information, eliciting automatic thoughts, identifying the underlying irrational beliefs, and recognizing their effects on mood and behavior. By challenging the irrational beliefs, alternative ways of thinking can then be introduced, replacing the irrational core beliefs.

Using the models

Rahe's model and the cognitive behavioral model are complementary and can be combined (see Figure 13.4). Cognitive behavioral theory delineates what is occurring in Steps One and Two in Rahe's model. It suggests a therapeutic technique for dealing with distorted cognitions that occur when certain schemas are triggered. It also introduces a wide array of heavily researched psychotherapeutic and behavioral techniques to deal with stress-induced reactions and interventions to increase coping responses. The cognitive behavioral model also has a long history of experience in dealing with anxiety and depression as well as maladaptive coping responses.

How can we use this formulation to reduce the negative impact of crossing cultures? The application of this formulation suggests that certain types of training would be useful. In Step One, the perception of

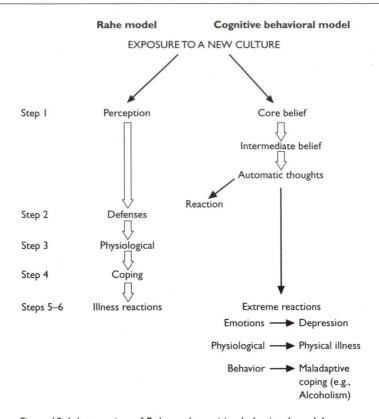

Figure 13.4 Integration of Rahe and cognitive behavioral models.

intercultural change can be affected by understanding the process of cross-cultural adjustment. It also suggests that the techniques from cognitive behavioral theory can be used to outline the automatic thoughts and core beliefs that distort perception. In terms of training, the use of the BaFá BaFá simulation (Shirts 1994) and other critical incident exercises can serve to sensitize participants to their perceptions of others in a foreign culture, their emotional reactions, and their misattributions.

Step Two suggests that modification of psychological defenses may also ameliorate some of the difficulties in cross-cultural adjustment. Bennett's (1993) Developmental Model of Intercultural Sensitivity, and his most recent work with Mitch Hammer (Hammer *et al.* 2003) in developing the Intercultural Development Inventory, which measures intercultural sensitivity, can be very useful in helping to recognize the individual's underlying cognitive orientation toward cultural differences. This would help in tailoring an educational program to facilitate development into the next stage of cultural sensitivity.

The control of the psycho-physiological symptoms of stress is suggested by Step Three. There are a wide variety of behavioral techniques used to deal with the psycho-physiological symptoms of stress. This would include relaxation training, visualization, biofeedback, and meditation (Davis, McKay and Eshelman 1995).

Step Four suggests that developing coping strategies that facilitate adjustment would reduce some of the stress. These skills might include language training and learning about the host culture, both prior to expatriation and on-site. The mobilization of social networks, as well as other coping strategies, would be extremely useful.

Finally, this formulation highlights the need for ongoing support after the initial training. The cross-cultural experience is not static and, as more experience is gained, a different degree of sophistication emerges about the host culture. Debriefing executives in a continual way would enhance their increasing effectiveness as they acculturate. Ongoing support would also permit the identification of executives for whom psychological and medical intervention is necessary.

This formulation also suggests a way of assessing a potential candidate's strengths and challenges in undertaking a cross-cultural assignment. It also highlights the need to get the families of the candidate involved in the selection process, as they too will undergo their own adaptation to changing cultures and are a potential help or hindrance to the executive's adaptation.

Conclusion

This module has attempted to introduce and synthesize two psychological models to elucidate a new model that might be useful in helping people cross cultures. It has attempted to outline the implications for training, selection, and monitoring of overseas personnel. While it cannot eliminate "culture shock," it may hopefully make the process of cross-culture adaptation easier.

References

Beck, J. S. (1995) *Cognitive Therapy: Basics and Beyond*, New York: The Guilford Press.

Bennett, M. (1993) "Towards ethnorelativism: a developmental model of intercultural sensitivity," in R. M. Paige (ed.), *Education for the Intercultural Experience*, Yarmouth, ME: Intercultural Press.

Black, J. S., Gregersen, H. B. and Mendenhall, M. E. (1992) *Global Assignments: Successfully Expatriating and Repatriating International Managers*, San Francisco: Jossey-Bass.

Davis, M., McKay, M. and Eshelman, E. R. (1995) *The Relaxation and Stress Reduction Workbook*, 4th edn, Oakland, CA: New Harbinger Publications.

Hammer, M. R., Bennett, M. J. and Wiseman, R. (2003) "Measuring intercultural competence: the intercultural development inventory," in R. M. Paige (ed.), *International Journal of Intercultural Relations*, special issue, 27 (4).

Kabat-Zinn, J. (1990) *Full Catastrophe Living*, New York: Delacorte Press.

Kealey, D. J. (1996) "The challenge of international personnel selection," in E. Landis and R. Bhagat (eds), *Handbook of Intercultural Training*, Thousand Oaks, CA: Sage, p. 83.

Marx, E. (1999) *Breaking through Culture Shock*, London: Nicholas Brealey.

Rahe, R. (1995) "Stress and coping in psychiatry," in H. I. Kaplan and B. J. Sadock (eds), *Comprehensive Textbook of Psychiatry*, 6th edn, Baltimore, MD: Lippincott, William and Wilkins, pp. 1545–59.

Sapolsky, R. M. (1998) *Why Zebras Don't Get Ulcers*, New York: W. H. Freeman.

Seligman, M. (1990) *Learned Optimism*, New York: Simon and Shuster.

Shirts, R. G. (1994) *BaFá BaFá: A Cross-Cultural Simulation*, San Diego, CA: Simulation Training Systems.

Solomon, C. M. (1994) "Success abroad depends on more than job skills," *Personnel Journal*, April: 51–60.

Tung, R. L. (1998) "American expatriates abroad: from neophytes to cosmopolitans," *Journal of World Business*, 33: 125–44.

Part V

Going deeper
Developing a global mindset

In the earlier parts of the book we have explored the nature of culture, how to scan and make sense of cultural processes, and the experiential challenge of actually crossing cultures. Here we are going deeper toward development of effective managers and leaders in cross-cultural contexts. In Part V, we offer modules that are aimed at evolution – i.e., growing effectiveness over time. Thus, they are broader in perspective and part of career-long learning.

Bennett presents the stages of intercultural competence and clarifies the operative behavior at each stage. She then cautions the teacher that modules that ignore the readiness (or stage) of the learner are seriously flawed. Thus, the instructor needs to appreciate the learners' position, and the teaching material must be adapted to the individual learner and the multiple levels of cultural competence within the classroom. Otherwise, the training may be ignored as old hat or resisted as too threatening.

Maznevski and Lane pursue similar goals as they urge the development of a global mindset, a meta-capability. In their model, developing self-awareness and other-awareness, at both the individual and organizational levels, is the goal. Emphasizing many alternative modes of instruction (lecture, sequential cases, experiential learning), they argue for "frame of reference" education. This is a highly interactive form of teaching where experiences are coupled with feedback to allow for the articulation of one's own schema as well as the development of systems thinking.

Kostova challenges the cultural vantage point in international business, seeing it as a necessary but insufficient perspective. Rather, she encourages the addition of an institutional point of view. Her institutional analysis of transitional economies provides us not only with a broader contextual perspective, but also takes us to a different level of analysis. Thus, she enriches the contextual frame for the development of effective "transnationals."

Adler takes us deeper into the realm of development over time. She argues that truly effective global leaders consciously pause for reflection. Her module on teaching reflective silence provides a straightforward method of modeling reflection in the classroom and the development of such skills for lifelong use.

Chapter 14

Turning frogs into interculturalists

A student-centered developmental approach to teaching intercultural competence

Janet M. Bennett

Introduction

The "frog theory of change" suggests that it is possible to boil a frog in a cauldron of water if you are careful to turn the heat up slowly. Turning the heat up too rapidly of course leads the frog to jump out. This metaphor provides educators with a very apt strategy for teaching intercultural competence. We can teach the hottest intercultural issues effectively only when we have approached them gradually and developmentally.

This chapter suggests a model for assessing the learner's developmental stage in terms of intercultural sensitivity and offers curricular recommendations that take into account learner readiness level. The discipline of intercultural communication will inform our perspective.

For purposes of promoting cultural competence in organizations, intercultural communication focuses on the face-to-face interaction between members of two significantly different cultures, with an emphasis on their subjective cultural patterns. By subjective culture, we refer to the learned and shared values, beliefs, and behaviors of a group of interacting people. Most scholars define subjective cultural diversity to include nationality, ethnicity, gender, age, physical characteristics, sexual orientation, economic status, education, profession, religion, organizational affiliation, and other cultural differences learned and shared by a group of people (M. J. Bennett 1998: 4–5).

This emphasis on subjective culture contrasts to many academic disciplines that focus instead on objective culture, which refers to the artifacts and structures created by a group of interacting people, such as their political and economic systems, artistic expressions, architecture, literature, theatre, history, heroes, and holidays. While these areas of study provide important knowledge for the student, they do not guarantee competence in relating to someone from the culture being studied.

However, unlike more benign topics such as botany or geography, intercultural relations are inherently challenging behaviorally and affectively. While the average management student may not rejoice in the pleasure of accounting, rarely does a spreadsheet challenge his or her identity or call into question basic beliefs. Intercultural encounters, whether domestic or international, may do precisely that. Therefore we are well advised to be aware of the typical fears and resistances inspired by the study of intercultural relations and the developmental reasons behind such discomfort.

For those interested in teaching about matters intercultural, careful audience analysis is essential. One way to approach this analysis is to assess the learners' level of intercultural sensitivity. How resistant to difference are they? How intrigued by other cultures?

The developmental model of intercultural sensitivity

A framework for analyzing the potential response to cultural difference is the Developmental Model of Intercultural Sensitivity (DMIS) (M. J. Bennett 1993). The underlying assumption of the model is that as one's *experience of cultural difference* becomes more complex and sophisticated, one's competence in intercultural relations increases. Each stage indicates a particular cognitive structure expressed in certain kinds of attitudes and behavior related to cultural difference. By recognizing the underlying cognitive orientation toward cultural difference, predictions about behavior and attitudes can be made and education can be tailored to facilitate development into the next stage.

The first three DMIS stages are *ethnocentric*, meaning that one's own culture is experienced as central to reality in some way; these stages reflect the worldview of "difference-avoiders."

| Denial | Defense | Minimization | Acceptance | Adaptation | Integration |

Ethnocentric stages | Ethnorelative stages

Figure 14.1 Development of intercultural sensitivity model.

Note
This is a visual approximation of the model developed in Hammer (1999) and Hammer, Bennett and Wiseman (2003).

- *Denial* of cultural difference is the state in which one's own culture is experienced as the only real one. Other cultures are avoided by maintaining psychological and/or physical isolation from differences. People at Denial generally are disinterested in cultural difference, although they may act aggressively to eliminate a difference if it impinges on them.
- *Defense* against cultural difference is the state in which one's own culture (or an adopted culture) is experienced as the only good one. The world is organized into "us and them," where "we" are superior and "they" are inferior. People at Defense are threatened by cultural difference, so they tend to be highly critical of other cultures, regardless of whether the others are their hosts, their guests, or cultural newcomers to their society.
- *Minimization* of cultural difference is the state in which elements of one's own cultural worldview are experienced as universal. Because these absolutes obscure deep cultural differences, other cultures may be trivialized or romanticized. People at Minimization expect similarities, and they may become insistent about correcting others' behavior to match their expectations.

The second three DMIS stages are *ethnorelative*, meaning that one's own culture is experienced in the context of other cultures; these stages reflect the worldview of "difference-seekers."

- *Acceptance* of cultural difference is the state in which one's own culture is experienced as just one of a number of equally complex worldviews. Acceptance does not mean agreement – cultural difference may be judged negatively – but the judgment is not ethnocentric. People at Acceptance are curious about and respectful toward cultural difference.
- *Adaptation* to cultural difference is the state in which the experience of another culture yields perception and behavior appropriate to that culture. One's worldview is expanded to include perspectives from other cultures. People at Adaptation are able to look at the world "through different eyes" and may intentionally change their behavior to communicate more effectively in another culture.
- *Integration* of cultural difference is the state in which the experience of different cultural worldviews is incorporated into one's identity. People at Integration often are dealing with issues related to their own "cultural marginality." This stage is not necessarily better than Adaptation in most situations demanding intercultural competence, but it is common among non-dominant minority groups, long-term expatriates, and "global nomads."

Content analysis research has supported the relevance of these stage descriptions. A theory-based instrument for measuring the major stages of the DMIS, the Intercultural Development Inventory, has been developed by Mitch Hammer and Milton Bennett (Hammer 1999; Hammer, M. J. Bennett and Wiseman 2003). It generates a graphic profile of an individual's or group's development, with a textual interpretation, providing educators with a valid and reliable profile of their intercultural sensitivity and readiness for intercultural learning.

In order to address appropriately the developmental needs of the learners, educators can borrow a framework from Sanford's *Self and Society* (1966). He suggests that educators must examine how to balance the level of challenge a learner faces with adequate supports to keep the learner engaged. If the students are overly challenged – if the heat is turned up too quickly – they flee the cultural context. If they are overly supported, they learn little or nothing. An example is a student at an ethnocentric level of defense against difference being overly challenged by being accused of racism, and resolving never to talk to a person of color again. A person who is in an ethnorelative stage, and is truly intrigued by cultural difference, would find a rhetorical lecture on "celebrating diversity" too supportive and lacking sufficient challenge. It is only when we have accurately assessed the developmental stage of our learners, and balanced the challenge and support in our curriculum, that we can effectively teach intercultural competence (J. M. Bennett, M. J. Bennett and Allen 1999; J. M. Bennett and M. J. Bennett 2003).

Further, the framework of challenge and support applies to both the *content* and the *process* of our curriculum. Depending on the DMIS stage, learners may find a particular subject (the content) more or less threatening. Culture shock, for instance, is more threatening to a learner in Minimization than one in Adaptation. Racism becomes more approachable for those in ethnorelative stages, a perspective widely ignored by overly eager trainers who often insist on sequencing it near the beginning of programs. Forcing the frog into the kettle of scalding water rarely works.

The methods used in training must also be balanced based on the audience analysis. In general, when the students have to take risks, or self-disclose, especially when trust has not yet been created, they may find the activity highly challenging.

Each of us recognizes topics in our courses that learners find very demanding, and those that are sure winners, whether it is that ever-so-dull review of economic policy or that fascinating material on negotiation. This model suggests that we balance out the content challenge with a compensatory method. For that challenging economics lesson, we design a low-risk, user-friendly process such as a video, a lecture, or a small-group activity. In other words, we support the students with the method, while challenging them with the content. Conversely, students are quite comfortable with more demanding methods (such as simulations or role-plays) if the topic is less threatening. By maintaining this balance, we are supporting the learners to take gradual risks around intercultural issues in a fashion that promotes their development.

When we are teaching students about intercultural issues, we can be reasonably sure that many of them will find discussions of culture quite challenging, perhaps even threatening to their worldview. Culture only becomes less challenging in the ethnorelative stages of acceptance, or beyond. Until learners are less challenged, therefore, our methods are supportive, and reasonably undemanding. Higher-risk, more-complicated activities are appropriately delayed until the later stages.

A wide variety of books are available that include collections of exercises, experiential activities, questionnaires, and models for teaching through the developmental stages. For an overall view of intercultural training and teaching methods, two volumes by Fowler and Mumford (1995, 1999) provide both activities and pedagogical rationales. From an organizational perspective, Brake and Walker (1995), Gardenswartz and Rowe (1993), Osland, Kolb and Rubin (2001), and Singelis (1998) offer activities appropriate for those studying business, management, and organizational behavior. Collections of intercultural activities easily adaptable to the organizational context include such classics as Pusch (1979) and Seelye (1996). A European perspective is offered by Fennes and Hapgood (1997), a cultural adaptation workbook has been created by Storti and Bennhold-Samaan (1997), and decidedly creative methods are outlined in handbooks by Thiagarajan (1991, 1994, 1995).

In the following discussion, we will apply this framework to the task of teaching intercultural competence, noting for each stage the developmental tasks the learners face, the challenge and support patterns for the instructor, and stage-appropriate competencies.

Developing intercultural competence at the Denial stage

At this stage, the typical learners involved in business or management may be surprised, if not dismayed, to find the subject of culture occurring in their courses. With an emphasis on maximizing productivity, they may see little reason to study the cultural patterns of other groups. Americans, for example, may take comfort in the idea that English is becoming an international business language, and "since we all speak the same language, that's all that matters." Other nationalities have similar causes of Denial.

Thus, our goal at Denial is simply to increase their recognition that cultural differences exist. We should avoid "proving" through complicated case studies the power of intercultural misunderstanding – that is simply too much heat. We should aim at competencies within the developmental grasp of the learner: the ability to recognize difference, to gather information about culture, and the inclination to do so. Knowing that the topic of culture presents a high challenge, we can provide supportive content using objective culture (trade practices, economics, human resource policies, etc.), illustrated with user-friendly activities that involve the students. One such activity is the "grocery store ethnography" (Kluver 1998), which involves the students in an anthropological analysis of a familiar situation. For an even more relevant context, students can use the "conceptual model for country/area studies" (Kohls 1999) to explore a multinational corporation's cultural patterns.

Developing intercultural competence at the Defense stage

Learners at the Defense stage are often labeled "resistant" since they are often overtly negative and sometimes even antagonistic about other cultures. They may be naïve dualists (Knefelkamp 1996), simply never having examined why they see their own culture as superior (e.g., "American business is the most successful in the world"), or they may be pernicious dualists, with the intent to denigrate others (e.g., "If the Chinese weren't so devious and manipulative, this negotiation would work better"). Naïve dualists are more amenable to educational efforts, once they have been exposed to the common humanity of their colleagues or classmates. Pernicious dualists require special training efforts that may be more than can be developed in the average classroom.

Our task is thus one of avoiding cultural contrasts and of providing a safe context for exploring human similarities. For this stage, and this stage only, the emphasis can be placed on characteristics the students share with other cultures. Essentially, the educator is trying to move the students to recognize that the perceived "other" is "just like me!" The "other" may be like me because we share interest in the same sports, in career success, or even in music. Seemingly minor similarities can help shift the perspective from "us/them" to "They're not so bad after all!" Classroom activities directed toward those at Defense should emphasize teamwork on tasks having little or nothing to do with culture. Therefore, ropes courses, building Lego-block models of group interaction, or "building a tower" (Fennes and Hapgood 1997) provide opportunities to work with others and to relax somewhat about cultural differences.

To challenge them to progress to more complex thinking about difference, we can emphasize basic intercultural competencies, including tolerance, patience, and self-discipline. For the international business student at Defense, to discuss economic policy with a Chinese scholar may be excessively challenging; for her or him to discuss a more culturally detached topic such as accounting might not be. Topics that are relatively free of culture, where learners can find commonality, can be seen to move them developmentally.

Developing intercultural competence at the Minimization stage

When the students begin to announce that, in essence, the world is full of people just like them, they have moved into Minimization. They might suggest various forms of cultural convergence: "Technology is bringing cultural uniformity" or "The key to getting along in any culture is just be yourself!" Often this position is considered the acme of intercultural sensitivity, in which we are metaphorically color-blind, and assume everyone is the same. In fact, it is merely another form of ethnocentrism, in which the standard for similarity is one's own culture: "Everyone is the same . . . and they're just like me!"

The primary task for students at this stage is to increase cultural self-awareness while acknowledging certain perceived similarities. Building on cultural self-awareness, the learners can examine the contrast between their own cultures and other cultures with which they will be working. Supportive content for this stage includes basic subjective cultural differences and knowledge of perception and worldview. The classic intercultural exercise entitled "Description, Interpretation, and Evaluation" (D.I.E.) helps students limit their instinctive negative evaluations of others while requiring them to develop multiple perspectives. The exercise (available at www.intercultural.org) is used to help students differentiate among what they can actually see (description), from what they think it might mean (interpretation), to whether they think it is good or bad (evaluation). When used to examine the policies and procedures of global organizations, the D.I.E. can bring out traces of ethnocentrism that inhibit intercultural competence. Osland, Kolb and Rubin (2001) have also developed a useful teaching unit on perception in the corporate context.

At this stage, the first task is to call into question the students' comfortable assumptions about similarity through examination of their own culture. Brake and Walker (1995) have developed a "cultural orientations model" useful for teaching cultural self-awareness as well as for comparing and contrasting other cultures. Frequently, using proverbs (see "U.S. proverbs and core values" by Robert Kohls 1996) can help the learners identify their own cultural values. One effective approach adapted from an exercise by Julie O'Mara ("Magazines," 1994) used annual corporate reports and asked the students to assume the perspective of an outsider arriving on the planet. What do these annual reports tell us about the culture of this place? Who has the power? How is it displayed? What are the values?

To increase the challenge, students can work with theoretical frameworks for analyzing culture, especially their own. Most business students are already familiar with Adler (2002), Hall (1981), Hofstede (2001), and Trompenaars and Hampden-Turner (1998). They may be less familiar with intercultural authors such as Brislin (2000), Kim (2001), Martin and Nakayama (2000), Samovar and Porter (2002), Stewart and Bennett (1991), and Ting-Toomey (1999), each of whom provides frameworks for intercultural interaction analysis useful in the business world. By assuming this interactive perspective, these theorists go beyond ethnographic cultural description to suggest the likely barriers that might occur when members of two cultures try to do business.

Challenge is further increased when we arrange contact with selected and coached members of other cultures and structured opportunities for difference-seeking. With students at Minimization, more sophisticated intercultural competencies need to be stressed: open-mindedness, cultural self-awareness, listening skills, nonjudgmentalness, and accurate perception.

Developing intercultural competence at the Acceptance stage

Learners at this stage recognize that there are differences in values and beliefs, and such differences need to be interpreted in their cultural context. Instead of being "difference-avoiders" they now can focus on the complexity of other cultures, even to the point of becoming "difference-seekers." Now they can be heard to query, "How can I learn more about Mexican culture before I begin to work with them?" or "The more cultures you know about, the better job you'll do."

The developmental goal at this stage is to systematically increase the complexity of categories they use for analyzing difference and to begin to develop their skills for frame-of-reference shifting. When learners have reached Acceptance, they tend to find the subject of cultural difference non-threatening and rather low-challenge. The instructor can therefore increase the challenge of methods used and stimulate the students with more complex risks such as role-plays, simulations, home-stays, and other experiential activities. Delaying these more challenging methods until students are developmentally ready has only recently been recognized as a pedagogical standard for intercultural trainers. Training in the 1970s often started out with a simulation, scheduled before students were ready to handle it, and often ended with unfortunate results – the heat having been turned up too quickly.

If the group is predominately in the Acceptance stage, simulations such as Barnga (Steinwachs 1995), BaFá BaFá (Shirts 1995), and Ecotonos (Hofner Saphiere 1995) help them to develop intercultural empathy and to recognize the complexity of intercultural relations. The use of cross-cultural dialogues (Storti 1994, 1999) designed around business issues emphasizes the relevance of culture to their future careers. To compare their own values to an organization's, "The Culture Compass" (Chu 1996) provides an excellent exercise, as does Min-Sun Kim's set of critical incidents on communication styles (1998). In addition, students are now open to dealing with issues of racism, and recognizing the impact of white privilege, vividly demonstrated in videos such as ABC *PrimeTime Live*'s "True Colors" (1991) or Rosabeth Moss Kanter's *A Tale of "O"* (1993).

Various videos can be used to compare and contrast cultural patterns, including Jaime Wurzel's *The Multicultural Workplace* (1990), *The Intercultural Classroom* (1994), and *The Cross-cultural Conference Room* (2002), Deborah Tannen's (1994) *Talking 9 to 5: Men and Women in the Workplace*, and David Matsumoto's (2000) *A World of Diversity*. Each of these videos provides complex and realistic intercultural critical incidents for analysis.

One content challenge persists at this stage. Students will ask, "If I 'accept' Indonesian culture, does that mean I have to think that everything they do is right?" This is a particularly delicate developmental task for the educator, since it requires walking the fine line between understanding another culture's behavior in the context of that culture and adhering to one's own moral judgments. Thus, one can comprehend the context and meaning of certain business practices in other countries and at the same time adhere to one's own country's standards. (See Moorthy *et al.* (1998) for a thoughtful model on how this can be approached.)

Developing intercultural competence at the Adaption stage

At the Adaptation stage, the students are ready to shift perspectives and actively use empathy skills. They now recognize that to succeed in the business, they may have to moderate their approach and accomplish tasks in a different way. They may comment on their adaptability to other cultural patterns: "I'm enjoying learning to bargain in Spanish!" or "Now I think I can use a go-between more effectively in Asia." Finally, the students are viewing cultural difference as low challenge, and we can indulge in nearly unlimited levels of challenge in both content and methods.

Students at this stage need to master skills of cultural observation, intercultural interviewing, and various ethnographic techniques in order to be able to continue their culture learning after their program. It is these learning-to-learn strategies that support lifelong learning during their professional careers. Additionally, they need to practice frame-of-reference shifting and intercultural empathy through the examination of critical incidents and more extensive case studies. Process challenges can include deeper exploration of more complicated constructs, including issues that may still be producing anxiety (e.g., "If I adapt to this other culture, does it mean I lose my existing cultural identity?" or "Do I have to abandon feminism to work overseas?").

Since the Adaptation stage asks the students to interact effectively across cultures, the stage-appropriate classroom activities are more risky and demanding. However, if the heat has increased gradually, the learners will now be ready to try more extensive role-plays (McCaffery 1995; Thiagarajan 1991, 1995), skits (Osland *et al.* 2001), or specific skills, such as learning to be indirect (Storti and Bennhold-Samaan 1997) or mastering negotiation (Ady 1998).

Developing intercultural competence at the Integration level

At this developmental level, the students are at least bicultural or bilingual and comfortable in many intercultural contexts. The subject of intercultural difference no longer threatens them and may in fact be perceived as supportive ("At last, someone understands I come from a different culture!"). They generally feel "at home" in most cultures, and enjoy shifting cultural frames to solve problems, analyze interactions, and mediate conflict. The last frontier of their intercultural exploration is their own cultural marginality, living at the edges of two or more cultures (J. M. Bennett 1993). They are challenged at this stage by investigating how they can establish personal boundaries for their identity, adhere to a set of values, and still live in the multicultural self that has evolved for them. They can be supported by validating their expertise, by participating as a cultural-resource person in other intercultural contexts, and by involvement in a "marginal peer group" of others who share this complex identity. This is not a stage most learners will achieve, and is not necessarily even a goal of intercultural learning. Most individuals should be aiming for acceptance and adaptation.

Developing intercultural competence in the multilevel classroom

Most of us rarely teach entire groups of students who are positioned in the later stages of development where there is great safety in pursuing intercultural issues. Therefore, it is imperative to sequence our content and methods cautiously to avoid the backlash that can so easily result from premature challenge for those in ethnocentric stages.

Further, it is fairly typical to have a classroom of students at various levels of development. In order to target our curriculum at the appropriate level of challenge, we need to assess, either through the Intercultural Development Inventory or, more informally, through audience analysis, where the majority of any given group is on the developmental continuum. For diagnosing levels, it is useful to picture a normal curve, with the preponderance of any given class located at a particular stage on the developmental line. It might be reasonable to expect in a large, diverse university 18–21-year-olds might cluster in the Minimization stage, with some students above the norm in Defense and with some at the other end of the curve in Acceptance. We can then design our curriculum to address the needs of Defense, Minimization, and Acceptance.

The most sophisticated interculturalists therefore have learned to preface their teaching with inoculations, a form of "dis-ease" prevention that preempts the potential negative response. The teacher introduces a controlled form of the objection early on in an attempt to reduce the reaction and avoid the dis-ease that may occur if we turn the heat up too fast for those in ethnocentrism. Examples of inoculations include: "Many of you may be wondering why intercultural competence is relevant to our work" (to address Denial); "Some of you may be thinking, 'The Internet doesn't have culture. As cultures merge through technology, our way is best'" (to address Defense); or "These intercultural concerns are soft skills anyone can pick up on the job" (to address Minimization). By starting with a well-developed series of inoculations, we can compensate for the few students who are not in the center of the normal curve and who still have issues to resolve in ethnocentrism.

When we intentionally sequence our curriculum based on learner readiness, the advantages are significant. It limits the stress and frees both faculty and students to explore delicate cultural matters in depth. It allows development of intercultural skills in a carefully scaffolded design. It provides a theoretical rationale for both the cultural content and the pedagogical choices we must make. And, finally, it allows us to recognize the challenges inherent in intercultural material and turn the heat up slowly, ever mindful of our task of turning frogs into interculturalists.

References

ABC News (Producer) (1991) *Prime Time Live*: "True Colors," television broadcast, New York: ABC News, available from corVISION Media, Inc., 3014 Commerical Avenue, Northbrook, IL 60062, (847) 509–8290, www.corvision.com

Adler, N. J. (2002) *International Dimensions of Organizational Behavior*, 4th edn, Cincinnati, OH: South-Western College Publishing.

Ady, J. C. (1998) "Negotiating across cultural boundaries: implications of individualism–collectivism and cases for application," in T. M. Singelis (ed.), *Teaching about Culture, Ethnicity, and Diversity*, Thousand Oaks, CA: Sage, pp. 111–20.

Bennett, J. M. (1993) "Cultural marginality: identity issues in intercultural training," in R. M. Paige (ed.), *Education for the Intercultural Experience*, Yarmouth, ME: Intercultural Press, pp. 109–35.

Bennett, J. M. and Bennett, M. J. (2003) "Developing intercultural sensitivity: an integrative approach to global and domestic diversity," in D. Landis, J. M. Bennett and M. J. Bennett (eds), *The Handbook of Intercultural Training*, Thousand Oaks, CA: Sage.

Bennett, J. M., Bennett, M. J. and Allen, W. (1999) "Developing intercultural competence in the language classroom," in R. M. Paige and D. Lange, (eds), *Culture as the Core: Integrating Culture into the Language Classroom*, Minneapolis: University of Minnesota Press.

Bennett, M. J. (1993) "Towards ethnorelativism: a developmental model of intercultural sensitivity," in R. M. Paige (ed.), *Education for the Intercultural Experience*, Yarmouth, ME: Intercultural Press, pp. 21–71.

Bennett, M. J. (1998) "Intercultural communication: a current perspective," in M. J. Bennett, (ed.), *Basic Concepts of Intercultural Communication: Selected Readings*, Yarmouth, ME: Intercultural Press, pp. 1–34.

Brake, T. and Walker, D. (1995) *Doing Business Internationally: The Workbook for Cross-cultural Success*, Princeton, NJ: Princeton Training Press.

Brislin, R. W. (2000) *Understanding Culture's Influence on Behavior*, 2nd edn, Fort Worth, TX: Harcourt College.

Chu, P. (1996) "The culture compass," in H. N. Seelye (ed.), *Experiential Activities for Intercultural Learning*, Yarmouth, ME: Intercultural Press, pp. 155–70.

Fennes, H. and Hapgood, K. (1997) *Intercultural Learning in the Classroom*, London: Cassell.

Fowler, S. M. and Mumford, M. G. (eds) (1995) *Intercultural Sourcebook: Cross-cultural Training Methods*, vol. 1, Yarmouth, ME: Intercultural Press.

Fowler, S. M. and Mumford, M. G. (eds) (1999) *Intercultural Sourcebook: Cross-cultural Training Methods*, vol. 2, Yarmouth, ME: Intercultural Press.

Gardenswartz, L. and Rowe, A. (1993) *Managing Diversity: A Complete Desk Reference and Planning Guide*, Homewood, IL: Business One/Irwin.

Hall, E. T. ([1959], 1981) *The Silent Language*, New York: Anchor/Doubleday.

Hammer, M. R. (1999) "The intercultural developmental inventory: a measure of intercultural sensitivity," in S. M. Fowler and M. G. Mumford (eds), *Intercultural Sourcebook: Cross-cultural Training Methods*, vol. 2, Yarmouth, ME: Intercultural Press, pp. 61–79.

Hammer, M. R., Bennett, M. J. and Wiseman, R. (2003) "Measuring intercultural competence: the intercultural development inventory," in R. M. Paige (ed.), *International Journal of Intercultural Relations* [Special Issue], 27 (4).

Hofner Saphiere, D. M. (1995) "Ecotonos: a multicultural problem solving simulation," in S. M. Fowler and M. G. Mumford (eds), *Intercultural Sourcebook: Cross-cultural Training Methods*, vol. 1, Yarmouth, ME: Intercultural Press, pp. 117–26.

Hofstede, G. (2001) *Culture's Consequences: Comparing Values, Behaviors, Institutions, and Organizations across Nations*, 2nd edn, Thousand Oaks, CA: Sage.

Kanter, R. M. (producer) (1993) *A Tale of "O": On Being Different*, video production available from Goodmeasure, P.O. Box 381609, Cambridge, MA 02238-1609, (617) 868-8662, www.goodmeasure.com.

Kim, M.-S. (1998) "Conversational constraints as a tool for understanding communication styles," in T. M. Singelis (ed.), *Teaching about Culture, Ethnicity, and Diversity*, Thousand Oaks, CA: Sage, pp. 101–9.

Kim, Y. Y. (2001) *Becoming Intercultural: An Integrative Theory of Communication and Cross-cultural Adaptation*, Thousand Oaks, CA: Sage.

Kluver, R. (1998) "Grocery store ethnography," in T. M. Singelis (ed.), *Teaching about Culture, Ethnicity, and Diversity*, Thousand Oaks, CA: Sage, pp. 23–8.

Knefelkamp, L. (speaker) (1996) *The Psychology of Bigotry*, video recording, Portland, OR: H.O.P.E. Conference, available from the Intercultural Communication Institute at 8835 SW Canyon Lane, Suite 238, Portland, OR 97225, (425) 297-4622, www.intercultural.org.

Kohls, L. R. (1996) "US proverbs and core values," in H. N. Seeyle (ed.), *Experiential Activities for Intercultural Learning*, Yarmouth, ME: Intercultural Press, pp. 79–81.

Kohls, L. R. (1999) "Conceptual model for country/area studies," in S. M. Fowler and M. G. Mumford (eds), *Intercultural Sourcebook: Cross-cultural Training Methods*, vol. 2, Yarmouth, ME: Intercultural Press, pp. 273–84.

Martin, J. N. and Nakayama, T. K. (2000) *Intercultural Communication in Contexts*, 2nd edn, Mountain View, CA: Mayfield.

Matsumoto, D. (director/writer) (2000) *A World of Diversity: Expanding Your Cultural Awareness*, video production available from Wadsworth Thomson Learning, P.O. Box 6904, Florence, KY 41022-6904, (800) 354-9706, www.thomsonlearning.com.

McCaffery, J. A. (1995) "The role play: a powerful but difficult training tool," in S. M. Fowler and M. G. Mumford (eds), *Intercultural Sourcebook: Cross-cultural Training Methods*, vol. 1, Yarmouth, ME: Intercultural Press, pp. 17–26.

Moorthy, R. S., De George, R. T., Donaldson, T., Ellos, W. J., Solomon, R. C. and Textor, R. B. (1998) *Uncompromising Integrity: Motorola's Global Challenge*, Schaumburg, IL: Motorola.

O'Mara, J. (1994) *Diversity Activities and Training Designs*, San Diego, CA: Pfeiffer.

Osland, J. S., Kolb, D. A. and Rubin, I. M. (2001) *Organizational Behavior: An Experiential Approach*, 7th edn, Upper Saddle River, NJ: Prentice-Hall.

Pusch, M. (ed.) (1979) *Multicultural Education: A Cross-cultural Training Approach*, Yarmouth, ME: Intercultural Press.

Samovar, L. and Porter, R. (eds) (2002) *Intercultural Communication: A Reader*, 10th edn, Belmont, CA: Wadsworth.

Sanford, N. (1966) *Self and Society: Social Change and Individual Development*, New York: Atherton Press.

Seelye, H. N. (ed.) (1996) *Experiential Activities for Intercultural Learning*, vol. 1, Yarmouth, ME: Intercultural Press.

Shirts, G. R. (1995) "Beyond ethnocentrism: promoting cross-cultural understanding with BaFá BaFá," in S. M. Fowler and M. G. Mumford (eds), *Intercultural Sourcebook: Cross-cultural Training Methods*, vol. 1, Yarmouth, ME: Intercultural Press, pp. 93–100.

Singelis, T. M. (ed.) (1998) *Teaching about Culture, Ethnicity, and Diversity: Exercises and Planned Activities*, Thousand Oaks, CA: Sage.

Steinwachs, B. (1995) "Barnga: a game for all seasons," in S. M. Fowler and M. G. Mumford (eds), *Intercultural Sourcebook: Cross-cultural Training Methods*, vol. 1, Yarmouth, ME: Intercultural Press, pp. 101–8.

Stewart, E. C. and Bennett, M. J. (1991) *American Cultural Patterns: A Cross-cultural Perspective*, Yarmouth, ME: Intercultural Press.

Storti, C. (1994) *Cross-cultural Dialogues: 74 Brief Encounters with Cultural Difference*, Yarmouth, ME: Intercultural Press.

Storti, C. (1999) "Cross-cultural dialogues," in S. M. Fowler and M. G. Mumford (eds), *Intercultural Sourcebook: Cross-cultural Training Methods*, vol. 2, Yarmouth, ME: Intercultural Press, pp. 203–9.

Storti, C. and Bennhold-Samaan, L. (1997) *Culture Matters: The Peace Corps Cross-cultural Workbook*, Washington, DC: Peace Corps.

Tannen, D. (writer) and ChartHouse International Learning (producer) (1994) *Talking 9 to 5: Women and Men in the Workplace*, video production available from ChartHouse International, 221 River Ridge Circle, Burnsville, MN 55337, (800) 328-3789.

Thiagarajan, S. (1991) *Games by Thiagi*, Bloomington, IN: Workshops by Thiagi.

Thiagarajan, S. (1994) *Lecture Games*, Amherst, MA: HRD Press.

Thiagarajan, S. and Thiagarajan, R. (1995) *Diversity Simulation Games*, Amherst, MA: HRD Press.

Ting-Toomey, S. (1999) *Communicating across Cultures*, New York: Guilford.

Trompenaars, F. and Hampden-Turner, C. (1998) *Riding the Waves of Culture: Understanding Diversity in Global Business*, 2nd edn, New York: McGraw-Hill.

Wurzel, J. (director) and Intercultural Resource Corporation (producer) (1994) *A Different Place: The Intercultural Classroom (part 1)* and *The Intercultural Classroom: Creating Community (part 2)*, video production available from Intercultural Press, Inc., P.O. Box 700, Yarmouth, ME 04096, (866) 372-2665, www.intercultural-press.com.

Wurzel, J. (director) and PBS Video (producer) (1990) *The Multicultural Workplace*, video production available from Phoenix Learning Group, 2349 Chaffee Dr., St. Louis, MO 63146, (800) 777-8100.

Wurzel, J. (director), Fischman, N. K. and Mayo, N. (producers) (2002) *The Cross-cultural Conference Room* [video and CD-ROM production]. Newton, MA: Intercultural Resource Corporation. (Available from Intercultural Press, Inc., P.O. Box 700, Yarmouth, ME 04096, (866) 372-2665, www.interculturalpress.com.)

Chapter 15

Shaping the global mindset

Designing educational experiences for effective global thinking and action

Martha L. Maznevski and Henry W. Lane

Introduction

In coping with globalization of markets, companies are establishing foreign operations and completing record numbers of cross-border mergers and acquisitions. However, globalization involves much more than geographical reach, whether that reach is expressed as operations in many countries or simply connecting through the Internet with computers in other countries. As the global economy continues to develop, managers must learn how to function as effectively in other countries as they do in their own country, and to bridge and integrate across the world by making use of both similarities and differences. Managers need to develop a global mindset.

A global mindset allows a manager to make decisions in a way that increases the ability of his or her company to compete effectively in the global economy. In this module, we argue that, although perhaps a global mindset cannot be *taught*, it can certainly be *learned*. To this end, we specify educational objectives to frame this learning. For these various objectives, we identify and discuss relevant pedagogical tactics (including educational experiences within traditional university curricula, executive education modules, and other types of programs) that can all be structured to facilitate and enhance the development of a global mindset.

Global mindset

The global mindset has mostly been discussed either in terms of personal characteristics and abilities possessed by managers, or in terms of its content, what executives need to know to function in the global economy. The four dimensions that tend to be included in the lists are: *attitudes*, such as curiosity and tolerance for ambiguity; *knowledge*, such as history and macro-economics; *business and management skills*, such as analysis and coordination; and *interpersonal effectiveness skills*, such as communication and team skills (e.g., Adler 1997; Bartlett and Ghoshal 1995; Czinkota *et al.* 1998; Francesco and Gold 1998; Govindarajan and Gupta 1998; Griffin and Pustay 1999; Harris and Moran 1991; Hill 2001; Jeannet 1998; John *et al.* 1997; Kets de Vries and Florent-Treacy 1999; Lane, DiStefano and Maznevski 2000; Mead 1994; Meier 1998; Rhinesmith 1992, 1995; Rosensweig 1998).

Content is important; it is necessary but not sufficient for success. The attitudes and skills described also are essential but not sufficient. A global mindset enables a person to adapt to the changing needs of global business. If we solely focus on content, we are preparing our students for the present, or perhaps the near future, but we do not help them prepare to meet long-term challenges. Conversely, solely talking about the right attitudes and skills does not necessarily develop such attitudes and skills.

Managers today do not have to be more capable than in the past, they must be differently capable (Wilson, Chapter 21 of this volume). The global mindset is a different capability. The heart of the global mindset is the ability to see and understand the world differently than one has been conditioned to see and understand it, and yet still to make sense of the world so as to act appropriately. A global mindset is a meta-capability that permits an individual to function successfully in new and unknown situations and to integrate this new understanding with other existing skills and knowledge bases. Our definition of a global mindset as a meta-capability is:

> The ability to develop and interpret criteria for personal and business performance that are independent from the assumptions of a single country, culture, or context; and to implement those criteria appropriately in different countries, cultures, and contexts.

A global mindset has two complementary aspects: a comprehensive cognitive *structure* that guides the noticing and interpreting of information; and a well-developed *competence* for changing and updating this cognitive structure with new experiences. A global mindset is a framework about global business that enables a person to pay attention, interpret, and behave effectively. The challenge in developing the cognitive structure that supports a global mindset is that it must allow for continuous change as the manager learns and as the environment changes. A useful structure, at least for initial development of a global mindset, is shown in Table 15.1.

The crux of developing a global mindset is achieving *self-awareness* and *other-awareness*, and more specifically the relationship between context – institutions, cultures, professions, and so on – and characteristics of the self and others. The second dimension – *individual* and *organizational* – provides a different perspective on global dynamics. It is important for managers to see themselves and others both as individuals and as

Table 15.1 An organizing structure for a global mindset

	Individual	*Organizational*
Self	Type 1: Myself Understand myself and how who I am is associated with the context I am in	Type 3: Own organizations Understand my own organizations and how their characteristics and effectiveness are associated with the context we are in
Other	Type 2: Others Understand how characteristics of people from other countries, cultures, and contexts are associated with the context they are in	Type 4: Other organizations Understand how characteristics and effectiveness of organizations from other countries, cultures, and contexts are associated with the context they are in

members of collaborative units, and to develop insights about individual and social behavior and perspectives.

A global mindset continually adapts universals of business to contextual contingencies. Since doing business globally is filled with uncertainty, amplified by numerous differences from country to country, the ability to tolerate ambiguity and to learn from new situations is critical to the global mindset.

Shaping the global mindset

A brief look at cognitive schemas illuminates some important processes for shaping a global mindset. A schema is developed through one of two processes – assimilation or accommodation (Furth 1970, writing about the research and psychology of Jean Piaget). In assimilation, new information is seen to be consistent with the schema and is incorporated readily, perhaps refining the details of the schema. In accommodation, new information contradicts the schema and thus the schema must be changed. As a cognitive structure, a global mindset should be developed initially through accommodation, and refined and redeveloped through iterations of assimilation and accommodation.

A key characteristic of accommodation is the *ability to articulate one's current schema accurately*. Without a realization that a current schema exists and shapes information processing, its limits cannot be identified and its inadequacy cannot be addressed with a new structure. Therefore, any learning aimed at the development of a new schema must incorporate explicit articulation of the current schema (Argyris and Schon 1978; Boyatzis 1995; Senge 1990; Tennant 1997; Woolfolk 1998).

Another important lesson from cognitive theory is the importance of feedback. A learner can only judge the appropriateness of a schema if its effects are made clear (Argyris and Schon 1978; Feldman 1986; Woolfolk 1998). Experiential learning is generally much more effective than passive knowledge acquisition in developing and influencing schemas: the experience usually provides immediate feedback (Kolb 1983). Research on schema development and change generates the following four statements that guide the development of educational experiences to shape the global mindset:

• Managers must understand their own schema and self, as an anchor point for any effective cognitive learning.
• Schema development and refinement require immersion in experiences together with accurate feedback.
• Effective complex schemas are developed through a process of building and bridging categories of knowledge and skills into a holistic, connected system of thinking.
• Effective learning is a continuous, ongoing process.

These four principles can be translated into educational objectives, which serve as foundations for developing educational experiences. The objectives are:

Objective 1: Develop students' ability to understand and describe their own schema;
Objective 2: Engage in relevant experiences with accurate feedback;
Objective 3: Develop students' ability to connect categories related to global business concepts and to develop generalizations; develop understanding of whole systems; and,
Objective 4: Provide opportunities to practice and to continue development.

It is also clear that using a broad variety of materials and methods is most effective for schema development and change. This is to capture different individual learning styles and to ensure information and principles are learned in many different ways. This finding generates a fundamental design principle:

Incorporate a wide variety of methods and materials (text, experiential, etc.), designed to maximize motivation, attention, retention, observation, and practice.

These educational objectives are summarized with the supporting research findings in the first two columns of Table 15.2. Pedagogical tactics flowing from each of the educational objectives are shown in column 3.

Table 15.2 Research-based educational objectives and pedagogical tactics for developing a global mindset

Educational objective	Research explanation	Suggested tactics[1]	Example
Describe own schema regarding universals/ specifics and relationships	• Effective schema development relies on explicit knowledge of own current schemas • Self is an important anchor in global mindset schema	• Provide discussion questions and assignments that explicitly require student to articulate his or her own worldview • Conduct self-assessments, debrief in context of schema development	• Self-assessment instruments measuring thinking style, learning style, values, culture, etc. • Ambiguous figure exercise, video cases, MBI framework • What criteria are important to you when you decide something is important? Explain them so others in the class will understand
Engage in relevant international experiences with accurate feedback	• Schemas developed from experiences • Effective schema development relies on accurate feedback concerning effects of behaviors	• Provide experiences, concrete as much as possible, vicarious when necessary • Engage students in experiences where they see and are faced with the consequences of behaviors, where they can receive answers they trust to questions about the effects of their own behavior in different contexts; concrete as much as possible, vicarious when necessary	• Travel experiences, cross-cultural and cross-situation experiences within traditional setting, with feedback concerning behavior • Experiencing Diversity Field Project • Cases (particularly sequential), videos • Simulations (behavioral, computer) such as BaFá BaFá with structured feedback session • Cooperative projects: stepped assignments or projects, distributed groups (over technology, members in different places)

1 Tactical Design Principle: use a wide variety of techniques, maximizing motivation, attention, retention, and observation practice. (From social learning theory, adult learning research.)

Table 15.2 continued

Educational objective	Research explanation	Suggested tactics[1]	Example

Develop connections, generalizations, categories related to global business; develop understanding of whole systems	• Schemas developed by drawing connections and relationships among experiences
	• Effective schema development from presentation of examples/non-examples, attributes/non-attributes
	• Effective schema development involves big picture, systems perspectives
		• Provide discussion questions and assignments that require student to develop his or her own connections
		• Students develop lists of examples/non-examples and categories of attributes/non-attributes themselves, with facilitation from instructor when necessary
		• Present students with perspectives and pictures that force them to move ever more broadly in their thinking (harder for younger students)
			• Fiction, foreign movies, and facilitation such as:
			  1 How was your first day at university like a trip to a newcountry? What skills do all business graduates need, regardless of their first job?
			  2 How was the decision in this case like/not like the decision in the last case? Did the video portray the same priorities as the case?
			• Projects for which each individual/group selects a different example of a category; class as a whole develops attributes by comparing the projects
			• Integrated project requiring students to understand a company's place in its global industry, industry's place in world economy

Practice ongoing development of universals, contingents, and relationships	• Effective schema development is ongoing, comes from inner and interpersonal dialect • Incorporates both assimilation and accommodation appropriately	• Require continual re-examination of the assumptions; integrate these strategies into whole program development • Encourage identification of assimilation and accommodation learning and situations that require them	• Disconfirming experiences • Integrating projects or themes that cross courses over time • Ongoing dialogue series; informal advisor relationships • Provide case examples of assimilation/accommodation in individuals, companies; require students to identify assimilation/accommodation learning in their own

1 Tactical Design Principle: use a wide variety of techniques, maximizing motivation, attention, retention, and observation practice. (From social learning theory, adult learning research.)

Shaping the global mindset in the classroom: frame-of-reference education

Many of our current educational tools (tactics) can be used effectively to pursue the objectives given above, but they must be implemented strategically, toward schema change and development, rather than exclusively toward knowledge acquisition – or even simple framework or tool development. Any international business curricular unit – a module, course, or entire program – can and should incorporate the methods that achieve the identified objectives.

Describe one's own schema

In developing a global mindset, it is important to be able to understand differences and similarities between "us" and "them." The need to understand "them" may be obvious. Understanding "us" is less obvious but critical to developing an effective global mindset. Describing our own schema can be uncomfortable and difficult, and is often resisted – it is just there, taken for granted. It is a skill in identifying universals and contingencies. How am I or we similar to and different from others?

Calling their schema into consciousness allows students to identify and examine aspects of their own views that they previously have taken for granted. Self-assessments provide one way to begin this process. To develop a global mindset, the self-assessment instruments should focus on dimensions that have been shown to vary by culture or context. Some of these include values (Schwartz 1994), learning or thinking styles (Abramson *et al.* 1993), and cultural orientation (Hofstede 1980; Maznevski *et al.* 1997; Trompenaars 1994). With standardized instruments, individuals can compare themselves with a set of norms, and also with classmates, to better articulate their own schemas. Students discover that context is associated with some very different basic assumptions we have about the world, and this leads to strong self-awareness. These revelations help people to build knowledge and categorize it in terms of universal truths and contingencies.

Ambiguous figures and perception exercises can be used to make the point about the relativity of the way in which people see and interpret the world around them. Perhaps the most well-known and most frequently used exercise involves the *Old Woman–Young Woman* image. The point of these exercises is to convey the idea that humans are limited information processors and that we select data from our environment to which we then respond. Data (behaviors, facts, etc.) are selected and interpreted based on our backgrounds such as education, life and work experiences, religious upbringing, culture, and language. These exercises also illustrate the point that we can interpret the same stimuli (data) differently. They can be used to examine the communication process (explaining the image from "my" viewpoint or trying to understand the other person's viewpoint) and the difficulty of helping people change their worldviews. Combining an understanding of cultural relativity with data about one's own schema in relation to others provides a base to begin examining differences in the work world.

Videos and case studies also can be used effectively to begin examining different maps that apply to the practice of management and the organization of work. Vignettes in videos such as those produced by Big World Media (www.bigworldmedia.com) can be used as "video cases" to create class discussions about different cultural views regarding task orientation, relationship building, management, empowerment, and collectivism versus individualism. Videos and other vicarious experiences can help build a broad understanding of what is universal, what is contingent, and how the two relate.

One framework that helps students to understand and compare different schemas and to integrate their learning is the Map, Bridge, Integrate (MBI) framework (Lane *et al.* 2000). The first component, Map, provides students with practice in identifying their own schemas (maps) about management practice and those of other cultures. The results of the self-assessment instruments or the analysis of the videos or cases provide the content of the "maps" which then can be compared and be the basis for rich discussions.

Engage in experiences with feedback

Experiential learning is usually highly motivating, and students report learning a great deal from it. However, experiences must be properly structured to provide feedback on the effects of one's behavior and to develop ideas about which concepts and behaviors are universal and which are contingent.

Simulations and role-plays provide opportunities for experience with feedback. One of the most popular behavioral simulations is BaFá BaFá, distributed by Simulation Training Systems (www.stsintl.com). In this simulation, participants are assigned to one of two "cultures" each with different rules. During visits to the opposite culture, participants try to play the other culture's "game" and to interact effectively in the other culture, without explicitly being told the rules. They obtain immediate feedback regarding their own behavior (with some individuals even being quickly and ruthlessly extradited for breaking a rule unknown to them). Well facilitated, it is highly effective at developing knowledge about cross-cultural interaction through experience and feedback (Sullivan and Duplaga 1997). Moreover, it also helps participants describe their own schemas and understand a schema's effect on cognition and behavior as well as possibly refine and change their mindset. It addresses multiple educational objectives simultaneously. In a careful debriefing, students see how their own perceptions, interpretations, evaluations, and behavior are strongly influenced by the rules with which they began. This provides them with the opportunity to revise their global mindset to incorporate this new insight (Sullivan and Duplaga 1997).

Field trips that provide opportunities to interact with people from other cultures and to shadow people conducting business in other countries are ideal. For maximum effectiveness, a field trip should include opportunities for action, then observing the effects of the action, reflection on this feedback, and another chance to interact in a different way. Any field trip aimed at developing a global mindset should require students to reflect on the experience in a formal way. This reflection should focus on what the student has learned about themselves, what they did well, what should be done differently next time, especially identifying some general and some context-specific ideas and guidelines for interaction.

If a trip abroad is not possible, then a volunteer or work experience in another local culture is a very good second choice. Some examples of cultural groups our students have entered include women's shelters, after-school programs for children, summer day-camp, child day-care, religious groups, the deaf community, the blind community, the gay community, food banks, senior citizens' residences, and various ethnic groups. We emphasize and reinforce the notion that culture does not necessarily mean national culture (Brannen 1999). Students then spend a period of time *in* the culture (at least two full days is recommended) in a way that allows participation rather than just observation. The emphasis in the fieldwork assignment is on experiential learning. The task is to *experience entering and dealing with another culture directly*. Students write a report (referred to as their "Diversity Field Report") about their reflection and insights – what they learned from the experience beginning with their entrance into the culture: feelings, lessons and insights, things confirmed or not confirmed, surprises – positive and negative. They should make links with the material covered in the course, international business, and previous experiences in another culture, if any. They should be striving to develop some patterns and some generalizations that might assist someone to function better in new cultural environments.

Develop systems thinking

To develop the systems thinking associated with a global mindset, students must generate generalizations. A *generalization* is a broad or general conclusion drawn from the observation of particular instances or situations. It has a quality of *insight* to it. The development of universal and contingent categories of knowledge and actions can be achieved through skillful questioning and facilitation of discussions. In every discussion on international management, instructors should guide students to build categories by continually asking how two or more things, ideas, or actions are similar or different. How is Coke like a Walkman? How is Nestlé like Procter & Gamble? How is NAFTA like the EU? And, of course, how are they different? Once students have begun to generate concepts and categories themselves, it is helpful to provide examples of concepts and associated characteristics already developed by others, for example through research – global products, global consumer goods companies, regional trading zones.

Published frameworks can also provide parts of the global mindset. For example, Hill (2001) has a useful framework for thinking about international strategic choices. However, given the importance of ongoing schema revision, students should also be guided in the process of how to evaluate others' concepts and frameworks, and to adopt only those that are valid by some explicit criteria (Gardner 1999).

Fictional pieces, movies from other cultures, and dialogue with people from other places are all very effective in the development of a global mindset, as they help to provide the contextual links for understanding how contingent knowledge and behaviors are related to universal ones (e.g., Puffer 1996).

A relatively efficient way of having students develop a more complex conceptual framework is to use a stepped approach. In this method, each student in a group, or each group in a class, completes an assignment or project on a single part of the category or concept. For example, in a course on doing business in Latin America, each group may complete a project on a different country or industry in this region. Next, the students share their learning with each other, through a presentation, circulation of report, web page, or some other means.

The final step is to have students explicitly develop a framework to compare and contrast the different elements of their own and each other's assignments, identifying dimensions that unite the ideas into one concept or category – Latin American business, in this case – while differentiating the ideas that need to be kept separate, such as effects of political systems. This framework can be constructed individually by students, for example as a class assignment or exam question, by the original project groups, by new groups composed of one member from each of the original groups. When this final step is incorporated into a module or course, students not only learn about business in Latin America, but they also learn how to develop their own generalizations and knowledge about global business.

Students must also develop a perspective that incorporates concepts into a larger systems view, seeing the relationship between, for example, being a global consumer products company and doing business in Chile. This is best accomplished over time throughout a course, and indeed throughout a curriculum. Students should be able to see, with guidance from the instructor if necessary, how the various topics and materials fit together. The objective of developing systems thinking requires instructors to guide the students as they connect the various elements in a course or other sequence. How does what we learned about interest and exchange rates earlier in the course help you understand the expatriate compensation issues here? We talked about the financial aspects of the DaimlerChrysler merger last month – how will the merged company deal with the cultural issues we've identified today?

Stepped assignments or projects can also be structured to facilitate systems thinking about global business topics. For example, a project on product entry into a new market can begin with product and potential target market (individual consumer characteristics) analysis, move to industry and cultural analysis, and finally develop an entry strategy taking into account potential competitor moves. As with projects to develop concepts and frameworks, sequencing is critical. If students are thrown the whole assignment at once, they may not develop an understanding of the individual components and the relationships among them. However, if the project's parts are sequenced carefully and the instructor guides the learning process, not the content or the outcome, the process is more likely to contribute to the development of a global mindset.

Practice ongoing development

In addition to developing specific categories of knowledge and behaviors and articulating the links between them, students must learn that a global mindset is continually being updated through new information. Moreover, they should become skilled at recognizing, rather than ignoring, information that disconfirms their current mindset and so sends a warning regarding possible need for revision of the mindset.

Obviously, ongoing development can only be practiced over time. Including this as an educational goal, then, requires deliberate coordination through a course and a program. One method is to have students complete an assignment, such as an analysis of a complex international business case, at two points in time separated by explicit course work addressed at developing a global mindset. The first analysis should be saved but not referred to in conducting the second analysis. Once the second analysis is completed, students should refer back to their first analysis. Some progress will be evident (hopefully), and the students should then analyze this progress in terms of how their thinking has changed in the interim.

Another effective but very difficult tactic is to present students with their own schemas, and engage the students either in defending the schema by agreeing with ridiculous propositions, or changing their schema. For example, a Latin American history professor once presented to a class of mostly U.S. undergraduate finance students a highly persuasive and eloquent argument that everyone in a capitalist society has free choice and equal opportunity, thus articulating their own schemas for them, while simultaneously giving them readings describing the lives and business of immigrant agricultural workers in California. The students responded immediately to the conflicting arguments and evidence the professor was providing. After they had convinced themselves that the professor was simply wrong in his lecture, they looked back at their own schemas and realized the need to change their own thinking as well. This frame-breaking experience opened them to reflection and revision in a way that other experiences could not have, and they also realized the importance of engaging in this kind of questioning frequently.

Modeling the process

The above analytical treatment gives several pedagogical suggestions and provides a way of thinking through curriculum design for developing a global mindset. However, its analytic nature does not question our own assumptions; it does not require us, as educators, to rethink how we conceptualize education. Until we do that, we cannot help our students effectively develop global mindsets.

Many business students have little or no international experience of the kind that would develop a global mindset and prepare them to take a strong role in global business. Indeed, their success throughout their academic and working careers has given them confidence in the mindset they have developed. To develop a global mindset, students must examine their own assumptions, question them, and re-contextualize them within a larger global picture. But given their high level of confidence in their current state of intellectual development, they are unlikely to engage in this process unless they are faced with strong evidence that their view of the world does not work as well as it should. We make this point in our textbooks, lectures, and discussions with students. But they are not likely to hear it if we deliver it in a way they are accustomed to learning in the first place.

In other words, we must confront our own schemas of teaching in order to help students develop their global mindset. If our program relies on lectures and discussions, instructors should consider how other methods could be used to at least begin the development of a global mindset. If a program is highly case-dependent, abstract lectures on in-depth topics from well-respected sources might signal that a new way of learning is important. Heretical as this sounds to most dedicated case teachers, it can actually work. For example, a graduating class of students who had engaged in case and problem-solving analyses for two straight years sat through a series of highly academic lectures on current global political economics and political analysis, and realized very quickly there were some important things about the world that they simply did not know. They began reading *The Economist* as thoroughly as the *Wall Street*

Journal, and sought other opportunities to understand global business from different perspectives, including history, religious studies, and other academic lectures at the campus. Then they returned to their case studies, but wearing a very different set of lenses and with much more comprehensive analyses and recommendations.

Most importantly, the pedagogical methods and materials must continually change with new students and new elements in the global business environment. As educators, we must model what we are trying to get students to do for themselves.

Conclusion

The global mindset is the ultimate international management tool. There is nothing more valuable we can impart to our students. But just as the global economy is asking managers and professionals to completely re-conceptualize what it means to do business globally, developing students who can do this requires us to re-conceptualize what it means to teach international business. In the business environment, this is a competitive imperative, and in our own institutions it is an educational imperative. The ideas and suggestions provided here can help us begin to address this dual imperative.

References

Abramson, N. R., Lane, H. W., Nagai, H. and Takagi, H. (1993) "A comparison of Canadian and Japanese cognitive styles: implications for management interaction," *Journal of International Business Studies,* 24 (3): 575–87.

Adler, N. J. (1997) *International Dimensions of Organizational Behavior,* 3rd edn, Cincinnati: South-Western College Publishing.

Argyris, C. and Schon, D. A. (1978) *Organizational Learning: A Theory of Action Perspective,* Reading, MA: Addison-Wesley.

Bartlett, C. A. and Ghoshal, S. (1995) *Transnational Management: Text, Cases, and Readings in Cross-border Management,* 2nd edn, Chicago: Irwin.

Boyatzis, R. E. (1995) "Cornerstones of change: building the path for self-directed learning," in R. E. Boyatzis, S. S. Cowen and D. A. Kolb, *Innovation in Professional Education: Steps on a Journey from Teaching to Learning,* San Francisco: Jossey-Bass, pp. 50–94.

Brannen, M. Y. (1999) "The many faces of cultural data," *AIB Newsletter,* first quarter.

Czinkota, M. R., Ronkainen, I. A., Moffett, M. H. and Moynihan, E. O. (1998) *Global Business,* 2nd edn, Fort Worth, TX: Harcourt Brace.

Feldman, J. (1986) "On the difficulty of learning from experience," in H. P. Sims Jr. and D. A. Gioia, *The Thinking Organization,* San Francisco: Jossey-Bass, pp. 263–92.

Francesco, A. M. and Gold, B. A. (1998) *International Organizational Behavior: Text, Readings, Cases, and Skills,* Upper Saddle River, NJ: Prentice-Hall.

Furth, H. G. (1970) *Piaget for Teachers,* Englewood Cliffs, NJ: Prentice-Hall.

Gardner, H. (1999) *The Disciplined Mind: What All Students Should Understand*, New York: Simon and Schuster.

Govindarajan, V. and Gupta, A. (1998) "Success is all in the mindset," *Financial Times*, February 2.

Griffin, R. W. and Pustay, M. W. (1999) *International Business: A Managerial Perspective*, 2nd edn, Reading, MA: Addison-Wesley.

Harris, P. R. and Moran, R. T. (1991) *Managing Cultural Differences*, 3rd edn, Houston, TX: Gulf Publishing.

Hill, C. W. (2001) *International Business: Competing in the Global Marketplace*, 3rd edn, Boston: Irwin/McGraw-Hill.

Hofstede, G. (1980) *Culture's Consequences: International Differences in Work-related Values*, Beverly Hills, CA: Sage.

Jeannet, J. P. (1998) "Strategists in the spider's web," *Financial Times*, January 14.

John, R., Letto-Gillies, G., Cox, H. and Grimwade, N. (1997) *Global Business Strategy*, London: International Thomson Business Press.

Kets de Vries, M. F. R. and Florent-Treacy, E. (1999) *The New Global Leaders: Richard Branson, Percy Barnevik, and David Simon*, San Francisco: Jossey-Bass.

Kolb, D. A. (1983) *Experiential Learning: Experience as the Source of Learning and Development*, Englewood Cliffs, NJ: Prentice-Hall.

Lane, H. W., DiStefano, J. J. and Maznevski, M. L. (2000) *International Management Behavior*, 4th edn, London: Blackwell.

Maznevski, M. L., DiStefano, J. J., Gomez, C. B., Noorderhaven, N. G. and Wu, P. (1997) "The cultural orientations framework and international management research," paper presented at Academy of International Business Annual Meeting.

Mead, R. (1994) *International Management: Cross-cultural Dimensions*, Cambridge, MA: Blackwell.

Meier, G. M. (1998) *The International Environment of Business: Competition and Governance in the Global Economy*, New York: Oxford University Press.

Puffer, S. M. (1996) *Management across Cultures: Insights from Fiction and Practice*, Cambridge, MA: Blackwell.

Rhinesmith, S. H. (1992) "Global mindsets for global managers," *Training and Development*, 46 (10), 63–9.

Rhinesmith, S. H. (1995) "Open the door to a global mindset," *Training and Development*, 49 (5), 34–43.

Rosensweig, J. A. (1998) *Winning the Global Game: A Strategy for Linking People and Profits*, New York: The Free Press.

Schwartz, S. H. (1994) "Beyond individualism/collectivism: new cultural dimensions of values," in U. Kim, H. C. Triandis, C. Kagitcibasi, S. C. Choi and G. Yoon (eds), *Individualism and Collectivism: Theory, Method, and Applications*, Thousand Oaks, CA: Sage, pp. 85–119.

Senge, P. M. (1990) *The Fifth Discipline: The Art and Practice of the Learning Organization*, New York: Doubleday.

Sullivan, S. E. and Duplaga, E. A. (1997) "The BaFá BaFá simulation: faculty experiences and student reactions," *Journal of Management Education*, 21 (2): 265–72.

Tennant, M. (1997) *Psychology and Adult Learning*, 2nd edn, London: Routledge.

Trompenaars, A. (1994) *Riding the Waves of Culture: Understanding Diversity in Global Business*, Burr Ridge, IL: Irwin.

Woolfolk, A. E. (1998) *Educational Psychology*, 7th edn, Boston: Allyn and Bacon.

Chapter 16

Limitations of the culture perspective in teaching international management

The case of transition economies

Tatiana Kostova

Introduction

Among the main objectives of international management education are making students aware of the differences that exist in individual behaviors and organizational practices across countries, providing theoretical frameworks that help students understand why these differences exist, and developing skills to analyze various environments and predict such cross-national differences. To achieve these objectives, international management research and education have typically focused on the concept of culture, which arguably shapes individual and organizational behaviors and leads to cross-national differences.

The teaching module presented in this chapter challenges the above approach by raising the question of whether examining culture and cultural variables is sufficient and/or effective for international management training. The module is built around the proposition that under certain conditions individual behavior becomes less influenced by national culture and more strongly influenced by other country-level variables, such as the dynamics of the political and the economic order in a given society. Thus, the culture perspective may be somewhat limited, and therefore should be supplemented by perspectives reflecting other country-level variables. For purposes of clarity of presentation, I refer to these other country-level factors as "institutional."

Module positioning and teaching objectives

This module can be taught as part of an International Management course at the undergraduate and graduate levels. I have used it in executive training as well, and in fact, this audience has had the most positive response to the proposed approach. It follows immediately after the culture module, which is toward the beginning of the course. It can be presented as an alternative to the culture approach and can be entitled, for example, "Institutional Context." Alternatively, it can be positioned as an extension and/or supplement to the culture framework. I personally like to begin the discussion of the module by framing it as a challenge (i.e., alternative) to the culture perspective, an approach which emphasizes the limitations of the traditional culture explanations and raises the interest level in the audience. However, it is important to end the discussion by framing it as an extension and a supplement to culture, a tool that further refines our conceptualization of social environments and helps develop a richer understanding of their effects.

The teaching objectives of the module are the following:

1   to demonstrate the limitations of the traditional culture perspective in explaining important cross-national differences;
2   to develop an understanding of the multi-faceted and complex social context in which individuals and organizations are embedded;
3   to recognize the impact of political and economic environments on individual and organizational behavior;
4   to discuss the relative salience of culture versus political and economic environments in different social conditions; and,
5   to develop and reinforce skills for analyzing cultural and institutional environments.

Session design

There are three major parts of the class session. Part One builds the case for the limitations of the culture perspective in explaining individual behaviors and organizational practices (objective 1 above). Part Two introduces an alternative conceptualization of external environments based on the institutional perspective (objective 2 above). Then it presents the specific case of transition economies as an illustration of the effects of political and economic changes on institutional environments, and consequently, on organizational behavior (objective 3 above). Part Three analyzes the conditions which determine the relative predictive power of the "culture" versus the "institutional" perspective (objective 4 above). Objective 5 is achieved through assigning pre-class individual research and by employing highly involved interactive teaching methods during the session. In my experience, ideally, the module should be taught in a one-and-a-half-hour session. However, it can be modified to fit shorter or longer sessions.

Part One: The limitations of the culture explanation

The goal in this part is to show that many patterns of organizational behavior and practices deviate from those that could be predicted from a cultural analysis of a country. I have used different approaches to initiate this part. First, students can be asked, in preparation for class, to do research on their own and bring examples of practices and behaviors that are inconsistent with the typical cultural profile of a nation.[1] This assignment can be formulated with different degrees of specificity, ranging from a broad question about practices that "strike you as very different from what you would expect given the cultural characteristics of the country" to a more specific question focused on a particular country or culture. Examples of such practices and behaviors can also be generated in class by asking similar questions. Alternatively, instead of involving students in the generation of examples, the instructor can prepare such examples and present them to the class. The advantages of the first approach are that students get more involved in the issues. The disadvantage is that some of the examples they suggest may not serve the teaching objectives very well. My preference is the second approach, as it saves class time and allows for a careful selection of instructive examples. The two criteria for selection of the examples are: (a) they must significantly deviate from the culturally predicted patterns, and (b) they must point to some similarities across otherwise culturally different environments. The latter point is important for developing the argument for the influences of institutional environments later in the class.

The following "caselet" is an example of a situation that could be brought to class for the above purposes. I will then use this case to illustrate the flow of the whole teaching module.

Behavior

The Kimberly-Clark Corporation started its Handan Comfort and Beauty Group joint venture in China with a Chinese partner in 1994 for the purposes of manufacturing feminine products for the local market. Despite the bumpy start and the many challenges in the start-up phases of the venture, it eventually took off and became successful. The operation in China was jointly managed by an American expatriate from the parent company and a Chinese manager appointed locally. In 1996, after three years of operation, the Kimberly-Clark officials in China noticed a nearby factory which was making similar products. Furthermore, they discovered that this "twin" plant used resources diverted from the joint venture, and most importantly, the Chinese manager of the joint venture was managing this plant as well. After trying to deal with this problem locally, Kimberly-Clark finally filed an official complaint with the U.S. embassy in Beijing, only to find out that they were not the only one to face this type of a problem and that there were dozens of American companies in a similar situation (Roberts, Power and Forest 1997).

Culture

After presenting this example, I ask the question, "Can someone describe for us the Chinese culture?" Typically, we would have covered China in our discussions on culture, but even if this had not been done in the previous class, students will be able to describe Chinese culture. Using Hofstede's (1980) work, for example, students would suggest that China is a highly collectivistic country with moderate power-distance and high masculinity, a country where people subscribe to the Confucian philosophy. Consistent with the culture perspective, it could be expected that these values will translate into attitudes and behaviors such as concern for others, putting societal and group interests above individual interests, an orientation towards social harmony and peace. Similar behaviors could also be predicted based on Trompenaars's (1993) work. For example, the high particularism on the "obligation" dimension of his framework, which he found typical for the Chinese culture, is associated with high levels of trust, long-lasting relationships between people, and a sense of duty to the group to which one belongs. The diffuse type of "involvement in relationships" is associated with non-confrontational attitudes and behaviors. Finally, the "saving face" concept, which is often recognized as a key cultural characteristic of the Chinese society, suggests avoidance of public humiliation, and therefore, compliance with behavioral rules, legal regulations, and social norms.

Consistency?

The next step of the discussion puts together the behavior and the cultural profile descriptions by asking the question, "Does what we know about Chinese culture explain what happened with Kimberly-Clark's joint venture?" The students see very quickly the inconsistency between the two. The more important question to address at this point is, "What, if not culture, could shed some light on why Chinese people behave in such a way?" Typically, the responses to this question will vary widely. Some will still try to "force" the example into the culture perspective by suggesting that perhaps the frameworks that we use (e.g., Hofstede, Trompenaars) are not good enough and miss on some important characteristics. Others may suggest that this particular case might be a cultural outlier as it falls out of the "culturally normal" profile. The problem with this explanation is that this is not an isolated case and, furthermore, there are other reported behaviors in China (e.g., bribery and corruption) which too are inconsistent with the cultural profile of that country. I have found that the most effective way to highlight the generalizability of such behaviors is to ask the Chinese students in class (if any) if this is in fact an exception or a frequent behavior. The answer has always been, "Of course, this happens a lot, we hear about such incidents all the time." The instructor could go a step further and challenge the Chinese students with the question, "Is it in your culture as a nation to cheat and steal?" Some may view such an approach as too aggressive and confrontational but it definitely helps make the point, once again, that the behaviors seen in this case, although widespread in China, cannot be predicted or explained by the culture perspective.

If time permits, the exercise can be repeated for another culture but I usually prefer to limit this part of the class session to one strong example only.

To summarize, Part One follows three main sub-parts:

- example of a widespread behavior in a particular country that seems surprising and unexpected given the cultural characteristics of the nation;
- analysis of the cultural profile of that nation;
- discussion of the inconsistency between the behavior and the culture.

This part ends with the conclusion that the culture perspective might be somewhat limited in explaining some typical behaviors in various countries.

Part Two: Introduction of the alternative "institutional" framework

The goal of this second part of the class session is to introduce additional aspects of national environments (e.g., political and economic) which may help explain better the "deviant" behaviors. I simplify the presentation by combining all these additional characteristics under the term "institutional."[2] The real challenge here is to be able to show: (a) that institutional characteristics are important dimensions of social context; (b) that they affect individual and organizational behaviors in a systematic way; and, (c) that people with different cultural background may engage in similar behaviors due to the similarity of the institutional environments they are facing.

A question that helps channel the discussion along these lines is, "Do you know of any other countries where people may engage frequently in such opportunistic behaviors like the ones shown in the Kimberly-Clark case?" Students, especially in culturally diverse classes, and those with richer experience, would quickly identify at least several such countries, for example, Brazil and Russia. Some would generalize to "the countries from the former Soviet Bloc" or "South American countries." The following question is, "Are the cultures of Brazil, Russia, and China similar in any way? If not [and the answer is, of course, no], why do we see these similarities in behaviors?" This usually triggers a lively discussion. If time permits it is interesting to allow several students to speculate on this issue. Eventually, the class will begin to identify several factors related to the social environments which seem to be similar across all these countries. The ones that most often emerge are political instability, vast economic changes and turbulence, and harsh social conditions (e.g., high unemployment).

Mini-lecture "The institutional perspective"

Building on the previous discussion, I suggest that, similar to culture, the economic conditions, the political order, and the social systems in a country are also important determinants of social behavior. I emphasize that there are a number of different organization theories interested in the influence of external conditions on organizations (e.g., Lawrence and Lorsch 1967). For our purposes, we focus on one of these perspectives, institutional theory (e.g., Scott 1995), which we find very instructive in explaining cross-national differences. I proceed with a short lecture on the institutional perspective, trying to specify, at a minimum, the following central ideas.

Central proposition

The main tenet of institutional theory is that societies tend to institutionalize, over time, certain structures and practices. These institutionalized practices and structures most often define what is considered legitimate (i.e., accepted and approved) in a given social entity. Consequently, organizations feel "pressured" to adopt such institutionalized practices because otherwise they may be viewed "illegitimate" by different constituents. As a result, organizations become similar to (or "isomorphic" with) each other. Thus, behavior and practices used by organizations are a product, not only of their national cultures, but also of the institutional environments they face.

Types of institutions

More specifically, institutional environments are characterized by three main types of institutions – regulatory, cognitive, and normative (Scott 1995, calls them "pillars"). The *regulatory* institutions consist of laws, regulations, and rules that define what is legally allowed. They serve as guidelines for reinforcing certain types of behaviors and restricting others. An example of a regulatory institution is the Foreign Corrupt Practices Act which was passed in the U.S. in 1977. Obviously, this regulatory institution has a direct impact on the behavior of people and on the organizational practices that companies use. *Cognitive* institutions are defined as the widely shared cognitive structures and social knowledge in a given environment. They reflect the shared understanding of how things are done in a given environment ("this is how we do things here"). As a result, certain behaviors become so common that they are taken for granted. An example of a cognitive institution could be the shared understanding among the members of a nation that you bribe customs officials if you want to get your job done quickly. Finally, the *normative* aspect reflects what is culturally acceptable in a given environment, what fits the social norms, the values of the people, and their belief systems. For example, a normative institution regarding bribery might suggest that there is nothing wrong with bribery, or the opposite – that it is completely immoral to bribe. The normative pillar is thus conceptually close to the concept of culture. Finally, the three institutional pillars tend to be interrelated and internally consistent. For example, the introduction of an environmental legislature (regulatory) is likely to create an understanding and a shared body of knowledge among people about environmental issues (cognitive), as well as a set of beliefs and values related to environmental protection (normative).

Emergence and evolution of institutions

Institutional systems are not fixed. They evolve and change over time as a result of the changing social factors in a particular environment. The impetus for a change may come from the macro social environment. In general, different configurations of key country-level characteristics, like the political system and the economic order, result in distinct sets of corresponding regulatory, cognitive, and normative institutions. These institutions, in turn, shape individual behaviors and organizational practices, as they make certain behaviors and practices allowed or required (regulatory), familiar, common, typical, or taken-for-granted (cognitive), and accepted or approved by the society at large (normative). For example, a changing political order may make certain behaviors illegal (e.g., communism banned free speech). A change in an economic principle may lead to a new understanding of what is legitimate business conduct (e.g., reducing trade barriers). The impetus for an institutional change may also come from within organizations and other social entities or even from an individual. Motorola's development of the Six Sigma practice, which was consequently adopted by General Electric and other companies, slowly rose to the status of an institutionalized way of managing quality in U.S. firms.

Furthermore, the change in the institutional system may be initiated in any of the three pillars – the regulatory, cognitive, or normative, and consequently, trigger changes in the other pillars. Continuing with the example from above, the impetus for institutional change in the area of environmental practices may have initially come from changing values and beliefs (i.e., normative pillar). These new emerging values communicated publicly have most likely led to creating an awareness of the implications of environmental practices among the wider population (cognitive pillar). Finally, under the pressure of changing values and awareness, a new legislation has been introduced to reflect these changes in values and social knowledge (i.e., regulatory pillar).

Environments and institutions

The goal here, after having introduced the main tenets of the institutional perspective, is to demonstrate that institutions affect business practices and organizational behavior. Instead of theorizing on this issue, I prefer using the case of transition economies as an example of how political and economic changes shape the institutional characteristics of these countries and how they, in turn, affect behaviors in organizations. While any type of a social environment can be used to illustrate these relationships, the transition economies example is very effective because it is extreme in many ways and helps build a strong case for the institutional perspective (versus culture). It is also very helpful for the analysis of the opening case of Kimberly-Clark.

Furthermore, for the purposes of flow and focus, I like to bring attention back to the behavior of opportunism and cheating that we considered at the beginning of the class. This can be done by asking a general question like, "How does the institutional perspective help us understand better the unexpected behaviors discussed in the beginning of the class?" To facilitate the discussion the instructor may offer additional questions such as, "How would you characterize the institutional environments in the countries that we discussed earlier – China and Russia, for example? Are they similar or different and in what ways? Do you see a link between these institutional characteristics and the tendency for opportunism that we have observed?"

I have found that this is a challenging task for students, and the most effective way to address it is to form small groups and ask them to discuss the question within the group. Eventually, the class will recognize that all these institutional environments share several common characteristics due to the state of transition in which they find themselves.[3] It is suggested to write these common characteristics on the blackboard for further discussion. Depending on the familiarity, or lack thereof, of students with transition economies, one might need to offer a brief description or even a mini-lecture on transition economies. In any case, it is important to frame this analysis within an institutional framework. The following presents briefly the main points that need to be emphasized.

Mini-lecture "Transition economies"

Goal of transition

In the mid-to-late 1980s, many countries from Europe, Asia, and South America launched massive social change programs for transition to a democratic political system and a free market economy.[4] For most Central and Eastern European (CEE) countries, the starting point was a centrally planned and state-controlled economy and an oppressive political system entirely dominated by a ruling communist party. While each country followed its unique model of transition, there were many common elements in the transition programs that reflect the core of the changes. The basic building blocks of the transition include liberalization, privatization, and industry restructuring. Although liberalization and privatization are common for Western market economies as well, the magnitude of the changes related to these programs in the former communist countries was unprecedented. For example, about 1,000 enterprises in the world were privatized in 1980–7. Compared to this, the number of state-owned enterprises subjected to privatization in some of the former communist countries after 1989 was much higher. In Hungary, there were about 2,000 large enterprises awaiting privatization, in Poland 7,500, and in China about 4,000. Thus, for example, if firms in China were to be privatized at the rate of one per week, it would take close to 80 years to complete the process.

Magnitude and scope

The transition to a market economy was accompanied by a large-scale and radical change in the regulatory system, as a myriad of laws and regulations supporting the market mechanism (often non-existent before or overthrowing the existing ones) had to be created and others had to be modified and adjusted. For example, each country developed and passed laws related to property, banks and credit, commerce and trade, international economic activity, taxes, bond and stock markets, antitrust, and social security, among others. The political changes were equally significant. For example, Bulgaria, formerly in the Soviet bloc, changed from a system in 1989 where the only players were the leading communist party, the agricultural union, and one trade union to a system with more than fifty political parties, three trade unions, three political blocs, and numerous public organizations (Kostova 1990). The biggest change, however, was related to the mindset and the philosophy of the people who not only had to learn the new rules of society and figure out how to live within the new system, but were also challenged to make sense of those changes, and to accept and approve them. Thus, the revolutionary changes in the regulatory institutional environment triggered equally substantial changes in the collective mindset of these nations as well as in their belief and value systems.

Social implications

Economic and political changes of such magnitude do not come without a social cost. The former full employment, fixed and secure jobs, stable wages, free healthcare and education, and many other social benefits were replaced by a sharp decline in employment (in some countries and periods the unemployment rate reached 25–30 percent), huge job uncertainty, four-digit rates of inflation, devaluation of currency, and loss of most social benefits. While the long-term goal of the reform was right, the short-term economic dynamics were traumatic. Figure 16.1 compares the fall of GDP in the CEE countries with that of the U.S. during the Great Depression and the Soviet Union during World War II. As seen, the economic distress experienced by CEE countries during the transition is far worse than in either of these historic periods. Data also show worsening of a number of indicators of the well-being of people. For example, in Russia the male life expectancy dropped from 64 in 1988 to 58 in 1995 and the death rate increased from 800 in 1988 to 1,100 per 100,000 population in 1995 (World Development Report 1996).

Institutional analysis[5]

It is important to conclude the presentation on transition economies with an explicit discussion of the main aspects from an institutional perspective. These can be summarized as follows:

- Radical change in all three types of institutions – regulatory, cognitive, and normative. For example, new laws and rules are introduced dealing with issues like competition and private ownership, new cognitive scripts gradually evolve that reflect societal knowledge about market economy (e.g., supply and demand, market pricing, marketing), and finally, new social values and beliefs emerge that make market behaviors acceptable and approved.
- Different pace and pattern of change of the three types. The regulatory institutions are usually the first to change. Furthermore, they tend to change in a more revolutionary rather than evolutionary manner. Thus, a law might be introduced at a particular point in time that automatically makes certain types of activities legal and others illegal. As a result, the changes in the regulatory environment typically have a direct and immediate effect on

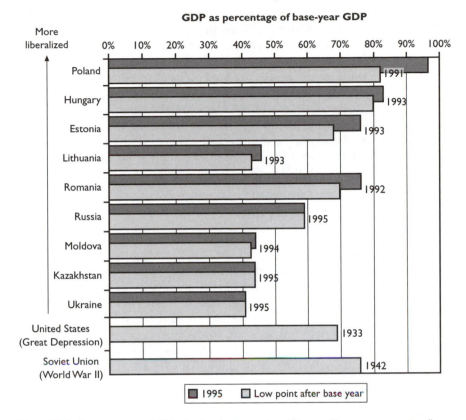

Figure 16.1 Comparison of GDP decline in Central and Eastern European counties (base year 1989) with United States GDP during Great Depression and Soviet Union GDP during WWII.

Note
The base year for the transition economies is 1989; historical base years are 1929 for the United States and 1940 for the Soviet Union. Data source: World Bank (World Development Report 1996).

behaviors and practices. Cognitive institutions are second in terms of rate of change and may have a more evolutionary or gradual change pattern. It takes time to create new cognitive scripts based on new individual experiences, to disseminate the scripts through the educational system or social interactions, and to form, as a result, new cognitive institutions shared among members of society about how "we do things here." Normative institutions are even harder and slower to change. Since the deeply ingrained cultural values and beliefs are at the core of self-identity, every change departing from those values and beliefs is typically viewed as a threat to individual and social identity. Consequently, people are likely to actively resist such changes.

- Turbulence and instability of the overall institutional environment. The broad scope of changes that take place in all types of institutions and with regard to almost all facets of social life in these economies creates an enormous instability. Furthermore, the different pace of change discussed above may lead to situations where the three pillars are inconsistent with each other in terms of what is required, typically done, or socially expected. That is, there will be a period of time during which the social norms or the social knowledge will be lagging behind and may be inconsistent with the regulations.

Transition and business behaviors

The next questions are, "Do you think that these characteristics affect in any way the behavior of people and the organizational practices used in transition countries? Would it affect you, for example, if the GDP in your country had shrunk by 50 percent and if the rules for doing business changed almost every day?" By this time, students should be able to clearly see the impact of such an institutional context. They will recognize that transition environments tend to send confusing messages about what is socially required, permissible, and desirable. As a result, social context becomes less salient in shaping individual behavior, and behaviors become less predictable and less isomorphic. People start experimenting with a variety of behaviors that might help them survive in the new system.

Furthermore, such a social context may in fact lead to the formation of a new "culture of transition" which guides behavior. Central characteristics of the culture of transition are high individualism and selfishness, as people are focused on their personal survival and the survival of their families during hard times. Thus, even those from traditionally collectivistic countries may become extremely individualistic during such a period. People will also become more opportunistic as they experiment with various behaviors and try to take advantage of the situation, and more "masculine" because of a strong pressure to compete for scarce resources and the related lack of concern for others. The culture of transition is also characterized by high uncertainty-avoidance (due to the lack of alternatives) and short- rather than long-term orientation. It is typical, in these countries, for employees to become cynical about work as they see how manipulation, "smartness," and "con-man-ship" flourish in the absence of well-established and enforced legal systems. Finally, they are likely to engage in "testing" and "trying out" foreign cultures or behaviors that were not allowed in the past (e.g., religion, pornography).

Rather than using the lecture format for this last section, I try to involve the students in deriving the common characteristics of the transition culture. It helps if there are students who are originally from or who have some experience in transition economies. This discussion usually produces very interesting (often peculiar) examples and students tend to enjoy it.

To summarize, Part Two of the module consists of three sub-parts:

- introduction of the institutional perspective;
- analysis of the institutional environment in transition economies;
- discussion of the impact on behavior and attitudes.

This part ends with the conclusion that the institutional perspective can be used to analyze different country environments and that institutions affect individual behavior as illustrated by the case of transition economies.

Part Three: Culture or institutions?

The goal of this final part of the class session is to compare the two alternatives – culture and institutions. I like to start with the question, "So far in this class, we have discussed two alternative ways of conceptualizing national environments and their influence on individuals: the culture perspective and the institutional perspective. Which one, do you think, is more powerful in explaining country differences in organizational behaviors?" For the purposes of engaging the students in active participation, I usually ask them to vote for one perspective, and I record the votes on the blackboard. After that, we have a short discussion of why they voted one way or the other. The two groups, formed as a result of the voting, usually present good arguments for "their" perspective. Many will suggest that it is difficult to choose one over the other because they are both relevant. There are several important points that need to be drawn from this discussion:

a   The two perspectives are not independent. On the contrary, political and economic environments which shape institutions also influence culture (i.e., values, norms, and beliefs). Thus, changes in the political and economic contexts are accompanied by changes of the culture as well.
b   However, culture and institutions change at a different pace. Due to its nature, culture usually lags behind the other macro-changes. While some of the regulations can change overnight, modifying value and belief systems may take a long time, especially when the change challenges the old values in a substantial way. Examples from transition economies again may help strengthen this point. Other examples may include intergenerational differences and how younger people in transition economies are quicker to adopt the new culture.
c   In stable environments with mature institutional infrastructure,

culture is consistent with the other parts. In such contexts, the regulatory rules, cognitive scripts, and social norms have evolved together influencing and shaping each other and, as a result, have formed a coherent and harmonious institutional system. Therefore, the effects of all three types of institutions on the behavior of people and organizations are likely to be similar, if not identical, and one could explain and predict variations based on any of these three elements including culture. For example, if we consider the institutional environment in China ten years ago regarding the particular issue of private ownership, we could suggest that the regulatory rules that existed in that country at that time, the social knowledge about private ownership, and the cultural norms and values that society used to attach to private ownership were all consistent with each other. Basically, private ownership was not legally allowed, was not something that people understood or took for granted, and also was considered morally wrong. The resulting behaviors of people and organizations relating to private ownership were in accord with all three elements of the institutional system.

d   In unstable and radically changing institutional environments, the predictability of individual and organizational behavior based on institutional context, and even more so based on culture, decreases significantly. When all key elements of the environment are changing and the different elements are not consistent with each other, it is difficult for people to make sense of the social context and to identify the best survival strategies. In an attempt to find those, people will tend to engage in a variety of behaviors not necessarily consistent with any one of the institutional pillars. Both individuals and organizations will start experimenting in ways which may go against their values and beliefs and break new cognitive ground. These attempts to find the most effective path within a contradictory and confusing social context will result in opportunistic behaviors and may even lead to criminal acts prohibited by the regulatory system. Furthermore, in such conditions, culture becomes less of a factor shaping behavior because the central cultural values and beliefs are questioned and challenged by the social changes, and because it is less proximal to behavior compared to cognition, and even more so to regulatory rules. Thus, due to the changing nature of the social environment and the different pace of change of its various aspects, behaviors in general will be less consistent, predictable, and guided by the institutional context. The regulatory institutions, if any at all, are likely to become the major contextual influence on behavior as most people and organizations will try to at least stay within the legally permissible range of activities.

This part of the class session concludes with the statement that under certain conditions (e.g., unstable, changing institutional environment), culture loses its predictive power and behaviors are better explained by the new regulatory and cognitive orders. Because of the similar patterns of social change in all transition economies and the similar effects of these changes on individuals, the culture of transition spans national borders. Thus, similar patterns of behavior are observed in countries which have significantly different traditional cultural profiles. This explains why most people from transition economies (Chinese, Brazilians, and Russians, among others) tend to engage in similar behaviors – some constructive and oriented toward learning and personal development to adapt to the new conditions; others opportunistic and less constructive, such as bribery and corruption.

Conclusion

In conclusion, it is important to note that the institutional alternative introduced in this class does not, in any way, question the undisputed value of studying culture. Instead, it extends further the culture paradigm by specifying its boundary conditions. The most effective learning about probable behaviors in a particular country will be achieved if both the culture and the institutional perspectives are used in combination and the links between them are explored. Together, these two perspectives provide a deeper understanding of social context.

Notes

1 It should be noted that, by this time, students already have been familiarized with culture and have developed cultural profiles of different nations in the preceding class.
2 It should be noted that, for our purposes here, the term "institutional" is used a bit loosely.
3 I find the case of transition economies very instructive for illustrating how the nature of the institutional environment influences and explains organizational behaviors.
4 For the purposes of this presentation, I will primarily use the case of the countries in Central and Eastern Europe.
5 If time permits, this can be done in small group discussions rather than in a lecture format.

Further reading

Adler, N. (1997) *International Dimensions of Organizational Behavior*, Cincinnati, OH: South-Western College Publishing.
Earley, C. and Erez, M. (1997) *The Transplanted Executive*, New York: Oxford University Press.

Erez, M. and Earley, C. (1993) *Culture, Self-identity, and Work*, New York: Oxford University Press.

Hall, E. (1973) *The Silent Language*, Garden City, NY: Anchor Books.

Kluckhohn, F. and Strodtbeck, F. (1961) *Variations in Value Orientations*, Evanston, IL: Row, Peterson.

Triandis, H. (1995) *Individualism and Collectivism*, Boulder, CO: Westview Press.

Zucker, L. (1987) "Institutional theories of organization," *Annual Review of Sociology*, 13: 443–64.

References

Hofstede, G. (1980) *Culture's Consequences: International Differences in Work-related Values*, Beverly Hills, CA: Sage.

Kostova, T. (1990) "Organizational innovations in Bulgaria," in R. Schwartz (ed.), *Managing Organizational Transitions in a Global Economy*, Institute of Industrial Relations, University of California, Los Angeles, pp. 169–90.

Lawrence, P. and Lorsch, J. (1967) *Organization and Environment*, Cambridge, MA: Harvard University Press.

Roberts, D., Power, C. and Forest, S. (1997) "Cheated in China," *Business Week*, October 6, pp. 18–20.

Scott, R. (1995) *Institutions and Organizations*, Thousand Oaks, CA: Sage.

Trompenaars, F. (1993) *Riding the Waves of Culture: Understanding Cultural Diversity in Business*, London: Economist Books.

World Development Report (1996) *From Plan to Market*, published for the World Bank by Oxford University Press.

Chapter 17

Reflective silence
Developing the capacity for meaningful global leadership

Nancy J. Adler

> We are a busy people in a busy corporate culture. But even the busiest person wants wisdom and sense in busyness. . . . All of us want to work smarter rather than harder. Yet all of us are familiar with frantic busyness as a state that continually precludes us from opening to the quiet and contemplation it takes to be smart.
>
> (Whyte 1994: 98)

Introduction

Following the experience of most profound wisdom traditions, Harvard professor Howard Gardner identifies reflection as one of the three competencies (along with leveraging and framing) that distinguish extraordinary leaders from ordinary leaders and managers. According to Professor Gardner,

> Reflection means spending a lot of time thinking about what it is that you are trying to achieve, seeing how you are doing, continuing if things are going well, correcting course if not; that is, being in a constant dialectic with your work, your project or your set of projects and not just going on blind faith [for extended periods] without stepping back and reflecting.
>
> (Gardner, 1998: 20)

Management and leadership, both as they are taught and as they are practiced, focus primarily (and in some cases, exclusively) on action, rather than reflection. This module is designed to bring back the possibility of extraordinary global leadership through reintroducing daily rituals of quiet, reflection, and contemplation.

The period of reflective silence

Introduce the concept of guarding time daily for reflection. Use the introductory paragraph (above) to explain the relationship between reflection and extraordinary leadership. Ask participants to brainstorm ways in which they currently guard time for reflection (such as by writing in a journal, meditating, closing the door and being quiet, taking a walk alone, practicing tai chi). Recognize that many of us, including many professors, guard little or no time for reflective silence. With participants, brainstorm forces in our organizational culture that support or undermine reflective silence. If participants come from multiple cultures, ask them how their particular culture supports people's choice to participate in a daily practice of reflective silence and how the culture undermines it.

Start with very short periods of reflective silence at the beginning of each session (two to three minutes). I use one of a number of ways to introduce sessions, including:

- Reading a brief inspirational or reflective quote. Some of poet David Whyte's quotes are particularly helpful for initially framing the necessity and challenge of contemplation in leaders' overly active lives. For example, "A soulful approach to work is probably the only way an individual can respond creatively to the high-temperature stress of modern work life without burning to a crisp in the heat" (1994: 98–9).
- Asking a deep, personal question about the implications of the material participants are discussing in the seminar.
- Inviting silence. Simply suggest that each person become quiet.
- Ringing a chime to signal the beginning and end of the period of reflective silence.

As the seminar progresses and participants begin to look forward to the period of reflective silence, it can be lengthened to approximately ten minutes and less structure can be used to initiate each session. Periods of reflective silence can be held at both beginning and end of each session.

Supporting structure for reflective silence

Introduce recommended, but optional, readings

Periods of reflective silence can be designed into seminar sessions with no pre- or post-session readings and with no accompanying assignments. The readings and assignments listed here are suggested strictly to deepen participants' understanding of the role of the reflective experience and more explicitly to tie reflection into global leadership.

Optional pre-readings to introduce the importance of reflection for managers and leaders

Peter Drucker's (1999) "Managing oneself" and Jim Loehr and Tony Schwartz's (2001) "The making of a corporate athlete" clearly and succinctly explain why reflection is crucial to effective leadership. Use the Drucker article to reflect upon the question: *To what extent do you think the ability to "manage oneself," as described by Drucker, is related to global leadership? How is it similar to and different from your personal conception of global leadership?*

Optional readings to introduce global leadership that makes a difference

Academic as well as popular management literature often confuses management with leadership, and rarely distinguishes ordinary from extraordinary leadership. Adler's *International Dimensions of Organizational Behavior* (2002b: Chapter 6) and her *From Boston to Beijing: Managing with a Worldview* (2002a) introduce the notion of global leadership as distinguished from both domestic leadership and management. Adler's brief article, "Leading: giving yourself for things far greater than yourself" (2001) challenges managers and leaders to address issues of significance, issues that make a difference.

Optional readings to introduce the relationship between extraordinary global leadership and reflection

Howard Gardner's book, *Leading Minds: An Anatomy of Leadership* (1995) supports, with research, the fact that extraordinary leaders – leaders who make a significant difference in the world – reflect on a daily basis. Recommended readings include the Preface and Summary chapter, or, for a more in-depth understanding of extraordinary leadership, the entire first section. Gardner's hour-long videotape program, *Creativity and Leadership* (Gardner 1998) is also excellent for introducing what we know about extraordinary leaders.

Optional readings to explore the relationship between action and reflection

Parker Palmer's books (including *The Active Life: A Spirituality of Work, Creativity, and Caring* (1990); "Leading from within," Chapter 5 in *Let Your Life Speak: Listening for the Voice of Vocation* (2000); and *The Courage to Teach: A Guide for Reflection and Renewal* (1999)) offer philosophical – rather than managerial – reasons why meaningful action in the world requires a balance between action and contemplation. *The Active Life* is particularly good for looking at the necessary relationship between authentic action and contemplation. *Let Your Life Speak* is excellent for looking at the issue of calling, of doing the work each of us is meant to do in the world. *The Courage to Teach* is recommended primarily for professors, rather than participants. While participants often find these readings quite meaningful, most also find them difficult and slow to read. Palmer at times uses Christian imagery to make his points, which creates a barrier for many participants. When I recommend the Palmer readings, I always warn participants that they are "slow reading" and to ignore the Christian imagery if it is not helpful to them.

Highly recommended, optional, readings to introduce leadership that address profoundly meaningful and significant global leadership issues

What Does it Mean to Be Human? (Franck *et al.* 2000) is a collection of very short, personal leadership stories. It unequivocally raises the issue of why leaders must address profoundly meaningful "big-picture" issues, and what the personal costs are both in addressing and in failing to address issues of meaning and substance. The stories address such issues as calling, authenticity, the ability to see reality (what Parker Palmer refers to as "collusion against illusion"), hope, despair, and optimism.

David Whyte is often referred to as the poet of corporate America. His book, *The Heart Aroused* (1994), addresses what it means to bring soul back into the workplace – what it means to hold courageous conversations on an ongoing basis with ourselves, our work, our colleagues, and the global society within which we live. In his most recent book, *Crossing the Unknown Sea*, Whyte defines work as "an opportunity for discovering and shaping the place where the self meets the world" (2001: jacket cover).

Sources of additional quotes for reflection sessions

Two of my favorite sources, in addition to *What Does it Mean to Be Human?* (Franck *et al.* 2000) and *The Heart Aroused* (Whyte 1994), are *Earth Prayers* (Roberts and Amidon 1991) and *Coming Home to Myself* (Woodman and Mellick 1998). *Earth Prayers* is a collection of 365 prayers, poems, and invocations from around the world for honoring the earth and our relationship to the earth. *Coming Home to Myself* is a collection of quotes, directed primarily at women, but highly meaningful for men also, taken from a number of the books by Jungian analyst Marion Woodman. Many echo the theme of reflection and knowing oneself as a precursor to acting effectively in the world. *The Circle and the Square* (Adler and Lew forthcoming) combines a number of quotes, stories, and paintings, many based on ancient Chinese wisdom stories, which echo today's challenges of global leadership.

Introduction to assignments

No assignments are necessary to include with the periods of reflective silence. The following optional assignments can be used, however, to further seminar goals and to support participants' understanding of the important relationship between reflective silence and profound leadership.

What Does it Mean to Be Human?

Introduce the book, *What Does it Mean to Be Human?* (Franck *et al.* 2000), by using the following assignment. The assignment can be included at the beginning of the seminar, or used in parts throughout the seminar.

I LEADERSHIP: WHAT DOES IT MEAN TO BE HUMAN?

To lead is to see reality for what it is. Yet to see the current state of our planet and civilization is to risk falling into despair. Returning to the question "What does it mean to be human?" – as opposed to the questions "Why is there such barbarity in the world?" and "Why do we treat each other with such inhumanity?" – is one way to transcend our despair and return to a clearer vision of what we, as human beings, are collectively capable of being and doing. Without clearly seeing reality and transcending despair, true global leadership remains impossible.

2 WRITE: WHAT DOES IT MEAN TO YOU TO BE HUMAN?

To choose to be a global leader is to choose to attempt to improve, in some way, the state of humanity and our planet while increasing the performance of the particular organization one leads. In 1–2 pages, describe what being human means to you.

3 READ: *WHAT DOES IT MEAN TO BE HUMAN?*

After personally responding to the question "What does it mean to be human?," read the responses of people from around the world in *What Does it Mean to Be Human?* (Franck *et al.* 2000). As you read others' responses, note any words, phrases, paragraphs, thoughts, or observations that are particularly meaningful or helpful to you as a person and as a current or future global leader. These are the thoughts that would be helpful to the people you work with for maintaining their sense of aspiration, vision, and motivation, as well as helping them to escape the inevitable descent into despair that accompanies any leader's worthy efforts. As you read the stories in the book, you may find yourself altering your own response to the question, "What does it mean to be human?" Go ahead and write new versions of your response, but keep a journal with each response so you can track the development of your thinking.

4 WRITING YOUR STORY: CALLING AND COMMITMENT

Many stories in the book describe people's calling – those life experiences and decisions that led them to make a life commitment to the type of work they are doing in the world and their particular approach to leadership. As you read the stories, think about the events and decisions in your own life that have led you, and are leading you, to make your own personal commitment to the work you are doing, or wish to do, in the world. How would you tell your story?

5 IN CLASS: TELLING YOUR STORY

Bring *What Does it Mean to Be Human?* (Franck *et al.* 2000) to class along with your thoughts on what it means to you to be human and your thoughts on your personal experiences and decisions that have led to your commitments. You will only be asked to share those aspects of your thinking that you wish to make public – so please be as honest as possible with yourself in your journal, even if you choose to share none of your current thinking with a wider audience.

Selected quotes for introducing periods of reflective silence

The following section lists a number of quotes that I use regularly from *What Does it Mean to Be Human?* (Franck *et al.* 2000) and *Earth Prayers* (Roberts and Amidon 1991) to introduce periods of reflective silence. In certain cases, I have altered or added material to the original quote to tie it more directly into global leadership. In all such cases, changes are bracketed and marked NJA, for Nancy J. Adler, to differentiate my wording from the author's original wording.

Professors and participants should select readings, quotes, and poems that best fit their particular seminar. After presenting the stories and quotes I have selected myself for the first few periods of reflective silence, I invite participants to select their own readings. Whether or not participants actually choose to select their own poems and quotes to read, it is important to invite them to do so.

Selected quotes from What Does it Mean to Be Human?
(Franck et al. 2000) that I have used to introduce periods of
reflective silence in various leadership seminars

INTRODUCING THE PRACTICE OF REFLECTIVE SILENCE

To live is to write one's credo, every day in every act. I pray for a world that offers us each the gift of reflective space, the Sabbath quiet, to recollect the fragments of our days and acts. In those recollections we may see a little of how our lives affect others, and then imagine in the days ahead, how we might do small and specific acts that create a world we believe every person has a right to deserve.

(Arthur Frank: 236)

VISION: WHY LEAD? WHY SOCIETY NEEDS EXTRAORDINARY GLOBAL
LEADERSHIP

To be human is not always to succeed, but it is always to learn. It is to move forward despite the obstacles. [NJA: To lead is not always to succeed, but it is always to learn. It is to move forward despite the obstacles.]

(David Krieger: 264)

[It is for us] to return to our original task of *Tikun Olam*, the restoration of the world.

(Rabbi Avraham Soetendorf: 26)

To be human is to find ourselves behind our names. [NJA: To lead is to find ourselves behind our names.]

(David Krieger: 264)

What you do in response to the ocean of suffering may seem insignificant but it is very important you do it.

(M. K. Gandhi: 66)

We have abandoned the concerns of the civilizations before us. We have forsaken the good, the true and the beautiful for the effective, the powerful and the opulent. We have abandoned enoughness for the sake of consumption. We are modern. We are progressive. And we are lost.

(Joan Chittister: 152)

At every opening talk [to refugee children of war], I would put a big picture of the planet up and we would start to relate to that planet as home, as a living entity. We would start to talk about what we were like as children. What were our hopes? What did you believe in? What did we believe was possible? How big was our vision? People would say, "My vision was big – anything was possible." Then I would ask, "What do you believe now?" and the reply would be, "Well, not as much is possible." [Leadership] ... is helping people to reconnect with the vision that anything is possible.

(Judith Thompson: 211–12)

What good is ascending the mountain if all we do is make ourselves holy? The point is to serve, to offer, to be the offering.

B. T. Glassman (from Franck *et al.*, 1988: 83)

We are all born with the potential to become human. How we choose to live [and to lead] will be the measure of our humanness. Civilization does not assure our civility. Nor does being born into the human species assure our humanity. We must each find our own path to becoming human. [NJA: We must each find our own approach to leading that reflects our humanity.]

(David Krieger: 264)

To be human is to give yourself for things far greater than yourself. [NJA: To lead is to give yourself for things far greater than yourself.]

(Joan Chittister: 151)

LEADING: GAINING AND OFFERING NEW PERSPECTIVES

If the signals we are sending into space hoping to contact extra-terrestrial intelligent life hit their targets, and such intelligent life has in turn detected and observed us, we don't have to fear invasion – even if minimally intelligent, they would prudently avoid all contact with our dangerous planet.

(Richard Chapman: 44)

LEADING TOWARD WIN–WIN SOLUTIONS

That victory never leads to peace is not a theoretical affirmation, but an empirical statement.

(Raimon Panikkar: 63)

LEADER'S RESPONSIBILITY FOR THE FUTURE

"Whatever we do today [NJA: How we lead today]," Dewasenta, clan-mother of the Onodaga Nation, said to me, "we should never endanger the seventh generation to come. As we walk through life, the seventh generation is looking at us from the ground. Therefore we should walk gently."

(Claus Biegert from Franck *et al.* 1998: 180–1)

INFLUENCE OF CULTURE

We are all culturally hypnotized from birth! It explains so much!

(Willis Harman: 80)

[A]waken in us a perspectival vision – the ability to see situations from many different perspectives and thus from a more compassionate vantage point. Perhaps ... technology, along with eco-crises and multinational commerce both of which transcend national borders, though they have the potential for gross misuse, can, if dealt with wisely, catalyze the expanded consciousness out of which generosity and compassion would arise spontaneously in our collective heart as a response to the barbarism of the day.

(Ram Das: 66)

To be human is to break the ties of cultural conformity and group-think, and to use one's own mind. [NJA: To lead is to break the ties of cultural conformity and group-think, and to use one's own mind.]

(David Krieger: 263)

All nations tell stories of wisdom and hope. In India, there is a story of a highly respected elder who was confronted by youngsters plotting to embarrass him. One youngster held a beautiful bird behind his back. The group said to the elder, "There's a bird, is it alive or dead?" If he replied, "It is alive," the youngster would kill the bird by squeezing its neck to prove the elder was wrong. If he replied, "It is dead," the youngster would release the bird to fly away and again prove the elder wrong. When the youngsters repeated three times, "There's a bird, is it alive or dead?" the elder thought deeply and replied, "It is in your hands." [NJA: Leadership; it is all in our hands.]

(Leonard Marks: 115–16)

I experience my culture and myself shaping each other in a dance. . . .

(Donella Meadows: 68)

I had the most extraordinary experience of love of neighbor with a Hindu family. A man came to our house and said: "Mother Theresa, there is a family who have not eaten for so long. Do something." So I took some rice and went there immediately. And I saw the children – their eyes shining with hunger. I don't know if you have ever seen hunger. But I have seen it very often. And the mother of the family took the rice I gave her and went out. When she came back, I asked her: "Where did you go? What did you do?" and she gave me a very simple answer: "They are hungry also." What struck me was that she knew – and who are they? A Muslim family – and she knew. I didn't bring any more rice that evening because I wanted them, Hindus and Muslims, to enjoy the joy of sharing.

(Mother Theresa: 86–7)

HOPE, DESPAIR, MEANING, AND THE SHADOW SIDE OF LEADERSHIP

The soul would have no rainbows if the eyes had no tears.

(Annelie Keil, Native American saying: 228)

Welcoming the dark as no more than the light's shadow, realizing all I am without, and all that I am within.

(Gillian Kean: 137)

At school we are programmed to give science and technology the last word, but in the maelstrom of our civilization we long to hear the first word.

(Ramon Munoz Soler: 251)

To be human is to take joy in meaning.

(Robert Aitken: 129)

Life is not a program. It seems to be an invitation.... [NJA: Leadership is not a program. It is an invitation.]

(Annelie Keil: 229)

Becoming more and more imprisoned behind the walls of separation and competition, our society is losing the human language of sharing and of communality. The gap between rich and poor, between nations, between races is increasing. Dizzied by our capacity to destroy, we have moved away from reality and have come to believe in a "virtual reality" produced for the purpose of making money. We are living in a century of arrogant stupidity. An ancient wisdom has been replaced by intellectual narcissism and extreme ignorance. Our true source of wisdom is life itself, and in the imperishable ever-present and specifically human there is hope. [NJA: Our true source of leadership is life itself, and in the imperishable ever-present and specifically human there is hope.]

(Annelie Keil: 230)

LEADERSHIP: ENOUGH IS MORE THAN ENOUGH

A Chinese proverb says that when a human being or a society or a community or a nation does not know when enough is enough, however much they have they will never have enough; but when a

human being or a community or a nation or a society knows when
enough is enough, they will realize that they already have enough.

(Satish Kumar: 184)

Carved in stone at a Zen Temple in Kyoto, "All I need to know is how
much is enough ... *nothing in excess.* It is time we balanced our long
pursuit of knowing the self with a deliberate pursuit of knowing how
much is enough – enough to enjoy to the full, enough to go around,
enough to sustain the earth. The vocation is to a higher culture, had
we only the ears to hear it."

(James Heisig: 216)

LEADERSHIP: WALK THE TALK

Years ago, when I became committed to the art of pottery, I had a
vision of the "perfect pot" ... [Now] I realize that if I ever were to
make that sublimely beautiful pot I must first become that sublimely
beautiful person.

(Thomas Bezanson: 237)

Throughout the centuries we have tried to ensure that we have peace
by preparing for war. And throughout the centuries we had war.... It
is of the utmost importance to recognize the folly of this policy and
adopt a new policy: ... If you want peace, prepare for peace.

(Joseph Rotblat: 50)

LEADERSHIP: THE CONTEXT

I cannot divorce myself from the nexus of history. I am shaped by the
thoughts and actions of others, and my own thoughts and actions co-
determine their lives and thus our collective existence.

(George Feuerstein: 91)

We do, with astonishing frequency, produce moments of nobility. Our
culture just doesn't choose to feature them on the nightly news. [NJA:
With astonishing frequency, our leaders produce moments of nobility.
Our culture just doesn't choose to feature them on the evening
news.]

(Donella Meadows: 69)

This is the issue before us at the end of one millennium and the
beginning of another. Will we humans accept the universe as the controlling context of existence or will we insist that the human be
accepted as the controlling context of existence? Controlling implies

the setting of limits and determining patterns of relationship. Will we accept our status as functioning within the greater community of existence or will we humans insist that the greater community of existence accept its status within the determinations imposed by the human? There is one lesson we should learn from our experience of the twentieth century. Our efforts to outsmart Earth will only bring about disastrous consequences.

(Thomas Berry: 35, 38)

Selected quotes and poems for reflection from the book
Earth Prayers

I particularly like *Earth Prayers* (Roberts and Amidon 1991) for introducing periods of reflective silence at global leadership seminars, because the collection of 365 poems and prayers represent all of the world's cultural and spiritual traditions. My personal preference is to draw primarily, but not exclusively, from those portions of the collection representative of aboriginal traditions, as these are often among the most inclusive writings (and therefore don't risk offending participants from other spiritual communities, including secular humanists who often define themselves as being outside of all spiritual traditions). I often choose to read only a couple of lines from a selected poem, thereby emphasizing the particular words that echo most directly the issues being discussed in the seminar. I also frequently add a sentence or phrase to more explicitly link the prayer or poem with global leadership. Below are several selections, among the many I have used, from *Earth Prayers*.

LEADERS SPEAK OUT

> [W]hile the stars and waves have something to say, it is through my mouth they'll say it.

(Vicente Huidobro: 9)

> As a leader, you have what it takes to make a difference: "Sometimes even a single feather is enough to fly."

(Robert Maclean: 27)

STATUS, MONEY, PROMOTIONS, AND RAISES ARE NEITHER THE ONLY,
NOR THE PRIMARY, SOURCES OF MEANING AND JOY

> The great sea has set me in motion
> Set me adrift,
> And I move as a weed in the river.
> The arch of sky

And mightiness of storms
Encompasses me,
And I am left
Trembling with joy.
     (Eskimo Song: 21)

And I thought over again
My small adventures
As with a shore-wind I drifted out
In my kayak
And thought I was in danger,
    My fears,
    Those small ones
    That I thought so big
    For all the vital things
    I had to get and to reach
And yet, there is only
One great thing,
The only thing:
To live to see in huts and on journeys
The great day that dawns,
And the light that fills the world.
          (Inuit Song: 41)

They've lost it, lost it,
and their children
will never even wish for it –
and I am afraid
that the whole tribe is in trouble,
the whole tribe is lost –
because the sun keeps rising
and these days
nobody sings.
     (Aaron Kramer: 68)

REFLECTIVE SILENCE

We declare a Sabbath, a space of quiet: for simply being and letting be, for recovering the great, forgotten truths; for learning how to live again.

     (United Nations Environmental Sabbath Program: 92)

PROFOUND LEADERSHIP

> Grandfather,
> Look at our brokenness.
> > We know that in all creation
> > Only the human family
> > Has strayed from the Sacred Way.
> We know that we are the ones
> Who are divided
> And we are the ones
> Who must come back together
> To walk in the Sacred Way.
> > Grandfather,
> > Sacred One,
> > Teach us love, compassion, and honor
> That we may heal the earth
> And heal each other.
> > > (Ojibway Prayer: 95)

CLOSING QUOTE

> Half an hour's meditation is essential except when you are very busy.
> Then a full hour is needed.
> > (Francis de Sales, from Andrews, *The Circle of Simplicity* 1997: 163)

Coaching and caveats

Specific versus diffuse cultures

For those participants who see reflection as a part of their religious or spiritual practice, but not as a part of leadership or their work within organizations, it is often helpful to introduce the concept of specific versus diffuse cultures. In contemporary North American culture, which is highly specific, we tend to compartmentalize aspects of our lives (such as separating professional life and private life, or seeing reflection as a part of a religious service but not as a part of organizational leadership). In other, more diffuse, cultures, this separation appears ludicrous. The fundamental human question is: Who are we? Not, who are we at work? Or at home? By giving a theoretical context explaining why reflection is a crucial part of global leadership, most participants will be able to let go of their reservations and engage in the reflective experience.

Universalism and particularism

In attempting to find the best way to introduce the relationship between reflective silence and profound global leadership, we often search for universals – quotes and stories that are meaningful to all humanity – that are expressed through our unique individual and cultural particularism. Especially in seminars on global or cross-cultural leadership, it is important to underscore the relationship, or dance, between universalism and particularism. Universals, which are true for people in all cultures at all times (such as reflective silence), do not deny individual identity or local definition. One of the unique challenges of global, as opposed to domestic, leadership is that it must address the concerns of all humanity while speaking in a language that is understood and meaningful to multiple particular subgroups (such as clients and employees from various cultural backgrounds). Discussing why certain quotes are particularly meaningful to some participants, while remaining less meaningful to others, helps all participants evolve beyond their cultural specificity toward an approach to leadership that could truly be labeled as global.

Moving from explicit to implicit

In selecting quotes, it is best to start with ones that have a more explicit connection to leadership and then progress to others that are broader and have more subtle or implicit connections. When selecting quotes that are more explicitly spiritual, I often initially choose aboriginal authors who use more inclusive imagery than authors from less inclusive, more traditional Western religious traditions.

Authenticity: walking the talk

In selecting introductory quotes, it is important that the professor personally believe in the truth and importance of each selected reading. Participants will sense immediately if you believe what you are saying. *Walk the talk!* If you don't take time to reflect, participants will receive the message that reflection is less important than loading PowerPoint or distributing handouts.

Quieting down: observing process

Developing the ability to become quiet and reflective is a learned skill. Invite participants to observe their own process. After three or four sessions, ask participants to comment on the differences they observe between the group's behavior during the fourth period of reflective silence and the first. My observation is that very little reflection takes place in the initial sessions because, to quote David Whyte, in "our buzzing-worker-bee mode" most managers and managerial students have difficulty becoming quiet (1994: 98–9). Within a few weeks, however, there is generally marked and noticeable progress. Before the first or second session, it is often valuable to read David Whyte's observation that:

> all of us are familiar with frantic busyness as a state that continually precludes us from opening to the quiet and contemplation it takes to be smart. The fast-moving mind rebels against slowing the pace because it intuits that it will not only have to reassess its identity but also the time to recover and recreate [who we are]. And, of course, when we are in the buzzing-worker-bee mode that would be a loss of momentum difficult to justify. We do not even have time to find out if our momentum is taking us over the nearest cliff. If we are serious about [who we are] all of us must confront the question of quiet and contemplation in the workplace.
>
> (Whyte 1994: 98–9, adapted by N. J. Adler)

Note that Whyte's original quote refers to soul in the workplace, a concept that I usually do not introduce in the first few sessions.

Spirituality and leadership

Introducing reflective practices and notions of profound global leadership often lead to questions about spirituality. Based on extensive reading and research, Professor André Delbecq at Santa Clara University created a course for MBAs and Silicon Valley CEOs on "Spirituality and leadership." Professor Delbecq does a superb job demonstrating the relationship between leadership and spirituality. I recommend his syllabus, readings, articles, and suggestions to anyone who is interested in this topic (see http://business.scu.edu/spirituality_leadership). He has been immensely helpful in guiding my colleagues and I in our personal explorations and in our professional design work around this topic.

References

Adler, N. J. (2001) "Leading: giving yourself for things far greater than yourself," *Reflections*, 2 (3): 26–9.

Adler, N. J. (2002a) *From Boston to Beijing: Managing with a Worldview*, Cincinnati, OH: South-Western/Thomson Learning.

Adler, N. J. (2002b) *International Dimensions of Organizational Behavior*, 4th edn, Cincinnati, OH: South-Western/Thomson Learning.

Adler, N. J. and Lew, Y. C. (forthcoming) *The Circle and the Square*, Montreal: McGill University.

Aitken, R. quote from F. Franck, J. Roze and R. Connolly (eds) (2000) *What Does it Mean to Be Human?*, New York: St. Martin's Press, p. 129.

Andrews, C. (1997) *The Circle of Simplicity*, New York: HarperCollins.

Arias, O. quote from F. Franck, J. Roze and R. Connolly (eds) (2000) *What Does it Mean to Be Human?*, New York: St. Martin's Press, p. 26.

Berry, T. quote from F. Franck, J. Roze and R. Connolly (eds) (2000) *What Does it Mean to Be Human?*, New York: St. Martin's Press, pp. 35, 38.

Bezanson, T. quote from F. Franck, J. Roze and R. Connolly (eds) (2000) *What Does it Mean to Be Human?*, New York: St. Martin's Press, p. 237.

Biegert, C. quote from F. Franck, J. Roze and R. Connolly (eds) (1998) *What Does it Mean to Be Human?*, Nyack, New York: Circumstantial Press, pp. 180–1.

Chapman, R. quote from F. Franck, J. Roze and R. Connolly (eds) (2000) *What Does it Mean to Be Human?*, New York: St. Martin's Press, p. 44.

Chittister, J. quotes from F. Franck, J. Roze and R. Connolly (eds) (2000) *What Does it Mean to Be Human?*, New York: St. Martin's Press, pp. 151–2.

Das. R. quote from F. Franck, J. Roze and R. Connolly (eds) (2000) *What Does it Mean to Be Human?*, New York: St. Martin's Press, p. 66.

Drucker, P. (1999) "Managing oneself," *Harvard Business Review*, March–April: 65–74.

Eskimo Song from E. Amidon and E. Roberts (1991) *Earth Prayers*, San Francisco: Harper, p. 21.

Feuerstein, G. quote from F. Franck, J. Roze and R. Connolly (eds) (2000) *What Does it Mean to Be Human?*, New York: St. Martin's Press, p. 91.

Francis de Sales quote from C. Andrews (1997) *The Circle of Simplicity*, New York: HarperCollins, p. 163.

Franck, F., Roze, J. and Connolly, R. (eds) (2000) *What Does it Mean to Be Human?*, New York: St. Martin's Press, originally published 1998: Nyack, NY: Circumstantial Productions Publishing.

Frank, A. quote from F. Franck, J. Roze and R. Connolly (eds) (2000) *What Does it Mean to Be Human?*, New York: St. Martin's Press, p. 236.

Gandhi, M. quote from F. Franck, J. Roze and R. Connolly (eds) (2000) *What Does it Mean to Be Human?*, New York: St. Martin's Press, p. 66.

Gardner, H. (1995) *Leading Minds: An Anatomy of Leadership*, New York: Basic Books.

Gardner, H. (1998) *Creativity and Leadership: Making the Mind Extraordinary*, videotape by R. DiNozzi (producer) with guidebook, Los Angeles: Into The Classroom Media.

Glassman, B. T. quote from F. Franck, J. Roze and R. Connolly (eds) (1998) *What Does It Mean to Be Human?*, Nyack, New York: Circumstantial Press, p. 83.

Harman, W. quote from F. Franck, J. Roze and R. Connolly (eds) (2000) *What Does it Mean to Be Human?*, New York: St. Martin's Press, p. 80.

Heisig, J. quote from F. Franck, J. Roze and R. Connolly (eds) (2000) *What Does it Mean to Be Human?*, New York: St. Martin's Press, p. 216.

Huidobro, V. quote from E. Amidon and E. Roberts (1991) *Earth Prayers*, San Francisco: Harper, p. 9.

Inuit Song from E. Amidon and E. Roberts (1991) *Earth Prayers*, San Francisco: Harper, p. 41.

Kean, G. quote from F. Franck, J. Roze and R. Connolly (eds) (2000) *What Does it Mean to Be Human?*, New York: St. Martin's Press, p. 137.

Keil, A. quote from F. Franck, J. Roze and R. Connolly (eds) (2000) *What Does it Mean to Be Human?*, New York: St. Martin's Press, pp. 228–30.

Kramer, A. quote from E. Amidon, and E. Roberts (1991) *Earth Prayers*, San Francisco: Harper, p. 68.

Krieger, D. quotes from F. Franck, J. Roze and R. Connolly (eds) (2000) *What Does it Mean to Be Human?*, New York: St. Martin's Press, pp. 263–4.

Kumar, S. quote from F. Franck, J. Roze and R. Connolly (eds) (2000) *What Does it Mean to Be Human?*, New York: St. Martin's Press, p. 184.

Loehr, J. and Schwartz, T. (2001) "The making of a corporate athlete," *Harvard Business Review*, January: 120–8.

Maclean, R. quote from E. Amidon and E. Roberts (1991) *Earth Prayers*, San Francisco: Harper, p. 27.

Marks, L. quote from F. Franck, J. Roze and R. Connolly (eds) (2000) *What Does it Mean to Be Human?*, New York: St. Martin's Press, pp. 115–6.

Meadows, D. quote from F. Franck, J. Roze and R. Connolly (eds) (2000) *What Does it Mean to Be Human?*, New York: St. Martin's Press, pp. 68–9.

Mollenkott, V. R. quote from F. Franck, J. Roze and R. Connolly (eds) (2000) *What Does it Mean to Be Human?*, New York: St. Martin's Press, p. 209.

Mother Theresa quote from F. Franck, J. Roze and R. Connolly (eds) (2000) *What Does it Mean to Be Human?*, New York: St. Martin's Press, pp. 86–7.

Ojibway Prayer from E. Amidon and E. Roberts (1991) *Earth Prayers*, San Francisco: Harper, p. 95.

Palmer, P. (1990) *The Active Life: A Spirituality of Work, Creativity, and Caring*, San Francisco: Jossey-Bass.

Palmer, P. (1999) *The Courage to Teach: A Guide for Reflection and Renewal*, San Francisco: Jossey-Bass.

Palmer, P. (2000) "Leading from within," *Let Your Life Speak: Listening for the Voice of Vocation*, San Francisco: Jossey-Bass, pp. 73–94.

Panikkar, R. quote from F. Franck, J. Roze and R. Connolly (eds) (2000) *What Does it Mean to Be Human?*, New York: St. Martin's Press, p. 63.

Roberts, E. and Amidon, E. (1991) *Earth Prayers*, San Francisco: Harper.

Rotblat, J. quote from F. Franck, J. Roze and R. Connolly (eds) (2000) *What Does it Mean to Be Human?*, New York: St. Martin's Press, pp. 48, 50.

Soetendorf, A. quote from F. Franck, J. Roze and R. Connolly (eds) (1998) *What Does it Mean to Be Human?*, New York: St. Martin's Press, p. 26.

Soler, R. M. quote from F. Franck, J. Roze and R. Connolly (eds) (2000) *What Does it Mean to Be Human?*, New York: St. Martin's Press, p. 251.

Thompson, J. quote from F. Franck, J. Roze and R. Connolly (eds) (2000) *What Does it Mean to Be Human?*, New York: St. Martin's Press, pp. 211–2.

United Nations Environmental Sabbath Program from E. Amidon and E. Roberts (1991) *Earth Prayers*, San Francisco: Harper, p. 92.

Whyte, D. (1994) *The Heart Aroused: Poetry and the Preservation of the Soul in Corporate America*, New York: Currency Doubleday.

Whyte, D. (2001) *Crossing the Unknown Sea: Work as a Pilgrimage of Identity*, New York: Riverhead Books.

Woodman, M. and Mellick, J. (1998) *Coming Home to Myself*, Berkeley, CA: Conari Press.

Part VI

The cultural context of work
Collaborative relationships today

While the earlier modules were focused upon the individual learner as an actor in a strange culture, here we focus upon the differences when the actors are purposefully thrown together in intercultural teams. With the earlier assertion that each individual carries multiple cultures, the existence of multicultural teams is a pervasive phenomenon.

Gibson begins Part VI by providing a classroom exercise for determining the differences between homogeneous and heterogeneous teams and their impact on team process. In this case, lecture precedes the use of a values questionnaire, which provides the data for the class to assemble into homogeneous or heterogeneous groups. Each team engages in an exercise and self-diagnosis that allow the members to appreciate the value and synergistic effects of diverse team membership.

Gluesing describes the work of a cultural coach with a long-term cross-cultural project team. Here the team functions in both real and virtual contexts, and the membership is ever-evolving as the project moves from stage to stage. Using cultural tensions as teachable moments and providing training "on the fly" reveals the need for a learning model significantly different from a traditional classroom. The coach must sense an issue and be prepared with an exercise that is "on point" and that can be contained in a short-term intervention.

Ting-Toomey turns the focus to conflict. She creates a negotiation simulation exercise that permits cross-cultural conflict to arise and the learners to "mindfully" consider their behaviors in light of the conflict at hand. Learners confront their ethnocentrism and develop a more "ethnorelative" perspective, allowing them to shift from position-based negotiation to a heightened awareness of shared interests across cultural groups.

Wilson concludes Part VI with an overview of key concepts in cross-cultural leadership development. She sees cross-cultural adaptability as the "extra capacity" needed by leaders and managers to successfully guide twenty-first-century organizations, and she presents the AHA! technique to develop this necessary expertise. This simple interactive and self-reflective exercise, grounded in previous learner experiences, expands the learner's repertoire of beliefs and behaviors to enhance effectiveness in leadership roles and collaborative relationships.

Chapter 18

Building multicultural teams

Learning to manage the challenges of homogeneity and heterogeneity

Cristina B. Gibson

Introduction

This chapter presents a set of exercises and techniques designed to increase student awareness of the challenges of interacting in multicultural collaborations and the strategies that might be employed to manage these challenges to create fully functional teams.

Culture is a shared meaning system (Hofstede 1991; Schweder and LeVine 1984). A multicultural team has members from two or more cultures (Earley and Gibson 2002). Cultures exist among people who share the same nationality (e.g., Canadians), the same organizational affiliation (e.g., Microsoft), the same function (e.g., engineering), or even the same gender. Members of the same culture share common views and they are likely to interpret and evaluate situational events and management practices in similar ways. In contrast, members of different cultures are more likely to respond differently to the same event or managerial approach.

Research on team composition suggests that homogeneous teams (all members of the same culture) are more satisfied and experience more positive reactions, while heterogeneous teams (with multicultural members) experience enhanced team creativity and breadth of solutions to a problem (Jackson, May and Whitney 1995; Earley and Gibson 2002). Empirical evidence also demonstrates that this benefit may diminish over time as a team becomes more homogeneous in its behavior during the later periods of its lifecycle (Cox, Lobel and McLeod 1991).

Some scholars have argued that teams of all types can be highly effective if they develop common norms for operating and shared work capability expectations (Earley and Gibson 2002). These elements make up a "hybrid culture" (Earley and Mosakowski 2000). This does not mean that everyone on the team has the same views, but that significant mutual understanding exists. This in turn facilitates individual and team performance and communication. A hybrid culture may derive from the overlapping cultures of team members (e.g., national, organizational, or functional cultures). Or a hybrid culture can be the newly developed patterns of team member interaction and shared understandings that are explicitly developed over time (Earley and Gibson 2002). Given both increasing internationalization and the prevalence of work groups in modern organizations, understanding the challenges that people face as they organize themselves in multicultural teams and how to build hybrid cultures to overcome these becomes an essential educational experience for all students of business, organizations, and psychology (Kirkman, Gibson and Shapiro 2001).

Objectives of multicultural team experience

This set of techniques is appropriate for an audience ranging from advanced undergraduates to master's level executives and can be utilized within a domestic context (e.g., in a U.S. Midwestern university setting) or in a cross-cultural context (e.g., an intercultural training program). By completing this experience, participants will:

a   gain greater understanding of team composition effects, with a focus on culture;
b   learn to address challenges in homogeneous versus heterogeneous teams;
c   develop skills in diagnosing strengths, weaknesses, opportunities, and threats that face teams;
d   gain teamwork expertise by working in teams and analyzing their own experience in those teams.

Basic components

There are <u>nine</u> basic components of this educational experience, including a series of activities during the class session in which team composition occurs. These nine components are presented below in sequence:

Activities *prior* to team composition session

Component One: An introductory set of readings that present the key elements of teaming and team composition, including the concept of culture, and multiple cultural identities.

> Lumsden, D. and Lumsden, G. (1993) *Communicating in Groups and Teams: Sharing Leadership* (Chapters 1 and 5), Belmont, CA: Wadsworth Publishing Company.
> Hackman, J. R. (1990) *Groups that Work (and Those That Don't): Creating Conditions for Effective Teamwork* (pp. 1–14, "*Work teams in organizations*"),San Francisco, CA: Jossey-Bass Publishers.

Hoeckin, L. (1995) *Managing Cultural Differences: Strategies for Competitive Advantage* (pp. 23–9, "*Culture: What it is...*"), Reading, MA: Addison-Wesley.

Component Two: Completion of a cultural values survey and a team member profile. A complete values survey might be utilized (Lane, DiStefano and Maznevski 1997) or a truncated values survey that assesses two or three dimensions of culture can be utilized if time constraints prohibit the longer format (Erez and Earley 1993). Appendix 18.1 is the Team Member Profile. On this, the students should be instructed to leave their preference for homogeneous versus heterogeneous team blank for the time being.

Activities *during* team composition session

Time allocation (75-minute class):
    Twenty minutes – lecture on team composition
    Twenty-five minutes – form teams (fill in style preference first)
    Fifteen minutes – team meetings
    Fifteen minutes – each team introduces themselves

Component Three: A brief lecture on team composition. Particular attention is paid to the concept of culture, the notion that culture exists at multiple levels, and that members of multicultural teams bring these multiple cultural identities with them into the team. The advantages and disadvantages of multicultural teams are also stressed. More specifically, lecture topics include:

1   Content of team composition

- Readily detectable attributes

  - task-related (tenure, department, credentials, education)
  - relations-oriented (gender, culture, age, membership in formal political groups, physical features)

- Underlying attributes

  - task-related (knowledge, skills, ability, experience)
  - relations-oriented (social status, attitudes, values, personality characteristics, behavioral style)

2   Individual input

- Mechanisms: cognitions; affect
- Process

  - member characteristics
  - cognitions/expectations
  - affect/emotion

      – individual behavior
      – member reactions to each other

3   Characteristics of culture

- Culture = the consistent way a group of people view the world
- Exists at many levels: national, organizational, group

4   Culture's impact on group members

- Values, priorities, focus
- Sources of self-knowledge
- Fulfillment of self-motives
- Evaluation of managerial techniques

5   Structure of membership

- Composition = configurations of attributes within small groups
- Heterogeneity = the degree to which members of a team as a whole are similar (homogeneous) or dissimilar (heterogeneous) with respect to individual-level attributes

6   Strengths and weaknesses of heterogeneous teams

- Strengths

      – improved decision quality
      – innovation and adaptation
      – inter-group and inter-organization coordination
      – personal growth

- Weaknesses

      – lower cohesiveness
      – less positive mood
      – decreased communication
      – turnover

7   Strengths and weaknesses of homogeneous teams

- Strengths

      – cohesiveness
      – warmth and acceptance
      – strong communication
      – stability

- Weaknesses

      – less creative
      – less stimulating
      – less personal growth

8   Staffing teams

- Job analysis
- Existing team members should be involved
- Staff for balance
- Screen for interpersonal skills and fit

Component Four: Student team preferences. Class members are asked whether they would prefer, as an experiment, to work in a homogeneous or heterogeneous team for the remainder of the course. Volunteer "recruiters" then use this preference to form some teams that maximize homogeneity and some teams that maximize heterogeneity.

Component Five: Formation of teams based on a "recruiting process." Instructors should:

a   Check for questions on the team member profiles. State: "Please take a few minutes to think about your preference for a homogeneous versus heterogeneous team. Now circle in the upper left hand corner of your team member profile your preference for homogeneous or heterogeneous."

b   State: "If you preferred a homogeneous team, pass profile to the right; if you preferred a heterogeneous team, pass profile to the left."

c   Announce: "We are going to try and accommodate your request for a homogeneous versus heterogeneous team, but we need the help of a set of volunteers to act as 'recruiters' to form the teams. Based on the team member profiles, you will select members to be a part of your team."

d   Select the number of recruiters for the number of teams needed in order to have four- or five-person teams (i.e., if you have twenty students, you will need five recruiters, one for each four-person team). Select enough homogeneous recruiters to create the appropriate number of homogeneous teams (e.g., if eight people indicated homogeneous preference, you will need two recruiters to recruit homogeneous teams); select heterogeneous recruiters to create the appropriate number of heterogeneous teams.

e   Recruiters come to the front and select teams from anonymous team member profiles (with help of instructor); homogeneous recruiters maximize homogeneity within their team; heterogeneous recruiters maximize heterogeneity; consider gender first; consider ethnicity/nationality second; consider age/class standing (tenure) third; consider academic field of study fourth; consider experience fifth.

f   Announce teams by ID numbers; have students move into teams.

Component Six: Team meetings. Instructor advises teams to meet to prepare a "social contract" and briefly explains the process of social contracting.

Following these meetings, have the teams introduce themselves to the class.

a   Discuss personal backgrounds, work history, current time constraints, strengths and weaknesses of working in a group, how you work best.
b   Reach consensus on a set of expectations. Write these down and hand them in. This is your team's social contract.
c   Social contract should include the following:

- Team name (be creative!)
- Expectations of each other
- Expectations for the team
- Expectations for the course

Activities *following* team composition

Component Seven: Team project work. Teams complete one or more projects together. These can be designed to fit other parts of the course. The content of the team project(s) is less important for this set of techniques to work: students simply need an opportunity to work together as a team.

Component Eight: Participant journaling. Students write one journal entry per week (Appendix 18.2). The ongoing process of experiencing, observing, analyzing, and recording experiences helps participants understand how teams function, how they can develop skills, and in what ways they can make their future in groups and teams positive and effective.

Component Nine: Final exam paper. As a final project, students analyze their experience in their team (Appendix 18.3). Students each prepare a formal paper (approximately ten pages) that demonstrates their understanding of the theories and practices associated with teamwork in organizations and analyzes the experiences of their project team using the theoretical and practical course material. The final paper represents the summary of their learning from the experience.

Time commitment required of students

- Pre-work: approximately three hours to complete reading and team member profile.
- Course sessions: one session (seventy-five minutes) for team composition lecture and forming teams.
- Team project work: varies from minimum of one outside class assignment to several.
- Journal: thirty minutes per week outside class on individual basis.

- Final project: students report that a ten-page paper requires two–three days to complete outside class.

Testimonials and learnings

Participants who have taken part in this set of exercises have reported numerous learnings from the experience, pertaining both to team composition on multicultural teams in particular and to team effectiveness in general. For example, "Kim," wrote the following:

> Our team was designed as a homogeneous team. . . . But while participants were similar in gender and age, they differed in terms of ethnic background. At first, members ignored the underlying differences in the team, failing to take advantage of the benefits associated with heterogeneous members and not avoiding the conflict that sometimes is associated with heterogeneous teams.

Kim devised a novel means of addressing this "underlying" set of differences in future teams:

> Each team could examine its potential heterogeneous nature by finding one similarity and one difference among team members. Perhaps participants could be directed to identify similarities and differences in communication styles, this might serve as a "cultural systems audit" that would inform the team about inequitable communication processes.

Kim's experience can be contrasted with that of "Tom" in a heterogeneous team.

> Our team was a very diverse group of individuals, in terms of gender, age, cultural background and work experience. At first, I was a bit apprehensive regarding the extreme diversity of the group and whether the diversity would negatively impact our performance. What I found over the past seven weeks was this diversity added considerably to creative problem solving, but was also a very rewarding experience. Heterogeneous teams profit from the differing perspectives of the various members because the diversity enables differing viewpoints to be brought to the table.

"Jennifer" had this to say about her experience in an equally heterogeneous team that was able to find commonalties among the diversity:

> Our team was a heterogeneous team from various cultural, social and

professional backgrounds ... although we had a number of individual differences, we shared a number of similarities that influenced our team level inputs. We developed a norm that treated everyone equally, respected our diversity, and listened to each other's opinions and suggestions. This made our members feel more a part of our team instead of like outsiders with different views. We also developed a norm of assisting each other in articulating our individual ideas and concepts for our group assignments. These are among the many factors that contributed to the success of our team.

As evidenced in these excerpts, the final papers that students have prepared in conjunction with this set of exercises are often very thoughtful and demonstrate numerous techniques the participants developed for managing team composition.

Potential problems or dilemmas

A common expectation is that students will have a strong bias toward homogeneity. In my use of this exercise, there have always been at least a dozen students who prefer each team type. In fact, more students tend to prefer heterogeneous teams when they hear of the potential benefits. However, if this does not occur, the instructor might first try to gently encourage a few students to reconsider and form a heterogeneous team. If they remain steadfast, the exercise could feasibly still be utilized, but the focus of the analysis becomes:

- What underlying differences were uncovered, even in the homogeneous teams?
- How did you encourage diversity of views in homogeneous teams?
- Would you do the same in the future?

Although the heterogeneous teams sometimes struggle at the outset when they are forming shared understandings and norms, this eventually passes. Instructors may want to schedule a midterm meeting with each team to check on progress, satisfaction, and potential problems. Teams should be reassured that intra-group problem-solving is one of the course objectives. The vast majority of students report very positive reactions to the systematic, intentional formation of teams. The process of struggling through challenges, guided by a set of tools and frameworks for framing the experience, and an opportunity to reflect on the learnings, all contribute to vastly increased insights into culture, team composition, and effective multicultural team functioning.

Appendix 18.1 Team member profile

MANAGEMENT OF TEAMS AND GROUPS
TEAM MEMBER PROFILE

PREFERENCE (circle one):
HOMOGENEOUS TEAM/HETEROGENEOUS TEAM

STUDENT ID #_____

(complete this option **after** the lecture on team composition)

Note: Providing the following information is completely voluntary. Leave blank any information you feel uncomfortable providing.

DEMOGRAPHICS

AGE _____   SEX _____

COUNTRY OF BIRTH _____ ETHNICITY _____
(1 = African American/Black; 2 = American Indian/Alaskan Native; 3 = Asian; 4 = Pacific Islander; 5 = Hispanic/Latino; 6 = White/Non-Hispanic)

EDUCATION

CLASS STANDING _____
(1 = Fr.; 2 = Soph.; 3 = Jr.; 4 = Sen.; 5 = Masters)

MAJOR _____
(1 = Accting./Info.Sys.; 2 = Fin.; 3 = Actuarial/Risk/Insurance; 4 = Real Estate; 5 = Operations/Info.Mgmt.; 6 = Mkt.; 7 = Mgmt/HR; 8 = Nonbusiness)

UNDERGRADUATE DEGREE RECEIVED/WILL BE RECEIVED FROM

_____
(1 = small private; 2 = large private; 3 = small public; 4 = large public; note small = less than 1000 students; large = more than 1000 students)

EMPLOYMENT

NUMBER OF YEARS EMPLOYED _____

NUMBER OF YEARS IN MANAGEMENT _____

FUNCTIONAL AREAS PREVIOUSLY EMPLOYED IN
(list all categories from below that apply): _____
(1 = Accting./Info.Sys.; 2 = Fin.; 3 = Actuarial/Risk/Insurance; 4 = Real Estate; 5 = Operations/Info.Mgmt.; 6 = Mkt.; 7 = Mgm/HR; 8 = Nonbusiness)

FUNCTIONAL AREA DESIRED FOLLOWING GRADUATION
(list category below that applies): _____
(1 = Accting./Info.Sys.; 2 = Fin.; 3 = Actuarial/Risk/Insurance; 4 = Real Estate; 5 = Operations/Info.Mgmt.; 6 = Mkt; 7 = Mgm/HR; 8 = Nonbusiness)

SIZE OF EMPLOYER DESIRED: _____
(1 = 1–100 employees; 2 = 101–1000 employees; 3 = Over 1000 employees)

INDUSTRY DESIRED FOLLOWING GRADUATION: _____
(1 = service; 2 = manufacturing; 3 = self-employed)

➡

Appendix 18.1 continued

TEAM EXPERIENCE

PROVIDE DURATION OF PARTICIPATION IN YEARS FOR ALL THAT APPLY:

ATHLETIC TEAM _____

MANAGEMENT TEAM _____

CLASSROOM TEAM _____

VOLUNTEER TEAM _____

WORK TEAM _____

COMMITTEE _____

CULTURAL VALUES

ENTER THE SCORES FROM YOUR CULTURAL VALUES SURVEY IN THE FOLLOWING CHART:

	TOTAL SCORE
SELF VS. GROUP FOCUS	
POWER DISTANCE	

OTHER THINGS WE SHOULD KNOW ABOUT YOU:

Appendix 18.2 Guidelines for journal preparation

Student Guidelines for Journal Entries

Objectives
This semester you will work intensively in class using and developing your skills in teams. The foundation of this work is lectures and readings. You will keep a journal about them. The ongoing process of experiencing, observing, analyzing, and recording your experiences will help you to understand how teams function, how you can develop your teamwork skills, and in what ways you can make your future team experience positive and effective.

Overview of Journal Components
- Your summaries of lectures and readings.
- Your notes about your experience in team exercises in class.
- A summary of what you have learned in each class.
- Your notes about your team meetings held outside of class.
- A final summary and analysis of what you've learned and experienced.

Process
- You should have an entry in your journal for each week.
- Each of the entries should have the following sections; (you are welcome to write as much as you please!):

  1   Preparation
  2   Observations
  3   Learnings
  4   Team notes

Format and Contents
1 Preparation Section
Before coming to each class session, you should write down a few notes about the reading and/or the case. You should write the key themes you noticed as you read and the major new things you learned. Also write any questions you might have or any additional issues you'd like to see addressed in class.

2 Observations Section
In this section, you should record any observations you make during the class sessions. If someone says something particularly insightful, record it here. Describe any strong reactions you have to the material and discuss it. Capture what you are thinking in process.

Appendix 18.2 continued

3 Learnings Section

After each class session, you should take five to ten minutes to make notes in your journal. Record anything new that you learned. "Reconcile" anything that now seems different to you than it did before the class session. For example, you may better understand a new term, see an aspect of your team in a new light, or learn something about another team you are currently on. Equally as important, you may now be confused about some aspect of team functioning (you should note this and follow-up on it in the next class session!)

4 Team notes

For each journal entry, jot down a few notes regarding your team. Your team should plan to meet at least once per week for the remainder of the course. When you meet, record a few "minutes" from each meeting in this section of your journal. Discuss how you felt during the meeting, what transpired, what was accomplished (or wasn't), and any other observations you make. These sections of your journal entries will become the "data" for your final paper.

On a final note, have fun with this and be creative! The more you let the thoughts flow, the more you will get out of this assignment!

Appendix 18.3 Guidelines for final paper

Final Exam Paper: Objectives And Guidelines

I. OBJECTIVES

The objective of the final exam is to demonstrate your understanding of the theories and practices associated with teamwork in organizations. More specifically, you should analyze the experiences of your case project team using the team behavior model and associated theoretical and practical material read and discussed in class. The final paper will represent a summary of your learning in this class. In essence, you are incorporating all of your journal material into one final deliverable.

II. CONTENTS

The paper should be divided into three sections:

A. Description (2–3 pages): describe each component of the team experience.
B. Analysis (5–6 pages):
    ☐ Analyze the key issues for the team members and the team, isolating specific components and applying theoretical frameworks from the course readings, lectures, or outside publications in order to discuss WHY those aspects of the system are key issues
    ☐ Be sure to answer the question, "Why did this occur?"
    ☐ To answer the WHY question, you must discuss causes, experiences, and consequences
    ☐ Be sure to provide enough detail regarding each key issue and link each key issue with concepts, readings, and lectures presented in class.
C. Recommendations (2–3 pages):
    ☐ Provide suggestions that would improve the effectiveness
    ☐ Discuss WHY and HOW your interventions will improve effectiveness; describe the expected impacts on each component
    ☐ Provide evidence that your suggestions will work (e.g., documented case examples from the literature, anecdotal evidence from corporate experience, research reports, or published theoretical frameworks)

The application of specific theories and frameworks utilized in this course is very important. For example, when you think about the composition of your team, what were the relevant cultural similarities and differences that impacted the team? (e.g., nationality? major? work background?) How did your team confront these? How might you do this differently in the future? Which readings, theories or frameworks helped you to think about these cultural issues?

   On a final note: use this paper as an opportunity to define the personal significance of your learning experience in this course and others that have utilized teams and group projects. Have fun, and be creative in your recommendations!

References

Cox, T. H., Lobel, S. A. and McLeod, P. L. (1991) "Effects of ethnic group cultural differences on cooperative and competitive behavior on a group task," *Academy of Management Journal*, 34 (4): 827–47.

Earley, P. C. and Gibson, C. B. (2002) *Multinational Teams: New Perspectives*, Mahwah, NJ: Lawrence Earlbaum Associates.

Earley, P. C. and Mosakowski, E. M. (2000) "Creating hybrid team cultures: an empirical test of transnational team functioning," *Academy of Management Journal*, 43 (1): 26–49.

Erez, M. and Earley, P. C. (1993) *Culture, Self-Identity, and Work*, New York: Oxford University Press.

Hackman, J. R. (1990) *Groups that Work (and Those That Don't): Creating Conditions for Effective Teamwork*, San Francisco: Jossey-Bass.

Hoeckin, L. (1995) *Managing Cultural Differences: Strategies for Competitive Advantage*, Reading, MA: Addison-Wesley.

Hofstede, G. (1991) *Culture and Organizations: Software of the Mind*, London: McGraw-Hill.

Jackson, S. E., May, K. E. and Whitney, K. (1995) "Understanding the dynamics of diversity in decision-making teams," in R. A. Guzzo, E. Salas and Associates, *Team Effectiveness and Decision-Making in Organizations*, San Francisco: Jossey-Bass, pp. 204–61.

Kirkman, B. L., Gibson, C. B. and Shapiro, D. (2001) "'Exporting' teams: enhancing the implementation and effectiveness of work teams in global affiliates," *Organizational Dynamics*, 30 (1): 12–29.

Lane, H. W., DiStefano, J. J. and Maznevski, M. L. (1997) *International Management Behavior*, Oxford: Blackwell Business.

Lumsden, D. and Lumsden, G. (1993) *Communicating in Groups and Teams: Sharing Leadership*, Belmont, CA: Wadsworth.

Schweder, R. A. and LeVine, R. A. (1984) *Culture Theory: Essays on Mind, Self and Emotion*, New York: Cambridge University Press.

Chapter 19

Teaching culture "on the fly" and "learning in working" with global teams

Julia C. Gluesing

Introduction

One of the emerging organizing forms for structuring work on a global scale is the global team, defined as a group of people who work interdependently across time and distance to achieve a common objective. They "think globally and act locally" to design products for the global marketplace and keep ideas and resources moving wherever they are needed to produce and deliver these products. Global teams are becoming more prevalent as communication technology becomes more reliable and allows the ready flow of more complex and detailed information including graphics, complicated mathematical data, video, and simultaneous transmission of information in multiple formats through multiple channels.

The structure and processes of global organizations utilizing global teams necessitate a qualitative difference in the way work is accomplished. Given an uncertain and non-routine environment, where multiple cultures intersect, incremental decision-making and small wins become absolutely crucial because they create some degree of order. As they enact and negotiate a new, shared culture over time (as shown in Brannen 1998), a global team jointly creates an achievable vision, basic working rules, and norms for interaction that will facilitate learning in non-routine settings.

The teaching challenge is to create learning opportunities within the natural flow of work that can convey both cultural concepts and intercultural communication skills in compact ways appropriate to the situation and to the readiness and skill levels of the members. Teaching culture in global teams is about teaching in context and helping teams achieve learning in incremental steps that promote mutual understanding and collaboration among the team members. "Teaching on the fly" to promote "learning in working" means that the teacher must take on the role of "cultural coach." The cultural coach is a roving observer of member interactions, selecting content and techniques to teach about culture, as it is appropriate to specific team members and situations. A cultural coach must be present with the team members in both their co-located and virtual contexts and learn enough about the team's work to customize the learning experience to team members' immediate needs.

In this teaching module, I will present an approach to teaching "on the fly" and promoting "learning in working" in global teams. This teaching approach is based upon a definition of culture as a system of "learned H.E.L.P.":

Habits – patterns of behavior and thought;
Expectations – for ourselves and others; accepted norms for behavior;
Language – language, both verbal and nonverbal, and symbols with shared meaning;
Perspective – about how the world works; assumptions about what is important and what is not that guides behavior.

This definition allows team members to readily grasp that they are already "multicultural" people because they have learned multiple H.E.L.P. systems (national, occupational, and organizational cultures). Team members learn that culture is something that can be both understood and immediately helpful by providing multiple perspectives and approaches. Multiple and different H.E.L.P. systems can foster innovativeness and help global team members become better problem-solvers when issues are complex. Their task then becomes creating a team H.E.L.P. system, or "working culture," that can enhance their performance. Defining culture as learned H.E.L.P. is non-threatening because team members understand it is possible and desirable to have multiple H.E.L.P. systems, and that they do not have to abandon the ones they already have to create and adopt a new cultural H.E.L.P. system.

For example, the challenge for American engineers working with French marketing staff is to negotiate a common way of working. The coach can help in as simple a way as bringing to their awareness possible differences in approaches to agendas that will enable them to avoid mis-understanding as much as possible and to create an agenda format accept-able to all. This negotiated approach to meeting management then becomes one "small win" in building a team H.E.L.P. system.

Approach to teaching "on the fly" and promoting "learning in working"

The approach to teaching "on the fly" and promoting "learning in working" in global teams is based on a four-phase process model with an instructional design that includes six basic teaching tasks (Gluesing 1998). Figure 19.1 displays the four phases and the six basic tasks.

Phase One, *Breaking down to open up*, involves three tasks that focus on

Global Teaming

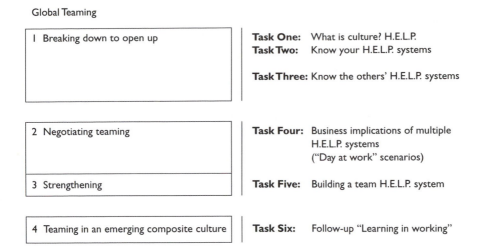

1 Breaking down to open up	**Task One:** What is culture? H.E.L.P.
	Task Two: Know your H.E.L.P. systems
	Task Three: Know the others' H.E.L.P. systems

| 2 Negotiating teaming | **Task Four:** Business implications of multiple H.E.L.P. systems ("Day at work" scenarios) |
| 3 Strengthening | **Task Five:** Building a team H.E.L.P. system |

| 4 Teaming in an emerging composite culture | **Task Six:** Follow-up "Learning in working" |

Figure 19.1 Instructional process tied to global teaming.

teaching basic culture concepts and on learning how culture influences thought and behavior. Task One helps members become familiar with the concept of culture as H.E.L.P. Tasks Two and Three involve teaching about the cultural systems that are most relevant to and likely to be the most influential in their daily work. For example, in a vehicle product development team there are likely to be at least two or three major organizational cultures (Division One etc.), four or five occupational cultures (engineering, finance, marketing, manufacturing, purchasing), and anywhere from two to six national cultures (e.g., U.S., Swedish, Japanese, British, German).

Not all cultures are relevant all the time. The cultural coach uses observation and knowledge about the team members and their work to decide which cultures (which values or behaviors) are most relevant in any situation and focuses teaching on these. In this phase it is important to make team members aware of the historical roots of culture, of the influence of business conditions on the development of national, organizational and occupational cultural beliefs, values and behaviors, and on the basic cultural axioms that guide behavior. By emphasizing the factors that have led to cultural patterns of thought and behavior, team members can understand that each culture has "logic." It is also important to uncover both similarities and differences as a basis for later negotiation of a teamworking culture.

Phase Two, *Negotiating teaming*, is when members begin to develop shared assumptions about their mission and some agreement about common objectives, how they will work together, and what each can contribute to achieving their common objectives. Phase Three is *Strengthening teaming*. In this phase the team members begin to work synergistically to achieve their objectives, and the team has become a viable system within their existing work structures and conditions. Phases Two and Three of the global teaming process rely on the success of Phase One. Both later phases involve teaching about implications of cultural patterns observable through behaviors in the work context.

This approach to teaching culture in global teams is rooted in the daily activities of doing work and takes advantage of learning opportunities as they arise. It is, of necessity, an improvisational approach. The cultural coach must be very well acquainted with the team's work contexts and processes in order to use this approach effectively. Although this process is applied and opportunistic, these tools and techniques are very useful because they are easily adapted across settings yet anchored in specific contexts.

Phase Four, *Teaming in an emerging "composite" culture*, happens when team members have composed a new cultural identity as a team. Their team H.E.L.P. system guides their interactions and becomes a source of experiences and skills strengthening the probability of their team's success. When the team is large and team membership fluctuates over time, a team may never develop a fully shared "composite" culture, but may continue to be composed of several networked cultural groups who learn to work together across boundaries. At Phase Four, Task Six may mean the reintroduction or reiteration of previously learned concepts and skills as team membership changes and to accommodate new team members' varying experiences, cultural awareness, and intercultural skill levels. Task Six may also include helping team members to renegotiate their team's H.E.L.P. system to respond to changing work conditions.

These phases of the global teaming process, and the instructional tasks associated with them, occur irregularly in a nonlinear fashion. Not all team members need to go through all instructional phases. Reversals and modifications of previously held assumptions about who the members are and how work should get done commonly occur. The phases are overlapping and fluctuate, especially when new members are added or new conditions warrant re-evaluating previously negotiated working cultural norms.

The teaching framework outlined above emphasizes the dynamic and systemic aspects of culture. Flexible strategies and tools include the teaching of basic core cultural axioms rooted in historical context to provide basic culture-specific knowledge as a starting point for intercultural negotiation. Examples drawn directly from the experiences of team members provide the basis for teaching tool development. These tools illustrate cross-cultural differences in creativity, in product development, in the use of knowledge, and in the approach to dealing with uncertainty, ambiguity, and problem solving that team members encounter on a daily basis.

The cultural coach introduces concepts by observing how team members interact in context, and customizes instruction "on the fly" to help them recognize culture at work. Team members are "learning in working" and then applying strategies to help them create shared understanding and a negotiated team H.E.L.P. system.

An example: A "day at work" scenario

The "day at work" scenario is a technique that can be employed rather easily by the cultural coach when "cultural" tensions are detected and an intervention would seem wise. The technique requires an hour and a half and can be successfully executed within an extended lunch hour. The "day at work" scenario works well when concepts and tools must be adapted to the salient cultures for the team members who are present "in the moment." Specifically, up to three scenarios about a day at work are presented and discussed, each based upon a different underlying set of cultural issues. These scenarios are particularly applicable to Tasks Two through Four of the instructional design and more specifically as a basis for teaching communication and negotiation skills required in Task Four to build the negotiated team H.E.L.P. system or "composite culture."

The teaching challenge in global automotive product development teams

To illustrate the application of the "day at work" scenario, I provide an example from my experience in the automotive industry. I have had the opportunity over the past three years to apply this process-oriented instructional design and to test a number of tools and techniques in a major automotive company headquartered in the U.S. Midwest. The company has initiated several new vehicle programs developing products spanning four continents: Europe, North America, South America, and Asia.

The Global Product Development Process, as it relates to the teaching challenge, is illustrated in Figure 19.2. The team moves through several different major milestones from initial concept and design to final product production. The team generally starts with a small multicultural leadership group that stays fairly constant throughout the product development process. As team tasks change, team members are added either incrementally or in large numbers. The team may begin with two or three co-located groups in different locations who travel periodically to each others' locations or work virtually. They may consolidate in a single location. These process phases and major changes in team composition

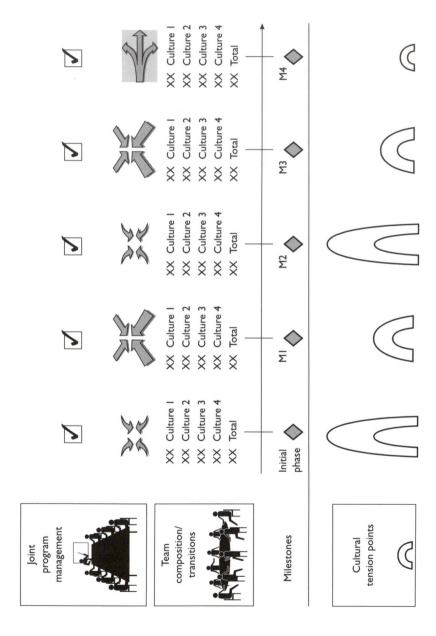

Figure 19.2 A global product development team.

represent cultural tension points of varying degree. This is when the cultural coach is most active, providing cultural orientation and facilitating negotiation among members.

The success of the global vehicle programs requires extensive cross-cultural collaboration in the development process that will integrate differing, often conflicting, market requirements with engineering and manufacturing practices. National cultural differences, as well as organizational and professional cultural differences, must be articulated, understood, and negotiated for the program to be successful. Divergent viewpoints about market needs, power struggles for control of product design and management, and conflicting approaches to product development processes are major issues that can heavily impact the ultimate success of the program and the achievement of company business objectives.

The overall educational challenge is to design a development program for creating multicultural awareness and skills among product development team members to help them work together to engineer and manufacture a global vehicle platform[1] that can be customized for diverse local markets. The specific teaching challenges include:

- complexity of multiple cultures in the global team work-setting, primarily national and regional, organizational, occupational cultures;
- temporary nature and continually changing make-up of team membership;
- changing "host culture" when team leadership moves from one organization and one national culture to another and/or when membership changes dramatically;
- large team size (100–400 people), with multiple networked sub-teams;
- different cultural adaptability and competence levels of team members, based on past experiences and acquired skills;
- geographically dispersed team members;
- quickly changing conditional context as company business strategy adapts to new marketplace challenges.

This is a long-term project and involves the use of different tools and techniques at different points in the team's development. It is rarely possible to teach the whole team at once (nor would you want to when needs and skills are highly variable and the team is large), and it is usually not possible to take the team away from their work for extended periods of time for formal classroom training. To respond to constantly changing conditions and time pressure, learning must take place quickly "on the fly" and must be grounded in daily practice to accomplish "learning in working."

The "day at work" approach can be easily adapted to teach about national, occupational, or organizational cultures, or any other cultural

H.E.L.P. system, because the scenarios are based on core cultural axioms, values and behaviors. Scenarios are designed to achieve three learning objectives:

1 Present recognizable and relevant situations illustrating common work practices influenced by cultural patterns of thought and behavior.
2 Create opportunities for team members to uncover the cultural patterns themselves and to see themselves directly in these patterns.
3 Engage in discussion and dialogue about the implications of these patterns for the team's work, including the identification of differences and similarities and the negotiation of new, shared cultural working norms.

The scenarios can be used with an individual, a sub-team working on the design of a vehicle component, or with a larger group. I have successfully used the approach with team members in 90-minute "brown-bag lunch" culture sessions. I have also used scenarios in large groups of 150 people as part of a larger working agenda and in private consultation with team leaders. Application of the scenarios in teaching culture is flexible and can even be spontaneous, provided the cultural coach is knowledgeable enough about the team and their work and has developed a few scenarios as part of a "teaching on the fly" portfolio. (See below for examples.)

There are several steps to creating and using a "day at work" scenario.

Creation

1 *Learn about the team.* Learn something about the specific work situation faced by the team members, the cultural make-up of the team, and their experiences. If you are coming from outside the organization, it is a prerequisite that you work with insiders to acquire as much knowledge as possible about the work challenges facing a particular team and about the team members themselves. It is also necessary to have general knowledge of the team's primary mission and of the countries, organizations, and occupations the team members represent.
2 *Decide which cultural patterns are most observable in the team and which cultural attributes you wish to stress.* To teach about a specific culture, the teacher must have general knowledge of that culture through experience and/or study, paired with consultation with someone who has specific experience in the particular culture. The attributes on which you focus depend on the work context. In general, I have found that attributes pertaining to styles of leadership, problem solving and decision making, motivation or commitment, and communication are relevant to most work situations. Write a brief narra-

tive that reflects the situation in a day at work from the perspective of someone who is part of the relevant culture. The three example scenarios focus on national culture. However, these could have been designed around occupational or organizational cultures or written to illustrate how different cultures interact in the workplace.

3   *Write the scenario with the help of a cultural "insider" to assure work accuracy and relevance.* Work with someone who is both an insider and trained in the "human" side of the business. If there is no such individual, gather as much information as possible from insiders, perhaps your "client" or other key individuals knowledgeable about the team. Read secondary documents to learn something about the industry as a whole. This takes time, but the investment translates into teaching opportunities and relevant learning. If I have enough knowledge about the people I am teaching and about their work, I know when to introduce learning tools so that they are relevant to the immediate work situation – true "teaching on the fly" and "learning in working."

Usage

4   *Look for a learning opportunity when at least half an hour is available.* Each scenario requires a minimum of half an hour. Sometimes you can get a larger block of time with team members and cover two or three scenarios at one time. It is not usually possible to do more than three scenarios in one session because the team members become overloaded. They need time to think about the learning and to observe patterns in the work situation. These scenarios are meant to increase self-awareness, awareness about others, and about the influence of culture on behavior in the workplace. They also help heighten people's observational skills.

5   *Use the scenario with a large or small group.* If groups are large, break the groups into subgroups (about five people) and ask them to read the scenarios and then discuss them among themselves, answering the three questions posed at the conclusion of each:

a   What behaviors does this description of a work situation illustrate?
b   What do you think are the beliefs and values underlying these behaviors?
c   What are your reactions to the primary character's thinking and to his or her behavior?

It takes about 10–15 minutes for the group to read and discuss the scenarios.

6   *Debrief the scenario.* Ask the group as a whole, or an individual from each subgroup, to volunteer responses to each of the three questions.

If the group has missed something, probe for responses to key passages in the scenario.

7   *Review and summarize the primary work behaviors and cultural values the scenario illustrates.* Emphasize the point that the scenario illustrates general, mainstream, cultural patterns and how these are typically manifested in a work situation. Ask how these patterns are like or different from the patterns they encounter in their own work situations. Stress also that there is individual variation in behavior and thought and that the patterns are meant to help them understand better culture's influence on work.

8   *Ask the group what they think are the implications of the values and behaviors for the group's work.* Probe for similarities and differences in patterns of behavior among the participants.

9   *Repeat these teaching steps with each scenario.*

Continuing dilemmas

Teaching culture "on the fly" is an experimental approach to learning in the work context for global team members. The "day at work" scenarios create small teaching wins and provide some ordered sense-making in complex and chaotic cultural work contexts. These scenarios are only one technique that can be used to create learning within the global teaming process. There still remains much work to be done to match teaching culture with how it is enacted in global teaming contexts. There are still several key questions to be answered through further research and collaboration among educators:

*   How can learning be shared quickly when it is "spontaneous" and "tacit"?
*   How can we measure "learning in working," and do we need to?
*   How can new communication technologies be better used to help teach?
*   How can "teams of teachers" better contribute to teaching culture in global teams?
*   How can we learn more about learning strategies that work "on the fly" when backgrounds and competencies vary widely?

Teaching culture "on the fly" means that we must do continuous "learning in working" ourselves to be good educators.

Three sample "day at work" scenarios for the United States, Japan, and Sweden

U.S. scenario: Jerry's day at work

Jerry Davis, an American engineer working for a major automotive manufacturer, was checking his e-mail in the office very early one morning. There were many e-mail messages that had been sent to him since the time he had left work late the night before to catch a few hours of sleep. However, there was one message in particular that caught his eye. His supervisor was announcing a last-minute meeting that had been called to convey the results of a management meeting and to discuss the next steps for the engineering team. Jerry knew this would be an important meeting to attend, so he rearranged his schedule to be there, even though it meant he would probably have to work late again to get everything done. For Jerry, the meeting would be an opportunity not only to learn about the latest turn of events, but also to participate more in the work of the team and to demonstrate how he could contribute to the team's success.

Jerry had joined the company just eight years ago, but in that time he had moved around quite a lot, accepting different job assignments and moving his wife and two children to a new city three times, but they didn't seem to mind. Jerry's wife had a career in real estate and saw the moves as an opportunity to learn more about the real-estate laws in different regions, as well as to experience first-hand what many of her own clients had to go through. The kids were young and were learning at an early age how to adapt to new situations. Jerry believed they would be stronger individuals because of these experiences. It was also true that each time the family moved it had been because of a promotion Jerry had received. His family was proud of him, and the evidence of his success was a bigger house and even a boat. The kids were just learning how to water-ski and loving every minute of it. Jerry had talked about his career plans with his wife before they were married. They both knew that Jerry had career goals and they planned each job move together, weighing the pros and cons of the decision to accept or reject a new assignment. So far, Jerry had made the right moves and he was on the fast track, recognized and rewarded by upper management as someone with a lot of potential.

Jerry arrived just in time for the meeting. There were about 20 people in the room, and he knew all of them, although he had only been with the team for two months. He had made the rounds and introduced himself to everyone when he joined the team. He was on a first-name basis with everyone, even those who were part of the team on a foreign service assignment. The team leader began the meeting by passing out a loosely structured agenda, then opened with a five-minute summary of what had happened at the management meeting the day before. A couple of the other team members who had been at the meeting chimed in to offer some of the details. As soon as the summary was complete, Jerry jumped into the discussion with a couple of pointed statements conveying his own opinions about the meeting's outcome, then turned to the whole group with a question "So, what are we going to do about it?" Many of the meeting participants were not yet ready to get to discussion, but Jerry was. He was a quick student and could see what had to be done to solve the problem that management had raised for the team. He got up from his seat and went to the whiteboard to lead the team in discussing how he thought they should drop the approach they had been taking and temporarily restructure their work and task assignments to solve the problem. He had seen this type of problem before in another situation and thought that business-as-usual would not solve it. He prided himself on being innovative and on doing whatever it took to get the job done. He thought the best teams succeeded when everyone rallied around the problem and figured out how to solve it. Some of the other people on the team did not agree with Jerry and were reluctant to drop the well-thought-out path they had been taking with their work so far. Jerry was so forceful in his presentation that he overruled objections and got them all to try it his way, especially when it looked to everyone like the team leader was open to Jerry's suggestions. When the meeting ended, Jerry was optimistic that the team would find a way to solve their problem just by putting their heads together to come up with a new plan and taking quick action on their decisions. Jerry was assigned the job of leading the special effort.

Japanese scenario: Yoshi's day at work

Yoshi Aoyama stepped off the train and onto the platform with the throngs of other workers beginning their workday. During his morning commute, he had time to think about the day ahead and begin preparing himself for the meetings he was to attend at the automotive company where he has worked for the past fifteen years, since he graduated from the university. Yoshi was hired into the company as an engineer, along with many others from his university who have been his cohort throughout the years.

Yoshi's work unit is best described in English as a "team," although they don't describe themselves as such. Yoshi's team works with other unit teams in the group on vehicle performance development, including safety, comfort, NVH (vehicle performance requirements for noise, vibration and harshness), and brakes. The team tries hard to take care of problems that arise, aiming at the project goal. However, the team members have recently encountered a problem with wind noise that they feel they cannot resolve themselves. Yoshi's team has kept the group manager informed about the problem from the start. The team carefully studied the problem and formulated a recommended solution, which they took to their team leader who in turn took it to the group manager. The group manager has suggested possible solutions to the team and has also incorporated suggestions from the team. Since the solution involves coordination with other teams in the project who are not part of Yoshi's group, Yoshi's team issued an invitation to the V Research Group and the G Design Team to attend a problem-solving meeting. This morning, Yoshi's team will meet with the other teams for four hours to work on the problem.

Yoshi and his team believe they have a good strategy in place to achieve the outcome they want. The team has prepared for the meeting over the past two weeks in close coordination with the other unit teams affected by the problem. Everyone involved in resolving the issue and everyone who will be affected by the suggested changes will be at the meeting. Yoshi thinks the meeting will run smoothly, and he is sure the chief, the final authority for the project, will adopt the recommended solution because it is the best solution for the project and for the company, even though his team will have to make some sacrifices.

The meeting will begin an hour after he arrives at the office, and Yoshi wants to make sure all the preparations are in order so the meeting will run smoothly. He checks the meeting room to make sure that the seating arrangements are all right and checks the agenda to see that it is accurate. When everyone arrives for the meeting, they exchange greetings and take their places, with the group manager in the middle.

Yoshi begins the meeting by referring to the common objectives of the group and their task to find the best solution for the company. Yoshi knows that everyone has read all the materials that have been exchanged prior to the meeting. The discussion flows from the agenda, and everyone is given the opportunity to speak about the issues. There is no confrontation or conflict, although Yoshi knows that the proposed solution will cause extra work and cost for some unit teams, including his own. The discussion proceeds with periods of silence and then reference to the details that will need to be executed, with the group manager contributing little. Finally, the group manager announces that he agrees to proceed with the accepted solution with a minor modification, which everyone knew would be the probable outcome. The meeting ends with an affirmation of everyone's commitment to the decision and praise for the teams' efforts.

Yoshi and his team leave the meeting knowing the decision is the right one, but they feel they will be sacrificing more than some of the other groups in the next few weeks. Later, after work when the team is having drinks together before the commute home, Yoshi and some of his team members vent some of their frustrations to the group manager, who reminds them of other situations when the roles (demand loads) have been reversed. Yoshi knows this is true, and in the future they will be able to call in a debt from one of the other group managers. One way or another, he is confident that his group manager will make sure that the chief knows what is going on.

Swedish scenario: Lars's day at work

Lars Olson arrived at the office on Monday morning at precisely at 9 a.m., as was his usual habit. He got a cup of coffee and said good morning to his co-workers, who were also getting their morning coffee, then went to his office to look at the day's calendar. He felt very refreshed from his weekend at the lake. He had been hiking alone along the shoreline and camped out overnight along the way. It had been a beautiful June weekend, and he was grateful just to be outdoors in the country and also for the solitude. He and several others at the office were part of a company-sponsored environmental group who were pitching in to monitor a portion of the lakeland to assure that it was not showing signs of over-usage.

The first scheduled item on Lars's agenda was a meeting to discuss the chassis design criteria for a platform being developed jointly by his car company and an American car company as a result of the American acquisition of the Swedish company. The car was intended for both Europe and the U.S. Lars was proud of the work the company had done on the current model sedan and of the initiative he had taken to learn on his own about new safety enhancements in materials for chassis construction. That car had received an industry safety award, and Lars was serious in his conviction that safety would not be compromised in the new design as a result of the acquisition. Lars also was concerned that his Swedish company would be able to maintain its status as a leading employer in the area and that, for the good of the regional economy, jobs would not be lost as a result of the merger. He remembered a previous joint-venture attempt that had failed in an uprising of union protest by the entire engineering community. He did not want to see that happen again with this joint program because it was important to the company's survival, and to Sweden's presence in the automotive industry, to be part of a larger global automotive company. His company also had a collegial and relaxed pace, and he was worried that the Americans would bring their habit of working excessive hours to the new venture. He did not want the company intruding on his private time. Lars also was concerned that those transferring to Sweden from the U.S. would arrive with the expectation that they should have bigger houses or higher incomes than their Swedish counterparts. That would not be a good start to cooperative relationships on the platform program.

Lars's manager was not as informed as Lars about the latest advances in materials, particularly steel, so the manager had asked Lars to attend the meeting and to facilitate it, suggesting that he try to get agreement on basic design criteria for safety. At 10 a.m., the meeting began with customary greetings. Even though the Americans had just arrived a week ago, the Swedes and the Americans had already comfortably slipped into calling each other by their first names, especially since the Swedes all spoke English very well. Lars shook hands with everyone and reviewed the agenda and procedures for the meeting, even though he knew everyone had received a copy of the agenda ahead of time. Lars and his colleagues had come prepared with photographs, drawings, and cost data, as well as documents outlining Swedish government concerns for environmental and passenger safety. Lars began the discussions by asking everyone to present their data and express their opinions with the goal in mind of reaching a consensus, particularly about safety design criteria.

However, the discussions soon took a surprising turn when one of the Americans interrupted and began to talk about how the Swedish approach to safety would not work in the U.S. Lars was patient and practical and could see the American's point of view, but he and his colleagues were caught off-guard by the interruption and by the American's rudeness from their point of view, especially in criticizing Swedish government policy. The Swedes were willing to listen and to be persuaded by any facts the American could offer, but they also wanted to make sure that everyone had the opportunity to present an opinion. They felt everyone should listen to everyone else before making any effort to reconcile contradictory positions. Lars calmly turned to his colleagues, checking their faces for signs that they were ready for negotiation. Not receiving it, he responded to the American's concerns with an offer to consider them in further discussion. When Lars was finished with his brief statement, the next person took his turn. After another hour or so of relaxed discussion, the Americans noticed that a decision seemed to be emerging from the discussion, and they were not sure if their concerns had been included. One of the Swedes reassured the Americans that they would all decide based on what was best both for the public and for the business. He asked the Americans to present any further data to make their case for less stringent safety criteria, which they did. The discussion of pros and cons continued until the appointed meeting ending time when the Swedes got up, nodding to each other and congratulating one another on the decision to proceed with the criteria listed on the flipchart. The Americans were taken aback since they did not realize at all that a decision had been made. They said they were not prepared to make a decision and didn't have the authority to do so anyway – the managers would make the final decision in the U.S. At this, it was the Swedes' turn to be surprised. They left the meeting room puzzled and frustrated, wondering why the Americans were there if they were not empowered to make a decision.

Cultural patterns emphasized in each scenario

Standard questions to be attached to each scenario:

1   What behaviors does this description of [Jerry's/Yoshi's/Lars's] work situation illustrate?
2   What do you think are the beliefs and values underlying these behaviors?
3   What are your reactions to [Jerry's/Yoshi's/Lars's] thinking and to his behavior?

Jerry's day at work

U.S. cultural patterns emphasized in Jerry's day:

*   Individualism

    –   personal gain – personal responsibility and self-reliance, personal initiative and control;
    –   achievement and material gain – external reward, individual recognition, moving up in the world (bigger house, boat, second home, career advancement, pragmatism – potential for bonus and promotion);

*   Freedom/equality

    –   mobility, autonomy, opportunity, freedom of choice;
    –   equality (lack of deference to his boss and others of higher rank, first-name basis, informality);

*   Pragmatism

    –   task-focused, inductive, a-theoretical, a-historical, what works;
    –   informal structure that suits the task and is specific to the situation – depending on the problem to be solved.

Yoshi's day at work

Japanese cultural patterns emphasized in Yoshi's day:

*   obligations, preparation and thoroughness, group interdependence, strong group identity and personal responsibility;
*   share information widely, leaders listen carefully, achieve group consensus, promote harmony, personal responsibility, collective decision-making, focus on overall goals, group consensus;
*   strategic thinking, individual and group sacrifice to reach objective,

collective decision-making, thoroughness and preparation, follow the chain of command;

- formal style to the meeting, silence is a part of the conversation, individual and group sacrifice for the objective, negotiation – everybody wins, confrontation avoided, personal responsibility, pride, self-esteem, attention to detail, harmony and peace;
- strong identity and loyalty to the group, follow the chain of command, after-hours socializing, peer competition discouraged, sense of reciprocal obligation and indebtedness, harmony and peace.

Lars's day at work

Swedish cultural patterns emphasized in Lars's day:

- punctuality highly valued;
- social responsibility: environmental consciousness and preservation of nature positively recognized; safety is a motivation in decision-making and is rewarded as a contribution to the public good; concern for material security;
- relaxed pace, value for egalitarianism (move quickly to first-name basis); business and personal relationships are kept separate, collegiality;
- self-development and personal initiative expected; person doing job knows more about it than anyone else, including manager, managers are not expected to have all the answers; coaching, managers suggest rather than direct or give instructions; procedures are designed to minimize uncertainty and the need for improvisation;
- avoidance of conflict, serious about business, patient, serial conversational style; turn-taking and listening without interruption are expected, unanimity and active consensus style; decisions emerge from discussion based on listening, persuasion and reconciling contradictory positions; negotiating based on personal conviction and self-restraint; flat and informal; open and direct, honest, reasoned.

Note

1 In the automobile industry, "platform" refers to the basic automobile architecture, "the core design comprising a common chassis and wheelbase" (Fine *et al.* 1996: 25), upon which different models and body styles can be built.

References

Brannen, M. Y. (1998) "Negotiated culture in binational contexts: a model of culture change based on a Japanese American organizational experience," *Anthropology of Work Review*, 18 (2, 3): 6–17.

Fine, C. H., St. Clair, R., Lafrance, J. C. and Hillebrand, D. (1996) *Meeting the Challenge: U.S. Industry Faces the 21st Century – The U.S. Automobile Manufacturing Industry*, Washington, DC: U.S. Department of Commerce, Office of Technology Policy.

Gluesing, J. G. (1998) "Building connections and balancing power in global teams: toward a reconceptualization of culture as composite," *Anthropology of Work Review*, 18 (2, 3): 18–29.

Chapter 20

Teaching mindful intercultural conflict management

Stella Ting-Toomey

Introduction

Intercultural conflict is defined as the "experience of emotional frustration in conjunction with perceived incompatibility of values, norms, face orientations, goals, scarce resources, processes, and/or outcomes between a minimum of two cultural parties from two different cultural communities in an interactive situation" (Ting-Toomey and Oetzel 2001: 17). Intercultural conflicts are sometimes based on deep-seated hatred and centuries-old antagonism, often arising from long-standing historical grievances. However, a majority of everyday conflicts can be traced to cultural miscommunication, lack of understanding, or ignorance.

Teaching intercultural conflict management is a challenging, yet rewarding, assignment. The theme itself can be approached from so many directions and angles. While classroom lectures can provide an initial grounding for explaining conflict concepts, I believe an active learning approach (Silberman and Auerbach 1998) helps students deepen their participation and enliven their learning in an intercultural classroom. Active learning experiences such as conflict role-play exercises, games and simulations, and conflict metaphors and journey visualizations, allow learners to confront their own values, attitudes, emotions, and culture-based behaviors. Learners can also become more aware of cultural strangers' feelings and reactions to dissimilar communication behaviors and events.

Intercultural conflict: conceptual background

The exercise introduced in this module simulates the communication aspect of an everyday intercultural conflict. Upon completion of a well-facilitated intercultural exercise, students should be able to:

- articulate their frustrations in dealing with cultural differences;

- identify the key factors that shape an intercultural conflict episode; and
- analyze their cultural roles and the cultural strangers' roles in contributing to the conflict situation.

Overall, participants should emerge from a simulated exercise with a sense of appreciation for the role of "mindfulness" in managing intercultural conflicts. To act "mindfully" in an intercultural encounter means paying full attention to an interaction at that particular moment without imposing their own evaluative lens on a cultural stranger's behavior. Simultaneously, to communicate "mindfully" means we pay close intrapersonal attention to our own reactive emotions, cognitions, behaviors, and cultural lens that we display in the conflict scene (Langer 1989, 1997; Ting-Toomey 1999). In mindful conflict management, we try hard to "catch" our own habitual ways of reacting to a conflict situation. Additionally, we are also willing to try out new thinking patterns, regulated emotions, and adaptive behaviors in managing the differences.

The conceptual grounding of the simulation, "Alpha-Omega Conflict Negotiation Exercise," can be located in Chapters 1–8 of *Communicating across Cultures* (Ting-Toomey 1999). The simulation is usually conducted in the 8th to 10th weeks of a 15-week semester. (I find it more useful to conduct the exercise, then discuss Chapter 8 in depth.) More specifically, cultural value dimensions such as individualism and collectivism, small/large power distance, low/high context-communication styles, ethnocentrism, and ethnorelativism would have been covered prior to the simulation. Also, the meaning of "mindlessness" and "mindfulness" would have been discussed extensively. Chapters on "managing intercultural conflict effectively" (Ting-Toomey 1994, 1997) have also served as supplemental readings. The simulation basically provides an excellent forum to help participants focus on what they consider as normal from the Alphan's or the Omegan's cultural frame of reference. The exercise also explores the emotional impact of dealing with communication differences – on both the verbal and nonverbal style levels – across cultural boundaries.

Intercultural conflict negotiation: a simulated exercise[1]

Title of the exercise: Alpha and Omega Conflict Negotiation Exercise

Overview

Two groups, the Alphans and Omegans, are assigned different cultural norms and given different outcomes to negotiate for one plot of land. During the negotiations the two groups enact their different cultural norms.

Overall purpose

To provide a context for students to experience communication style differences, underlying value clashes, and multiple goal conflicts.

Objectives

Upon completion of the exercise, students will be able to:

1 integrate affective, cognitive, and behavioral learning in managing intercultural conflict;
2 be mindful of their own ethnocentric tendencies in intercultural conflict episodes;
3 increase their awareness of differentiating mindless from mindful conflict behaviors;
4 suspend "snapshot" evaluations of cultural differences; and
5 compare the differences between position-based and interest-based conflict negotiation.

Time

Time allowed is 60 minutes. There are four phases:

- exercise introduction phase (5 minutes);
- in-group orientation phase (10 minutes);
- inter-group negotiation process phase (15 minutes);
- debriefing phase (20–30 minutes).

Facilitators

While one instructor can conduct the exercise, co-facilitators are better.

Facilities

Two separate areas or rooms where each of the groups can confidentially discuss and practice their cultural norms and their task instructions.

Materials

1 Two handouts for each culture (see Appendices):

- cultural norms and task instructions for each culture (see Appendices 20.1 and 20.3);
- negotiation contract (see Appendices 20.2 and 20.4; contract is different for each culture);

2   flipcharts, colored markers, and name-tag labels;
3   whistle or other signaling device.

Teacher's directions for conducting the exercise

1 Exercise introduction phase (5 minutes)

Explain the basic format of the exercise as follows.

> *You are going to participate in a fun exercise as a member of either the Alphan or the Omegan group. The groups have never met before. However, they will get a chance to meet each other today at a cocktail party. We will now split you into two groups. Your facilitator will give you more instructions about your role in the party. Enjoy yourself and have fun with your group. You will have 10 minutes to get acquainted with members of your own group. Then you will come to meet each other at the cocktail party. The cocktail party encounter will last about 15 minutes.*

Then randomly assign the class to the two groups.

2 In-group orientation phase (10 minutes)

Have the students read their group's characteristics and task instructions. (The facilitator should do an oral summary of the core values and communication styles of the group. She or he should demonstrate and dramatize the particular communication styles with ample verbal and nonverbal examples.) The facilitator should emphasize the task instructions of the group and answer questions about the group's norms or task. Do not answer any questions or provide information about the other group.

Process instructions: within each large group, divide the students into clusters of three. Instruct them to discuss and practice their group norms with each other within the triad and think of appropriate verbal or nonverbal behaviors or effective reasons to convince the others of the importance of their relationship or task goals. Encourage the group to come up with a greeting ritual in accordance with their group norms (i.e., Alphans are more digital and low-context, and Omegans are more analogic and high-context).

3 Intergroup negotiation phase (15 minutes)

Have the Omegans join the Alphans in one classroom – the Alphans (who are monochronic and clock-bound) should be complaining now about the tardiness of the Omegans (who are polychronic and relational). One facilitator should direct each Omegan triadic group to join and greet an Alphan triadic group. Make sure that both Alphans and Omegans are standing and remain standing during the entire negotiation session. Remind the students that each Alphan–Omegan team has complete authority to negotiate for their group and sign the contract with all signatures appearing on one contract. They do not need to sign both contracts – one signed contract is good enough. Remind them that they have 15 minutes to accomplish their goal and that the dinner banquet will follow right after their cocktail-party getting-to-know-each-other session. Blow a whistle after about 10 minutes and inform the students that they will have only 5 minutes to finish their negotiation and the banquet will be served shortly. Post flipchart papers on the wall and encourage each team to finalize their contract negotiation and create a diagram or draw a consensus plan on a flipchart paper. Blow a whistle to end the team negotiation session at about 15 minutes; stop the interaction even if some teams could not come to a consensus agreement.

4 Debriefing session (20–30 minutes)

Students return to the large classroom format. Use some of the following questions for debriefing:

- How many teams have actually completed their negotiation sessions with a signed contract?
- How many teams did not? Why, or why not?
- How did you feel during the negotiation session? How do you feel now?
- What happened? Why did it happen?
- What did you notice during the negotiation session?
- What were the stressful moments? What were the pleasant moments?

After an individual venting or voicing process for several minutes, invite each team to summarize for the class what went on in the negotiation session and explain their contract diagram to the class. Encourage them to discuss both the content negotiation issues and the verbal and nonverbal behaviors exchanged in the session. For the purpose of drawing out ethnocentric viewpoints, you can also make four columns on the board:

- 1st column: Alphans' view of Omegans
- 2nd column: Alphans' view of themselves
- 3rd column: Omegans' view of themselves
- 4th column: Omegans' view of Alphans

Ask members of one group and then the other: "How did you feel about the other group?" or "What did you think of the members of the other culture?" List responses in the appropriate columns, then invite the insiders of the culture to share their perceptions of their cultural traits, for the purpose of generating alternative cultural description: "How would you describe your own culture?" List responses in the appropriate columns. Wrap up the debriefing session by asking:

*   What did you learn from the exercise or simulated experience?
*   To what extent can you relate to the Alphan or Omegan experience?
*   Can you draw examples from your real-life interactions in the workplace that parallel the Alphan–Omegan experience?
*   What constructive suggestions or recommendations do you have in managing real-life intercultural conflict differences?

5 At the end of debriefing

You may now want to switch off the classroom light, instruct the students to close their eyes and ask them to breathe deeply and de-role. The facilitator should count down from 10 to 1 and encourage the students to breathe away their Alphan or Omegan role.

Intercultural conflict: debriefing concepts

The key debriefing concepts regarding the Alpha–Omega conflict negotiation exercise are: moving from an ethnocentric to an ethnorelative mindset; identifying mindless versus mindful conflict behaviors; and, moving from positionally based negotiation to interest-based negotiation.

Moving from ethnocentric to ethnorelative mindset

The initial debriefing questions to evoke mindfulness in the students' interpretations of each other's culture are: *Why did Alphans evaluate Omegans as "lazy, tardy or irresponsible"*? Conversely, *Why did Omegans evaluate Alphans as "uptight, boring, or aggressive?"* Point out that they are using their own cultural baseline reactions to evaluate the other culture's attributes. Explain the differences between the ethnocentric mindset and the ethnorelative mindset (see Bennett's Chapter 14 in this book). The ethnocentric mindset means that we hold views and standards that are "own-group-centric" and are making snapshot evaluations about another group based on our own in-group standards. The ethnorelative mindset, on the other hand, means that we mindfully suspend our judgment and conscientiously use the other group's cultural frame of reference in interpreting their behaviors. When we act mindlessly, we use our "own-group-centric" standards to downgrade the out-group's conflict practice. When we act mindfully, we catch ourselves in the moment of snapshot – ethnocentric judgment – and are willing to take time to understand the reactive emotions of the culturally dissimilar.

Further questions can move students from an ethnocentric mindset to an ethnorelative reflection stage. For example,

- What differences do you see in the words used to express the views of each culture (compare the 1st column with the 2nd column, compare the 3rd column with the 4th column)?
- What is the basis of your evaluation or interpretation? What verbal and nonverbal behaviors did you observe that influenced your perception?
- How did these interpretations and perceptions further influence the conflict negotiation process?
- Can you think of any ways to rephrase or reframe your interpretations?

By learning to reframe the conflict situation from the other culture's frame of reference, we can suspend our snapshot evaluations in judging unfamiliar behaviors in a prejudiced direction.

Identifying mindless versus mindful behaviors

In mindful conflict practice, we conscientiously come up with alternative explanations for unfamiliar conflict behaviors from the other culture's point of view. We are able to pair the cultural logic (i.e., the underlying cultural values and beliefs) with the communication behaviors in question. We also conscientiously adjust and adapt our behaviors to signal intercultural sensitivity.

In teaching the role of "mindfulness" to students, draw out their comments on how they have behaved "mindlessly" or "mindfully" in the simulated exercise. For the most part, students should have no problems identifying their own mindless judgmental thoughts or reactions. Their comments often contained the following sets of words: anxious, defensive, frustrations, not listening, mindless listening, judgmental, not getting my point across, acting ethnocentrically, acting evaluatively, impatience with the other group, total communication breakdown.

Next, ask each group to describe their underlying cultural values and norms. Now that both groups have a clearer understanding of the value patterns that guide the Alphan and Omegan cultures, probe their thoughts on how to explain the different behaviors (e.g., Omegans never get to the point in their negotiation and never give a clear "yes" or "no" answer) in conjunction with their newfound understanding of the other culture's values (e.g., Omegans are very relationally centered and they try not to offend others by being indirect and effusive).

More debriefing questions can be posed as follows:

- What do you think are the underlying value assumptions that drive Alphans' or Omegans' conflict behaviors?
- Now that you understand the Alpha or Omega cultural values, can you understand why they behave so differently from your cultural group?
- How many of you feel very stressed because you were playing an entirely different role in the simulation?
- How would you prepare yourself better to meet the people from the other culture?

Other follow-up probing questions can then center on how they might have behaved differently in the simulation. Under the "mindful" column, they would typically suggest, e.g., be more observant, suspend judgment, learn more about the culture beforehand, have patience, do not react quickly, learn their values, learn the meaning of their communication style, do not take things personally, lower defensiveness, learn to adapt, learn to identify common ground. More specifically, *how can we change our mindset from a mindless orientation to a mindful orientation in managing cultural differences?*

Students, at this point, are able to enthusiastically offer their insights, such as mindful observation, empathic listening, mindful reframing, refraining from over-generalizing, the difference between cultural and personal trait levels, and the importance of understanding both differences and similarities between members of different cultures. They also often comment on the various situational factors (e.g., the importance of conflict goals, the setting, the time constraint, family conflict script) that enter into analyzing a complex intercultural conflict case (see Ting-Toomey and Oetzel 2001).

Moving from positional-based negotiation to interest-based negotiation

Lastly, intercultural conflict parties should also learn to engage in a common-interest dialogue process. Rather than emphasizing positional differences, both Alphans and Omegans should learn what they have in common. Positional-based negotiation emphasizes polarized differences, coercive power, fixed conflict objectives, and win–lose to lose–lose outcomes. Interest-based negotiation, on the other hand, emphasizes common interests, shared power, negotiable conflict objectives, and a win–win outcome. For example, the fact that Alphans desire a high-tech parking lot is because they want to attract tourists in order to generate additional funds for building better schools and playgrounds for their children. Similarly, Omegans desire a beautiful park because they want their children to have a safe, relaxed place to play and get to know each other. By digging deeper into common interests, Alphans and Omegans may discover that they have much in common. For example, both Alphans and Omegans desire a safe environment for their families and children to live, work, and play together. Neither enjoy conflicts. Both groups want to be respected. Both groups realize that they have to do something constructive to revitalize their commonly shared space or else deterioration will set in and the space will be wasted. As they learn to engage in more mindful interest-based negotiations, their polarized positions can be softened and their commonalities explicitly shared. Their win–win outcome may consist of building a four-level recreational structure with the ground level as a park and the top three levels as parking spaces. Alternatively, they may dig downward, with the ground level as a beautiful park, and the underground levels as a high-tech parking lot.

To achieve this level of win–win problem-solving dialogue, both Alphans and Omegans have to display good faith in an effort to modify their culture-based conflict styles. They have to adapt and modify their own communication styles so that the language, the verbal style, and the nonverbal style they use do not appear to be too "aggressive" or "passive" in dealing with culturally dissimilar others. In flexibly adapting our communication behaviors, we are also signaling to the others that we respect their ways of communicating and living.

Debriefing challenges

Some of the challenging questions from the students include:

1   *Do Alphans or Omegans represent a real-life specific culture?* No. Each group may have some attributes that make you imagine that it is about a particular culture. However, this is only a 15-minute intercultural simulation. The groups have only a few cultural norms and rules to follow in a short simulation. In a real-life culture, there are a great number of conflict norms and rules that may exist in a particular situation. Encourage the students to always underestimate their understanding of a new culture. Let them know that the experience of culture shock or culture stress is an inevitable crossing-culture experience. It is part of a transformative, learning process.

2   *Who should adapt to whom in a real-life intercultural conflict situation?* The answer is "it depends." Try to deepen students' analytical framework by bringing in situational factors that are critical in deciding who should adapt to whom in different types of intercultural situations. To do so, you can ask, for example,

- Who wants what from whom?
- Is this a one-time conflict relationship or a long-term interpersonal or team relationship?

- What are the different power resources that team members possess?
- What are the scarce resources that are involved in the intercultural conflict? Are the scarce resources really scarce or only perceived as scarce?
- Are they operating within a larger organizational cultural context? How would that affect their conflict negotiation choices?

Creative variations

There are many creative ways that an instructor can modify the Alphan–Omegan Conflict Negotiation Exercise. Here are some suggestions:

1   Experiment with different group compositions: for example, 4 Alphans and 2 Omegans, or 2 Alphans and 4 Omegans. The discussion can focus on majority and minority conflict negotiation by the sheer majority–minority size composition.
2   Experiment with female–male group composition: for example, 4 female Alphans and 2 male Omegans, and compare that with 4 male Alphans and 2 female Omegans. Alternatively, make some teams all-female, and others all-male. The discussion can focus on differences and similarities of negotiation patterns and conflict outcomes between groups.
3   Experiment with sex or age categories: designate female or male groups, older or younger groups, and assess which has more power in each group, and play with the small/large power-distance value orientation and leadership/followers dimension.
4   Give the Alphans and Omegans a "time-out" caucus period so that they can communicate privately with their own Alphan or Omegan team members. Encourage them to strategize and talk to each other and plan what they should do next in the simulation. Send them back into their original team and let them know that they will have only 5 minutes left to round-off their negotiation phase.
5   Offer them time to debrief each other: write some debriefing questions on a flipchart. The questions should focus on drawing out their feelings and sharing their experiences (e.g., the most stressful aspects, the most pleasant aspects, the most satisfying aspects, the most disturbing aspects, and the most surprising aspects) in participating in the simulation. The facilitator should still do a full-blown debriefing process after this "venting" discussion.
6   If there is time, let them diagram (via pictures or words) the different stages they went through – from initiation, through middle-negotiation, to the closure phase – in the intercultural Alpha–Omega

conflict process. Invite them to share and explain the picture with the large class.

7   Form a fish-bowl, and request an unsuccessful team (i.e., the group that did not sign the contract) to continue the simulated exercise. Ask this team to continue their interactions for 5 minutes, ask observers in the outer circle to identify mindless conflict behaviors. Next, request the players to start practicing some mindful conflict skills and to engage in interest-based negotiation patterns in the next 10 minutes. Ask observers to identify mindful conflict characteristics.

8   The totally unmotivated students or students who have high apprehension of any role-play exercise can be assigned the role of a journalist from a third culture. Instruct them to play the role of an objective journalist, and ask them to take notes and report back to the larger class all the observed behaviors and events that contributed to a destructive or a constructive conflict episode.

In summary

A well-guided, semi-structured debriefing process moves the students from the ethnocentric mindset stage to the ethnorelative perspective-taking stage, from increasing mindless reaction to choosing to act mindfully, and from positional-based negotiation to interest-based negotiation.

Mindful conflict management requires us to be sensitive to the differences and similarities in conflict encounters between diverse cultural groups. It demands that we be aware of our own ethnocentric biases and be ready to move from ethnocentric thinking to viewing through an ethnorelative lens. It encourages us to increase our alertness to our own and others' mindless behaviors. It propels us to understand more deeply the cultural logic that guides our own and others' conflict behaviors.

Appendix 20.1 (For Alphans only)

ALPHA GROUP CHARACTERISTICS (Confidential Information)
1   Alphans equate time with money. Time is considered very valuable and should be utilized to the fullest extent.
2   Alphans live by the philosophy, "Live to work." They place business before pleasure because it gives life purpose.
3   In the Alpha culture, the individual is considered the most important. As a member of the Alphas, you are primarily concerned with meeting your individual needs and goals.
4   When in conversation, Alphans like to be direct and straight to the point. Alphas like to stick to business related talk. They believe that showing emotions in their talk is improper. They also like to cross their arms to guard their emotions when they feel tense or vulnerable. Finally, Alphas like to snap their fingers when they think someone expresses a good, logical idea or suggestion.

INSTRUCTIONS FOR MEMBERS OF THE ALPHA GROUP
1   You are meeting members of the Omega group for the first time at a pre-dinner cocktail party. Although your two groups have never met, you have to correspond with each other about a plot of land in the community, which is co-owned by the Alphas and the Omegas. In the correspondence, both groups agreed that the plot of land should be utilized to better serve the community.
2   Your plan for the meeting is to persuade members of the Omega group of the necessity for a new, high-tech parking structure. You expect that the Omega group will go along with your plan.
3   YOUR PRIMARY GOAL IS TO HAVE THE OMEGAS CO-SIGN THE CONTRACT SO THAT CONSTRUCTION CAN BEGIN IMMEDIATELY. Wasted time means wasted money. You have your contract ready, and as soon as it is signed by all parties involved, construction can begin on the parking structure.
4   You would like to get business out of the way first so you can relax and enjoy your dinner.

YOU HAVE COMPLETE AUTHORITY TO MAKE A DECISION FOR THE MEMBERS OF YOUR GROUP.

(REMEMBER, DO NOT DISCUSS YOUR GROUP'S SOCIAL NORMS OR INSTRUCTIONS)

© A. Hoppe, D. Michalis and T. Reinking (1991) California State University, adapted by S. Ting-Toomey. Used with permission.

Appendix 20.2 (For Alphans only)

CONTRACT

WE PLEDGE OUR FULL SUPPORT AND CONSENT FOR THE BUILD-
ING AND THE DEVELOPMENT OF A PARKING STRUCTURE IN THE
ALPHA–OMEGA LOT.

CONDITIONAL CLAUSES (IF ANY):

SIGNED AND SEALED ON THIS DATE:

_____

ALPHA MEMBER'S SIGNATURE:

_____

ALPHA MEMBER'S SIGNATURE:

_____

OMEGA MEMBER'S SIGNATURE:

_____

OMEGA MEMBER'S SIGNATURE:

_____

© A. Hoppe, D. Michalis and T. Reinking (1991) California State University,
adapted by S. Ting-Toomey. Used with permission.

Appendix 20.3 (For Omegans only)

OMEGA GROUP CHARACTERISTICS (Confidential Information)
1   Time is of no concern for Omegas. For instance, an Omega may arrive at appointments as much as 45 minutes late and not consider it inappropriate. Omegas live by the philosophy "Enjoy life to the fullest this moment."
2   Omegas place people before business. In the Omega culture, the values of the family/group are the most important. Omegas place family group goals before individual needs and goals. When in conversation, Omegas like to inquire about the families of others and also to talk about their own families with others.
3   Omegas like to engage in small talk and people oriented issues.
4   Omegas also feel comfortable showing their emotions to the fullest extent. Omegas use many hand gestures when they talk. They also like to touch each other on the shoulder when they get excited during conversations.

INSTRUCTIONS FOR MEMBERS OF THE OMEGA GROUP
1   You are meeting members of the Alpha group for the first time at a pre-dinner cocktail party. Although your two groups have never met, you have to correspond with each other about a plot of land in the community, which is co-owned by the Omegas and the Alphas. In the correspondence, both groups agreed that the plot of land should be utilized to better serve the community.
2   Your plan for the meeting is to really get to know members of the Alpha group better and, if the opportunity arises, to chat with them about your group's dream of building a beautiful park in the empty lot. You expect that the Alpha group will go along with your plan.
3   YOUR PRIMARY GOAL IS TO GET TO KNOW THE ALPHAS. Although you have your contract ready, you do not expect Alpha members will co-sign the contract until after dinner. However, you also know that life is very unpredictable and you may have to talk about the contract earlier than you prefer. As soon as all parties involved sign the contract, construction can begin on the beautiful park. YOU HAVE COMPLETE AUTHORITY TO MAKE A DECISION FOR THE MEMBERS OF YOUR GROUP.
4   Your approach to the cocktail party is to get to know members of the Alpha group and the family histories so you and they will feel comfortable and at ease before any serious business discussion.

(REMEMBER, DO NOT DISCUSS YOUR GROUP'S SOCIAL NORMS OR INSTRUCTIONS)

© A. Hoppe, D. Michalis and T. Reinking (1991) California State University, adapted by S. Ting-Toomey. Used with permission.

Appendix 20.4 (For Omegans only)

CONTRACT

WE PLEDGE OUR FULL SUPPORT AND CONSENT FOR THE BUILD-
ING AND THE DEVELOPMENT OF A PARK IN THE OMEGA–ALPHA
LOT.

CONDITIONAL CLAUSES (IF ANY):

SIGNED AND SEALED ON THIS DATE:

_____

OMEGA MEMBER'S SIGNATURE:

_____

OMEGA MEMBER'S SIGNATURE:

_____

ALPHA MEMBER'S SIGNATURE:

_____

© A. Hoppe, D. Michalis and T. Reinking (1991) California State University,
adapted by S. Ting-Toomey. Used with permission.

Note

1 Exercise and Appendices: Hoppe, A., Michalis, D. and Reinking, T. (1995)
  "Alpha–Omega intergroup negotiation simulation," adapted and modified by
  Dr. Stella Ting-Toomey, CSUF. In S. Sudweeks and R. Guzley (eds), *Instructors'
  Resource Manual for Building Bridges – Authored By Gudykunst, Ting-Toomey, Sud-
  weeks, and Stewart*, Boston: Houghton-Mifflin, 77–83. Used with permission by
  the first author, Angela Hoppe.

References

Hoppe, A., Michalis, D. and Reinking, T. (1995) "Alpha–Omega intergroup nego-tiation simulation," in S. Sudweeks and R. Guzley (eds), *Instructors' Resource Manual for Building Bridges – Authored by Gudykunst, Ting-Toomey, Sudweeks, and Stewart*, Boston: Houghton-Mifflin, pp. 77–83.

Langer, E. (1989) *Mindfulness*, Reading, MA: Addison-Wesley.

Langer, E. (1997) *The Power of Mindful Learning*, Reading, MA: Addison-Wesley.

Silberman, M., with Auerbach, C. (1998) *Active Training: A Handbook of Techniques, Designs, Case Examples, and Tips*, 2nd edn, San Francisco: Jossey-Bass/Pfeiffer.

Ting-Toomey, S. (1994) "Managing intercultural conflicts effectively," in L. Samovar and R. Porter (eds), *Intercultural Communication: A Reader*, 7th edn, Belmont, CA: Wadsworth, pp. 360–72.

Ting-Toomey, S. (1997) "Intercultural conflict competence," in W. Cupach and D. Canary (eds), *Competence in Interpersonal Conflict*, New York: McGraw-Hill, pp. 120–47.

Ting-Toomey, S. (1999) *Communicating across Cultures*, New York: Guilford.

Ting-Toomey, S. and Oetzel, J. (2001) *Managing Intercultural Conflict Effectively*, Thousand Oaks, CA: Sage.

Chapter 21

Effective cross-cultural leadership

Tips and techniques for developing capacity

Meena Surie Wilson

Introduction

A child born in any part of the world today is heir to a variety of complex political, legal, economic, educational, and technological systems embedded in cross-cultural contexts. The expertise, beliefs, and behaviors needed to effectively lead and manage today's institutions within these complex systems can be learned. However, successful leadership and management in these new contexts require an "extra capacity" – cross-cultural adaptability.

I believe that the quality of leadership[1] matters and makes a difference to the way we live. My overall intent is to aid students to become informed practitioners and consumers of leadership involving people from different cultures. Therefore, this module offers an instructional exercise – the AHA! technique – for developing the essential extra capacity of cross-cultural adaptability. A description of this exercise follows a conceptual introduction to the topic of cross-cultural leadership.

A conception of leadership

For thousands of years and in cultures around the world, intelligent and competent individuals have come together to lead change and manage complexity. Now these tasks have become so formidable that many more of us have to learn new and useful ways of thinking through and solving problems cooperatively. Simply to orchestrate and evolve the systems we have created, we need to bring together combinations of spiritually, intellectually, and emotionally grounded people.

Future scenarios, willing workers, orchestration, combinations of people – this is the language of leadership and management. These tasks of leadership have endured across historical eras and cultures. As captured by the phrases above, these tasks are:

- facing adaptive change: by creating compelling future scenarios through navigating, learning, regulating stress, and obtaining resources;
- maintaining commitment: by inspiring willing workers through showing trust, building teaching–learning relationships and community, and developing norms that help individuals and groups to become accountable;
- setting direction: by orchestrating events and resources through creating a shared mission and sometimes challenging the status quo; and
- creating alignment: by combining people in ways that are productive through building processes and systems to select between initiatives, to pool efforts, and to surface and contain conflict.

Successful leaders work to accomplish these tasks and help their groups to survive and thrive (Kotter 1990; McCauley 2000; Schein 1992; Yukl 1989).
   Key questions then become:

- How do individuals learn to lead and manage?
- What must they know?

I present two models. Both can be used with students to orient them to their personal leadership journey. The first model is a generic formula to help adults to learn and develop. The second model describes the scope of expertise individuals must gradually accrue if they wish to succeed as leaders or managers at senior levels.

How leadership capacity develops

Successful leaders push themselves to acquire expertise and evolve in their beliefs and behaviors. All of us endure a lifetime of challenging work and personal experiences, but effective leaders are somehow able to use their experiences to extract insights about themselves. These insights inform their ongoing journey of personal development. At each step, they garner other people's support for continuing development and, one way or another, they resolve their challenges and learn from them.
   A formula for learning from experience is the assessment–challenge–support or ACS model (see Table 21.1).[2]
   "The most powerful drive in the ascent of man is his pleasure in his own skill. He loves to do what he does well and, having done it well, he loves to do it better" (Jacob Bronowski in McCall, Lombardo, and Morrison 1988: ix). The individuals who are most likely to become effective fortify themselves with accurate self-assessment. Then they seek out challenges and muster other people's support so that they learn from their challenges. The A–C–S elements in combination are one formula for

Table 21.1 Elements of a developmental experience

Element	Motivation	Resources
Assessment	Desire to close gap between current self and ideal self	Clarity about needed changes; clues about how gap can be closed
Challenge	Need to master the challenge	Opportunity for experimentation and practice; exposure to different perspectives
Support	Confidence in ability to learn and grow; positive value placed on change	Confirmation and clarification of lessons learned

Source: Adapted from McCauley, C. D., Moxley, R. S. and Van Velsor, E. 1998, p. 9.

using work and personal experiences to develop capacities for leading and managing.

I am suggesting that effectiveness at leading and managing is simply a matter of knowing oneself and learning from experiences with some help from other people. But what is effectiveness? It is the combination of expertise with appropriate beliefs and behaviors. Furthermore, expertise, beliefs, and behaviors are all <u>learned</u>.

Regarding "expertise," in earlier research on factors leading to success on international assignments (Wilson and Dalton 1998), my colleague and I asserted that:

$$\text{Expatriate effectiveness} = \text{Technical/functional/professional expertise} \\ + \text{Business expertise} \\ + \text{Cross-cultural expertise}$$

Layers of sophisticated expertise are not enough, and the limitations of expertise become quickly apparent in cross-cultural situations. For effectiveness, the leader's beliefs and behaviors must evolve and mature. This evolution toward maturity calls for the extra capacity of cross-cultural adaptability.

Effective cross-cultural leadership: the extra capacity

Culture is a worldview shared among a group of people, based on learned beliefs and behaviors, and resulting in a collective way of thinking, feeling, and acting. The shared learning process for developing beliefs and behaviors helps the group to integrate internally and adapt externally. Thus, this worldview is dynamic and evolving.

Starting at birth, we learn culture from the inside out. We assume that this worldview is "correct" and that everybody sees the world in the same way. Usually, we are unconscious of holding a worldview until we experience another culture. For most, discovering our worldview and its differences from that of people who live in another neighborhood, region, or country is initially a surprise – even a shock.

At the same time, we learn regional and country culture from the outside in. During primary and secondary school, we learn about our country's political, legal, and economic institutions and our forms of self-expression via sports and the arts. We grow up practicing particular religious, secular, and social customs. Later, we learn professional culture by pursuing higher education and affiliating with professional associations.

Cross-cultural adaptability, the capacity to move back and forth between different worldviews more easily, can trigger further learning and the continuing evolution of individuals' beliefs and behaviors. Most of us belong to many groups – such as family, sex, ethnic, religious, regional, national, professional, organizational, and so on. By participating in multiple cultural groupings, we are opened up to having our beliefs and behaviors progressively shaped by many influences. As we move from group to group, we naturally adapt and develop our ability to think and respond differently in different situations.

Moving back and forth between different ways of approaching situations is even more difficult in international settings. For example, in the U.S. culture, "sincerity" means speaking your mind, while in the Japanese culture "sincerity" means conducting social relationships with respect for others' feelings. In the U.S., seating oneself next to a stranger in an empty railway compartment would be intrusive, while in India, seating oneself at a distance from a stranger would be considered unfriendly. In a Middle Eastern country, using language in an elaborate or poetic way would be moving, while to northern European ears such expressions could sound pompous or sentimental. By learning and practicing such differences, individuals further evolve their beliefs and behaviors, and their evolution helps them build even greater adaptive capacity.

The pivotal nature of cross-cultural adaptability is highlighted by two major research projects: Global Leadership and Organizational Behavior Effectiveness (GLOBE)[3] and Global Leadership Development Research (GLDR).[4] GLDR researchers found cross-cultural adaptability to be one of four contributors to effective performance.[5] GLOBE research findings of three categories of leader behavior – behavior effective everywhere, that effective in some but not all countries, and that effective nowhere (see Table 21.2) – also imply that effective cross-cultural leadership calls for adaptability. This adaptive stance includes: the willingness to practice behaviors that are universally acceptable, learning behaviors that are culturally specific, and minimizing behaviors that are ineffective.

Table 21.2 Globe leader scales – behaviors and characteristics listed by sub-scale

Sub-scales	Generally endorsed	Endorsed sometimes	Not endorsed
Charismatic/value-based leadership			
Visionary	Foresight, plans ahead	Anticipatory	
Inspirational	Positive, encouraging, motive arouser, confidence builder, dynamic, motivational	Enthusiastic	
Self-sacrificial		Risk taker, self-sacrificial	
Decisive	Decisive	Willful, logical, intuitive	
Integrity	Honest, just, trustworthy	Sincere	
Performance orientation	Excellence-oriented		
Team-oriented leadership			
Administratively competent	Administratively skilled	Orderly	
Diplomatic	Win–win problem-solver, effective bargainer	Worldly, intra-group conflict-avoider	
Malevolent (reverse)	Dependable, intelligent		Irritable, non-cooperative
Team integrator	Communicative, team builder, informed, coordinator		
Self-protective leadership			
Conflict inducer		Intra-group competitor	
Face saver		Evasive	Indirect
Procedural		Formal, habitual, cautious, procedural	
Self-centered			Loner, asocial
Status-conscious		Status-conscious, class-conscious	
Participative leadership			
Autocratic		Elitist, ruler, domineering	Dictatorial
Non-participative		Micro-manager	
Humane leadership			
Humane orientation		Compassionate	
Modest		Self-effacing	
Autonomous leadership			
Autonomous		Individualistic, independent, autonomous, unique	

Source: Adapted from Dorfman (forthcoming).

Adaptable leaders can flex their behavior and relate more effectively with people who are different from them. They adjust more quickly to unfamiliar, uncomfortable, and unpredictable situations. Culturally adaptable leaders do not necessarily change their objectives when they enter a new culture – they simply learn to entertain other perspectives and change the way they behave.

Developing cross-cultural adaptability: the AHA! technique

In this section, I present an exercise to guide aspiring leaders toward becoming culturally mindful. This exercise, the AHA! technique, can be used to instruct beginning, intermediate, or advanced students, provided they are interested in self-consciously developing cross-cultural adaptability by opening themselves to new perspectives and making behavioral changes. AHA! invokes a questioning process, the first step to be taken by those who wish to become cross-culturally adaptable. Since the technique involves students learning from each other, this exercise is well suited to a mixed group of people – from novice to expert – bringing a range of previous cross-cultural experiences.

AHA! is introduced in four phases:

1 Warm-up: in dyads, students talk about their own cross-cultural experiences. AHA! structures their conversation without students realizing this. Volunteers then share their stories with the larger group.
2 Mini-lecture and application: AHA! is explained as an adaptation of methods that are often used in cross-cultural training. Dyads join, become groups of four, and apply AHA! to their earlier stories.
3 Role-plays: in dyads, students role-play cross-cultural scenarios; this is followed by a structured debrief with each student answering the debriefing questions in turn.
4 Goal setting and practice: students are asked to identify 3–5 future situations that will give them an opportunity to practice AHA! They may later be asked to submit a paper describing what they learned from their practice.

Warm-up

After pairing up, students tell each other a story based on their own experience or on the experience of someone they know. Depending on the maturity of the students, the exercise may have to be orchestrated one step at a time. The instructions are as follows:

• Take a few minutes to list a few different incidents or situations in which you (or a friend) became strongly aware that there are people in the world who think, feel, and act differently from you.

- From your list, select one incident or situation. The situation should be one that surprised, frustrated, or embarrassed you (or your friend). Tell a story about what happened. Include as much detail as you can. What did you/friend see and hear? What did the other person/ people say and do? What did you/friend do? What were your/friend's thoughts and feelings?
- At the time, what was your interpretation of the other person's/ people's words and actions?
- At the time, what did you/friend learn about yourself and the other person/people?

The instructor opens up the large group storytelling session by talking about one of his or her own experiences.

Time: paired conversations 10–15 minutes; whole group storytelling 10–20 minutes.

Mini-lecture and application (use overhead slides to explain AHA!)

AHA! is a simple technique for paying full attention to cross-cultural situations (see Table 21.3).

Assessing and hypothesizing can be instinctive and rapid, but must be slowed down. Asking will have to be learned and practiced. An individual cannot always know how another person is experiencing a situation. Taking the time to "ask" a cultural informant to help interpret the situation is one way of learning to look at situations from other people's points of view.

To explain the AHA! process, link a few of the stories told during the large-group storytelling with the AHA! structure as follows:

- assessing the situation is equivalent to being able to tell a story in detail;
- hypothesizing or making guesses about the other person's motivations – "Where is he/she coming from?" – is equivalent to coming up with an interpretation of another person's words and actions; and

Table 21.3 The AHA! process

A	Assess:	Look, listen, and describe in detail
H	Hypothesize:	How did you interpret the others' words and actions?
A	Ask:	Gather more information before you act
!		

- asking for additional information is equivalent to starting a questioning process to learn more about another person/people and oneself.[6]

To anchor the AHA! technique, ask students to link their own stories to the AHA! structure. In their groups of four, they then brainstorm ways in which each earlier situation could have been handled differently.

- How many interpretations can the group generate to explain the culturally different person's/people's words and actions?
- In each earlier situation, what questions could the storyteller have asked to check his or her hypotheses?
- How could the main character in the story have responded differently, thereby creating a different ending to the story?

Time: 20–40 minutes.

Role-plays

The role-plays help students to practice AHA! One scenario, "At the tradeshow," is included as a handout sample (See Appendices 21.1 and 21.2). Students are paired, and each one is assigned a role and given the appropriate handout. The debriefing that follows the role-play is as important as the role-play itself.

Debrief questions (to be answered by each role-player):

Assess

1   Based on your observation of the other person, describe what you saw and heard.
2   Describe anything the other person said that surprised or annoyed you or made you uncomfortable.

Hypothesize

3   What cultural beliefs may have influenced the other person's words and behaviors?
4   What personality or other factors may have influenced their words and behaviors?

Ask

5   What information were you and/or the other person missing that could have led to the situation being handled in a different way?
6   What are the ways in which you could have obtained this information?

Time: reading and preparation for role-play 5 minutes; role-play 5 minutes; debrief 10–15 minutes.

Many scenarios can be developed from real-life cross-cultural incidents, such as those frequently reported in the news media or available on the web sites of leading newspapers and magazines. Experienced students will be able to generate their own scenarios.

In constructing scenarios, is it useful to incorporate the three types of interactions in which opposing cultural orientations often lead to tension (Hay Group 1995):

- using personal vs. contractual basis for building relationships;
- emphasizing planning vs. implementation; and
- demonstrating centralized vs. participatory leadership practices.

Asking students to generate and enact their own scenarios (after the model has been provided) is a tactic for accelerating learning. Students often back away from learning about the emotionally volatile aspects of cultural differences. Inviting them to craft role-plays in which they learn from each other's experiences – and at the same time, learn a language for talking about cultural differences – is a way around the resistance to this type of learning.

Goal setting and practice

Goal setting in the context of personal and leadership development is identifying a behavior that one would like to change in order to interact more effectively with other people. Having learned AHA!, one goal for students could be to diligently practice this technique. A 3-to-5-page paper can be required in which students describe several situations in which they applied the technique and reflect on what they learned.

Summary

This module has provided an overview of cross-cultural leadership development. I suggest that students can become effective leaders or managers by learning to be cross-culturally adaptable. One approach to becoming adaptable is to practice the AHA! technique. AHA! is a useful starting point for expanding one's personal repertoire of beliefs and behaviors over a period of time. Leaders and managers who do not possess an expanded repertoire of beliefs and behaviors are missing the cultural savvy they need to succeed.

Central to leadership is a mysterious bonding of people with each other, but the nature of the power, influence, and authority that people exercise over each other is not easy to understand. Social scientists have tried to explain these patterns of interaction between leaders and followers, much as television newscasters try to explain patterns of weather. But, like weather predictors, they have only been partially successful. What we do know is that leadership lives in the middle of relationships between people.

We may not as yet understand leadership completely, but learning to accommodate differences between people and cultures is one step in the right direction. To this end, cross-culturally adaptability is *de rigueur* for leaders and managers in the twenty-first century.

Appendix 21.1 At the trade show

INSTRUCTIONS FOR THE EXPORTER
- You are an exporter who is about to meet an importer to discuss how your companies can do business for the export-import of several lines of dining room furniture. Trade agreements between your countries are in place.
- A trade show of Home Furnishings is being held in the home country of the exporters.
- You wish to make the importer feel welcome and close on a sale. From previous experience you have learned that:
    - Informality is key to establishing rapport.
    - Always pitch your newest product lines – you have brought models and samples (furniture and various woods used) and are ready to point out the new features.
- You expect to close on a sales contract by the end of your conversation with the importer.
- The importer has approached you with great interest and has traveled from quite a distant country to get to this trade show. You fully expect that he/she will want to return home with a contract in hand, due to the high travel expenses.

YOUR CULTURAL ORIENTATION
- Informality (often related to low Power Distance)
- Focus on innovative product lines (often related to low Uncertainty Avoidance)
- Getting the sales contract signed as a basis for business relationships (often related to low Family Collectivism)

Appendix 21.2 At the trade show

INSTRUCTIONS FOR THE IMPORTER
- You are an importer who is about to meet an exporter to discuss how your companies can do business for the export-import of several lines of dining room furniture. Trade agreements between your countries are in place.
- A trade show of Home Furnishings, hosted by local business organizations, is being held in the home country of the exporters.
- You are pleased that you have been able to arrange a personal meeting with one of the exporters.
- This is the first year that you have attended this trade show, and your main objective is to get to know the rep from the company with which your company expects to do business for a long time.
- From previous experience you have learned that:

  - To make a good impression, it is best to behave in a formal and reserved way until you get to know the other person quite well.
  - It is important to learn about the product lines that have been marketed successfully for the longest period of time, and are still popular with purchasers.

- You plan to extend the exporter an invitation to visit your company headquarters.
- You would like to know the background and history of his company, and the ideals that guide the company owners.
- You expect this to be the first of several meetings that will lead to a good personal and business relationship.

YOUR CULTURAL ORIENTATION
- Formality and reserve (often related to high Power Distance)
- Focus on traditional product lines (often related to high Uncertainty Avoidance)
- Respect for tradition (often related to high Uncertainty Avoidance)
- Getting to know the people running the business as a basis for business relationships (often related to high Family Collectivism)

Notes

1 I use the words "leadership" and "management" interchangeably, since these activities are complementary and synergistic.
2 Based on principles of adult development, the ACS model formalizes thirty years of research and leadership development practice at the Center for Creative Leadership.
3 GLOBE (House, Javidan and Dorfman 2001) is a multi-phase, multi-method study of culture and leadership implemented in 62 countries worldwide. Over 170 country co-investigators participated in gathering and analyzing data from over 17,500 middle managers in 800 organizations representing financial, food

processing, and telecommunications services. To accentuate cultural differences, only country-based (not multinational or global) organizations were selected.

4 GLDR (Dalton *et al.* 2002) is a study of 214 managers from four multinational companies, each representing a different industry group: automotive, pharmaceutical, telecommunications, and hospitality and service. Corporate headquarters were located in Switzerland, the United States, and Sweden; participants were from 39 countries and working in 30 countries. The research focused on differences between domestic and global managers to identify the "extra" capabilities needed by those working globally. Half the managers from each company were operating in their own country; the other half were "global," working across multiple time zones, national business infrastructures, and cultural orientations.

5 The three other capabilities identified are: seeing the world through others' eyes; specialized knowledge of international business; and innovativeness that uses cultural differences to introduce new products and services.

6 Caution: Remind students to select informants who have objectivity about their native culture, i.e., individuals who have worked and/or lived in two or more cultures. To guard against individual bias, several informants should be consulted.

References

Dalton, M., Ernst, C., Deal, J. and Leslie, J. (2002) *Success for the New Global Manager: How to Work across Distances, Countries, and Cultures*, San Francisco: Jossey-Bass.

Dorfman, P. W. (forthcoming) "Leadership prototypes and cultural variation: the identification of culturally endorsed implicit theories of leadership," in R. J. House, M. Javidan, P. W. Dorfman and P. J. Hanges (eds), *The GLOBE Project*, Thousand Oaks, CA: Sage.

Hay Group (1995) *Mastering Global Leadership: Hay/McBer International CEO Leadership Study*, Boston: Hay/McBer Worldwide Resource Center.

House, R. J., Javidan, M. and Dorfman, P. W. (2001) "Project GLOBE: an introduction," *Applied Psychology: An International Review*, 50 (4): 489–505.

Kotter, J. P. (1990) "What leaders really do," *Harvard Business Review*, 90, May–June: 103–11.

McCall, M. W. Jr., Lombardo, M. M. and Morrison, A. M. (1988) *The Lessons of Experience*, Lexington, MA: Lexington Books.

McCauley, C. D. (2000) "A systemic approach to leadership development," in D. Day (chair) *Systemic Leadership Development: Conceptual Models and Best Practices*, symposium at the meeting of the Society for Industrial and Organizational Psychology, New Orleans, LA, April.

McCauley, C. D., Moxley, R. S. and Van Velsor, E. (1998) *The Center for Creative Leadership Handbook for Leadership Development*, San Francisco: Jossey-Bass.

Schein, E. H. (1992) *Organizational Culture and Leadership*, San Francisco: Jossey-Bass.

Wilson, M. S. and Dalton, M. A. (1998) *International Success: Selecting, Developing, and Supporting Expatriate Managers*, Greensboro, NC: Center for Creative Leadership.

Yukl, G. A. (1989) *Leadership in Organizations*, Englewood Cliffs, NJ: Prentice-Hall.

Part VII

The cultural context of work
Impacts on functional performance

As instructors, in many circumstances, we are faced with opportunities to enrich the common functional courses by adding a cultural element. This is particularly challenging because the initial discipline-based framework is often designed to build on earlier work that does not contain cultural issues. Here we provide modules to supplement otherwise functionally oriented learning. We find that, by incorporating a cultural perspective, these modules permit the instructor to bring a richness to the experience and a complexity to the learning that carries the class to a higher level in many ways.

Vernon presents the question of ethics in multicultural settings, where the situation is complicated by the "fact" that each culture may have a different set of ethics. She uses a "caselet" method to challenge learners intellectually and emotionally to consider why they may think something is wrong while others believe it is right.

Spich extols the value of simulations in the teaching of negotiations where cultural values are not shared. For Spich, simulated negotiations provide a context where "hot-mode learning," mindfulness, and risk-taking are pedagogical elements that create a powerful learning environment.

Frayne offers a course design that features international human resources management as a strategic issue. Using a systems approach, she weaves the cultural dimension throughout as a central and integrating issue that adds complexity. Thus, she broadens our understanding of the scope and responsibilities of management in international context and of the importance of comprehensive management development.

Geringer and Frayne present a framework for describing the evolution of joint ventures and alliances. This is then employed in an Alliance Culture Exercise to heighten learners' ability to engage, reflect, rework, and recognize developmental patterns in these collaborative relationships.

Bird brings new insight into the necessary complication of adding cultural modules to the integrative capstone strategy course. He helps learners see that culture's influence on "micro" organizational behavior, as well as on the external political, economic, and social order, profoundly affects the firm's assessment of and response to the "macro" organizational environment, impacting both strategy formulation and implementation. He argues that, at this juncture in their training, it is imperative for learners to tackle the discomfort of striving to combine viewpoints and integrate value sets – precisely what a cultural perspective demands.

Chapter 22

Global ethics

Heidi Vernon

Introduction

People develop ethical standards based on myriad and often subtle factors inherent in each culture. Cultural components such as ethnicity, religion, politics, social status, sex, group affiliation, and legal system all contribute to an individual's standard of ethical behavior. *Culture* can be defined as a set of values, beliefs, rules, and institutions held by a specific group of people. *Ethics* is the study of what constitutes right or wrong behavior. In the workplace, employee behavior is affected by the employee's specific culture and the company's own ethical standards and codes of conduct. When that employee manages or works abroad, the culture into which he or she goes increases the complexity of that individual's ethical decision-making process. In today's global business environment, people often work in many cultures, confronting and adapting to different standards and different expectations of ethical behavior.

As corporations have become more global and their operations and personnel cross national boundaries, accrediting bodies, faculty, and prospective employers have encouraged universities to address ethical issues that transcend national borders and cultures. There is an ongoing debate among a wide variety of groups about how to identify, understand, and deal with ethics across cultures and on a global scale. The immediacy of this task is exacerbated by the role of technology and instant access to events worldwide. The media report in minute detail every corporate crisis, every governmental blunder, and every appearance of ethical transgression. The following examples represent only a very few of the organizations that focus our attention on global ethics.

- In 1999, groups of U.S. university students held campus demonstrations demanding that universities force companies making items with school logos to release the names and addresses of factories that made the goods.

- Berlin-based Transparency International, an independent organization that tracks corruption among government officials worldwide, issues a Corruption Perceptions Index and a Bribe Payers Index each year. These indices are based on polls taken by organizations such as Gallup International and surveys from ten independent institutions. Former World Bank official Frank Vogl, who founded Transparency International in 1993, noted an "explosion of public demand that business and governments stop corrupting one another" (Crossette 1999).
- The Organisation for Economic Co-operation and Development, the Paris-based organization of the world's most developed countries, introduced a code in April 1999. The code prohibits bribery and requires ratifying countries to introduce domestic legislation making it a criminal offense for their corporations to bribe foreign officials to win business contracts (Lewis 1999).
- In November 1999, United Nations Secretary-General Kofi Annan hosted Rev. Leon H. Sullivan who announced that a dozen companies with international operations signed the Global Sullivan Principles. Chevron, Colgate-Palmolive, KFC, and General Motors agreed to adhere to a far-reaching set of socially responsible and ethical guidelines. These principles are an extension of the 1977 Sullivan Principles that set standards for U.S. companies doing business in South Africa during the 1970s.

Teaching global ethics

Is there any best way of approaching the task of teaching global business ethics within a cultural framework? Teaching ethics within a single culture is far easier than teaching ethics across cultures. For example, in a single culture, especially one with a Western foundation, one can use a framework of one or more of the following five approaches to deal with ethical issues (Mill 1985):

- The Utilitarian Approach of Jeremy Bentham (1974) and John Stuart Mill (1985) in the nineteenth century suggested that ethical actions are those that provide the greatest balance of good over evil.
- The Rights Approach of Immanuel Kant (1974) focused on the individual's right to choose for him- or herself. In effect, Kant urged people to adopt principles or actions that everyone can adopt without inconsistencies.
- The Fairness of Justice Approach of Aristotle (1974) asked how "fair" was an action and whether it treated everyone alike.
- The Common Good Approach presents a vision of society as a community of members who share a common set of values and goals.

- The Virtue Approach assumes there are certain ideals like honesty, courage, generosity, and fidelity to which people should strive in order to reach their full potential (Velasquez *et al.* 1996).[1]

Most assumptions about ethical actions, such as good should prevail over evil and fairness is desirable, are entrenched in Western European cultural bias. However, good, evil, and fairness are culturally determined and change from culture to culture. It is easy to imagine that absolute good is to protect one's family at any cost or that evil is to abandon the prevailing ideology. Fairness has little or no meaning in a culture in which resources are scarce and one's own family is at risk. Often a community's goals and values are in conflict, leaving the individual with little or no guidance for establishing an ethical anchor.

What happens when business people cross national boundaries and their ethical standards conflict with those of other countries? Whose ethics should they follow? Is it possible to develop standards that transcend national boundaries? Are there absolute rights and wrongs? Does the Virtue Approach help us develop transcendent ethical standards? What is the task for educational institutions in helping individuals and companies understand their own ethical standards and developing broad ethical guidelines that help them better manage the ethical challenges they surely will face?

What teaching techniques are most effective in the classroom and produce the greatest benefit for the prospective or practicing manager? In my view, using "caselets," or short cases, is by far the most exciting method I have found for teaching ethics on the undergraduate, MBA, and executive training levels.

The caselet method

I develop caselets that address ethical issues currently being discussed in newspapers, magazines, television, or other media outlets. A caselet is no longer than two pages in length and has four to six questions that follow the text. This kind of exercise can be written in a short period of time from easily available media sources. Topics can be tailored to an audience and can be specific to their interests. Using this tool, it is critical that the faculty member follow the issue as it evolves and be prepared to add the newest information for discussion. The following are examples of current issues that could easily be crafted into caselets.

- Sweatshops: Wal-Mart, Payless Shoes, Nike, and Toys "Я" Us and other U.S. companies appear to be disregarding their own code of basic labor standards. Auditing systems miss serious problems (Kristof and WuDunn 2000a, b).

- Global linkages: The Securities and Exchange Commission is investigating a surge in Asian sales at Belgian software firm Lernout and Hauspie Speech Products NV. The sales are to corporate customers with which L&H has financial ties and which share a common address and corporate officers (Maremont and Eisinger 2000).
- Genetic tampering: The ongoing debate about genetically modified food and the risk to human health and the environment. This issue pits American and European farmers, consumers, and huge agricultural producers against one another and builds on the unrelated food scares caused by mad cow disease in the UK and dioxin-tainted chicken in Belgium.[2]
- Hazardous products: The sale of tobacco products in developing countries at the same time that sales in the U.S. are diminishing. Developing-country governments subsidize and often encourage smoking because they have a monopoly on sales and distribution of cigarettes.

The following caselet about Bridgestone/Firestone and Ford can be used as it stands or with the latest news bulletins.

Bridgestone/Firestone and Ford

What happened

On May 8, 2000, the National Highway Traffic Safety Administration (NHTSA) issued a letter asking Ford and Bridgestone/Firestone for information on tire problems. On July 28, Ford received the tire warranty data from the tire maker and began around-the-clock analysis. On August 4, Ford found a pattern in the data pointing to problems with 15-inch ATX and ATXII tire models and Wilderness AT tires made at the Decatur, IL plant. Ford called in Bridgestone/Firestone experts. The firms worked together over the weekend to verify the findings. Finally on August 6, Ford decided to issue a recall and company officials discussed the issues with the NHTSA in Washington. The next day, the recall was announced at a news conference in Washington.

Immediately after the recall, chaos erupted at Ford and Firestone dealerships. Thousands of car owners showed up demanding replacement tires although very few were available. More than 6.5 million tires were needed for the recall, representing half Bridgestone/Firestone's annual production for Ford. Ford began to study the idea of diverting tires from new car manufacturing to use in the recall. Ford also contacted Goodyear and Michelin to supply extra tires.

By August 18, lawsuits were filed and Ford Explorer sales fell. On August 20, Ford announced it was suspending production in three plants for two weeks to free up 70,000 tires for replacement. Lawsuits were filed and continued to mount. By August 30, there were reported complaints about tire failures in Venezuela, Saudi Arabia, and Thailand.

As Labor Day 2000 arrived, the rift between Ford and Bridgestone/Firestone had widened into a chasm. The companies disagreed on how to handle the crisis in the media and how to meet the need for replacement tires. Wall Street was increasingly concerned, and Ford and Bridgestone/Firestone stocks fell sharply. The tire maker's stock went down 39 percent between the time of the recall and the end of August. Each company asserted it had acted responsibly in the matter. The *Asian Wall Street Journal* wrote that the two companies were:

> writing the most important chapter in the history of product recalls since the Tylenol case 18 years ago, when the pain reliever was recalled after pills that had been sabotaged with cyanide killed seven people. In this case, instead of one firm, two companies with a long complex relationship are involved, and they are struggling to save customers' lives and corporate reputations as they deal with a suspect product that is out on the road, not on a store shelf.
>
> (Simison *et al.* 2000)

Ford issues

Ford was named in lawsuits against Bridgestone/Firestone. The Ford Explorer, the hottest sport-utility vehicle (SUV) on the market was associated with 88 deaths. Initially Jacques A. Nasser, Ford's CEO, said he would not testify before Congress but, on August 31, changed his mind. He asserted that the company had behaved properly and acted as soon as it had identified which tires were defective despite evidence that Ford had received complaints about tire problems in Venezuela as early as 1998. NHTSA began an on-going investigation about what Ford knew about the tire problem at home and abroad and when Ford knew about it.

Bridgestone/Firestone issues

The company is a joint Japanese–U.S. company. Parent corporate headquarters in Japan sets company policy for the U.S. operations. In fall 2000, retail sales of Firestone tires dropped 40 percent. Masatoshi Ono, the Japanese CEO, went willingly to testify before the U.S. Congress and abjectly apologized while the company in Japan continued to stonewall. Bridgestone/Firestone replaced the Japanese CEO of its U.S. operations and appointed an American for the first time. As the company struggled to discover what caused the tread to separate from the tire, its engineers blamed a unique combination of tire and vehicle design, tire manufacturing, and customer abuse for tire failures linked to the deaths of now more than 100 Americans, almost all in Ford Explorers.

The road ahead

In January 2001, Ford launched an effort to settle all pending individual suits in the U.S. over injuries and deaths from rollovers of the Ford Explorer. Although Ford did not address foreign claims or class-action consumer suits, it authorized generous settlements and made apologies to the injured and their families in state suits. Ford laid the blame for the rollovers squarely on the tires. Bridgestone/Firestone spokespeople did not comment on Ford's action but did not follow Ford's lead with apologies or settlements. In May 2001, Bridgestone/Firestone suddenly ended its 95-year relationship as a supplier to Ford and accused the car makers of refusing to acknowledge safety concerns about the Explorer.

In October 2001, Ford announced that Henry Ford's great-grandson, William Clay Ford, would replace Jacques Nasser as Ford's CEO. Shortly thereafter, Bridgestone/Firestone agreed to pay more than $50 million to settle charges that the company engaged in deceptive and unfair trade practices when it sold tires that were subsequently ordered recalled by the U.S. government.

By the beginning of 2002, both companies had made significant changes in management and had suffered huge financial losses. The tire company had spent more than $1 billion to settle suits, pay lawyers, and develop public-service programs. Ford had spent more than $3 billion on recalls and design changes in the Explorer. Both companies were left with questions about whether this crisis could have been handled differently, whether management took the right actions, and how they would face crises in the future.

Teaching note

I use this caselet at the advanced undergraduate, MBA, and executive training levels. The case can be assigned prior to class or can be handed out in class. It takes students about 10 minutes to read it. I divide the students into six groups and give each group one question from the seven examples listed below. They have 15 minutes to discuss the question among themselves, then present their responses to the class as a whole. The answers depend on the age, sophistication, and experience of the students. There is a tendency for the class to want to participate after each question is addressed by the group and it usually works better to let that discussion take place rather than waiting until all groups have presented. Discussion on this particular case usually lasts about 45 minutes to an hour. If the caselet is handed out in class, the entire time allotted is about one hour and a half.

Questions

1   Is this a Ford problem? Why, or why not? Is this solely a
    Bridgestone/Firestone problem? Why, or why not?

Issues to be addressed by faculty member:
Should Ford assume responsibility for every component on its car? Should
Ford have the same responsibility for tires as it does for axles, steering
wheels, or other components? If Ford expressed concern about tire failures to Bridgestone/Firestone should it assume that its responsibility has
been discharged? How far should Ford be expected to go to pursue the
issue of tire failure? Is Bridgestone/Firestone completely responsible for
the tire failures? Are there compelling reasons that Ford shares responsibility? The *Washington Post* (Keating and Mayer 2000) reports that Ford
Explorers have a higher rate of tire-related accidents than other SUVs,
even when equipped with Goodyear tires. Should Bridgestone/Firestone
be held responsible for rollovers caused by bald tires, faulty brakes, and
blowouts unrelated to tread?

2   What are the differences between this crisis and the Tylenol
    situation?

Issues to be addressed by faculty member:
Does Ford and/or Bridgestone/Firestone have more responsibility for the
tire failures than Johnson and Johnson had for the several bottles of
Tylenol that were tampered with after they reached the drugstore? Does it
matter how the deaths or injuries occurred? Is the manufacturer always
responsible regardless of how the product failed? What was J and J's top
management's response? Why did it have that response? What did it rely
on to guide its actions?

3   If you were the CEO of Ford would you have handled this
    situation differently? If you were the CEO of
    Bridgestone/Firestone are there other steps you should have
    taken? What steps will you take now? Are there cross-cultural
    (Japanese–U.S.) issues that affect or have affected top
    management actions?

Issues to be addressed by faculty member:
Ford's CEO Jacques Nasser initially refused to testify before Congress
although Ono went readily. Ono gave an abject apology although the
company in Japan continued to stonewall. What is the symbolism of an
apology in Japan that has no counterpart in the U.S.? In the U.S., does
taking responsibility imply legal culpability? How do companies handle,

identify, and manage cultural differences, particularly in times of crisis? How does an absence of cultural understanding hurt their legal positions? How helpful are joint defense pacts to share information, costs, and strategies? What happened in the Ford and Bridgestone/Firestone crisis to destroy their relationship even though they had a pact?[3]

4   Why is this crisis complicated by problems with the Ford Explorer and tires in foreign countries (in this case, Venezuela)? With whom does responsibility for the tire failures lie outside the U.S.?

Issues to be addressed by faculty member:
Why has Bridgestone/Firestone refused to join Ford in negotiating settlements with victims of Explorer rollovers due to tire–tread separation in Venezuela? Why do Ford and the tire company blame each other and how do they make a distinction between what happened in Venezuela and in the U.S.? What are the legal differences? Venezuela does not have a strong consumer protection movement and does not allow class action suits. Although Venezuela's new Constitution guarantees consumers the right to safe, high-quality products, the provision cannot be implemented because of lack of funds and personnel. Courts are widely believed to be corrupt and judges poorly trained.

5   What role should government regulatory agencies such as the U.S. National Highway Traffic Safety Administration play in this crisis?

Issues to be addressed by faculty member:
The U.S. Department of Transportation database is one of the few tools by which the government could track defects that cause fatal accidents. NHTSA administrator Sue Bailey said that since tires wear out naturally (unlike seatbelts) some fatalities were likely to occur. Federal data showed no tire-related fatalities from 1991 to 1993. For years 1995 to 1998, the federal database showed that fatal accidents involving Explorers were nearly three times as likely to be tire-related as fatalities involving other SUVs. How many fatalities have to occur before a red flag goes up? What is the mechanism NHTSA uses to make companies issue a recall? Can NHTSA's response be improved?

6   What are the lessons for all companies facing crises?

Issues to be addressed by faculty member:
There are rules that companies should follow when presented with a crisis. What are some examples of effective crisis management? What are examples of poor crisis management? There is a vast literature on crisis management (Vernon 1998).

7   What responsibilities do global companies have in each of the environments in which they operate? Are they the same or different? Who bears the responsibility of ensuring that consumers are protected – the host government or the company?

Issues to be discussed by faculty member:
Both Ford and Bridgestone/Firestone are global companies whose products cross national boundaries. Students should be encouraged to question whether global standards should be applied to them, question who is responsible for quality and also for remediation if there is a problem. The global issue, interestingly, falls off the cliff in this caselet. Venezuela disappears as an issue. I think the important point here is that industrialized countries can afford the discourse and have the means of remediation. Poor countries and those that devalue the harm to certain portions of the population (women, children, and minorities) have entirely different ethical standards. It might be a good exercise to ask students to put themselves in the position of the head of a small factory in a poor Muslim country and apply the five approaches to the work lives of women and children.[4]

Finally, my suggestion for introducing these dilemmas is to make it very explicit that there are dilemmas that arise and that sometimes they cannot be solved. Nevertheless, the process of trying to resolve them is at least as important in students' thinking as a right or wrong answer. I tell students that their task is to deal with the dilemmas through the case.

Notes

1 To be candid, I find that students are wildly uninterested in the classic approaches when they are presented as philosophical discussion. They want the discussion to relate to something with which they can identify. Recently I have tried to discuss ethics in light of September 11, 2001. I think it is particularly important that students realize that some cultures have a totally different ethical system that can seem to be the antithesis of the Western approach to ethics. For example, it seems worthwhile to me to ask students how people in other poverty-stricken, ethnically diverse countries like Afghanistan would approach issues of product safety, pollution, behavior toward women and minorities, and other ethical issues.

2 Multiple sources including the *New York Times* and *Financial Times*, and the Internet in January 2000.

3 I try to push the students very hard on managerial responsibility and the importance of leadership from the top. It is useful to note that both companies fired their CEOs. That almost surely would not have happened without this crisis.

4 One of the best books dealing with ethical standards internationally is Wartick and Wood (1998). This uses a stakeholder approach that is very useful but is not based on the classics. See also Donaldson (1989), which is based more on the classics.

References

Aristotle (1974) in O. A. Johnson (ed.), *Ethics: Selections from Classical and Contemporary Writers*, 3rd edn, New York: Holt, Rinehart, and Winston, pp. 47–76.

Bentham, J. (1974) "An introduction to the principles of morals and legislation," in O. A. Johnson (ed.), *Ethics: Selections from Classical and Contemporary Writers*, 3rd edn, New York: Holt, Rinehart, and Winston, pp. 228–39.

Crossette, B. (1999) "A new index tracks bribe-paying countries," the *New York Times*, 27 October: A6.

Donaldson, T. (1989) *Ethics of International Business*, New York: Oxford University Press.

Kant, I. (1974) "Foundations of the metaphysics of morals," in O. A. Johnson (ed.), *Ethics: Selections from Classical and Contemporary Writers*, 3rd edn, New York: Holt, Rinehart, and Winston, p. 205.

Keating, D. and Mayer, C. E. (2000) "Explorer has higher rate of tire accidents; analysis shows Ford SUV outpaces others in class regardless of tire brand," *Washington Post*, 9 October: A01+.

Kristof, N. D. and WuDunn, S. (2000a) "Two cheers for sweatshops," *New York Times Magazine*, 24 September.

Kristof, N. D. and WuDunn, S. (2000b) "Two cheers for sweatshops," *Business Week*, October: 122–8.

Lewis, P. (1999) "Corporate conduct code is proposed for Third World nations," the *New York Times*, 29 April: A7.

Maremont, M. and Eisinger, J. (2000) "SEC probe focuses on Asian revenues of Belgian tech firm," the *Wall Street Journal*, 22 September.

Mill, J. (1985) *Utilitarianism*, Oxford: Blackwell.

Simison, R. L., Shirouzu, N., Aeppel, T. and Zaun, T. (2000) "Spat between Ford, Firestone grows as recall proceeds," *Asian Wall Street Journal*, 29 August: 1+.

Velasquez, M., Andre, C., Shanks, T. and Meyer, M. J. (1996) "Thinking ethically," *Issues in Ethics*, Winter: 2–5.

Vernon, H. (1998) *Business and Society: A Managerial Approach*, McGraw-Hill: 132–52.

Wartick, S. L. and Wood, D. J. (1998) *International Business and Society*, Malden, MA: Blackwell Business.

Chapter 23

Negotiating culture

Robert S. Spich

Introduction

Culture refers to values, practices and institutions used by individuals and groups to define, create, and organize a society. The study of culture focuses on how societies cope with universal problems, e.g., work, justice, community, transactions. Getting learners to understand and appreciate the role of culture in shaping the development and resolutions of conflicts or the processes and outcomes of negotiated transactions is an important objective.

Negotiations as universal technique

Negotiation is a universal practice. It is "culture-free" in the sense that most of the elements of negotiation are universal: agendas, bargaining, power, persuasion. Culture is about "how" negotiations are practiced as a technique. Thus, to teach about culture in negotiations, one begins with a universal model of negotiations. Once the universality of the practice is established, the cultural effects on key practices and techniques (e.g., bargaining behavior, transaction evaluation, resolving conflict, making trade-offs) can be studied. The learner builds from a universal base and then analyzes the specifics of cultural impacts on the universal case. This provides a rich opportunity to engage in cross-cultural comparisons as well.

Negotiation learners are not novices

In technical courses, the teacher is expert, usually in front of a room with the role of delivering the information in a one-way communication to neophytes. In this case, the teacher controls the learning because of the expert power she or he possesses. The learning is discipline- and teacher-centered.

In contrast, for negotiations, the learners already are negotiators and have been so all of their lives. They bring considerable (and often cross-cultural) experience to bear on the issues, have developed their own theories for success, and can show good examples of success in the field. They are not neophytes. Thus, an opening statement in this class should be:

> We are not here to teach you how to negotiate. You already know how to do that. We are here to help you become better negotiators! We are here to show you how culture is the context that shapes much of what we achieve in our negotiations.

Thinking and analyzing something they have been doing all of their lives makes people better negotiators. By helping them recognize when they are in a negotiation situation, they can better understand how to handle it. So, in contrast to the expert teacher delivering "technique knowledge," the key task here is to get the learners to understand their own present performance as negotiators and to pose the challenge of negotiation learning as performance improvement, not new learning. Thus, reflection and analysis of the rich and long-term experience of the learner provides a strong incentive and interest to learn, especially when one is called on to explain failure in a past negotiation.

Negotiation learning is all about the learner

The focus of negotiation learning is the learner. Negotiation learning is less about "what is out there," than it is about what is going on within the learner during the activity of negotiation. The value of the teacher in negotiations lies in assisting with self-assessment, identification of applicable skills, and putting ideas into practice. Negotiation improvement cannot come from a book alone. Since much of negotiation learning is really learning about oneself as a negotiator, a mentor and a guide is needed who organizes the learning experience. For that reason, we often turn to trainers and coaches. The teacher is there to point out that the outcomes of a negotiation are determined by what happens in the negotiation situation and, further, that the learner is not a victim of other people's tactics – rather, one's own behavior is essentially all that one controls during a negotiation. The learning is about self and social dynamics. Managing such dynamics is a skill that can be learned and is critical to success.

Negotiation learning is intensely about the learner themself! What they do or do not do well in a negotiation, how they do it, when they do it, and the like are all matters of choice and control with direct impact on results and performance in the classroom exercise. A learner who does poorly in a negotiations exercise cannot distance themself from that experience. For that very experience is the data that need analysis. This kind of learning is close, analytically hot, present and timely, and risky! Under these circumstances, the learner tends to pay more attention to the lessons, for these have practical and immediate meaning and implications for learning. It is here that cultural insights are often the strongest and longest-lasting. The learners directly experience the effects of a cross-cultural miscommunication and have an opportunity to talk about it and understand the dynamics of what happened. This is learning in real time.

Negotiation learning is about breaking habits first

Much of our behavior, especially in negotiations, results from long-term habit. A negotiation situation arises and we tend to "go on automatic" to deal with the situation. Habit is learned over time and by its nature tends to be below active levels of awareness and consciousness. Habit tends to be reactive, not contemplative and analytic. With this in mind, negotiation teaching develops awareness and consciousness of self, context, structure, and process. This is a fundamental first step in re-learning and fixing bad habits. Three kinds of awareness are important.

The first is *awareness of context and environment.* Culture is not always obvious or readily noticed by negotiation learners. Making them aware of how cultural context impacts negotiations is a first important learning. This can be done via the study of current events. For example, in a class session, I created a living case around a U.S.–China confrontation over a crashed spy plane. Once the basics of the conflict were analyzed based on a collected set of press articles, the discussion moved to the much richer cultural context and background factors that were essentially the subtext and drivers of the real negotiations that were just beginning between these two nations. Having students from China in the class was particularly powerful in making the culture issue paramount. Of particular interest was how the subtle aspects of language in apology, treated so differently from the U.S. and the Chinese perspectives, needed to be diplomatically worked out so that key constituencies could be satisfied. The result of that hour-long conversation was an enhanced appreciation for how the larger context of a problem impacts the options and decisions made in a negotiation. A regular reading of the international press yields a large number of timely issues that lend themselves to making poignant what seems common.

The second kind of awareness is *awareness of process and structure* of the negotiation activity. As a social process, negotiation has identifiable parts and processes that are amenable to analysis and intervention. Some of the many "parts" to the negotiation, e.g., stages of development, agendas and their creation, the physical setting of the site, time resources, and roles, are not always so obvious nor understood. For example, bargaining is not a simple activity but made up of sub-activities like communications, exchange and evaluation, argumentation and persuasion, and relationship making. Each of these in turn is a complex social process. Thus, there is a hierarchy of complexity that needs to be identified and learned.

As the learning proceeds, learners become increasingly cognizant that negotiation is not just the simple give and take between parties. Cognizance of these very complex social processes promotes respect for what it takes to become a good negotiator. Like any activity, its more subtle aspects become apparent and powerful tools over time. The learners need to have the parts identified, defined, and labeled, show their workings and interrelationship, and demonstrate both good and bad states of the structures and processes to know what makes for a good negotiation situation and how to "fix" one when it is not so good.

The third kind of awareness is *self-awareness* of one's own individual behavior. Most of negotiations is really about behavior – what people do, say, think, perceive, hear, learn, and the like. For this, a mind experiment can be set up whereby the negotiator imagines that they are negotiating in a room of mirrors. Then the question arises: How would being in a room of mirrors affect a negotiation? This puzzle forces the learner to be both in the negotiations as participant and outside of the negotiations as observer. Once they start to watch themselves as negotiators, they begin to see behaviors as worthy of analysis. This has one curious beneficial effect of demonstrating that "soft skills" of studying behavior can have very hard outcomes. This gives increased credibility to the externally oriented learners who feel safe in the analysis of numbers and the "other." They then begin to notice differences in style and interactions. This leads to the why and how questions and eventually to culture as one of the explanatory variables.

In learning sessions with strong feedback periods, the mirrors are the comments of others about the particular effectiveness or ineffectiveness of actions taken. Some of the most powerful learning moments come when individuals, assured of their own intentions and past actions, are informed that what they intended was never acted out in reality. This has a soft shock value and calls immediately into attention the need to create consistency between intentions and actions. In this way, the value of culture learning comes from direct discovery, as the learner observes differences in negotiation techniques and styles and explores the assumptions that underlie behavioral actions.

Negotiations learning in cold and hot modes

Learning about negotiations is done best when understood as two modes which are both necessary but insufficient unto themselves. They are *cold learning* (cognitive learning with emphasis on models and frameworks for analysis) and *hot learning* (affective learning with an emphasis on practice, application, and real-time analysis).

To improve the "stick" of cultural ideas to memory, the learner needs to become emotionally involved, either vicariously (as in watching filmed negotiations and analyzing a particular person in that negotiation) or directly via experiential learning with real-time feedback. In this way, the learner gets to experiment with behavioral tactics and styles as they develop their own more effective repertoire of negotiating behavior. The caveat here is to make sure there is a linkage between the hot and cold learning. In the review of an exercise, the teacher can get students to reflect on how the cold learning was present and active in the exercise. Hot learning is fun but can be spurious when not linked to the cold learning of models, frameworks, and techniques of analysis. Former students often report, even years later, their memory of a certain class session, memorable because of the presence of both of these modes in the learning process.

Negotiation as self-interested discovery

The argument here is that good cultural learning is about self-interested discovery. Discovery is based on the larger motives of curiosity and self-interest. It is also based on a long-observed "fact" that most students of negotiation are in class either because they have had poor past experiences that they want to learn from or they are unsure just how good a negotiator they really are. They are curious about their own capabilities and are interested in learning from and testing the abilities of others as well. This motivates a self-interested desire to learn and improve.

Next, comes an interest in prediction and forecasting. In getting what one wants from the world, it helps immensely to learn from the past. This means not repeating mistakes and reading the situation and context better. Thus, learners want frameworks for analysis that help them understand better what went on in the past and how to avoid repeating bad history. It is here that learners often come to the simple realization that the other side they are dealing with is in exactly the same situation as they are. Other people populate the world and they may have goals very different from ours! Thus they come to appreciate the reality of conflict and the importance of mutual understanding of interests.

At this point, an interest in preparation for a future event such as negotiations arises. This means the learners want to know the basics of good common practice in planning, some tools for scenario planning and number crunching, how to deal with difficult people, and the like. Finally, in all these stages of learning comes an interest in better and best practice: how do you open an international negotiation; who should make the first offer and how should the deal be framed and in what language; how should translators be used? This is addressed via the analysis of formal cases, discussions of real experience, and the creation of experiential exercises that allow for the application of ideas and the development of skills through repetition in learning situations.

Thus, this view argues that cross-cultural negotiation learning can grow from the particulars of individual self-interest and discovery. Following a developmental stages model, learners discover, first in themselves, then in others, the larger issues and theory that give a more complete understanding of culture and its consequences.

Some pointers on debriefing cross-cultural negotiations

1   Establish a set of descriptive categories you want students to address. It is particularly good to start the discussion with an open question for the whole class on a neutral issue like, "Just how does this industry work and what are the context drivers behind this deal? What is making these two sides seek this deal?" This gets the discussion going and people into a more relaxed analytic learning mode about the general drivers behind the deal before the specifics of their own bargaining session come under scrutiny.

2   Pose questions on the board. For example, one I use often is, "What things (actions, behavior, inaction) helped or hindered the initiation, development, progress, and/or closure of this negotiation?" With this question you can get to "soft behavioral stuff" without making the "finance guys and engineers" too uncomfortable with the "touchy-feely" aspects of bargaining. It also gets them to see how micro-behaviors and habits (e.g., failing to shut off a cellphone during a bargaining session) have an impact on the other side's perceptions of them. They usually get laughed at for these, but they learn quickly and suffer only mild red-faced discomfort.

3   Begin with a review of the negotiation outcomes. Was there a deal? What are the deal's details? How did you arrive at this agreement? Students enjoy most when details are quantitative and comparable across teams so they can see how well they did (they like to compete). It is also an eye-opener to see how many different solutions exist to the same problem.

4   To create the sense of "us versus them," you can physically separate the class into the two sides of the negotiation and conduct an open interview with teams, moving back and forth freely between the sides to get a fuller picture of the events of the negotiation and to allow free questioning about tactics and justification of decisions. This works particularly well with MBA classes.

5   The quality of the debriefing is in part a function of the quality of the preparation for class. The better prepared the learner is to negotiate, the more likely that the negotiation will be an interesting experience.

Interesting experiences are more interesting to talk about! Therefore, reward for preparation.

Audience issues and pedagogical challenges

To understand culture's impact on negotiation, you have to deal with the issue of cultural determinants of behavior versus idiosyncratic sources of behavior. How a person in a case or exercise behaves may or may not reflect a cultural trait of the object culture of interest. This means you have to be careful to point out how stereotyping is a cognitive sense-making activity that can be subject to both bias and prejudice.

Generally, the younger the audience, the more careful you need to be about how feedback is given in class. Younger learners are often more aggressive and insensitive to the subtle aspects of feedback. They readily laugh and make fun of others without realizing how quickly the tables might turn on them. Thus, for this group, it is probably better to have more structured feedback based on questions that they can follow clearly and take notes on. Alternatively, older students with experience have a deeper knowledge and appreciate more the subtle issues and the counter-intuitive insights as well as contradictions. They like puzzles and conundrums. They also like application to the workplace. An effective instructor will know when and how to turn an issue in the case or exercise into a general issue by asking a question like, "How many of you have experienced something like this in the workplace? What happened in that case?" This can often lead to very rich discussions, but you must be attentive to time or you may not cover all you had planned.

Conclusion

This thumbnail sketch of key issues in the teaching of the culture identified a set of fundamental pedagogical ideas that play a role in the successful planning and execution of a negotiations course. Culture is one of those themes that, like the weather, we all know something about from our experience, but on closer look really do not, especially when we have to explain it. Yet cultural knowledge for cross-cultural interactions is increasingly a core knowledge and skill of successful international ventures. We hope the reader comes away with a feeling of confidence and curiosity when they attempt to bring cross-cultural materials into their negotiations courses.

Chapter 24

Conceptualizing and designing a course in international human resource management

Colette A. Frayne

Introduction

Developments during the last decades of the twentieth century have produced what may be termed an era of globalization. As business has continued to globalize, one of the most challenging aspects has focused on how a firm manages its human resources to sustain a competitive advantage.

Scholars from several disciplines are addressing these issues – coming at them from the perspective of strategy, cross-cultural management, international business, organizational theory, sociology, and human resource management (HRM) (Evans, Pucik and Barsoux 2002). It appears that the traditional boundaries between academic disciplines and functional areas (e.g., HRM and strategy) are becoming more highly integrated and that the globalization of business is having a significant impact on human resource management and organizational performance (Dowling, Welch and Schuler 1999). This chapter presents an integration of various approaches to designing and delivering courses on the topic of international human resource management.

Approaches to international HRM

The field of international HRM is generally characterized by three broad approaches (DeCieri and Dowling 2000). Initial approaches in this area emphasized a cross-cultural approach to examining human behavior in organizations. Another approach studies comparative HRM practices within and across countries. A third approach focuses on various functional aspects of HRM in multinational firms. However, a recent undertaking by Evans, Pucik and Barsoux (2002) integrates the orientations of strategy, culture, and HRM and presents international human resource management from a general management rather than a functional perspective. These authors suggest using an organizational systems perspective and argue that we must consider implementation of various

HRM strategies within a context of conflicting needs of the organization, such as local responsiveness versus global integration, coordination versus control, and short-term profitability versus long-term innovation. This orientation expands the traditional curricular focus to be more comprehensive and interdisciplinary, drawing on multiple theoretical perspectives and clearly promoting a general management view. The theoretical rationale draws upon fit and contingency theory, the resource-based view of the firm, different contextual schools (comparative management, institutional theories from political science), while building links to social capitalism and network theories, as well as theories of organizational learning (Evans, Pucik and Barsoux 2002). This approach clearly fits with recent demands of scholars and practitioners that international HRM be interdisciplinary and focused on contributing to company performance.

A course designed to teach students about human resource management in international settings has been identified at different schools. The course is usually designed to introduce students to the nature of managing human resources in international, multinational, global, and transnational firms. The purpose of the course is to provide students with an in-depth understanding of the basic problems inherent in international HRM. The intention is to either prepare the students for further work in the field or to give them a sound basis for understanding the international corporate dimensions of their own careers – sometimes both. Utilizing Evans, Pucik and Barsoux's (2002) framework, I developed a course entitled *Managing People in Global Markets*. The overall framework stipulates that the relationship between HRM and organizational performance must be separated into three different faces or roles, namely, "the builder," "the aligner," and "the navigator" who steer through the dualities confronting organizations today. This course, which consists of case studies, readings, videos, and projects, has been designed to reflect an integrative strategic approach to understanding and practicing international HRM.

Managing people in global markets

The *Managing People in Global Markets* course is designed for students of international management and general management, rather than for specialists in human resource management. The course is intended to introduce students to the major issues associated with managing people in the context of the global marketplace. The emphasis in the course is upon skill development. In this regard, an effective manager must evidence fluency in the theories and concepts required to achieve congruence between an organization, its environment, its organizational systems and structures, the key tasks that the organization has to perform, and the organization's human, technological, financial, and other resources. Yet, conceptual skills alone are not sufficient. An effective manager must also evidence the skills required to manage the task, people, structures and systems, as well as the ability to apply those skills to complex situations. This course uses the case study method as a primary pedagogical approach, in an effort to create an environment conducive to active and participative learning, as opposed to more passive lecture-based instructional approaches.

Pedagogical objectives for course

I have various objectives for this course:

• to facilitate students' understanding of the impact of cultural differences on the management of people in multinational organizations;
• to enhance students' ability to assess the impact of global conditions on the strategic management of human resources in the context of overseas subsidiaries, acquisitions, and joint ventures and alliances;
• for the student to compare and contrast critical human resource issues in the contexts of domestic and international operations and the stages of a firm's internationalization.

In order to increase students' awareness of the complexity of managing multinational operations, I continually ask them to identify key environmental, strategic, and organizational variables that influence international operations, how these variables interact, and how these variables affect the management of an organization's human resource capabilities. This course was designed for graduate students and practicing managers; however, I am teaching it to an upper division undergraduate class. The course materials are complex and rigorous and certainly present challenges to any audience, particularly to undergraduates.

Outline of the course

The course is divided into four modules:

1   Historical overview of HRM and global competition
2   Foundation components of HRM
3   Aligning or changing HRM practices
4   Leveraging HRM capabilities

I use the term "module" to reflect focused learning on a specific topic within the overall course. These modules vary in length and depth, depending on the overall topic area being addressed, and are discussed in greater detail in the following sections.

Module One: historical overview of HRM and global competition

Module One provides a historical overview of human resource management and global competition, building, aligning, and leveraging HRM capabilities. The overview seeks to establish the scholarly disciplines inherent to the design of the course, including HRM, strategy, cross-cultural management, international business, international economics, and trade theory. The interdisciplinary nature of international HRM is distinguished from traditional HRM and the changing role of HRM in international organizations is highlighted. I have found the article by Harry Lane, "Implementing strategy, structure, and systems" (1999a), to be very useful for students in the beginning phase of this course. This reading provides students with a framework for assessing the various elements of an organization's design. This module also emphasizes the need for students to understand and assess the importance of cultural biases that may exist in an organization's normal modes of operation. Culture and context, central to the entire course, are presented so that students focus on being aware of the cultural assumptions underlying their systems and practices and the implications of their use in other countries and cultural contexts. The contextual issues considered extend beyond the realm of national and organizational culture and challenge the student to simultaneously balance these variables with the external context of the firm, its international context and stage of internationalization, the business strategy context, and the key structures, tasks, and mode of operation in the business environment. In this way, students are continuously challenged to examine the cultural and non-cultural contextual variables and their impact for the HRM context within the firm.

Module Two: foundation components of HRM

Module Two introduces the first face of building HRM – getting solid foundations of selection, development, and performance management into place. I use the *Lincoln Electric: Venturing Abroad* case (Bartlett 1998) to illustrate getting the basics of human resource management into place and ensuring internal coherence. This case has been used previously to show how human resource management can contribute to sustainable business performance. The largest manufacturer of welding equipment in the world, Lincoln Electric, motivates its employees in the United States through its incentive and performance appraisal system. The company enjoyed unrivaled growth and prosperity until they decided to embark on a bold strategy for internationalization, under the guidance of a management team that had never worked outside the United States. The *Lincoln Electric: Venturing Abroad* case sets the foundation for the entire course by raising many important issues about how HRM contributes to organizational performance as a company goes international. Issues and concepts raised in the case include those of core competencies, culture-bound management practices, and the need to adapt, transfer, or create new systems as a company operates in one country as opposed to another. Students get to see international acquisitions as a growth strategy, the duality of control versus coordination during the process of internationalization, and the overall importance of developing managers with international experience. I teach this case over a four-hour time block and complement the case study by showing a video of an interview with Lincoln Electric's former CEO, Donald Hastings, and NBC's Leslie Stahl from an excerpt of the television program *Sixty Minutes* (CBS 1992). The video is excellent and brings the plant, the workers, and Cleveland, Ohio, into your classroom.

Module Three: aligning or changing HRM practices

Module Three introduces the second face of "aligning HRM" – aligning or changing HRM strategy and internal practices so as to implement that business strategy effectively. The relationship of HRM with the organization's business strategy is key and is seen as a critical partnership. During this module, I emphasize the role of strategic HRM and the importance of "fit" with the external environment. I use the *Colgate-Palmolive: Managing International Careers* case (Rosenzweig 1994) to illustrate the critical issues of human resource management and career development as the firm's activities span nations and continents. Colgate-Palmolive, the U.S.-based consumer products company best known for its toothpaste and detergents, has long emphasized overseas experience for its managers. In the 1980s, Colgate-Palmolive developed a comprehensive policy regarding expatriate assignments, which addresses many personal, financial, and logistical concerns. By the 1990s, a new problem emerged: dual careers and the reluctance of some prospective expatriates to accept these critical international assignments. By examining these topics, students are exposed to the many issues involved in the management of international careers, as well as to the impact of social and environmental trends driving the company to re-examine this policy and its emphasis on international experience as a prerequisite for promotion to top management. Can a firm with 65 percent of its sales in international markets, selling consumer products that must be adapted to local tastes and customs, not alter its expectations that managers obtain international experience through these types of assignments? The case provides a rich discussion of expatriate management, dual careers, business strategy, and the link of HRM strategy, international markets, and competence development. I also teach this course over a four-hour time period and end with a brief lecture on dual careers and the critical role that expatriates can play for a global firm.

To further "round out" the module on aligning capabilities, I continue the examination of global staffing and the key role of expatriation management. The *Marconi Telecommunications Mexico* case (Lane 1999b) allows the students to study personal accounts of expatriation, adjustment, and repatriation in the context of a firm that has continued global expansion through acquisitions while perhaps outdistancing its ability to staff the acquired companies in Mexico, Chile, and other parts of Latin America. We once again revisit the systems framework provided in Module One by the Lane (1999a) article and examine the role of "fit" between strategy and systems as Marconi embarks on a global strategy with implications for its human resource capabilities. Continuing with an examination of the systems model and the concept of "fit," the *ABB Poland* case (Frost and Weinstein 1998) provides a wonderful case for examining international strategy, structure, and staffing in acquisitions, as well as the need to manage change initiatives in the newly acquired Polish companies. The students struggle with issues of national versus organizational culture, how to implement changes, and how to maintain the matrix structure and mindset of ABB with a host of companies in an ex-Soviet-bloc area. We conclude this module and the *ABB Poland* case analysis with a discussion of the challenges of transferring systems within another organizational entity – namely, international joint ventures – and we address the continued difficulty of adaptation versus creation of new systems to fit the strategy, culture, or administrative heritage of either the foreign parent company or the host-country partner. Throughout this module, I introduce various regions of the world (e.g., Latin America, Poland, Russia, Southeast Asia) so that the students are continuously challenged to think about HRM practices in a context of country comparisons, issues of globalization and localization, and stages of the firm's internationalization. I expect that the students will prepare each case with a clear recognition of the country or region in which the case is depicted. I challenge the students to use current Internet sources, newspapers, magazines, and Culturegrams (see References) to understand the HRM practices particular to the country or region of study. When we do the *ABB Poland* case, for example, I provide them with the article "Business success in Eastern Europe: understanding and customizing HRM" (Kiriazov, Sullivan and Tu 2000). This article gives the students a good grasp of the disparate and complex factors that influence human resource practices in some of the formerly communist countries.

Module Four: leveraging HRM capabilities

The final module of the course focuses on making use of HRM capabilities. The emphasis in this module is on the development of organizational capabilities for competitive advantage. The tensions between the "dualities" that are faced by international organizations are highlighted, including short-term results versus long-term profitability and global integration versus local responsiveness pressures. Each of the cases that I have selected for this module focuses on a different stage of leveraging HRM capabilities. The *Bristol-Compressors, Asia Pacific* case (Morrison and Black 1998) focuses on the efforts of the president of the Asia–Pacific region and his management committee as they try to increase the quality and quantity of managers in the region. Lack of depth in management ranks is viewed as a critical problem for Bristol Compressors and the students are faced with action alternatives that balance training current managers, recruiting locals, or returning to the use of expatriates. Continuing with the theme of leveraging capabilities, students are exposed to cases in China (*Mabuchi Motor Co., Ltd* – Beamish and Goerzen 1998); Vietnam (*HCM Beverage Company* – Black and Morrison 1998a); Indonesia (*Building Products International* – DiStefano and Everatt 1999); and Korea (*LG Group: Developing Tomorrow's Global Leaders* – Black and Morrison 1998b). Each of the cases exposes the students to different cultural contexts, different phases of leveraging capabilities (e.g., managing, protecting, and steering), and different phases of HRM activities (e.g., training and development programs; crisis management programs; global leadership development, recruitment, and selection). The focus of this module is truly integrative and is supported with readings dealing with the global manager and with the challenges of aligning the functional areas with the global strategies.

Conclusion of the course

After completing the fourth module, I conclude the course with an integrative review and summary of the key concepts, frameworks, and learning points. To promote active involvement and interaction in this final review and learning session, I require the students to bring their three most important learning points from the course and to share these points during the class discussion. Not only do these learning points promote active involvement of the students in the context of a review session, this session also allows for additional concepts to be raised and for concepts to be discussed in greater depth and with further emphasis on integration. The learning from this session enables me to reflect on the challenges as well as successes that I have experienced in teaching this course. The key challenge for me is presenting each module and clearly articulating the keen differences between the three faces of HRM in international firms. For each face, I highlight four main areas: namely, the *activity*, the *focus*, the *theory* and the *role* of HRM within each distinct face. For example, during the Building HRM face, the *activity* involves getting the basics in place, the *focus* is on internal coherence, the *theory* is one of "fit" from an internal organizational design perspective, and the *role* of HRM is that of a builder. It often takes students some time to understand each of the faces and the challenge for me is to highlight these four main areas throughout the selection of cases that I use. The key to success for me in teaching this course is my preparation and selection of the various cases for each of the modules as well as the corresponding readings and activities. Through the extensive use of relevant, current, and meaningful case studies, I find that the students leave the course with a richer appreciation of the human resource management challenges that are involved in the process of internationalization. They also understand the need to operate in an increasingly global and complex environment where people are considered a precious and sustainable competitive advantage.

Organizational field project

As an additional integral means of applying concepts from the course, student groups are asked to complete a field project that examines in some detail the management challenges of globalization. The student team conducts this project on an organization that they select. The project incorporates analysis, critique, and recommendations. In order to place responsibility on the students for accessing and interpreting primary as well as secondary data sources for the chosen organization, interview and first-hand data are required in this project. The field project tests the students' deeper understanding of how an organization actually manages the global workforce and how well each of the students is able to integrate the materials and learning that we have collectively developed throughout the course. Most importantly, this project is intended to help the students internalize and integrate the issues discussed in the course in a practical, useful, and career-enhancing way. Past students have reported that they learned an enormous amount about the organization that they were interested in as well as knowledge of current global management challenges. Critical skills of how to collect data, conduct analyses, and apply the knowledge that they have gained in this course are also important to project success.

Personal learning journals

Coupled with the field project, a final and perhaps potent form of organization learning resides in the requirement for each student to keep a personal learning journal as we proceed through the course. The purpose of this journal is to ask each student to reflect on the daily learning in the class and ask the question, *"What does all of this really mean for me as I try to enhance my ability to effectively manage and work with others?"* After each session, students are asked to draw upon the session's mix of cases, readings, role-plays, discussions, simulations, etc., and apply these various instructional activities to their own personal learning objectives for the course as well as their ability to maintain and enhance their overall effectiveness as global managers. I ask the student to do this reflection after each class. The student, via integration and prioritization efforts, should strive to translate this reflection into at least one journal entry for each class session topic and activity. For example, if a class session consists of a case, a reading, discussion, and a lecture, the student will have at least four entries for that day. Each entry should reflect a significant discovery, insight, connection, guideline, observation, concern, or other kind of learning that integrates session context and experience with the student's own current or future managerial reality.

It is within these entries that students often reflect on another key aspect of culture, namely, individual variations and interpretations of their own cultural beliefs, norms, values, and perspectives. This activity often aids the student in making sense of the various challenges presented in the cases when national culture confronts organizational culture. Rather than broadly interpreting cultural differences and making generalizations across cultures and/or countries, students are able to personalize such learning based on individual cultural backgrounds and experiences. Three or four entries per class session, for seventeen classes (based on a quarter system), means that the student should possess at least 50 entries by the end of the course. Based on a review and integration of the journal entries, each student is required to prepare an essay. The essay should reflect their ability to sort out, integrate, and interpret their own entire collection of entries throughout the course. This essay provides the students with the opportunity to synthesize their learning from this course and apply the learning to their personal managerial effectiveness and their career.

Conclusions

Managerial development is the single biggest challenge presented by increased globalization of firms and markets. Developing tomorrow's generation of global managers requires a need to develop a global mindset and the specific task of developing leaders for the future. These challenges only serve to heighten the need to conceptualize, design, and deliver courses on managing human resources in international firms that emphasize a broader perspective of what operating internationally involves. The course discussed in this chapter is one effort to meet this important educational and managerial challenge.

References

Bartlett, C. (1998) *Lincoln Electric: Venturing Abroad*, Boston: Harvard Business School: 9-389-095.

Beamish, P. W. and Goerzen, A. (1998) *Mabuchi Motor Co. Ltd.*, Boston: Harvard Business School: 98M034.

Black, S. and Morrison, A. (1998a) *HCM Beverage Company*, London, Ontario, Canada: Ivey Publishing: 98C003.

Black, S. and Morrison, A. (1998b) *LG Group: Developing Tomorrow's Global Leaders*, London, Ontario, Canada: Ivey Publishing: 98G009.

CBS (1992) *Sixty Minutes* video, New York: Columbia Broadcasting System: November 8.

Culturegrams published on the Internet at www.culturegrams.com, Lindon UT: Axiom Press.

DeCieri, H. and Dowling, P. (2000) "Strategic human resources management in multinational enterprises: theoretical and empirical developments," in P. Wright *et al.* (eds), *Research and Theory in SHRM: An Agenda for the 21st Century*, Greenwich, CT: JAI Press.

DiStefano, J. and Everatt, D. (1999) *Building Products International – A Crisis Management Strategy (B)*, London, Ontario, Canada: Ivey Publishing: 99C002.

Dowling, P., Welch, D. and Schuler, R. (1999) *International Human Resource Management: Managing People in a Multinational Context*, Cincinnati, OH: South-Western College Publishing.

Evans, P., Pucik, V. and Barsoux, J. (2002) *The Globalization Challenge: Frameworks for International Human Resource Management*, New York: McGraw-Hill.

Frost, A. and Weinstein, M. (1998) *ABB Poland*, London, Ontario, Canada: Ivey Publishing: 98C011.

Kiriazov, D., Sullivan, S. E. and Tu, H. S. (2000) "Business success in eastern Europe: understanding and customizing HRM," *Business Horizons*, January 43 (1): 39–43.

Lane, H. (1999a) "Implementing strategy, structure, and systems," in H. Lane, M. Maznevski and J. DiStefano (eds), *International Management Behavior: Text, Readings, and Cases*, Cambridge, MA: Blackwell, pp. 181–205.

Lane, H. (1999b) *Marconi Telecommunications Mexico*, London, Ontario, Canada: Ivey Publishing: 8A98C09.

Morrison, A. and Black, S. (1998) *Bristol Compressors, Asia-Pacific*, London, Ontario, Canada: Ivey Publishing: 98M001.

Rosenzweig, P. (1994) *Colgate-Palmolive: Managing International Careers*, Boston: Harvard Business School: 9-394-184.

Chapter 25

Incorporating culture in joint-venture and alliance instruction

The Alliance Culture Exercise

J. Michael Geringer and Colette A. Frayne

Introduction

Fundamental environmental and organizational changes, trends toward internationalization and the increasing cost and complexity of technology have caused many companies to utilize inter-organizational collaboration, including joint ventures and other forms of alliances, as a key element of their international strategies (Harrigan 1988; Yoshino and Rangan 1995). However, despite their increasing frequency and strategic importance, many joint ventures and alliances (JVAAs) fail to achieve their performance objectives due to the unique challenges associated with managing these inter-organizational ventures (Geringer and Hebert 1991; Yoshino and Rangan 1995). The challenge results from the presence of two or more partner organizations that are often competitors as well as collaborators (Geringer 1988, 1991; Hamel 1990). Partners often simultaneously have convergent or complementary and divergent or even opposing alliance motivations, goals, and operating policies, as well as disparate national and organizational cultures (Buckley and Casson 1988; Frayne and Geringer 1990; Laurent 1986; Lynch 1993). As a result, a large proportion of JVAA failures have been attributed not to financial or technical problems, but instead to "cultural," factors, such as conflicts in management styles and operational practices (Devlin and Bleackley 1988; Ganitsky and Watzke 1990; Geringer and Frayne 1990, 1997, 2000; Shenkar and Zeira 1987). Indeed, these factors help to explain why many JVAAs begin to experience operational problems even after years of relatively stable performance.

Despite the challenging context and the critical role of cultural factors in JVAAs' operations and performance, issues of culture have received relatively limited attention in JVAA research or teaching. The objective of this chapter is to describe the "Alliance Culture Exercise," an instructional tool that can facilitate an instructor's efforts to introduce culture and its relationship to the structure, management, and performance of JVAAs, and promote insightful discussion of culture and culture-related issues within the context of JVAAs.

Culture and the structure, operation, and performance of JVAAs

Research in JVAA success has shown that a critical issue is the need for the partners to identify a common, or at least compatible, vision of the proposed alliance (Geringer and Frayne 2000). A shared vision among the respective partners' organizations should take into account the respective strategic and environmental pressures and should also be consistent with the environmental context in which the partners and the JVAA will operate, including the industry or industries in which they compete and the respective home and host countries in which they operate. Developing a shared vision is not always an easy task, due, in part, to barriers created through cultural differences.

In order to operationalize their shared vision and achieve their respective strategic objectives, the partners' organizations must establish an appropriate structure and set of operating procedures and practices for the JVAA and for relations between the partners and the JVAA (Geringer and Frayne 1990, 1997; Geringer and Hebert 1989). But, managers often confront pressures arising from the different needs for local responsiveness and global integration (e.g., at the function, product, or market level) among the JVAA participants, as well as with and among the partners' organizations (Bartlett 1986; Doz and Prahalad 1984). These pressures may influence a host of decisions, such as the degree of centralization of decision making, management style, recruitment or reward practices for managers and other personnel, the integration mechanisms that are employed, and a host of other culture-related issues (Davidson 1984; Gates and Egelhoff 1986; Prahalad and Doz 1981; Prahalad and Bettis 1986). Tensions between the partners' organizations and the JVAA as a result of integration and responsiveness pressures and their relationship to national or organizational culture of the partner organizations (and perhaps the host nation of the JVAA) therefore have fundamental implications for the structure, operation, and performance of the JVAA.

The challenge for the instructor is creating among students an awareness of the nature of this tension and skills for better managing it.

The Alliance Culture Exercise

1 Focal audience and instructional contexts for employing the Alliance Culture Exercise

The Alliance Culture Exercise has proven to be a robust instructional technique. We have successfully utilized this exercise with senior executives, more junior managers, and non-managerial personnel from a range of nations (all six major continents) and a variety of organizations (small and large, governmental and private, for-profit and not-for-profit). We have also used the Alliance Culture Exercise with undergraduate, graduate, and executive MBA audiences, both as part of focused seminars (e.g., one- to three-day training programs) and in more traditional degree-oriented programs (e.g., quarter-length or semester-length classes).

2 Pedagogical objectives for using the Alliance Culture Exercise

A pedagogical objective for this exercise is to facilitate students' ability to identify both the potential and realized gaps between different national and organizational culture perspectives of the entities involved in a JVAA (e.g., North American versus Japanese perspectives, engineering versus marketing orientation of the partner organizations). Students are expected to consider why these gaps originate, and what implications they have for the structure, operation, and performance of JVAAs. The Alliance Culture Exercise provides one approach for exploring the general issues associated with culture and JVAAs. This exercise can address such issues as:

- challenges of managing different cultures in an alliance;
- three types of organizational cultures that can be developed in an alliance;
- the determinants of or considerations in selecting an alliance culture;
- implications of alliance culture decisions, including the emergence of management of divided loyalties and associated problems.

For the purpose of a strategy course in Joint Ventures, we use an operational definition of culture. Culture can be seen as the pressures from national and organizational histories to define the JVAA management style and operational practices. Examples are the degree of centralization or decentralization, recruitment and reward practices, and the orientation to geographically local adaptation.

3 Instructor guidelines for using the Alliance Culture Exercise

We typically proceed with the Alliance Culture Exercise in the following manner.

a Introduction of JVAAs

The instructor introduces the concept of JVAAs, their potential as strategic tools, and the kinds of challenges that they often confront. The instructor can use examples from the business press to illustrate the use and performance of alliances in well-known fields (e.g., the Ericsson–Sony joint venture in cellular phones). We have usually kept this discussion to about five to ten minutes, unless the context is a focused JVAA component of a broader-focused course.

b Introduce typology of culture types

The instructor can introduce three general types of alliance culture. These are somewhat generic types, but this typology of "alliance cultures" is an excellent base for generating discussion. The introduction of the typology of alliance culture typically takes only a few minutes and tends to be primarily definitional.

1 One-culture dominance: The alliance and its employees adopt the culture of one of the partner organizations. An example of this culture can be found in the Japanese American Seating Case (Geringer and Miller 1998).
2 Cultural mosaic: The culture of individual employees varies and reflects practices in their respective partner organizations. Siebel Systems (available from Harvard Business School) is an example which illustrates this cultural type.
3 Cultural melting pot: The different backgrounds and experiences of the alliance's employees are integrated into a new, emergent culture. Caterpillar, Inc., (available from the authors) is an excellent case to illustrate this cultural type.

c Assess and compare culture types

The instructor can facilitate a discussion of the potential strengths and weaknesses of each of the three types of alliance culture (both short-term and longer-term), and the contexts in which their use might be more or less appropriate. This discussion can be completed in as little as five minutes, or as long as half an hour, depending on the evidence and the degree of detail the instructor wishes to pursue. For example, this discussion can be extended by asking the students to consider whether managers should assume that they *cannot* completely overcome national or organizational cultural differences, or conversely whether they should assume that managers *can* overcome and manage such differences. We have found that fifteen to twenty minutes of discussion is usually adequate for most audiences, or about twenty-five to thirty minutes of discussion if the individual or small-group activity option is used (see Table 25.1).

To structure this discussion, the instructor can use either individual/small-group activity or group discussion:

- Individual/small-group activity: Begin by asking the students to spend a few minutes (individually or in small groups) identifying and writing down a list of strengths and weaknesses of each of the three culture types, as well as considerations on when and how to use them. This activity can then be followed by a group discussion (see next point below) to help identify and explore the different perspectives and points identified by each individual or team. This approach can be particularly valuable in a diverse group of students.
- Group discussion: After presenting the three culture types, the instructor can draw three columns on the whiteboard, chalkboard, or flipchart. Label these columns: "One-culture dominance," "Cultural mosaic," and "Cultural melting pot." Under each column, the instructor can draw a row for each of: "strengths," "weaknesses," and "other considerations," as suggested below (see Table 25.1).

The instructor can then facilitate a discussion of strengths and weaknesses on a culture type-by-type basis, completing the first type ("one culture dominant") before moving to the next. After completing the strengths and weaknesses of each, we then discuss the considerations on when and how to most appropriately use (or not use) each of the three culture types. This tends to be a lively and insightful discussion.

Typically, the types of strengths and weaknesses of each culture type would include such factors as the following:

- For one-culture dominance:
  - Strengths: can be implemented quickly; enhances ability to integrate the JVAA with the culturally dominant partner; may facilitate low-cost and relatively easy implementation of policies and procedures since they can be imported nearly completely from existing practices of the culturally dominant partner.
  - Weaknesses: may make subordinate culture partner and its personnel feel "left out" and less motivated; may hinder ability to

Table 25.1 Assessment and comparison of culture types

	One-culture dominance	Cultural mosaic	Cultural melting pot
Strengths			
Weaknesses			
Considerations			

Source: Osland 1995.

attract and utilize highly qualified personnel from the subordinate culture; may hinder ability to integrate with subordinate culture and make use of that partner's people and other resources; may hinder the dominant partner's ability to learn from the subordinate culture.

- For cultural mosaic:

  - Strengths: may place more emphasis on an individual's background; may allow differentiation of the JVAA's activities and approaches based on each partner's contributions.
  - Weaknesses: may provide less incentive for cooperation in the alliance between individuals or groups from the different cultures; may promote politics and divisiveness; may slow the rate at which agreements are reached to coordinate between the different cultures and approaches of the partners.

- For cultural melting pot:

  - Strengths (perceived): often viewed by students as an "ideal" culture adapted specifically for the JVAA's unique context and needs.
  - Weaknesses: slow to accomplish; does not just "happen," rather must be managed; often accompanied by ambiguity and disagreement about, e.g., what is important, how to do things; difficult to develop if the JVAA involves continual rotation of managers or other employees from the partner organizations or experiences high turnover; may be difficult to integrate the JVAA with the partner organizations since the melting-pot culture causes it to look and act differently from the partner cultures.

d Extension of discussion into other culture-related topics

Optionally, depending on the amount of time available, the instructor can extend the Alliance Culture Exercise discussion into topics such as:

- the relationship of alliance culture to other structural or operational factors (e.g., alliance control, human resource practices); or

- the processes, procedures, and skills necessary to promote the emergence of certain types of alliance cultures (e.g., team building, management of divided loyalties).

This discussion can take anywhere from five to ten minutes (e.g., a brief discussion of the management of divided loyalties) to as long as an hour. Sample discussions on two topics follow.

TOPIC: JVAA CULTURE AND CONTROL

A company that agrees to participate in a JVAA inevitably complicates its life. Due to the shared ownership and decision-making nature of these ventures, each partner must relinquish some control over the JVAA's activities. Yet, for reasons intimately related to their home organization's corporate strategy and objectives, partner-company managers often resist such a move. Therefore, in order to fully achieve their strategic objectives, it is essential that partner organizations be able to effectively control their JVAAs (see Geringer and Frayne 1997; Geringer and Hebert 1989).

The level of costs associated with effective control is related to the level of interdependence between the JVAA and other operations of the partner organization. Partner companies will encounter the lowest level of costs when the level of interdependence with the JVAA is minimal. This may allow more flexibility regarding the JVAA's culture. However, as the level of interdependence increases, costs associated with effective coordination, monitoring, enforcement, and so forth also tend to increase. This often encourages the partner experiencing high levels of interdependence to focus on controlling the JVAA culture.

TOPIC: JVAA CULTURE AND THE MANAGEMENT OF DIVIDED LOYALTIES

Divided loyalties occur when employees confront situations in which they are asked to be loyal to two or more different organizations, managers, or cultures, and there is inconsistency between the different individuals or groups. This conflict can hinder efforts to effectively motivate and integrate the JVAA's human and other resources, thus threatening the ability of the venture and/or its partners to achieve the intended objectives of the alliance. Managing divided loyalties, therefore, becomes an important issue – one closely linked to the culture developed within the alliance.

Students can be asked to identify bases for divided loyalties as well as examples they may have confronted (or can imagine). Factors hindering identification of alliance employees with the alliance might include career systems tightly linked to partner, strong manager identification with partners, a leadership vacuum in the JVAA, perceptions of emergent domination or inequality, poor or unclear mechanisms for performance feedback, language difficulties or differences, multi-site alliances (especially JVAAs with sites near partners), and/or intensive dependence of alliance on partner(s). In contrast, actions that help promote employee identification with the JVAA might include such things as resource and task independence of the JVAA, HRM controlled by the JVAA's management rather than HRM controlled by a partner organization, a leader who commands the admiration or trust of all team members and who helps set clear standards for interaction, timely feedback loops, and/or the existence of a clear source of external threat.

Conclusions

Here we have identified factors related to the issue of culture within the context of JVAAs and other alliances. We have briefly discussed the nature of these factors, particularly partner organizations and their strategies, the environmental context of the partners' organizations and the JVAA, the shared vision underlying the JVAA itself, and organizational requirements. We have also presented a basic instructional technique, the Alliance Culture Exercise, which introduces and addresses issues of culture with respect to the design, management, and performance of JVAAs.

Clearly, the successful management of culture in JVAAs represents a challenge to all of the parties involved in the venture. The Alliance Culture Exercise presented in this chapter is intended as an instructional technique for initiating an introductory level of discussion of culture and its relationship with the structure, operation, and performance of JVAAs. We have found that the Alliance Culture Exercise is robust in terms of the audiences with which it can be employed, as well as in its ability to extend the discussion into a range of related topics.

References

Bartlett, C. A. (1986) "Building and managing the transnational: the new organizational challenge," in M. E. Porter (ed.), *Competition in Global Industries*, Boston: Harvard Business School Press, pp. 367–404.

Buckley, P. and Casson, M. (1988) "A theory of cooperation in international business," in F. Contractor and P. Lorange (eds), *Cooperative Strategies in International Business*, Lexington, MA: Lexington Books, pp. 31–53.

Davidson, W. H. (1984) "Administrative orientation and international performance," *Journal of International Business Studies*, Fall: 11–23.

Devlin, G. and Bleackley, M. (1988) "Strategic alliances – guidelines for success," *Long Range Planning*, 30 (3): 12–18.

Doz, Y. and Prahalad, C. K. (1984) "Patterns of strategic control within MNCs," *Journal of International Business Studies*, Fall: 55–72.

Frayne, C. A. and Geringer, J. M. (1990) "The strategic use of human resource management techniques as control mechanisms in international joint ventures," in G. R. Ferris and K. M. Rowland (eds), *Research in Personnel and Human Resource Management*, Greenwich, CT: JAI Press, pp. 53–69.

Ganitsky, J. and Watzke, G. (1990) "Implications of different time perspectives for human resource management in international joint ventures," *Management International Review*, 30 (special issue): 37–51.

Gates, S. R. and Egelhoff, W. G. (1986) "Centralization in headquarters–subsidiary relationships," *Journal of International Business Studies*, Summer: 71–92.

Geringer, J. M. (1988) *Joint Venture Partner Selection: Strategies for Developed Countries*, Westport, CT: Quorum.

Geringer, J. M. (1991) "Strategic determinants of partner selection criteria in international joint ventures," *Journal of International Business Studies*, 22 (1): 41–62.

Geringer, J. M. and Frayne, C. A. (1990) "Human resource management and international joint venture control: a parent company perspective," *Management International Review*, 30 (special issue): 103–20.

Geringer, J. M. and Frayne, C. A. (1997) "Controlling IP in alliances is ideal goal," *Les Nouvelles*, 32 (1): 24–9.

Geringer, J. M. and Frayne, C. A. (2000) "Strategic human resource management in international joint ventures," in P. C. Earley and H. Singh (eds), *Innovations in International and Cross-cultural Management*, Thousand Oaks, CA: Sage, pp. 107–28.

Geringer, J. M. and Hebert, L. (1989) "Control and performance of international joint ventures," *Journal of International Business Studies*, 20 (2): 235–54.

Geringer, J. M. and Hebert, L. (1991) "Measuring performance of international joint ventures," *Journal of International Business Studies*, 22 (2): 249–63.

Geringer, J. M. and Miller, J. (1998) *Kasai-Banting Inc. (A)*, London, Ontario, Canada: Ivey Business School.

Hamel, G. P. (1990) "Competitive collaboration: learning, power and dependence in international strategic alliances," unpublished doctoral dissertation, University of Michigan, Ann Arbor.

Harrigan, K. R. (1988) "Strategic alliances and partner asymmetries," in F. Contractor and P. Lorange (eds), *Cooperative Strategies in International Business*, Lexington, MA: Lexington Books, pp. 205–26.

Laurent, A. (1986) "The cross-cultural puzzle of international human resource management," *Human Resource Management*, 25 (1): 91–102.

Lynch, R. P. (1993) *Business Alliances Guide: The Hidden Competitive Weapon*, New York: Wiley.

Osland, J. (1995) *The Adventure of Working Abroad: Hero Tales from the Global Frontier*, San Francisco, CA: Jossey-Bass.

Prahalad, C. K. and Bettis, R. A. (1986) "The dominant logic: a new linkage between diversity and performance," *Strategic Management Journal*, 7: 485–501.

Prahalad, C. K. and Doz, Y. L. (1981) "An approach to strategic control in multinationals," *Sloan Management Review*, Summer, 5–13.

Shenkar, O. and Zeira, Y. (1987) "Human resources management in international joint ventures: directions for research," *Academy of Management Review*, 12: 546–57.

Yoshino, M. Y. and Rangan, U. S. (1995) *Strategic Alliances: An Entrepreneurial Approach to Globalization*, Boston: Harvard Business School Press.

Chapter 26

Teaching culture in the capstone strategy course

Allan Bird

Introduction

The strategic management course is identified at different schools under a variety of names, e.g., "Business Policy," "Corporate Planning and Strategy," or "General Management." This course is usually designed to give the student a capstone experience in which the concepts, models, techniques, and tools learned in separate, functionally focused courses are integrated into a single unified body of knowledge. The objective of such a course is to imbue within the student an understanding of the firm as a complex system that interacts with a larger, more complex, environment and, further, to provide students with concepts and tools appropriate to managing the firm as a whole. The underlying assumption is that if one understands the firm and its place within the environment, as well as the application of strategic concepts and tools, one can make the firm an active master of its environment.

Given such an orientation, and in light of widespread recognition of the globalization of business operations and competition, one might expect that discussion of culture and its influence on business should occupy an important position within the strategy course. One's expectation would not be met. A review of numerous strategy books would lead one to conclude that culture has little impact on the firm or its environment in ways that matter strategically.

There are several possible explanations for the current situation. First, there is often an assumption that students have already received substantial training in the influence of culture through prior coursework, particularly in courses on organizational behavior or the typical international business management course. However, as Bird and Osland (2000) note, this is a questionable assumption. It is also doubtful that strategy instructors who do want to cover the matter more thoroughly in their courses have received a solid grounding in culture and the cultural dimensions of their discipline as part of their training. Finally, the underpinnings of the field of strategy and its various concepts and models are based on an assumption that culture does not matter. Strategic concepts and methods are usually seen as universally applicable. The field of strategy is situated squarely within a social science perspective that includes notions of a "technological imperative" and "convergence." Lincoln and Kalleberg succinctly present this position (1990: 20):

> the forces of scale, production technology, and market constraint determine the internal organization of a firm, regardless of the social setting in which it is embedded. At both levels, society and organization, the mechanism that constrains the range of organizing options from which the firm can viably select is the imperative of performance/efficiency – survival.

With these considerations in mind, let us focus on the issue of how to teach culture within the strategy course. As the case method of instruction is widely used in teaching strategy, my approach has been to select cases that illustrate not only various strategy issues but also surface cultural issues. This means that, almost invariably, I use cases with an international dimension or that reflect comparative differences between two or more countries. In discussing how to teach culture below, I reference specific cases. These cases reflect personal preferences and in no way represent the only, or even the best, cases.

Culture at the micro level

One approach to teaching culture is to focus on the cultural background of the top management of the firm and the way culture influences managerial perceptions of the environment as well as the selection of appropriate company strategies in light of those perceptions. Rather than introducing different dimensions for comparing culture, e.g., Hofstede's (1980) work-related values or Kluckhohn and Strodtbeck's (1961) value orientations, I work from what is known about the way culture influences values, attitudes, beliefs, perceptions, and the selection of schemas and scripts to guide action. This approach employs cases that demonstrate such differences.

For example, contrasting the perceptions of Honda and Harley-Davidson executives can surface fundamental differences in the way cultural history and cultural values influence managerial thought and behavior. I assign the Honda (A) (Christiansen and Pascale 1987) and the Harley-Davidson (Kotha 1999) cases for consecutive class sessions.[1] During each of these sessions, we address typical strategic issues, e.g., market entry, market segmentation, organizational restructuring. While comparisons between the two companies are common during the second session,

I try to keep discussion in this area from going too deep. In the third session, I ask the students to compare managers' perceptions in both cases. I start with a simple question for the students themselves, "What is the function of a motorcycle?" This question, after some general discussion about motorcycles as transportation and as material symbolic expression, leads to an exploration of how Honda and Harley-Davidson managers see motorcycles, how motorcycles should be manufactured, who should ride them, and how to market them. Once we have some basic differences up on the board, I ask why managers from these two companies see motorcycles so differently. I try to zero in on the rationale behind the perception. For example, Honda managers in the case appear to see motorcycles less as a symbolic expression of self-identity than as an inexpensive form of transportation. I push students to explain why the Honda managers see things this way, and why the Harley-Davidson managers see things so differently. Because many students may be unfamiliar with Japanese history or culture (although the case has rich detail), it may be necessary to provide cultural and historical detail that will assist students in developing logics for explaining differences. It is often also useful to ask, "Why do Harley-Davidson managers have such a hard time seeing the things that Honda executives see?"

My intent in addressing culture in this fashion is to help students see that culture's influence at the "micro" or organizational behavior level can have a profound impact on how a firm understands its environment and fashions a response to that environment at the "macro" level. Even if students have received instruction on culture's effect through other courses, often this is the first time they see how wide-ranging its effect on an organization can be. To reinforce this point throughout the course, all subsequent discussions involving perceptions and behaviors of individual actors include a consideration of cultural influences.

Culture at the macro level

A second approach to teaching culture in the strategy course is to focus on the cultural environment in which firms operate. Again, I employ a range of cases to demonstrate culture's effect. However, I often preface the cases with a short "lecturette" that focuses on one dimension that has been found consistently to be the most useful in contrasting cultures (Gudykunst and Ting-Toomey 1988; Triandis 1995): individualism versus collectivism. I use the lecturette in advance because I have found students have a very difficult time with the abstract activity of identifying cultural influences at the institutional level.

After a short discussion of individualist and collectivist values as reflected in the behavior of people, I ask if these values are also reflected in a country's institutions. Students often quickly conclude that they are.

However, when I push for examples, they struggle. I then lay out a simple framework identifying three broad areas: political ideologies, economic governance, and social governance.

I point out that political ideologies can be distinguished in terms of how they define the relationship between the firm and the state. An individualistic ideology seeks to clarify the rights of individuals and firms. It does so primarily by defining and adjudicating individual claims and defending rights. The individualistic political ideology prefers that decisions be made in open, competitive political markets where there is a competition of ideas and interests. The government acts primarily as a referee responsible for enforcing "fair play," while individual actors align themselves with various political interests and seek to defeat those with whom they disagree. Laws and regulations provide a framework within which social order evolves and changes in accordance with the preferences of individuals, as reflected by decisions in the political marketplace.

In contrast, a communitarian[2] ideology seeks to clarify and protect community rights, often by emphasizing citizens' duties. Individuals are expected to be loyal to groups, which, in turn, demand conformity. Within a communitarian society, the preferred mode of decision making is through consensus among groups, rather than majority vote. Through consensus the social order is protected and stability maintained.

The lecturette then moves on to consider individualist and communitarian ideologies as reflected in assumptions about how governments should intervene in the economy. These assumptions parallel those in the political arena. In an individualist society, economic activity is seen as a separate sphere of life. The government must monitor economic activities to protect individuals and firms from unfair practices but, otherwise, needs no further involvement. Based on these assumptions, government should:

- distance itself from economic activity;
- delegate rights to pursue economic activities;
- monitor economic activity; and
- seek to promote benefits for consumers over the interests of producers.

If governments intervene in the marketplace it is for purposes of achieving these aims.

In communitarian societies economic activity is seen as a central aspect of life and, therefore, requires the involvement of the state at many levels. Government should make economic plans in order to push economic activities in directions that will serve the general welfare of the community. Government agencies:

- formulate economic strategies in consultation with firms;
- implement strategies by providing support in the forms of credits, subsidies and regulation;
- favor home-country firms over foreign investors; and
- promote strong economic growth overall.

Finally, we move into a consideration of these two ideologies as they are reflected in social governance. Social governance, like its political and economic counterparts, is usually directed toward promoting social order or social freedom. In an individualist society, social activities are seen as belonging within the sphere of individuals' private lives. The state should protect people from social abuse, but otherwise ensure they are free to pursue whatever social life interests they choose. For example, in the U.S. the government guarantees freedom of the press, political freedom, religious freedom, and other freedoms associated with human rights. Government adopts a monitoring role to ensure that individual social freedoms are not infringed or abused.

Communitarian societies do not ignore social freedoms, but are more concerned with maintaining social order and the underlying discipline necessary to sustain that order. The government tends to exercise greater control (though not necessarily explicit censorship) of the media. It determines what sorts of social activities are legitimate and controls facilities and services that are viewed as being critical for national development. Government controls schools and their curricula to ensure the perpetuation of the belief that, to achieve national goals, loyalty and obedience are imperative. It rewards those who are loyal to its policies with favors and preferences and punishes those who challenge or question its policies.

To explore these institutional differences in a strategic context, students analyze two cases following a format similar to that previously described. We begin by analyzing the Sanyo Manufacturing Corporation's experience with entry and subsequent management of an acquisition in Forrest City, Arkansas (Clark and Hayes 1981). The focus of the case is on typical strategy issues of core competence and industry competitiveness. We also branch explicitly into issues of government regulation, political pressure, and social change. I encourage students to evaluate instances where Sanyo was surprised by events (e.g., an acrimonious labor strike), exploring Sanyo's expectations based on their past experiences back in Japan. In the second session, we go the other direction, analyzing the entry into Japan by Toys "Я" Us (MacKenzie and Spar 1995). Again, we focus on typical strategy issues of core competence, local responsiveness, and consistency across operations; but we also focus on variations in the institutional environment of Japan in comparison to the U.S. and on how Toys "Я" Us must adapt to be effective.

By this point, students are now highly sensitized to both the "micro" and "macro" influences of culture on strategy development and implementation. I push the students further by stepping away from case discussion and putting them through an exercise that involves developing their own dimensions for comparing and contrasting cultures. I ask them to identify a social issue basic to society and relevant to businesses. Often students struggle with this. So, after letting them work on it for a while, I often suggest a question for them to work on. (One of my favorites – "Who is responsible for bearing the cost of structural economic change?" – was asked by MBA students at New York University in the early 1990s. They were particularly interested in this question because at the time U.S. corporations were pursuing widespread layoffs and downsizing.) Working from the perspective of Kluckhohn and Strodtbeck (1961), I suggest to students that there are probably a limited number of answers to this question and ask them to see how many they can come up with. Following this exercise, I search for a case that can bring such issues to the surface in a strategic context. For example, for exploring the issue of who should bear the cost of economic restructuring, I use an INSEAD case, *Lufthansa: The Turnaround (A)* (Lehrer 1995). In discussing the question of economic restructuring and who should bear its costs, students often conclude that the cost is borne by one of three entities: the government, the firm, or the individual (or some mix of those three with one bearing more of the burden than the other two). With this as a foundation, we explore Lufthansa's experiences, which differ dramatically from what U.S. students are familiar with. U.S. students are often puzzled as to why "codetermination" and workers' councils are so easily accepted by Lufthansa.

The outcome of this exercise is twofold. Students acquire an understanding of yet another area of the firm's environment where culture matters, and they learn that they can and should seek to develop their own approaches for bringing to the surface and explaining cultural influences on firms and their strategic behaviors.

Conclusion

It is unrealistic to expect any one class to teach business students all that they need to know about the role of culture in business. That is not the issue. My conversations with colleagues who teach strategy, however, often revolve around whether culture can or should be taught in a capstone course, particularly given that many instructors may not be well trained. I view it as essential to teach culture in the capstone strategy course for two reasons. The purpose of the course is to integrate all that has been learned about the various functional areas of the firm. Students may appreciate the influence of culture in, e.g., marketing, organizational behavior, and accounting; however, the capstone also represents the one course where the influence of culture can also be presented in an integrative manner.

Finally, because it is a capstone experience, students often take this course in the last or next-to-last term prior to graduation. What better opportunity exists for faculty to reinforce the importance of understanding culture's influence on business management than to incorporate it in this significant and integral course?

Notes

1 My class sessions run to 75 minutes in length. For longer class sessions it may be possible to combine the cases.
2 I purposely use this term rather than "collectivist" because it has become more popular in political science and sociological discourse, and because it focuses on the notion of community, which is often easier for U.S. students to comprehend.

References

Bird, A. and Osland, J. S. (2000) "Beyond sophisticated stereotyping: cultural sensemaking in context," *Academy of Management Executive*, 14 (1): 65–87.

Christiansen, E. T. and Pascale, R. T. (1987) *Honda (A)*, Cambridge, MA: Harvard Business School: 9-384-049.

Clark, K. and Hayes, R. (1981) *Sanyo Manufacturing Corporation – Forrest City, Arkansas*, Cambridge, MA: Harvard Business School: 9-682-045.

Gudykunst, W. B. and Ting-Toomey, S. (1988) *Culture and Interpersonal Communication*, Beverly Hills, CA: Sage.

Hofstede, G. (1980) *Culture's Consequences: International Differences in Work-related Values*, Beverly Hills, CA: Sage.

Kluckhohn, F. and Strodtbeck, F. L. (1961) *Variations in Value Orientations*, Evanston, IL: Row, Peterson.

Kotha, S. (1999) *Harley-Davidson*, Seattle: University of Washington.

Lehrer, M. (1995) *Lufthansa: The Turnaround (A)*, Fontainbleau, France: INSEAD.

Lincoln, J. R. and Kalleberg, A. L. (1990) *Culture, Control and Commitment*, New York: Cambridge University Press.

MacKenzie, J. and Spar, D. (1995) *Toys "Я" Us Japan*, Cambridge, MA: Harvard Business School: 9-796-077.

Triandis, H. C. (1995) *Individualism and Collectivism*, Boulder, CO: Westview Press.

Part VIII

Not the end

Chapter 27

As we go forward

Richard A. Goodman, Margaret E. Phillips and Nakiye Avdan Boyacigiller

Introduction

The opening chapter, "Culture, passion, and play," spoke of an ongoing community of colleagues engaged in dialogue and exploration of issues cultural and teachers, trainers, coaches, consultants, researchers, therapists, and practitioners. We have learned much from this community and expect to continue to learn from them in the ensuing years. Active learning is a fundamental requirement of an increasingly complex world. We are grateful to the community and expect to enlarge the dialogue through our collective work presented here. We have presented a consolidation of our insights, albeit a transitory one. While there are many, many great ideas and practical solutions embedded in this book, the text reveals that we still deal with a vast array of dilemmas in teaching a cultural perspective.

Inherent dilemmas

It is clear to us that some dilemmas are inherent – they cannot be resolved. Yet they are what foster, benefit from, and are best dealt with through *dialogue*. To the end of promoting this dialogue and challenging the community at large to seek further answers, we asked each author to speak of the dilemmas they still face with the content or process of their module. As a result, many of the chapters above have raised these dilemmas, some identifying creative ways of dealing with them. But from these discussions, we recognize that some overarching, intransigent dilemmas remain:

- The dilemma of power versus humility, that is, our goal of giving learners the confidence to act without the arrogance that often blocks further learning. We need to help learners develop a sense of power over the material, but also a sense of humility that there is so much more to learn. To do so, we need to have this ourselves. We must be willing to go into the classroom (or to the workplace) on any day and teach (or work) knowing full well that we do not know full well. Therefore, we need to have openness to revelatory comment whenever and wherever it happens and help learners develop the same.

- We all recognize the complexity of the issues we are dealing with, and we want learners also to appreciate this complexity, yet do so with (again) a feeling of confidence. They are challenged to live with and use the resultant tension, both in the classroom and in their workplaces, and we too must live with this challenge in our teaching.

- Coupled with the complexity of the issues is the complexity of the learning group itself. Our learners are differentially knowledgeable and differentially interested in learning. Thus, they are differentially ready and differentially able to learn. This dilemma of the non-homogeneous learning group – persistent in any teaching situation – is heightened by the developmental nature of cultural learning.

- Organizational culture is dynamic for external reasons, because the organization is a permeable membrane with participants constantly entering and leaving and because, frequently, organizations recombine, forming brand new entities. While it is clear from this assertion that a learning stance is therefore required, such forces and the ensuing organizational dynamics create a serious teaching challenge. Our dilemma becomes when to tell a learner that "x" is true, when in point of fact "x" is just an abstract description of an ever-changing phenomenon.

- We all feel the constant pressure of time: do we have the time to teach the way we want to be teaching? In this volume, we have presented some ways colleagues have found to bring more time-consuming issues into the classroom in compressed timeframes. But time constraints and the demands of a developmental learning process continue to pose a dilemma.

- Similarly, a common dilemma in all learning circumstances is the issue of time versus depth, and the concomitant ontological issues of what to study. This leads to questions of emphasis – are we overemphasizing cultural factors or are they absolutely basic to the learners' process?

- We all know from our engagements in cultural issues that some learners have great difficulty decoding cultural incidents. While they can be right on target about the issues in a cognitive sense, they have serious trouble in the field or at work. Even with experiential learning – a decided bias among the authors in this volume – the ability to develop or not to develop "sight" into one's real life experiences remains puzzling to many of us. Are we effectively moving our learners away from stereotypes toward real understanding? Have we been successful in creating classrooms where mindfulness and risk-taking are prevalent?

- The educational process for professionals is itself a dilemma. We either teach about culture in a separate course or culture is alluded to in a wide range of courses. In the former, it is not integrated with or into the other topics of professional training; in the latter, it is not taught with sufficient depth to become a serious capability of the learner. Some argue that we need to reconceptualize professional education to find much better ways to be integrative, holistic, and systemic.

The power of community

These dilemmas, and many more, face us all as a community interested in culture in organizational settings. We have made much progress over the last few decades within an increasingly dynamic organizational ecosystem. But as a community we need to continue to persevere. We expect to find further enlightenment in the larger community, and to this end we invite all to share their thoughts and their solutions (tentative to well-formed). We expect to see more published, we anticipate more opportunities in convention and colloquium for face-to-face dialogue, and we look for the development of more colleagiums for issues cultural. Let us join you and you join us in pushing on the cultural boundaries of knowledge and pushing forward our knowledge of culture.

eBooks – at www.eBookstore.tandf.co.uk

A library at your fingertips!

eBooks are electronic versions of printed books. You can store them on your PC/laptop or browse them online.

They have advantages for anyone needing rapid access to a wide variety of published, copyright information.

eBooks can help your research by enabling you to bookmark chapters, annotate text and use instant searches to find specific words or phrases. Several eBook files would fit on even a small laptop or PDA.

NEW: Save money by eSubscribing: cheap, online access to any eBook for as long as you need it.

Annual subscription packages

We now offer special low-cost bulk subscriptions to packages of eBooks in certain subject areas. These are available to libraries or to individuals.

For more information please contact webmaster.ebooks@tandf.co.uk

We're continually developing the eBook concept, so keep up to date by visiting the website.

www.eBookstore.tandf.co.uk